496

W9-BVM-135

A SHORT HISTORY OF Christianity

A SHORT HISTORY OF Christianity

GEOFFREY BLAINEY

ROWMAN & LITTLEFIELD
Lanham • Boulder • New York • Toronto • Plymouth, UK

Published by Rowman & Littlefield
4501 Forbes Boulevard, Suite 200, Lanham, Maryland 20706
www.rowman.com

10 Thornbury Road, Plymouth PL6 7PP, United Kingdom

British Library Cataloguing in Publication Information Available

Library of Congress Cataloging-in-Publication Data

Blainey, Geoffrey.
    A short history of Christianity / Geoffrey Blainey.
        pages cm
    Includes bibliographical references and index.
    ISBN 978-1-4422-2589-3 (cloth : alk. paper) — ISBN 978-1-4422-2590-9
    (electronic) 1. Church history. I. Title.
    BR145.3.B57 2013
    270—dc23

                                                        2013029361

Printed in the United States of America

CONTENTS

LIST OF MAPS

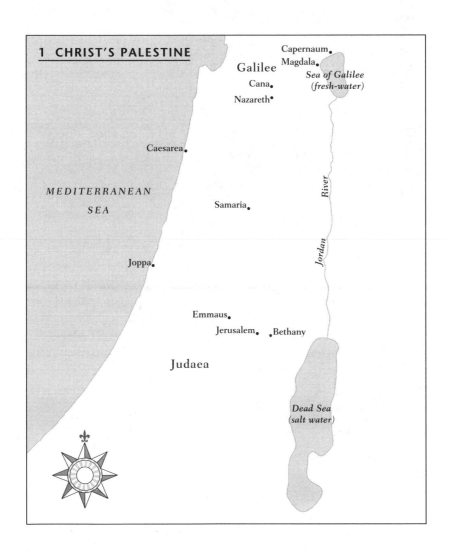

1 CHRIST'S PALESTINE

Galilee

Capernaum.
Magdala.
Cana.
Nazareth•

Sea of Galilee
(fresh-water)

Caesarea.

MEDITERRANEAN
SEA

Samaria.

Joppa.

Jordan River

Emmaus.
Jerusalem. .Bethany

Judaea

Dead Sea
(salt water)

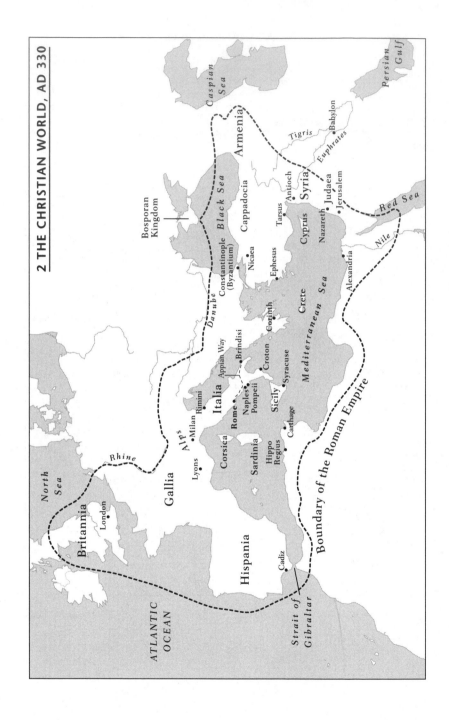

2 THE CHRISTIAN WORLD, AD 330

Persian Gulf

Caspian Sea

Tigris

Babylon

Euphrates

Armenia

Black Sea

Antioch
Syria
Judaea
Tarsus
Jerusalem
Nazareth

Red Sea

Bosporan Kingdom

Cappadocia

Cyprus

Nile

Constantinople (Byzantium)

Nicaea

Ephesus

Crete

Alexandria

Danube

Corinth

Mediterranean Sea

Brindisi

Appian Way

Croton

Syracuse

Rimini

Milan

Italia

Naples
Rome
Pompeii

Sicily

Alps

Corsica

Sardinia

Carthage

Lyons

Hippo Regius

Rhine

Gallia

North Sea

Britannia

London

Hispania

Cadiz

Boundary of the Roman Empire

ATLANTIC OCEAN

Strait of Gibraltar

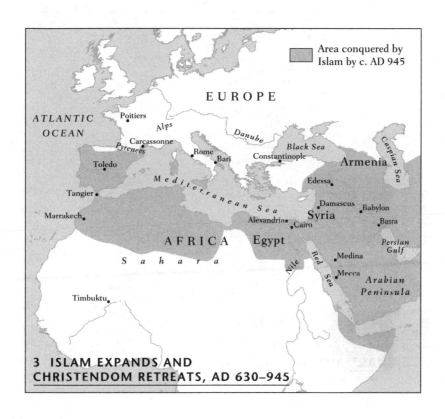

Area conquered by Islam by c. AD 945

EUROPE

ATLANTIC
OCEAN

Poitiers

Alps

Danube

Carcassonne
Pyrenees

Rome

Bari

Black Sea

Constantinople

Armenia

Caspian Sea

Toledo

Mediterranean Sea

Edessa

Tangier

Damascus

Babylon

Marrakech

Alexandria

Cairo

Syria

Basra

AFRICA

Egypt

Persian
Gulf

Sahara

Nile

Red Sea

Medina

Mecca

Arabian
Peninsula

Timbuktu

**3 ISLAM EXPANDS AND
CHRISTENDOM RETREATS, AD 630–945**

North Sea

Baltic Sea

Jarrow

Roskilde • Lund

Armagh •

York •

Dublin •

London • Louvain

EUROPE

Cologne •

Canterbury Aachen

Prague •

St Denis • Paris

Speyer •

ATLANTIC
OCEAN

Mont
St Michel

Clairvaux

Vienna •

Chartres

Freiburg

Einsiedeln •

Citeaux

Alps

Cluny •

Milan •

Venice •

Clermont •

Ravenna •

Santiago de
Compostela •

Albi •

Avignon •

Genoa •

Loreto •

Assisi •

Pyrenees

Rome •

Monte
Cassino

Burgos •

Mt Athos •

Constantinople •

Avila •

Mediterranean Sea

Monreale •

Athens •

AFRICA

**4 MEDIEVAL EUROPE:
MONASTERIES AND PILGRIMAGES**

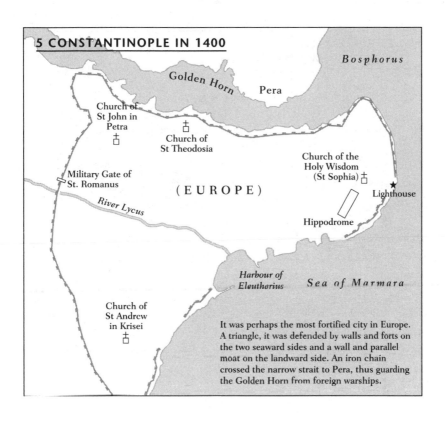

5 CONSTANTINOPLE IN 1400

Bosphorus

Golden Horn　Pera

Church of
St John in
Petra
✝

Church of
St Theodosia
✝

Church of the
Holy Wisdom
(St Sophia) ✝

Lighthouse

Military Gate of
St. Romanus

(EUROPE)

River Lycus

Hippodrome

*Harbour of
Eleutherius*　*Sea of Marmara*

Church of
St Andrew
in Krisei
✝

It was perhaps the most fortified city in Europe.
A triangle, it was defended by walls and forts on
the two seaward sides and a wall and parallel
moat on the landward side. An iron chain
crossed the narrow strait to Pera, thus guarding
the Golden Horn from foreign warships.

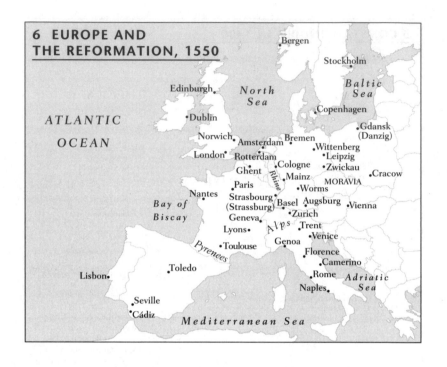

6 EUROPE AND THE REFORMATION, 1550

Bergen

Stockholm

Edinburgh

North Sea

Baltic Sea

Copenhagen

ATLANTIC OCEAN

Dublin

Gdansk (Danzig)

Norwich

Amsterdam

Bremen

Wittenberg

Leipzig

London

Rotterdam

Zwickau

Cracow

Ghent

Cologne

Rhine

Mainz

MORAVIA

Paris

Worms

Nantes

Strasbourg (Strassburg)

Basel

Augsburg

Vienna

Bay of Biscay

Geneva

Zurich

Lyons

Alps

Trent

Toulouse

Genoa

Venice

Pyrenees

Florence

Lisbon

Toledo

Camerino

Rome

Adriatic Sea

Naples

Seville

Cádiz

Mediterranean Sea

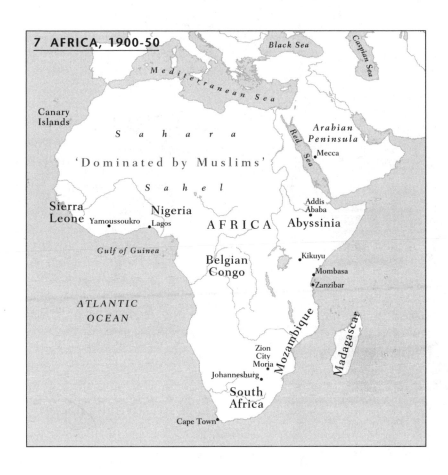

7 AFRICA, 1900-50

Black Sea

Caspian Sea

Mediterranean Sea

Canary
Islands

S a h a r a

'Dominated by Muslims'

*Arabian
Peninsula*

Red Sea

Mecca

S a h e l

Sierra
Leone

Nigeria

Yamoussoukro

Lagos

AFRICA

Addis
Ababa

Abyssinia

Gulf of Guinea

Belgian
Congo

Kikuyu

Mombasa

Zanzibar

ATLANTIC
OCEAN

Mozambique

Madagascar

Zion
City
Moria

Johannesburg

South
Africa

Cape Town

8 THE WORLD'S CHRISTIANS IN 2010

In 1900, of the nations with large Christian populations, at least eight of the
top ten were in Europe. By 2015 Europe probably will hold none of the top ten.
If the European Union, however, was counted as one nation, it would rank first.

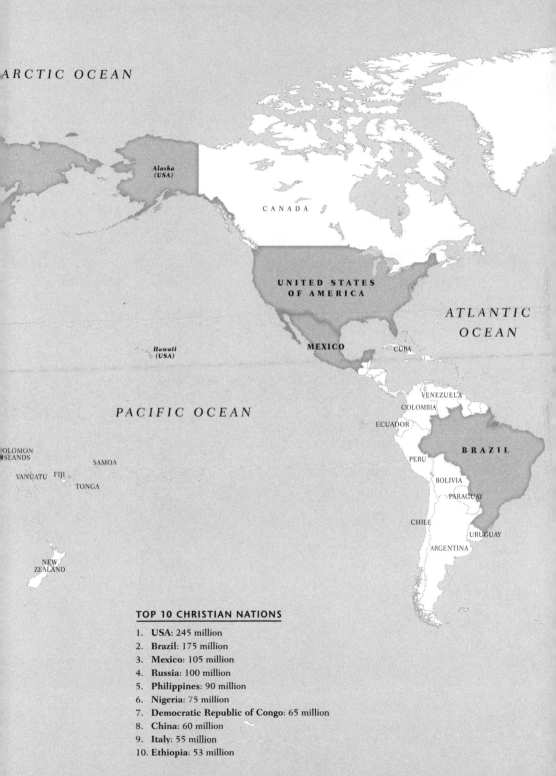

ARCTIC OCEAN

Alaska
(USA)

CANADA

UNITED STATES
OF AMERICA

ATLANTIC
OCEAN

Hawaii
(USA)

MEXICO

CUBA

VENEZUELA

COLOMBIA

ECUADOR

PACIFIC OCEAN

BRAZIL

SOLOMON
ISLANDS

SAMOA

PERU

VANUATU FIJI

BOLIVIA

TONGA

PARAGUAY

CHILE

URUGUAY

NEW
ZEALAND

ARGENTINA

TOP 10 CHRISTIAN NATIONS

1. **USA**: 245 million
2. **Brazil**: 175 million
3. **Mexico**: 105 million
4. **Russia**: 100 million
5. **Philippines**: 90 million
6. **Nigeria**: 75 million
7. **Democratic Republic of Congo**: 65 million
8. **China**: 60 million
9. **Italy**: 55 million
10. **Ethiopia**: 53 million

PREFACE

To write a history of Christianity is fascinating, frustrating and even perilous. It is fascinating because of the way it shaped western civilisation, and the long periods in which it affected people's way of life. It is frustrating because some parts of the history are wrapped in mystery. In its opening years the miraculous is rarely far away, and some of the Christian precepts come down to us in the form of parables, allegories and even riddles. To write its history is also perilous because it is punctuated with controversy, and on each opposing side those who argued – and even fought – were backed by what they believed were invincible arguments. I have tried to see both sides with some sympathy.

A few scholars argue that Jesus Christ, the founder of the religion, did not even exist. They rightly point out that contemporary references to him were extremely rare. My own conclusion is that, by the standard of the times, his life is astonishingly documented. He did not become well known until the last few years of his life, and then only in one small outpost of the Roman Empire. And yet, of all the people who were his contemporaries and achieved no high office and won no fame outside their own country, Jesus's life and teachings are amongst the most documented.

Numerous small books or gospels were written about him, and four are famous. Known as the gospels of Matthew, Mark, Luke and John, all except one were finalised within fifty years of Jesus's death. Other stories and memoirs were written, by hand, of course. The problem is the sheer multitude of detail and its inconsistencies and contradictions. Eventually, there arose a huge industry based on discussions of those gospels and a shelf full of other early writings. In the following 1800 years, more handwritten and printed books in the western world centred on the life of Jesus than on any other topic. This intellectual energy was generated, century upon century, partly because the evidence about him was abundant and divergent. Therefore, anyone writing about his short life and the long history of Christianity has to weigh conflicting or inconsistent evidence again and again. The notes at the end of this book are brief guides to some of the evidence I used.

I investigated this story as a historian, not as a theologian. I wished to educate myself as well as others. In writing it, I had in mind a variety of general readers and also historians who work in other fields and have faint knowledge of Christian history. On the assumption that many readers would have little knowledge of Christian theology, I have avoided, as far as possible, the more technical terms.

In some chapters the beliefs of the mass of people receive attention. Though it is not easy to ascertain what stonemasons and housewives thought 500 or 1500 years ago, I sometimes attempt this difficult task, finding clues along the way. Thus, I describe a Christian woman travelling as a pilgrim to Jerusalem in the fourth century and the funeral of a Christian slave in the United States in the nineteenth century.

One dilemma was deciding how many pages to give to continuity as distinct from change. If change is always allowed to hold the central place in a history, then dispute gains undue emphasis; for in the history of a religion nothing of importance changes without disagreement. As Christianity covers twenty centuries, and many lands, the disputes can seem endless. And yet many centuries are quiet rather than disputatious.

The book is not intended to be a short encyclopedia. Much is omitted. When I was about three-quarters of the way through the writing, I deleted more than twenty of every 100 pages I had written. Some episodes were omitted or pruned to allow more space, in the final version, for Paul of Tarsus, Francis of Assisi, Zwingli of Zurich, John Wesley of England, and dozens of other influential individuals. Doubters and rationalists also have a place in this book, for they are part of the many-sided history of Christianity.

Geoffrey Blainey
Melbourne

PART ONE

1

THE BOY FROM GALILEE

Of all the known people of the world, living or dead, Jesus is the most influential.

His birth was viewed as a momentous event, and still is. When the chronology now used in the world was created, the assumed date of his birth was singled out and named as Year One. The decision was not quite accurate. The exact year of his birth is not known. Even today, various facets of his birth, life and death are veiled in mystery and argument, and yet his influence on human history has been profound.

Jesus was Jewish, in race and culture and religion. The name 'Jew' is derived from 'Judah', which occupied half of the narrow strip of the territory flanking the Mediterranean Sea long known as Palestine. Long ago, Jesus's ancestors had lived elsewhere. Traditionally they were known as the Hebrews, meaning the people who 'crossed over': in essence they were travellers or wanderers.

No matter in what land the Jews lived, they viewed Jerusalem as the holy place. It stood on a mountain ridge, held a permanent spring of fresh water, and was easily fortified. After it was captured by King David for the Hebrews in about 1000 BC, it became the site of the great temple, one of the most lavish buildings in the western world. Built by King Solomon, the son of David, it became the heart of the Jewish religion. Here sacrifices and prayers could be offered to God, and holy words read aloud by the chief priest and his attendants. Because the Jews, unlike other peoples and kingdoms of the Mediterranean and the Middle East, believed in only one God, and because the temple in Jerusalem was considered his only shrine, it is likely that no other place of pilgrimage in the Middle East and Europe was imbued with more awe. The final crisis in Jesus's life – the start of the quick chain of events that led to his death – was on the site of King Solomon's temple.

After the death of King Solomon his kingdom was divided into two: Israel to the north and Judah to the south. In 587 BC Jerusalem was conquered by the powerful Babylonians. The capture of Jerusalem was one of the traumatic events in the long history of a people who endured many mishaps and disasters. Many of the leading Jews were deported to Babylon. In exile they dwelt on their misfortunes and wondered whether they had so offended God that this was their punishment.

In less than half a century the Persians captured Babylon, and most of the Jews were able to return to their own land, where, in about 520, they began to rebuild the temple. Living under a succession of foreign rulers, and ultimately under a Greek-speaking regime, they eventually recaptured their own land in 142 BC. For almost eighty years they rejoiced in their independence; they would not be independent again until the twentieth century.

THE ROMANS CONQUER

In 63 BC the Romans invaded Palestine. Already possessing the largest and most diverse empire in the world, they conferred some independence on those colonies that were subservient and dutiful and which paid their taxes. Finally, appointing a local ruler under the title of King Herod, the Romans delegated power to him, and in turn he allowed the Jewish authorities considerable freedom in supervising religious life. It was near the end of the reign of Herod that Jesus was born, possibly in 6 BC.

Under the occupation of a small Roman army, the Jews maintained their unusual culture and religion. As far as possible they ignored the Romans' gods and paid only a formal respect to the distant Roman emperor, who was increasingly worshipped as a god by those around him. Jews continued to obey the rules of their own religion. Their daily life was ruled by powerful traditions. Thus, baby boys had to be circumcised soon after birth, and it was judged unholy and unclean to neglect that rule. Certain foods, including pork, were never to be eaten. Widows and the very poor had to be cared for. The Sabbath, or Saturday, was a day of rest and worship, a strict rule that made it difficult for Jewish soldiers to serve honourably in the Roman army, although some did.

So a distinct Jewish world operated inside the Roman Empire. It is doubtful whether any other province of the empire survived as such a distinct cultural and religious entity. This was the miracle of the Jewish religion – its sheer tenacity through century after century. Jesus inherited this religion and culture.

God dominated the Jewish culture. He was their God, though not exclusively. Called the Eternal One, he was invisible and immortal, the possessor of enormous power and knowledge and an immense capacity for love as well as anger. Having created human beings in his own image, and given them a free will, he thereby gave them the opportunity to choose evil as well as good. If they obeyed his laws, his help could be relied on. He was their father – they were his children: the children of Israel. Most of the hymns they sang to him, called psalms, were written during the time of the exile in Babylon and the jubilant return to Jerusalem. In the light of their experience they could confidently proclaim: 'God is our refuge and strength, a very present help in trouble.'

According to the Hebrews, God was everywhere. Sometimes he was seen to be in 'his holy temple' or sometimes in heaven, but his spirit and his presence and his knowledge were such that he could be in ten thousand places at the same time. As Psalm 139 proclaimed, nobody could escape from him: 'Whither shall I go from thy spirit? Or whither shall I flee from thy presence?'

When the Jewish people fled to Babylon, God was waiting for them. They returned to Jerusalem, and he was already there. God even knew 'when I sit down and when I rise up'. One psalm explained that God knew one's inner thoughts even before they were spoken.

The Hebrews' emphasis on their all-powerful and perfect God stood side by side with their understanding of the human condition. Mankind, in contrast to God, was imperfect, with a capacity for evil as well as good. 'Sin' was the word widely used, but it did not equate fully with the modern meaning of sin. A sinner was disobedient to the will of God. A sinner disobeyed not only moral precepts but also cultural and ceremonial rules laid down by Moses and recorded in the books now called the Old Testament. Disbelief – atheism or agnosticism – was also a sin.

Hebrews held the view that humans had an innate disposition to be sinful: they should therefore be acutely conscious of their failings and should seek forgiveness. This sounds like a gloomy view of life but it was actually optimistic. The individuals who came to terms with their human nature could live in harmony with God, and feel deep comfort, peace and even joy. That joy might even continue after death, although personal immortality was not a common theme in the Jewish scriptures.

To many modern eyes, the Jewish attitude to God seems subservient, but to Jewish eyes God was just. Nothing on earth could approach his sense of justice. He would richly reward the good and the 'righteous'. His love was boundless and endured forever, a message that Psalm 136 repeated two dozen times. On the other hand, God would exact vengeance on those who seriously disobeyed him, and on those who, having infringed his rules, did not repent. The Jews could not readily comprehend the idea of an unjust God. If their world was turned upside down by a natural disaster or a foreign conqueror, it was because they deserved it.

These were the Jewish beliefs that Jesus absorbed as a child. A few of them he reshaped towards the end of his short life, but most he accepted instinctively and followed wholeheartedly.

STARS AND COMETS

In the time of Jesus, the stars in the night sky were more fascinating to most people than they are today. It was believed that an unusually bright star was a sign that momentous events would soon take place. Thus, the great Roman poet Virgil described how a brilliant star had once guided the founder of Rome to the exact place where the city grew. The birth of the founder of a religion might also be announced by his own star.

According to the gospel of Matthew, three wise men or sages living in a faraway land saw a brilliant light shining in the night sky, beckoning them in the direction of Palestine. Believing it signified the birth of an exceptional child, they collected gifts for him and followed the star in the hope, indeed the certainty, that they would find the child: 'We saw his star in the East and have come to worship him.'

The star finally halted above a small building where a mother named Mary nursed her newborn son, Jesus. On entering the doorway, the wise men 'fell down and worshipped' him. From their bags they unpacked their gifts, which included gold – the emblem of kings – and frankincense and myrrh.

This charming story, or allegory, was later set down in writing, to be recounted century after century, and altered a little in the retelling. The baby was so important that the three wise men were thought to deserve more prestige, and they eventually became three kings. About five hundred years later they were belatedly given names.

The birth of Jesus eventually caught the imagination of a large part of the world, and even The Three Kings, now spelled in capital letters, became the unseen passengers in major voyages of exploration. When Christopher Columbus discovered Cuba, which he first thought was somewhere near the Holy Land, he told his crew he expected to go ashore and find the source of the gifts that The Three Kings had placed at the feet of Jesus. When Abel Tasman, the Dutchman, discovered New Zealand and named some of its headlands and adjacent islands during his fleeting visit, he selected one biblical name. He conferred on several rugged islands not the name of an apostle but the title of The Three Kings.

Independent evidence suggests that unusual events did indeed occur in the skies around the time of Jesus's birth. One was the brilliant spectacle of Halley's comet, which made one of its rare appearances in 12 or 11 BC. Another was the uncommon convergence of three planets – Jupiter, Saturn and Mars – in 8 BC.

The place of Jesus's birth is not known with certainty. Mark, the author of the earliest gospel or life of Jesus, did not specify a birthplace. The other gospel-writers nominated Bethlehem, a small town only a morning's stroll from Jerusalem. Being the home of David, the hero of Jewish history, Bethlehem was a fitting birthplace for someone soon to be hailed as the saviour of the Jewish people. It is said by Luke that Jesus's parents actually lived in Nazareth but were compelled by a coming census to be present in Bethlehem at what proved to be the time of his birth. In fact, the records reveal that no census was held at that time, and even if it had been held, the officials would not have compelled inhabitants to make a long journey simply in order to be counted in the place where their family originated.

The town of Nazareth in Galilee, where Jesus spent most of his life, is seen by some as the alternative birthplace. Indeed, his followers were initially called the Nazarenes, and Jesus himself is described in the New Testament as Jesus the Nazarene. Several modern biblical scholars, after surveying the evidence, can affirm no more than that he was a Galilean: 'We must conclude that we do not know where he was born.'

Jesus's father's name was Joseph, and his mother's name was Mary, and it was she who would rise to fame as the centuries passed. According to Mark's gospel, Jesus also had younger brothers and sisters, but some scholars say that these were really cousins or other relatives who shared his upbringing,. A matter of deep importance to the people who came to be called Christians, it will be discussed later.

There can be little doubt that Joseph and Mary nurtured their family. From an early age, Jesus attended a synagogue and learned the highlights of the books now called the Old Testament. He also learned to read and write, accomplishments that were not attained by most people living in his home town.

It is reported that Jesus, as a boy of twelve, went with his parents to Jerusalem. A journey that took several days on foot, it was made at the annual feast of the Passover, the foremost festival of the Jewish calendar. It was a wonderful time to be in that small city, in the company of Jewish pilgrims from near and far; and in the temple, Jesus listened to the various teachers and to readings from the Jewish scriptures. He was so eager to explore that his parents could not find him. Discovered at last 'sitting among the teachers, listening to them and asking them questions', he explained his disappearance with surprising authority: 'Did you not know that I must be in my Father's house?'

These are his first recorded words. The word 'must', emphasising the nature of his relationship with God, is significant. Luke, in his gospel, reports Jesus using that word on eighteen different occasions. The young Jesus, as depicted in the various gospels, conveys an unusual air of duty.

Jesus became a carpenter and also acquired some of the skills of the stonemason. Presumably he made the simple wooden furniture used in the houses, the wooden yokes worn by beasts of burden, the wooden ploughs, the wooden gates and doors and animal pens, and the commodious barns needed by the nearby farmers. To work daily at the crafts of carpentry and stonemasonry was to receive wages that were on the top half of the income ladder.

A VOICE FROM THE RIVER JORDAN

While Jesus worked as a carpenter he gained a wealth of religious knowledge. He attended the synagogue, a place of teaching as well as preaching, and the stories of the great Jewish kings, prophets and warriors filled his mind. Influenced by discussions with his neighbours, he acquired views on the Roman occupation of his homeland.

In about the year AD 27 or 28, Jesus's absorption in religious and political matters – the two were closely linked – became intense. He began to gather like-minded followers, of whom eventually there were twelve, the same number as the original tribes of Israel. Most of his disciples were local men who lived near the Sea of Galilee, and several were initially the followers of an evangelist named John, who dressed in a rough cloak of camel skin and preached at various places along the River Jordan.

Crowds came to hear John the Baptist. Jesus himself fell under his influence: indeed, they were cousins, according to Luke. Living on the edge of civilisation, John ate the simplest foods, including wild honey and locusts. He believed in the ancient prophecy that God would one day send a new King David to free Palestine from foreign rule. Perhaps in a forthcoming year God would preside over a momentous Day of Judgement, reward the pure and the repentant, and punish the Romans. Predictions of similar events could be found by those who carefully scanned the Old Testament with its intermittent air of great expectations.

The River Jordan was the only stream in Palestine worthy of being called a river. It passed through an inland lake, the Sea of Galilee, and flowed on again as a narrower waterway, penetrating a corridor of dry, rocky terrain before entering the Dead Sea. When rain fell or snow melted in the mountains, the Jordan ran fast, even overflowing its banks. In a typical year, however, there were several months when it was scarcely a river, its shallow stretches being easily crossed on foot.

Presiding over one of the crossing places, John the Baptist ceremonially baptised those of his followers who wished to repent. The water was coloured brown by the soil that washed down the river's banks, but in the eyes of John the Baptist's followers it was sacred, especially when it was flowing. Baptism washed away their sins and brought them close to God, and to him they formally dedicated their lives.

So Jesus himself was baptised, probably being immersed totally in the river as John uttered the sacred blessings. Witnesses vowed that the event was crowned by the miraculous. A dove seemed to descend from the sky at the moment of baptism, and from on high a voice was heard: 'This is my beloved Son, in whom I am well pleased.' It was a landmark in the life of Jesus that he, and not John, was declared to be God's beloved son.

High officials from the temple went to the River Jordan to see whether John the Baptist was claiming to be the long-awaited Messiah, the 'anointed one' who would rescue the Jews from their overlords. John replied that he was just the street crier. He liked to repeat the words of the old prophet Isaiah: 'I am the voice of one crying in the wilderness. Make straight the way of the Lord.' The real Lord was Jesus, hidden in the crowd near the riverbank, invisible to the officials, so John told them.

The exact site of the baptism of Jesus is not known, but the episode itself would be long remembered. In the space of a few centuries, as Christianity spread, Jordan became the most famous of rivers in the minds of Europeans. The majestic Rhine, Rhône, Danube and Volga, in all their width, and even the long Nile and Euphrates, conveyed no mystique compared to this brown thin river that ran mostly parallel to the sea, which at its nearest point could be reached in a day's walk. Some seventeen hundred years after Jesus's baptism, the name of the Jordan would be, for Americans, more evocative than the Mississippi and the Amazon.

A YOUNG TEACHER AND HIS PARABLES

Jesus now began to teach and preach, in the open air and in the synagogues. Early in his new calling he went, one Saturday, into the synagogue at the lakeside town of Capernaum. 'And they were astonished at his teaching, for he taught them as one who had authority, and not as the scribes.' Here was a young amateur making the professionals themselves seem amateurs.

It is possible that at first he was a disciple of John the Baptist. The very first narratives or gospels are unanimous in depicting John as simply a faithful precursor of Jesus, but many of John's own disciples held a different view. After all, John was a preacher of authority before Jesus appeared. Why should he necessarily bow down before Jesus, a much younger preacher? Perhaps it was a little later that Jesus began to develop his distinctive message. Such is the tentative theory outlined by one leading theologian in recent years.

The recorded sayings of Jesus leave behind a remarkable story of rural life in Palestine, where at least half the working inhabitants were farmers, rural labourers, owners of orchards and vineyards, keepers of flocks and herds, diggers of wells and carriers of water. The tasks and instruments of farming are mentioned by Jesus more often than those of carpentry and building. Again and again Jesus plucks a religious or moral message from rural life. He talks of a farmer perplexed because his tree produced no figs, and of another farmer who set out to grow grain by hand, but soon found that many grains were eaten by birds before they could germinate, and others fell on stony ground, where they died for lack of soil and moisture. Fishermen – of the lakes rather than the deep sea – also appear in his stories and parables.

As Jesus walked past villages he noticed the minor crops being harvested. 'The kingdom of heaven is like to a grain of mustard seed,'

he announced to his listeners. He talked of someone paying a tithe –
a tax – in the form of 'mint and anise and cumin'. The seeds of
cumin, a herb with a display of pink or white flowers, gave an aroma
to freshly baked bread and served as an ingredient of medicine.

How well he knew the countryside and the crops, the vineyards
and livestock. His speeches describe a hen protecting her chickens,
and the cock or rooster crowing. At the end of his life he sadly prophesied that 'this night, before the cock crow', his disciple Peter would
not be loyal to him at the very moment his loyalty was desperately
needed. Jesus talked of the highways and byways and the hedges
that run near them, of the shepherds and their sheep, and the travelling hawkers who sold sparrows to be cooked in the pot – five for a
mere two farthings. He clearly knew about prices and everyday commodities – the superior price always paid for old wine rather than
new, and the daily wages paid for this or that task.

Harvest time was the crucial month in the life of his district,
when the grain had to be cut with a sickle at just the right time.
'The harvest truly is plenteous, but the labourers are few,' said Jesus.
Determined to change people's thinking before it was too late, he
urgently needed the help of all to bring in the harvest.

Jesus's words either startled or delighted people. He seemed to
love the world and its daily life, but he was also resolving to turn that
world upside down. Thus, it was a strong Jewish tradition to honour
one's parents, and never was the act of honouring them more important than when they died. But here was Jesus telling a follower not
to worry about attending his father's burial: 'Let the dead bury their
dead.' A poetic but provocative command, its disrespect for the dead
did not go unnoticed in strict Jewish circles.

He did not respect the Sabbath in the rigid way favoured by Jewish authorities. As he told them, 'The Sabbath was made for man,

and not man for the Sabbath.' Approached by a sick man who had been lame for thirty-eight years, Jesus did not wait until tomorrow but promptly healed him on the Sabbath. The laws handed down by Moses in his wisdom were sacred to most Jews, but were not always sacred to Jesus.

Preaching in his home region, Jesus gave a sermon in the presence of his twelve disciples, a sermon that is now famous. Called the Sermon on the Mount in one gospel, and the Sermon on the Plain in another, its message is consistent with most of Jesus's other teachings:

And he opened his mouth and taught them, saying:

Blessed are the poor in spirit, for theirs is the kingdom of heaven.
Blessed are those who mourn, for they shall be comforted.
Blessed are the meek, for they shall inherit the earth.
Blessed are those that hunger and thirst for righteousness, for they
    shall be satisfied.
Blessed are the merciful, for they shall obtain mercy.
Blessed are the pure in heart, for they shall see God.
Blessed are the peacemakers, for they shall be called sons of God.
Blessed are those that have been persecuted for righteousness' sake,
    for theirs is the kingdom of heaven.
Blessed are you when men revile you and persecute you, and utter
    all kinds of evil against you falsely on my account.
Rejoice and be glad, for your reward is great in heaven, for so men
    persecuted the prophets who were before you.
You are the salt of the earth: but if salt has lost its taste, how shall
    its saltiness be restored?

There is something presidential about the prose of this version of his sermon, as if it were written for a grand occasion by an orator.

Many of its additional thoughts are memorable. 'You are the light of the world,' said Jesus. It was on this same occasion that Jesus probably taught his followers what became known as the Lord's Prayer:

Our Father who art in heaven,
Hallowed be thy name.
Thy kingdom come,
Thy will be done
On earth as it is in heaven.
Give us this day our daily bread;
And forgive us our debts,
As we also have forgiven our debtors;
And lead us not into temptation,
But deliver us from evil.

The Lord's Prayer refers to the kingdom, one of Jesus's central concepts. By this he meant a realm ruled by God's love and mercy. It was something already in many people's hearts, in Palestine and elsewhere, but it also represented a time that was to come.

His short prayer turns twice to heaven. It was a word sometimes used to signify the vast vault in which the sun, moon and stars could be seen. But heaven to the early Christians was to become more than a vast canopy, all of which was visible on a clear night. Heaven was a series of places or layers, one above the other, so arranged that the upper six were not visible. In the most distant layer, far from sight, God was said to reign along with the angels.

We cannot be certain how often Jesus spoke of heaven. Every known version of his speeches, sermons and parables was set down in writing some time after his death. Written mostly by people who were not present, the words were handing down an emphatic oral tradition.

'I SAY UNTO YOU'

So far, Judaism had been mainly a religion for the Jewish people, although occasional sayings – visible in the Psalms – encompassed all human beings. The Book of Jonah, written at a time when the Jews tended to be a tightly knit people, made it clear that God could also save Gentiles, meaning the people who were not Jews. Jesus showed signs of belonging to this wider tradition. In the Old Testament, the Book of Leviticus had commanded: 'Thou shalt love thy neighbour as thyself', a radical morsel of advice but spoken probably on the assumption that most of the neighbours were Jews themselves. Jesus himself tended to see all people as his neighbours.

He repeated a message of love. Every kind of person was entitled to be loved: the young and the old, female and male, black and brown and white, Roman as well as Jew. He himself loved the leper and the lame and the healthy, and the law-breaker and the law-keeper. Even the collectors of the taxes that sustained the Roman regime were entitled to be loved. 'I say unto you, Love your enemies, bless them that curse you, do good to them that hate you.' Thus Jesus expressed his wide sympathies – unimaginably wide, in the view of most people.

He rebuked those who retaliated. He looked askance at those who were mean-spirited, or who held the typical human resentments. He told of the prodigal son who went away and enjoyed his wild 'time on the town' until his money ran out. When the son returned, everyone in the family rejoiced, except his brother, who had done the hard farm work day after day. The brother, resenting the favouritism, wondered why the prodigal one received all the hugs and kisses. As many of us would probably have felt as the dutiful son did, we feel some surprise that Jesus did not sympathise with both brothers. But

Jesus's first sympathies always lay with the lost ones, especially those who strayed and then tried to redeem themselves.

Jesus was wary of the motives of those who went about doing good deeds in a conspicuous way. It was best to give money privately to the synagogue or to the poor. It was more pleasing to God when a poor widow gave a tiny sum than when a rich landlord gave a large sum.

He saw personal wealth as a burden and a peril: 'But woe unto you that are rich,' he warned. Riches were a moral hazard, a sign of selfishness and a source of pride. Jesus, along with the old Jewish prophets whom he revered, respected humility and hated pride. While he did not hate individuals – all were the children of God – he hated certain forms of behaviour, especially those that led others astray. He especially despised hypocrisy. His overwhelming message was of God's love and compassion.

2

THE DEATH AND REBIRTH OF JESUS

Jesus soon attracted thousands of sympathisers and followers. Initially curious about him, many became ardent. Most probably came from humble parts of society. They were the poor, the sick, the residents of cramped houses in the towns, farmers who lacked enough land to feed themselves, wage-earners who scythed the harvest and brought the sheaves to the threshing floor, people who carried supplies on their back or walked beside their heavily loaded donkeys. Jesus spoke especially to those who, because of the erratic or lawless life they led, were not acceptable to the high priests and rabbis.

Women, too, were attracted to Jesus and his teachings. In no other decade in the first thousand years of Christianity were women as influential as they were during Jesus's own brief ministry. Thus he conversed at length with a Samaritan woman who gave him a drink of the water she drew from the well. Though Samaritans and Jews were not usually friends, he addressed to her one of the best known messages in the Bible: 'God is a spirit; and they that worship him must worship him in spirit and in truth.'

Other women appear in significant episodes of his teaching life. Mary of Bethany rubbed his hair with precious ointment, and Mary Magdalene, whom he cured of the 'seven devils', stood loyally nearby when he was dying. In healing the sick, he often attended to women, one of whom was the mother of the disciple Peter. He publicly expressed admiration for the poor widow who donated a few thin copper coins to the temple in Jerusalem. He vigorously defended women of poor reputation, and once stepped forward to save the life of a female adulterer who had been condemned to die by the punishment of stoning. 'Let him who is without sin cast the first stone,' he defiantly declared. As the standing of women was not high in Palestine, Jesus's kindnesses towards them were not always approved by those who strictly upheld tradition.

INSIDE THE NEW TEMPLE

The temple erected by King Herod the Great was a marvel of its age, even though it remained uncompleted. Built on the site of King Solomon's temple, it was larger than that ancient and celebrated building. The Jewish anthology, the Talmud, rejoiced in Herod's massive square building, 250 metres long on each side and rather like an Olympic stadium in area: 'He who has not seen the Temple of Herod, has never seen in his life a beautiful structure.' The adjacent gardens, buildings and courtyards magnified the site. Work on it did not proceed after Herod died in 4 BC because nobody was willing to pay the ten thousand workmen said to be on the building site at its busiest.

The heart of the temple was the Holy of Holies, which was approached through a sanctuary. Close by, in the Court of Priests, cells were available to house thirty-eight priests. Another notable place was the Court of Women, where they observed the ceremonies from a gallery but did not take part in them.

It had long been the tradition for Jews to sacrifice birds and animals to their God and these were killed in large numbers. Herod's temple contained a slaughterhouse close to the altars, and the butchers used 'rinsing chambers' to wash themselves, while at their feet was a sewer that conveyed blood and offal along a conduit to the Kedron Valley. Hygiene was honoured: much water was used in the temple, even though the people of Jerusalem had to use water with care, for it depended on springs and not on a reservoir or aqueducts. Later, Christianity did not adopt these acts of sacrifice from its mother religion, but it did continue to sing the psalms and read the passages of scripture in which animal sacrifices were extolled or remembered. A climax in Handel's *Messiah*, composed in the eighteenth century and still sung widely, is the cry 'glory to the lamb that was slain'.

Jews living in distant ports on the Mediterranean Sea and beyond sent an annual tribute of money to the temple in Jerusalem. Each year, thousands of pilgrims crossed the seas and land to visit it. Jerusalem's economy gained much from the fame of its temple and the devoutness or nostalgia of Jews who lived far away; but not everyone venerated the temple and its dazzling processions, its religious ceremonies, and the playing of musical instruments. Some Jews claimed God was too mighty to be confined and worshipped in one space; he could equally be worshipped on the high seas, in the wilderness and on the busy roads.

It is said that Jesus visited Jerusalem only once, but others write of three possible visits. He certainly appeared in the temple towards the end of his life, and slighted the high officials with their grand robes and self-satisfaction, for so he saw them. He thought poorly of the rich who displayed self-importance by placing their donations in the temple treasury in front of everyone, and he praised the widow who donated two flimsy copper coins. To his disciples he explained that 'she out of her poverty has put in everything she had', whereas the rich put in a mere fraction of their wealth.

Jesus rebuked those who were conducting commercial business in the temple. To all intents, however, they were doing nothing unusual; they were simply changing money for Jews who had come from foreign lands and wished to make an offering, or they were assisting worshippers who wished to purchase a bird or animal for sacrifice. But Jesus knocked over the tables of the money-changers and upended the chairs on which sat the sellers of doves. It was his own deliberate action, and his disciples, if present, took no part.

The authorities at the temple were astonished at this assault on practices that had gone on, perhaps less obtrusively, for decades. They concluded that Jesus was a troublemaker. That indeed was his intention: he saw the temple as a place of worship, but he could not see the spirit of worship prevailing inside its walls.

THE SUN WILL BE DARKENED: A PROPHECY

The Jewish leaders must have heard of Jesus's dramatic prediction that one day the temple itself, the shrine for all the Jewish people, would be destroyed. Luke recorded Jesus's dramatic words: 'There will not be left here one stone upon another.' Jesus is said to have made this declaration while teaching in the temple, but according to Mark, the disciples were resting on the Mount of Olives and looking towards the temple when Jesus predicted its end. Such differences are frequent in the New Testament, but the message of both authors was essentially the same. Meanwhile, the disciples had to go out and spread the Christian message of love and repentance. 'The Gospel must first be preached to all the nations,' said Jesus.

We know that one generation later, in AD 70, the temple was indeed destroyed by the Romans – their severe act of retaliation for a Jewish revolt. What Jesus apparently predicted had come to pass. But we should not accept too readily the assurances of the gospel writers that Jesus had predicted this specific event. We have to be cautious because it is possible that the earliest gospel was written just after the destruction of the temple. In short, the prediction could have been made and dressed up after the event.

On the other hand, the gospel writers did not primarily use this catastrophe to prove that their leader had been far-seeing. His fore-telling of the destruction of the temple was followed by his more shattering prediction. The world that they knew would come to an end. Two gospels set down spellbinding accounts of his prediction of the time of troubles. According to Luke, Jesus said: 'Nation will rise against nation, and kingdom against kingdom; there will be great earthquakes, and in various places famines and pestilences; and there will be terrors and great signs from heaven.' And according to Mark: 'The sun will be darkened, and the moon will not give its light, and the stars will be falling from heaven, and the powers in the heavens will be shaken. And then they will see the Son of Man coming in clouds with great power and glory. And then he will send out the angels, and gather his elect from the four winds, from the ends of the earth to the ends of heaven.'

These predictions were to exert a profound effect on the first Christians. They were promised a time of troubles, perhaps of long duration, a time that would severely test their faith.

WHO IS THIS MAN?

The high officials in the temple challenged the credentials and intentions of this itinerant preacher who made crystal-clear predictions of disaster. In fact, while there was a strand of social revolution in Jesus's message, his was not a call to overthrow the Roman or the Jewish leaders. At the same time, he further aroused the Jewish authorities when he reportedly raised a friend named Lazarus from the dead.

The episode was reported to the high priest, who, either astonished or suspicious, decided to take action. He feared Jesus had become too powerful, too popular, and was too widely perceived as exercising supernatural powers.

At about this time, Jesus was dining in a private house in Bethany when a woman performed the gesture of a loving disciple. She broke open an alabaster jar of expensive ointment, took the scented fluid in her hand and anointed his head. She possibly knelt down, too, and wiped his feet with her hair and anointed them. Soon the whole house was filled with the scent. This is not the only instance of Jesus being anointed by female admirers.

A few who sat at the table recognised her gesture as a reminder of the historic anointing of the kings of Israel and quietly applauded her. Others were indignant; they knew the price of the jar and exclaimed: 'Why was the ointment thus wasted?' Jesus, his hair moist with ointment, defended her conduct. Intensely moved, he added: 'She has done a beautiful thing to me.' As for the suggestion that her money should have gone to the poor, he replied with a prediction that would be quoted for centuries: the poor will always be with us, 'but you will not always have me'.

Jesus hinted that he would soon be put to death by the authorities. He told those at the table, the atmosphere having turned tense, that the woman had actually anointed his body 'for burying'. The next sentence he spoke was also memorable: 'And truly, I say to you, wherever the gospel is preached in the whole world, what she has done will be told in memory of her.'

The disciple Judas was apparently sitting at the meal. Secretly, he had already turned traitor, in return for the promise of a handsome sum of money.

AT THE LAST SUPPER

Knowing that he would soon be arrested, Jesus called together his disciples for a final meal. It is not completely clear whether they all met on the evening before his execution or one or two days earlier, but they were probably celebrating the Jewish Passover.

Their last supper was poignant. Together in an upper room they sat, the disciples and Jesus, and as they ate and drank he taught them, conversed with them, and questioned them: a leader delivering his last message. The traitor, Judas Iscariot, was amongst them. To the astonishment of the disciples, Jesus announced, 'Truly, I say to you, one of you will betray me.'

Whether he said this in an accusatory voice we do not know, but the disciples responded uneasily. Now sensing how dangerous it was to be the followers of Jesus, and conscious of their own weakness under pressure, they possibly feared that they might be forced publicly to disown him. Furthermore, they believed he could see into their minds with a power that far surpassed their own powers of scrutiny. After he talked of betrayal, the disciples one after another anxiously asked, 'Lord, is it I?' When it was Judas Iscariot's turn to speak, he inquired, 'Master, is it I?' Jesus knew that Judas was the betrayer.

Jesus eased the tension around the table. He took up a loaf of bread, blessed it and pulled it apart, after which each disciple accepted a piece and waited for Jesus to speak. His words were simple: 'Take, eat; this is my body.' When they had eaten the bread he took up a cup of wine, blessed it and passed it to them in turn, saying, 'Drink of it, all of you. For this is my blood of the covenant.'

This emotion-filled ceremony was followed by a few words of prophecy from their master: 'I tell you I shall not drink again of this fruit of the vine until that day when I drink it new with you in my Father's kingdom.' The disciples assumed that Jesus was talking of his own impending departure to a higher place, the kingdom of which he sometimes spoke.

In the Last Supper, as imagined and painted by some of Europe's finest artists, Judas Iscariot can usually be recognised. No halo is set around his head. Sometimes his hair is painted red. It was one of the events that was to fascinate distinguished painters. For western civilisation, it remains one of the most symbolic of all meals.

After the supper was over and a psalm had been sung, Jesus went into a garden to pray. There his presence was disclosed by Judas to the Jewish authorities, and the temple soldiers arrested him. Was he a danger to the governing powers in Jerusalem? That was their fear and dilemma. While preaching, he had not openly expressed the belief that he was the prophet coming to rescue the Jews from Roman rule. But now, when questioned by high Jewish officials, he was forthright, making it clear that the hand of God was on his head. In response to the question from the Chief Priest, 'Art thou the Christ?', he answered simply, 'Yes'. Of course the word 'Christ' signified the anointed person – the Messiah who would transform Israel. 'You have heard his blasphemy,' announced the Chief Priest with an air of triumph.

In the sad words of Mark, the disciples 'all forsook him and fled'. Even Peter, who had vowed to follow his master to prison or to death, was seen by him no more. Under official questioning Peter insisted that he had had nothing to do with Jesus, saying it not once but three times. The cluster of disciples was not to be seen at Jesus's brief trial, nor were they standing loyally near him when he was about to be executed. Three of the gospels do not mention the presence of a disciple at the end, and only John's gospel reports that a disciple was present – the only one out of the twelve.

Jesus was a political as well as a religious leader. Some see him as supporting the poor against the rich, rural Galilee against the elite of Jerusalem, and the Jewish people against the Roman occupiers. What is clear is that both the Jewish and the Roman authorities saw him as a danger to their prestige or authority, and a possible threat to their ability to govern in their respective spheres. Pontius Pilate, the Roman governor who condemned Jesus to death by crucifixion, knew that Palestine was a potentially turbulent place, and some thirty-five years later a serious revolt did occur.

It is feasible to argue that the accounts of Jesus's very short and almost arbitrary trial, which were all penned at a later time, were motivated partly by a wish not to offend the Roman rulers. They therefore assigned more blame to the Jewish leaders than to Pontius Pilate. But the fact remains that Jesus was sentenced to death on the orders of a Roman governor, not a Jewish judge.

In the rush of events from his arrest to the eve of his death, Jesus knew that he was innocent. He also seemed to believe that he was ordained to die, that his birth and death were part of a divine plan, that his chosen disciples would triumphantly spread his creed, and that he would take his place with God himself. During the ordeal that began after the Last Supper he remained mostly silent. The teacher and preacher, the man who had spoken tirelessly in public, now had, according to Mark, almost nothing to say. Only four times did he speak, two of which were in answer to questions, and all of which were brief.

Death by crucifixion was a punishment for foreigners rather than citizens of the Roman Empire. A slow, gruesome and humiliating way to die, it was imposed when a strong warning had to be delivered; and after a revolt in southern Italy, some six thousand slaves were crucified along the roadsides.

So in public Jesus was nailed by the hands and feet to a cross on a Friday morning. Two minor criminals were nailed to crosses on each side of him. On Jesus's cross was posted a scornful caption written in Hebrew, Latin and Greek, and proclaiming, 'Jesus of Nazareth, the King of the Jews'.

Both Mark and Matthew record that the last words of Jesus were spoken in agony: 'My God, my God, why have you forsaken me?' Spoken in his native tongue, Aramaic, these words have puzzled many readers. But the Roman soldier standing near the cross heard Jesus's cry, and indirectly he answered it: 'Truly this man was God's son.' In another gospel the soldier was not quite so full of praise, simply saying that Jesus was innocent.

John's gospel has its own affectionate narrative about those last hours on the cross. Jesus, still conscious, looked down and saw, standing near the cross, his mother and one unnamed disciple, 'the disciple whom he loved'. To his mother Jesus reportedly said, 'Woman, behold your son!' And to the disciple he said, 'Behold your mother!' The episode ends with John's own words: 'And from that hour the disciple took her to his own home.' A new Christian community was being formed.

Jesus, now close to death, finally said, 'It is finished.' Another gospel, while sharing most of the details, reported that Jesus's last sentence was more positive: 'Father, into thy hands I commit my spirit.'

Jesus died that afternoon. Before nightfall his body was wrapped in spiced linen cloth and placed in a cave-like tomb, with a heavy stone to block the entrance. The year of his death was possibly AD 30, although other years are also suggested by learned scholars. The exact date of his death has long been overshadowed by an event that occurred two days later.

'HE IS NOT HERE'

On the Sunday following his death, Mary Magdalene resolved to pay her tribute. That morning, hoping to anoint his dead body with precious ointment, she spoke to a man she thought was the gardener. Instead, to her astonishment, he responded in the voice of Jesus, and actually greeted her by name, 'Mary'. In the gospels of Mark and Luke, other women – they are named – were present at this extraordinary event. The gospels give different accounts but in spirit they agree. The evidence is strong that the blocking stone had been rolled away from the cave, and the tomb was now empty, except for the living presence of a young man – or an angel – who was very well informed. To the women who came in search of Jesus's body he said, 'Do not be amazed; you seek Jesus of Nazareth, who was crucified. He has risen; he is not here.' The women's instinctive response was to run away, 'for trembling and astonishment had come upon them'.

That afternoon, two of Jesus's disciples were travelling from Jerusalem to the rural village of Emmaus. That they were walking away from the city and from the scene of his humiliation was a sign that the once-exciting religious movement was in retreat. As they walked they were joined by another traveller. They continued to talk, not recognising that the third man with them was Jesus. At the village that night the three ate supper together, and suddenly the stranger became familiar to them, for he proceeded to re-enact the last meal they had memorably shared several evenings before. According to Luke's gospel, 'he took the bread, and blessed, and broke it, and gave it to them'. Presumably he said not a word. 'At once, the disciples' eyes were opened and they recognised him.' Then Jesus 'vanished out of their sight.' Shaken but overjoyed by what they had seen, the disciples hurried seven miles back to Jerusalem to tell others the astonishing news.

While the two disciples were still describing their miraculous encounter, Jesus again seemed to appear amongst them. Aware of their confusion and uncertainty, he showed them his hands and his feet, where bruises and nail holes could be seen. 'Have you anything here to eat?' he asked, and they gave him some broiled fish, which he ate in front of them. He walked with them in the dark as far as Bethany, urging them to preach his message of forgiveness 'in his name to all nations'. Then, lifting his hands and blessing them, he vanished.

According to Matthew, the resurrected Jesus also met his astonished disciples – all except Judas – on a mountain in Galilee and informed them that they were now the leaders of the movement. The task he gave them was global: 'Go therefore and make disciples of all nations, baptising them in the name of the Father and of the Son and of the Holy Spirit, teaching them to observe all that I have commanded you.' Jesus finished with words of comfort: 'And lo, I am with you always, to the close of the age.'

His reappearances were not yet over. It is claimed that he was seen by many others who had once heard him speak or knew him by sight. To his followers – except for the doubters among them – Jesus was now seen as the long-awaited Messiah, the saviour of the Jews. Probably he was not yet seen as the potential saviour of all people everywhere, but the time would soon come when the king of the Jews would be hailed as the king of all.

A week after the crucifixion, the loyal and unfailing believers in the resurrected Christ numbered perhaps only a few hundred. Such a small group, deprived of their leader, seemed unlikely to survive. Moreover, death by crucifixion was humiliating, and ran contrary to the glorious triumph assumed to be the destiny of a Messiah. But so intensely did these early faithful believe they shared Jesus's love that they were willing to die for their belief. In the following half-century the hundreds multiplied into thousands. They became millions, and eventually a billion, and still they increased. There had been nothing like it in the recorded history of the world.

Early Christianity soon possessed three main beliefs, which were shared in full by most believers. The first was that God exists and reigns, and that he sent Jesus Christ, his son, into the world to save all those who merited or attracted his mercy. The second was that Jesus Christ, after death, came to life again, and reappeared briefly on earth before ascending to heaven, where he reigns, a permanent presence, alongside God. The third and vital belief, one not well known now to the general public, was that God and Jesus together, in the form of the Holy Spirit, can inhabit the hearts and minds of Christians. And when the Holy Spirit descends on true Christians, they are filled with a sense of the nearness of God and the presence of Jesus himself.

Even in its early days, Christianity was faced with critics who wondered how the resurrection could have happened. Christians themselves were among the doubters, for their religion was to become so many-sided that it generated its own critics from within. We will hear their voices later.

AT HOME IN THE SYNAGOGUES

When Jesus was a young carpenter, the largest cities of the Roman Empire were Rome and Alexandria. Some historians say Rome held close to a million people, but a leading economic historian has argued that the number was closer to one-third of a million. Alexandria, near the delta of the Nile in northern Africa, held some 216 000 people – rather than the million and more attributed by one of its most learned sons, Philo of Alexandria. Even half a million is difficult to accept, fine scholar though he was.

These two powerful cities, Rome and Alexandria, held more than the next eight largest cities of the Empire combined. Antioch and Smyrna, both of which are in present-day Turkey, were probably the third- and fourth-largest cities in the Empire, and not far behind was Ephesus, today a ruin. What is now the economic heartland of Europe, the western half, was the home of only two of the top cities – mighty Rome and the Spanish port of Cadiz, which held 65 000 people. In this population map, Jerusalem was a town of little significance, and Palestine a province of small importance.

Five years after the death of Jesus, it seemed inconceivable that one day his doctrines would extend to Rome and Alexandria and right across the Empire, that it would eventually be the religion of the Roman ruler as well as those he ruled – who could imagine that? Or that Christianity would long outlive the Roman Empire and extend much further than the Empire's armies ever reached? At first such a miraculous growth of a minor religion was utterly impossible to imagine, but the impossible would happen.

The Jewish people, dispersed as they were across the Roman Empire, provided the first network through which Christianity spread, slowly at first. They formed perhaps 9 per cent of the total population of the Empire, and that was actually a larger percentage than lived in Europe on the eve of World War II. In the time of Jesus, the Jews were influential in the cities and towns of Spain, Italy, Sicily, the Greek mainland and islands, coastal North Africa, Arabia, Persia, Syria and other parts of Asia minor. Only a small proportion of the total number of Jews lived in Palestine, and many were compelled to move elsewhere after the failure of their rebellion against the Romans in the years 65 to 70.

In whatever corners of the Mediterranean coastline or hinterland the Jews settled, they founded one or more synagogues. Even as early as 200 BC many Jewish synagogues could be found in Egypt, and especially in Alexandria, where it was probably easier to find a synagogue than in some regions of Palestine. A vital social as well as religious centre, a synagogue was a house of worship, a place for meetings and social gatherings, a school for both children and adults, and a kind of courthouse. It probably owed much to the Egyptian temple, which also combined education and worship.

Many synagogues were small but others catered for large crowds: the one at Sardis in the south-west of the present Turkey was 90 metres long and possibly held a thousand worshippers, seated and standing. It is exultantly recorded of the largest Egyptian synagogue: 'He who has never seen the double colonnade of Alexandria has never seen the glory of Israel in his life.'

Just before the time of Christ, many synagogues, especially those far from Palestine, were not frequented solely by people of Jewish ancestry. A missionary spirit was abroad, and some synagogues welcomed visitors, who were attracted by the moral code and the uplifting atmosphere. Female outsiders were especially attracted and some became generous benefactors. The newcomers, known as 'God-fearers', were not usually considered as equals, for they belonged to none of the tribes of Israel. They could not, for example, recite the prayer 'Our God and God of our Fathers'.

As the first Christians were Jewish, they attended the synagogues and seized opportunities to spread their own distinctive message. Some synagogues in Asia Minor and North Africa became more Christian than Jewish in their loyalties. The two religions were able to live side by side in the same house of worship because they still had so much in common.

Together the people listened to readings from the Old Testament, sang the psalms, joined in the formal prayers, and followed the rituals and calendar of the Jewish religion. They listened to readings from the Song of Solomon at Passover, and from Ecclesiastes or Samuel on other holy days. On occasion they might be visited by one of Christ's disciples – now called the apostles – who spoke of his teachings. For years, Peter and James, the latter of whom was called the brother of Jesus, were prominent in and around Jerusalem, and they were respected – except by those who thought them too revolutionary, or out of tune with mainstream Judaism. A few brief manuscripts were soon in circulation, recording some of the sayings and doings of Christ, and they too were expounded in the synagogues.

Even when a Christian congregation broke away from a synagogue and met on its own, and even when completely new Christian groups, consisting mainly of Gentiles and other pagans, began to meet, they relied heavily on the Jewish traditions and atmosphere. They relied especially on the words of the Septuagint, being those parts of the Old Testament translated into classical Greek in

Alexandria before the time of Christ. The Jewish voice remained a crucial part of Christianity.

A thousand years later, even fifteen hundred years later, the long history of Palestine was almost as familiar to serious Christians as was the short life of Jesus. And while Christians and Jews slowly moved apart, every Sunday the Christian congregations still sang the psalms more than any other hymns, and still heard more readings selected from the Old Testament than from the New. When the Protestants emerged in the sixteenth century, they separated themselves from the Catholics but did not move away from the Jewish traditions and writings.

3

'WHO CAN BE AGAINST US?'

While Christ himself and his short life were extraordinary, and while the belief that he again came to life spurred the Christian movement, it is by no means certain that his message alone would have created the institution that has lasted some two thousand years. Most of his disciples had let him down during his lifetime, though all but one returned to the faith. Other brave leaders had to step forward.

THE RISE OF AN UNEXPECTED LEADER

Paul was born in Tarsus in what is now southern Turkey. Lying nearly 300 kilometres north of the Sea of Galilee, Tarsus held a flourishing Jewish quarter, such as were found in many cities and larger towns of Asia Minor. Paul was both a Jew and a Roman citizen, not a common combination. He was perhaps in his late twenties when Jesus was delivering his final sermons in countryside so far away that the name of the Nazarene was probably unknown in Tarsus. When Paul first heard of him is unclear, but when he went to Jerusalem to be tutored by the celebrated Rabbi Gamaliel, he would have been given an unfavourable impression of Jesus, who was not popular among the leading Jews.

Paul became a damaging opponent of the Christians, who were still small in numbers. He was determined to see their influence wane. When Stephen, a disciple of Christ, was stoned to death by a mob in Jerusalem, Paul was there urging on the stoners. He also spent time in charge of a small team that arrested and brought to trial Christians who offended against Jewish law; and he was travelling with his servants to a synagogue in Damascus to collect suspects when he had an overwhelming experience. It was midday and sunny, but the sunlight was suddenly outshone. 'I saw on the way a light from heaven brighter than the sun, shining round me and those who journeyed with me.' In shock, all present fell to the ground.

Suddenly they heard a voice call to them in Hebrew, 'Why do you persecute me?' Paul, in alarm, cried out, 'Who are you?' The voice replied, 'I am Jesus of Nazareth who you are persecuting.' Paul was deeply troubled by these words. It is said that for three days he could not eat, drink or even see, for the bright light had physically blinded him. His consolation was the belief that he was now, and forever would be, a follower of Christ. As his sight and composure returned, Paul was strong in his new conviction that Jesus was the Son of God.

Others later expressed doubt about whether a blinding light had struck him. Scholars of the Bible wonder whether he actually was on the Damascus road at the time, and whether it was a public event or a private experience, but nobody who knew Paul doubted that his spirit and personality had changed. Such moments of a heightened sense of awakening are well known to great inventors, religious reformers, and people of acute insight and creativity. They have their flashes of insight and all is changed.

Fervent as an opponent, Paul was also fierce and fervent as a disciple. Baptised, he set about his Christian duties as he saw them. He spent three years in pagan Arabia, where a few clusters of Jews and Christian Jews lived, probably working at ports or trading posts. Nothing resulted from his stay there, except perhaps self-knowledge and determination.

After much hesitation he finally met Peter, James and some of the other apostles living in Jerusalem, and quickly became their ally. They were accustomed to new converts but this man was contentious. In the mainstream Jewish synagogues and in the temple at Jerusalem, the news of Paul's change of heart must have caused dismay. The more single-minded rabbis could hardly tolerate or remain friends with somebody who had changed sides so suddenly and passionately. Most of the dedicated Jews whom Paul knew well did not forgive him.

As a disciple of Christ he still revered the Old Testament, took pride in the Jewish people and their traditions, and saw himself as 'a Hebrew of the Hebrews'. Being Jewish, he was probably inclined to think that Romans, Greeks, Samaritans, Syrians and others who became Christians should first adopt the Jewish way of life of Christ and other Jews. Thus, they should cease to eat pork, shellfish and other foods not allowed by Jewish law, and should not work on a Saturday, that being the Sabbath. A true Christian man should also undergo the minor surgery and major ceremony called circumcision.

The debate about these vital matters was probably conducted in the city of Antioch, not far from Paul's home town of Tarsus, and in the course of the debate he changed his mind. He came to believe that Christianity should not remain a branch of Judaism but become a religion for all people, Gentiles as well as Jews. It was in Antioch that the term 'Christian' was first used. Paul was also one who emphasised the new courtesy of calling Jesus primarily by the name of Christ or 'the anointed one'. In the congregation at Antioch it was agreed that Gentiles and Jews should each be free to follow their own rules on diet, circumcision and marriage. It was agreed that all people were welcome to become Christians. In persuasive words, Paul set out a credo for the infant church: 'There is neither Jew nor Greek, there is neither slave nor free, there is neither male nor female, for you are all one in Christ Jesus.'

A TRAVELLING CYMBAL

The young Christian movement slowly began to make use of Paul's talents. He knew how to organise, and to do the work himself if others let him down. He was a negotiator, able to link clusters of dedicated Christians with groups in other towns. He could juggle complex ideas, he possessed a gift with words, and he was willing to travel at his own expense to distant cities where the Christian message had arrived and was likely to spread. Moreover, his previous record as a dedicated anti-Christian made him a talking point when he spoke in public.

The indirect evidence suggests that Paul was not living in marriage at this time and could therefore move easily from city to city. He could also practise as a tentmaker – a craft that employed tens of thousands of people in the empire – wherever he worked as a Christian activist.

Several of Paul's letters, or epistles, are the earliest surviving documents written by a Christian. He was living at the Greek port of Corinth – then one of the largest cities of Europe – when he composed his first epistle, addressed to Christians living in the Greek city of Thessalonica. He had already preached to the people there, and in about AD 51 he wrote to them, expressing his faith that Jesus Christ would return to earth. He himself hoped to be present on that Day, which he spelled with a capital D.

In which year would Jesus Christ return? Paul himself was convinced that this would be in his own lifetime, or soon after. He became impatient, however, with those Christians in Thessalonica who, thinking that Jesus's return was imminent, neglected their ordinary tasks and duties. He told them to be strong; a time of trouble would come before the time of joy. An evil person called the Antichrist – perhaps the Roman emperor in disguise – would pretend to be Jesus Christ and do enormous harm, and create confusion too. In that preliminary time of trouble, the main duty of Christians would be to serve the 'living and true God, and to wait for his Son from Heaven'.

In his zeal, Paul gave parts of Christ's teaching a new emphasis. He pointed, more than did Christ, to the idea of original, or inherited, sin. To Paul this was part of human nature, and he repeated the strongly believed story, passed from generation to generation, that it had originated with the very first man and woman, Adam and Eve, when they disobeyed God in the Garden of Eden. Only Christ could lift the weight of sin and the spectre of pain and death from human beings. Those who were saved by Christ, and by their faith in him, would be rewarded with a place in heaven and a victory over death. As Paul wrote, 'Death, where is thy sting?'

Paul had travelled a long way from the Jewish teachings of his childhood, for the Old Testament did not generally support the idea of the resurrection of the body, and did not often discuss a heaven for individual people. Christ himself, however, believed in hell and heaven.

In his call for love and charity, Paul was closer to Christ than to

Judaism. For him, charity was a way of thinking and feeling, and much more than good deeds: 'Though I bestow all my goods to feed the poor, and though I give my body to be burned, and have not charity, it profiteth me nothing.' Being human, however, he did not feel charitable to all the people he met. He was disappointed to find believers with a 'counterfeit faith' who pretended to be receptive to the Holy Spirit but were really 'in love with this present world' – he met them often. He had no time for the 'tattlers and busybodies' and their chattering tongues. He even criticised himself and his constant teaching and arguing; he almost conceded that he was just a 'sounding brass and a tinkling cymbal'.

Paul made three long missionary journeys, mainly in Asia Minor and the lands around the Aegean Sea. In the cities and towns he corresponded with or visited, he often left behind one message in particular that, in the following centuries, was learned by heart: 'And the peace of God, which passes all understanding, will keep your hearts and minds in Christ Jesus.'

THE SILENCE OF THE WOMEN

Whereas neither the Jewish nor the Roman family would warm the heart of a modern feminist, the early Christians were sympathetic to women. Paul himself insisted in his early writing that men and women were equal. His letter to the Galatians was emphatic in defying the prevailing culture, and his words must have been astonishing to women encountering Christian ideas for the first time: 'there is neither male nor female; for you are all one in Christ Jesus'. Women shared equally in what is called the Lord's supper or Eucharist, a high affirmation of equality.

Readers of others of Paul's letters might gain the impression that he thought women inferior. In a letter to the Greek Christians in Corinth – people whom he knew well – he warned: 'let your women keep silence in the churches; for it is not permitted unto them to speak'. While silence was probably the custom for women in many congregations, they must have spoken during religious services in Corinth, since Paul laid down rules for their dress and conduct while praying or prophesying. He insisted that, unlike men, women should wear a scarf or other head covering. Here and there in his later letters are unfriendly comments on women, prompting some modern theologians to suggest that Paul's changing attitude in later years came from a fear that the infant Christian Churches were inviting official disapproval by becoming too radical and too sympathetic in their attitudes to women and slaves. Scholars also argue, with some authority, that Paul wrote only parts of the later epistles, particularly those to Timothy. The debate about Paul's attitude to women will go on and on.

In some cities, female Christians were activists. The evidence of their activities is abundant. Apollos, a Jewish intellectual, sailed to Ephesus in about AD 54 and became 'mighty in the scriptures' and almost a rival to Paul as a preacher; and he was helped to become mighty by his tutor Priscilla, the daughter of a Jewish tentmaker. Mentioned six times in the New Testament, she was Jewish, came from Rome, and along with her husband might even have been a founder of the Christian circle in Corinth. Certainly they both sailed on a missionary voyage with Paul. Likewise, the four unmarried daughters of Philip the Evangelist, then living in the port of Caesarea in Palestine, were all said to be prophets, and Paul stayed in their house for many days.

Women also served as deacons in the church and even as financiers. Lydia of Philippi in Macedonia was a seller of that expensive raw material called purple, and her money must have been vital for that infant congregation. Indeed, so influential did women become that the pagan philosopher Porphyry, who was flourishing in about AD 300, complained that Christianity had suffered because of them. But the period of female influence was already ending, and the all-male hierarchy of full-time bishops and priests was taking control.

'I HAVE FOUGHT THE GOOD FIGHT'

Paul was an outspoken perfectionist, a sure formula for making enemies. His loyalty to the new Christian Churches was unshake-able. Roman officials in the provinces suspected that he gave such loyalty to Christ that he could give no loyalty to the emperor, let alone the Roman gods. Paul knew he was in peril. Unlike Jesus and most other leaders of the infant church, he at least held the privileges of a Roman citizen and could seek the protection of the law. Nonetheless, he spent time in prison and was flogged with whip or rod on several occasions in Asia Minor. He landed in Rome under custody in about AD 60, and the accusations against him were handled slowly.

Finally sentenced to death, he was executed near the banks of the Tiber during the emperor Nero's brief persecution of the Christians. On the eve of his death Paul was entitled to use again his own words: 'I have fought the good fight, I have finished the race, I have kept the faith.'

Paul is said by many theologians – especially German Protestants – to be the second-mightiest person, after Christ, in the entire history of the church. On the basis of his prose, one English literary critic called him 'the first romantic poet in history'. Many of his reported sayings live on, with the aid of fluent translators, in everyday speech in many languages. We still talk of a 'labour of love'. We still say that the love of money is the root of all evil, and not long ago many used to tell their children in more formal moments to 'hold fast that which is good'. One of Paul's sentences became a kind of Christian war cry: 'If God be for us, who can be against us?'

The sixties was a perilous decade for the new church and its leaders. In AD 62, James, the brother of Christ and at that time the bishop of Jerusalem, was killed on the orders of the High Priest and the official council, the Sanhedrin. Peter, his predecessor, had fled Jerusalem but was eventually imprisoned and put to death in Rome. That city was later to become significant not only for its active Christian congregations but also as the burial place of the two most famous martyrs, Peter and Paul.

LANGUAGES OF THE CHRISTIANS

Christ had given nearly all his teaching in the Semitic language called Aramaic, now spoken by few people and in only a few corners of the Middle East. He also spoke some Hebrew and a little Greek, but Aramaic came naturally to him. The word 'Abba', meaning 'Father', used by Jesus when he prayed in the Garden of Gethsemane, was Aramaic. Several of the sentences he spoke when crucified were Aramaic, but Aramaic was probably used by few of the Christian Churches that were founded in the first decades after his death.

In Palestine most of the earliest Christian Churches preached, sang and prayed in Hebrew, for Jews were the main members. Most Jewish Christians who met far from Palestine worshipped in Greek, the main language of the eastern half of the Roman Empire, and most of Jesus's parables and sayings were translated by others into Greek before they finally appeared in writing. The four gospels that formed the core of the New Testament, and the numerous letters of Paul, were written in Greek. As late as AD 200, Christians in such westerly cities as Rome and Lyon worshipped in Greek. Even in Carthage in North Africa the first generations of Christians worshipped in the Greek language.

Today, Greek words are still important in Catholic and most Protestant churches, and of course the Orthodox Church. 'Christ' and 'Bible' are Greek words. 'Angel' has a Greek pedigree, being the word for a messenger. The twelve disciples, especially after the death of Christ, were honoured with the Greek name of 'apostle', and later Paul and Barnabas – a Jew from Cyprus – were given that title too. 'Bishop' came in a zigzag way from the Greek word for an overseer. 'Eucharist', the main ceremony of the Christian Church, is the Greek word for thanksgiving. 'Dogma' derives from the Greek word for opinion. 'Pentecost' is also Greek, meaning fifty days after the Passover. The letters 'IHS', which appear above the Christian cross in church buildings, are the Greek equivalents for 'JES', meaning Jesus. Even today in many scattered parts of the Christian world the prayer 'Lord have mercy' is chanted in its original Greek version, 'Kyrie eleison'.

In Rome, the language of the Christians was Greek rather than Latin. A North African man, Victor, who died in AD 198, was the first pope to forsake Greek and write in Latin. But even a century later, most burial inscriptions of Jews in Rome were in Greek, with only a few in Latin. Perpetua, a brave woman who died in North Africa in 203, was probably the first well-known Christian woman to write in Latin. Eventually that became the language of the western Christians and the eventual split between the western and eastern Churches was probably widened by the lack of a shared language.

It was the spoken and not the written word that was vital for the early Christians. For the first twenty or more years after Jesus's death, nearly all his teachings were passed on by word of mouth, often by those who had heard him speak, privately or publicly; and it is possible that occasionally a meaning was altered in the process. The day finally came when no one remained who had known Jesus personally. When the last of the twelve disciples died – when and where is not recorded – the news must have been heard in Christian places of worship with an acute sense of loss.

It became more and more important that the story of Jesus's life and teachings be set down in writing. Some leaders of the church did not think the need was urgent, since any day Christ might return to earth and decide to tell his story and even add to it. The common opinion was that Jesus's own words were still vital for Sunday worship. Fortunately, some sayings had been set down in writing, and copies were taken along to many Christian meetings and read aloud. The learned scholar Justin, writing in Rome in about 150, described the meetings: 'On the day called Sunday all who live in cities or in the country gather together to one place, and the memories of the apostles or the writings of the prophets are read as long as time permits.'

THE SORTING OF THE BOOKS

The oldest surviving record written by an early Christian is a short letter from Paul. The First Epistle to the Thessalonians, it appeared about twenty years after the death of Christ. In the following half-century were written numerous minor and major gospels, containing infinitely more detail than Paul knew.

Of the four major works, The Gospel According to Mark is the earliest. Consisting of no more words than appear in a daily tabloid newspaper, it is eloquent, vivid and quick-moving. A record of Jesus's last and productive years, it begins with a simple proclamation: 'The beginning of the gospel of Jesus Christ, the Son of God.' Its first story is the sensation caused by John the Baptist when he began to baptise people by the thousands, and the last is the discovery by three women that the tomb of Jesus is empty and he is alive again. The three women, we read, 'said nothing to any one, for they were afraid'. These were Mark's last words; thus he ended with an air of mystery, and vital questions awaiting an answer.

Much of Mark's life is unknown. Some claim that he served as secretary to Peter, and there are grounds for thinking that he wrote part of his gospel from a memoir written by Peter himself. We do know that Mark was Jewish and that he knew Paul and other early leaders. His gospel had a strong influence on that of Matthew. For long the best known of the gospels, Matthew's was read aloud in churches more often than any other, such were its literary merits, its clarity and air of authority. At the very end of the gospel were recited the assuring words said to have come from Jesus: 'And lo I am with you always, to the close of the age.' Some critics maintain that the disciple Matthew did not write the gospel.

The author of the third gospel, Luke, was not a personal friend of Jesus, and according to some historians was not a Jew. Said to be a physician and certainly a friend of Paul, he was often sympathetic to Paul's distinctive point of view. His story begins with the assertion that the author has 'followed all things closely' and will tell the truth. The fourth gospel was written by John. Few would deny that he painted a unique, loving and, in places, first-hand view of the life of Christ. Appearing in the nineties, it is slightly later than the other gospels and has little to say about the parables Jesus taught. In 1924 an English biblical scholar caused a stir when he argued that John's gospel was written not in Greek, as were the other three, but in the Aramaic language spoken by Jesus himself. Many Christians prefer it to all other gospels. It concludes with the confident statement that Jesus did and said far more than was ever recorded. If they had all been written down, John supposed 'that the world itself could not contain the books that would be written'.

In about AD 160, a Syrian named Tatian happily resolved to write an account of the life and teachings of Christ based on a selection from these four gospels. Among the many other gospels that had been written by then, these four were already receiving preference and were regularly read aloud in churches. As the gospels sometimes contradicted one another, with each highlighting different episodes, Tatian set out to reduce the four competing stories to one; and in the process he made countless decisions about what to delete and what to thread together. Called 'The Diatessaron' and probably written in Greek, Tatian's account helped worshippers to see the life of Christ as a whole, rather than in four separate versions. Remarkably popular, it was translated into Arabic, Latin, Armenian and other languages. More than a thousand years later, a medieval Dutch scholar produced his own version of a single gospel, calling it a 'Harmony of the Scriptures'.

Three centuries after the death of Christ, there was still no agreement on which of the scores of gospels, memoirs, epistles and histories should be chosen as the truest. While four gospels stood out, other works were added one by one, and the remaining sources of dispute were resolved. Rome and Constantinople were now the centres of the Christian Church, and at last, in about AD 400, Constantinople accepted the Revelation to John, and Rome accepted the Epistle to the Hebrews. At about the same time, St Jerome was busily translating the books of the Old and New Testament into

Latin, and revising the existing Latin editions, but the resultant Bible, known as the Vulgate, did not appear in the one volume until the sixth century.

Long before the modern era of agnostic activism, acute minds were at work challenging or defending the accuracy and authenticity of early manuscripts, and selecting the best. Until the twentieth century, more scholarly hours were devoted to the life of Jesus than to physics, chemistry and perhaps all the combined sciences. Amidst all their disagreements, most Christians did agree. They believed that a man called Jesus lived and died, and that his life and spirit transmitted a magnetic message.

It is often contended that present-day scepticism about facets of Christianity is the product of our more educated, more rational world. But the first three centuries of the religion were alive with such doubts and with certainties too.

CHRIST SEEN FROM MANY ANGLES

By the year AD 200 the Christians had meeting places over much of the Roman Empire, but their adherents were still outnumbered by those of several rivals. Supporters of the various pagan gods far exceeded the ranks of the Christians, and they erected grand monuments and temples in Rome and elsewhere. Judaism also remained a popular religion, though it had lost many followers to Christianity. While the synagogues and the Christian Churches both endured episodes of persecution, the Christians suffered more frequently; at times the Jewish religion was actually favoured by Rome because its members were more willing to offer loyalty to the emperor.

One obstacle for Christians during the first two centuries was the fact that they were competing with very old religions. Romans tended to appreciate the old. They admired the old Roman gods. Part of the reason they admired Homer, Plato and Aristotle was because they were ancient. If Christianity embodied a vital truth, the Romans asked, why was that truth not known to the great men of earlier eras? One way of overcoming this prejudice was for Christians to emphasise their links with the much older Jewish religion.

Of the religions competing in the Roman Empire in the period to 250, Christianity was probably the most criticised. Its novelty and vitality made it vulnerable. Celsus, a pagan philosopher in Alexandria, wrote the first major critique, titled 'True Discourse', in about AD 178. Most of the pages have vanished, but a few sections written on papyrus were found near Cairo during the Second World War. Celsus dismissed Jesus as a bastard son of a Roman soldier and his disciples as a disreputable rabble of ten boatmen and two tax collectors. He repeated some of the Jewish criticisms of Christianity and added more. He thought the Christian leaders were too intolerant and their faith in miracles went too far. Proud of the Roman Empire and its gods, Celsus feared that any creed which was disloyal to the Empire must weaken the fabric and spirit of Rome. He did see merit, however, in Christians' high emphasis on morality.

On the fringes of Christianity, just inside or just outside, were numerous dissenters. From about AD 70 the followers of Docetism argued on philosophical grounds that Jesus had not died and therefore had not been resurrected. Some of these arguers saw themselves as Christians in spirit but refused to take Holy Communion. How, they argued, could they partake of the body and blood of Christ to commemorate a death that had not occurred?

Ebionites – the Hebrew word for poor men – were Christians who lived an austere life somewhere east of the River Jordan. They argued that the reason Jesus was special was because he had been baptised in the Jordan, where the Holy Spirit descended on him. They approved of only a few of the biblical writings. Perhaps not too far away from them theologically were the followers of John the Baptist, who had spread out to the city of Ephesus, where Paul came across them.

Another opponent of early mainstream Christianity was Mani, who blended it in a sophisticated way with eastern cults to create a universal religion. Known as the Apostle of Light, Mani was born in April AD 216 in Babylonia, in present-day southern Iraq, and travelled to India before making Persia his home. His religion spread along the trade routes with a speed that Christianity in its first two hundred years did not surpass, and many of his followers in Spain, North Africa and Italy were former Christians. A thousand years after Mani's birth, a version of this religion was to be revived with vigour in south-west France by the Albigensians and Cathars.

Mani's sect, known as the Manicheans, held to a strong sense of the presence of evil. They contended that the world itself had been created by the evil one, and that the servants of the real God, the Kingdom of Light, had to be alert to prevent disaster. The followers of Mani prayed seven times a day while they waited for the Day of Judgement, which they prophesied would set the world on fire and keep it alight for 1468 days. The fear that the world was about to end was widespread in many groups on the fringes of Christianity. Why and when the world would end became a topic of intense debate and speculation.

Another well-known dissenter was Bardesanes, who gathered an army of followers on the eastern edge of the Roman Empire. Born Bar-Daisan in AD 154 at Edessa, an inland city on a vital trade route east of Antioch, he was converted to Christianity but later insisted that Christ was a phantom and could not have been resurrected.

Influenced by Persian ideas, he ranked the stars as second to God in their ability to shape human events. With his son Harmonius he wrote many Syriac hymns before he fled to Armenia, an early stronghold of Christianity.

Origen, born in Alexandria in about AD 185 and for part of his life a contemporary of Mani and Bardesanes, showed in his massive writings the wide range of controversies simmering in the church at the one time. He himself created or heightened a few of them. In his travels across the Roman Empire, he left behind a trail of arguments and counter-arguments all the way from Arabia to Rome. Origen offered mystical advice as well, explaining that if people learned to pray effectively, they would raise their soul into union with Christ, but he also disputed many of the major teachings of the church to which he proudly belonged. He doubted whether Christ was as important as God; he thought the power of the Holy Spirit on earth had been exaggerated; he hoped it might be possible to convert even the enemy Satan; and he hinted that God possessed such love and mercy that he would not allow hell to inflict too much pain. Origen was one of many Christians who insisted that reason must go arm in arm with religious faith. A religion that today is sometimes seen as not fully rational actually placed a very high emphasis on the rational in numerous debates of the second and third century.

Those scholars who today call for a more secular world occasionally echo the arguments used by these early critics of the church. A few go much further and argue that Christ did not exist. Oddly, the ancient writers, from whom the moderns have unknowingly inherited several of their arguments, had no doubt that there was such a person as Jesus. They did not debate whether or not he lived, but whether in origin he was human or divine or both.

4

BREAD, WINE AND WATER

As the first Christians met mainly in private homes, children were present and expected to take part. Frequently baptised at the same time as their parents, they joined with them in the vital ceremonies. If slaves were part of the family, they too participated.

Most of the early Christians believed that the Second Coming of Christ was near. When finally he did appear amongst them 'in all his glory', no church would be needed, so the local leaders did not think too much about creating a permanent arrangement for Christian groups. As the church was highly decentralised, local leaders were as important as Empire-wide leaders, and they were accustomed to finding their own solutions.

The early leaders of individual churches were called bishops, from a Greek word meaning overseer or inspector. A bishop led the act of worship, guided members in their thoughts and actions, and helped to solve disputes. Later, when formality became the fashion, the bishop dressed in white, for that was the colour of purity: saints in heaven were robed in white, according to the Book of Revelation.

The early bishop, in duties and prestige, was a pale predecessor of today's bishops.

The young church must not fall into unfit hands. Who then should be chosen as a bishop? Paul is said to have argued that the ideal bishop must not be a recent convert, he must have been married no more than once, and in conduct he must be 'temperate, sensible, dignified, hospitable, an apt teacher'. Of course, being 'God's steward', he must be capable of teaching sound Christian doctrine and 'be well thought of by outsiders'. Obviously he must not be drunk in public, or violent, conceited or quarrelsome. Such precepts suggest that Paul, in his travels or in the complaints he received, had already come across a few questionable bishops.

One way of testing a candidate for this highest of posts was to seek knowledge of his family. 'He must manage his own household well, keeping his children submissive and respectful in every way; for if a man does not know how to manage his own household, how can he care for God's church?' We can almost hear Paul's tone of voice in that argument, though some scholars now insist that these views attributed to him were written after his death. The sterling qualities required of a bishop's wife are not mentioned.

Presbyters, or elders, assisted the bishop and gave him authority. The church in Rome had forty-six presbyters in the year 251, but such a large number suggests that they were spread amongst various congregations that met in different suburbs of the city. Deacons were also appointed as officials. When seven deacons were appointed to help administer and serve a town congregation of worshippers they were described as 'men of honest report, full of the Holy Ghost and wisdom'. Most of the early officials in their duties did not really resemble today's bishops, deacons, priests and elders: their duties and prestige evolved.

Soon, in the growing world of the Christians, there were a few thousand deacons, of whom some were all-rounders and some little more than messengers who carried food to the houses of the sick and the poor. The apostle Paul had enough experience of deacons to know that they had to be selected with skill. 'They must hold the mystery of the faith,' he announced, 'with a clear conscience.' It was almost elementary that they should not be 'double-tongued'. He gave the strong impression that women could serve as deacons.

The early churches usually appointed a member to act as prophet. It also allowed any trusted member to make a prophecy or speech, outlining God's plan for his people, pointing to omens that might herald Christ's return, and reminding listeners of the warnings uttered by Isaiah and other esteemed Jewish prophets. As the decades passed and the Second Coming was less prominent in Christians' minds, the local prophets became minor performers. Eventually, they were replaced by the professional bishop and priest.

SUNDAY AND EASTER

As Christ was resurrected on a Sunday, that day was likely to be sacred for Christians. But Saturday had long been the sacred day for Jews, and many early Christian groups continued to worship on Saturday. Initially, a few groups honoured both Saturday and Sunday.

By finally selecting Sunday as their holy day, the early Christians alienated many of their Jewish worshippers. Moreover, as Sunday was a work day in the Roman Empire, the Christians – unless they were self-employed – had to set aside time for worship either before or after the day's work. More often than not, the religious service was probably held on Sunday evening.

A meal was part of that religious service. Most Christians actually said they met in order 'to break bread', and in some congregations the custom arose of serving a meal especially for the poor. Worshippers welcomed the food and drink, for they were hungry after a hard day at work, which consisted mostly of manual labour. Slowly, however, over the years, the meal evolved from a hunger-satisfying one into something symbolic, restricted to bread and wine or water and preceded by fasting. It was intended to recall Jesus's last supper, when he had taken the bread and called it his body, and declared the wine to be his blood, and had commanded the disciples to eat and drink in remembrance of him. Known as Holy Communion, the Lord's supper, the mass or the Eucharist, it was a deeply moving ceremony for participants. At that 'joyful meal' they felt Christ was truly amongst them.

Easter Day, the annual celebration of the resurrection of Christ, did not immediately become a special feast day shared by all Christians. Christians in Rome were slow to take it up, preferring to view every Sunday as their Easter. Further east, the church honoured Easter annually, choosing the weekend on which the Jews celebrated Passover. As the exact date of Passover was determined by the spring equinox and the full moon, the date varied from year to year, falling somewhere between 22 March and 25 April.

Official calculations of the exact date had to be made well in advance. At first many Christian bishops followed the Jewish calculations, but the city of Alexandria, a busy centre of astronomy, issued its own pronouncement on when Easter would fall each year. Occasionally, Christians in some parts of the Mediterranean celebrated Easter seven days in advance of their sister churches elsewhere. In 387 the Christians in Gaul celebrated Easter on 21 March, Alexandria celebrated it on 25 April, with Rome in between those two dates.

Christian leaders had long thought it would be appropriate if all churches chose the same day for Easter, but it was not a matter of life and death. Even Milan and Rome were, in travelling time, much further apart than are the South Pole and the North Pole today. As for Alexandria and Rome, they were different worlds, and ninety-nine out of every hundred Romans probably did not set foot in the Egyptian city even once in their whole life. Agreement on Easter was finally reached in east and west in 525, but the Irish monasteries still dissented.

THE VIRGIN BIRTH

Christmas was not celebrated by the early Christians, the exact date of Jesus's birth being unknown. Other things must also have worked against the idea of Christmas. In AD 245 the brilliant theologian Origen dismissed the idea of celebrating the birth of Christ 'as if he were a king Pharaoh'. A century and a half later, the three honoured patriarchs of the east – in Constantinople, Alexandria and Antioch – accepted 25 December as the special day. This was precisely the time when, after weeks of living with fallow fields and cold winds, most people rejoiced that the days were beginning to lengthen. Christians sensibly took over a day already favoured as a pagan Roman holiday, 'the birthday of the unconquered sun'. For Christians the day now honoured the 'Sun of Righteousness'.

Christianity was almost four hundred years old before it began to celebrate Christmas confidently, and the long delay is puzzling. Understandably, Christ's birth was not held to be symbolically as important as his resurrection. But in the eyes of the church's leaders, the celebration of Christmas – meaning Christ's mass – had not even been viewed with the same fervour as the feast of Pentecost, which was in praise of the Holy Spirit.

There was an increasing fascination with Christ's mother, Mary; her status was rising, and a feeling of deep reverence for her was widespread along the eastern Mediterranean, whether in Alexandria or Antioch. While the gospels were not unanimous in claiming that Mary was a virgin when she gave birth to Jesus, the idea that Christ's birth was unique gained credence. By AD 432 it was widely accepted that Mary had always been a virgin – thus pushing aside Mark's assertion that Jesus possessed brothers and sisters – and in that year the council of Ephesus gave her the precious title of God-bearer. A feast in honour of the Blessed Virgin Mary, as she was now called, was widely celebrated in Antioch and nearby regions.

Another idea, not emphasised in early writings, became prominent. It was increasingly believed that when Mary died, she was raised bodily from the earth to heaven. Known in the western Church as the Assumption of the Blessed Virgin Mary, and in the eastern Church as the Dormition, or Falling Asleep, this concept formally placed her with Jesus in heaven. In AD 594, Gregory of Tours, a bishop and historian of his religion, gave his blessing to the event, and his verdict was accepted. Prayers to Mary therefore acquired a new prestige and intimacy. The next step in her enthroning was to be made in the Middle Ages. Called the Immaculate Conception, it assumed that she herself, like her son, had been born without sin.

The rising tide of reverence for Mary as a mother increased the reverence for Christ's own birthday, on what is now called Christmas Day. The veneration of Mary was accompanied by increasing veneration for the three wise men, now known as the Magi, or magical men who had followed the bright star in the winter sky to pay homage to the infant Jesus.

BAPTISM: THE WATER THAT SMILED

A new Christian was initiated into the church by the water cere-mony called baptism, the term coming from Greek words meaning to be purified. It was a Christian, not a Jewish, ceremony. Most of those baptised were adults, and the act of immersion symbolised their sacred contract with God, not to be broken. The day when Jesus as a young man was baptised in the river by John the Baptist was the beginning of his life as a prophet and teacher, and so the days when his followers were baptised were hailed as the beginning of their new lives.

When conducting a baptism the early leaders naturally preferred a stream of running water, another Jordan. But Christianity was a town religion at first and few wild rivers were at hand. Therefore, water from the town's river had to be used. Even stagnant water was acceptable, for all kinds of water were seen as possessing an intrinsic virtue. The learned Tertullian explained to his North African audi-ence that in the beginning the world was a place of total darkness, 'a melancholy abyss', lacking in form and not yet possessing stars and moon. In that dark desolation, water was the only perfect sub-stance – 'smiling, simple, pure in its own right'.

So long as the Christian Church consisted of a thousand relatively isolated places, customs varied. In the port of Alexandria the sea was used for baptising, and dawn was the preferred time. In about AD 250 the routine was well established: 'at cock crow the baptis-mal party shall take their stand near waving water, pure, prepared, sacred, of the sea.' In many inland towns the baptism ceremony, at first held on the river bank, was transferred to the church. So arose the practice of blessing the water inside the church. It was timely when the water carried up from the river was brown after heavy rain or smelly after a long period of no rain. The water was used not only for baptising. Placed in a stone font near the main door the 'holy water' was used by worshippers to make with their hand the sign of the cross.

Many adults were already living as Christians but had not yet been baptised. Perhaps they awaited the visit of a bishop to their town, or perhaps they postponed the ceremony because they were sailors at sea, or soldiers far from their home church. If they died suddenly, without being baptised, could they go to heaven? While the answer was usually 'no', the question led to intense discussion. A special provision had to be made for Christian martyrs who, not yet baptised, chose to die rather than publicly renounce their religion. They were now deemed to have been baptised by their very death: it was called 'the baptism of blood'. It signified emphatically the importance of baptism.

Various Christian leaders argued that people who died before being baptised could not enter the kingdom of heaven, since the 'original' sin with which every child was born had not been washed away. They advocated the practice of baptising babies, but many Christians disagreed. Baptism was a conscious act of dedicating one's whole life to following Christ – how could week-old babies be expected to choose it? A debate that neither side could win decisively, it was revived with emotional force in the sixteenth century in Germany and Switzerland.

The baptism ceremony practised widely in AD 200 called for adults who wished to become Christians to prepare themselves. For a day or two they fasted. They also learned a prayer by heart, perhaps the Lord's Prayer, and one or two creeds. To learn the words by heart was driven partly by a need for secrecy. Late in the second century, possibly in fear of persecution, a phase of secrecy – called the Discipline of the Secret or *Disciplina Arcani* – enveloped the church.

Before the moment of baptism, the bishop delivered a warning to Satan: 'But do thou flee, O Devil, for the judgement of God is at hand.' Those about to be baptised then turned their faces and bodies to the west to evade Satan. After again turning, to the east, they recited a creed. Almost certainly, in baptisms in Rome in the second century, the Apostles' Creed was recited. Still pronounced in most churches today, it is a simple and fervent statement of belief ending with the words: 'I believe in the Holy Ghost, the Holy Catholic Church, the communion of saints, the forgiveness of sins, the resurrection of the body, and life everlasting.' The Apostles' Creed was believed to have been composed mysteriously by the twelve apostles, with each contributing thoughts plucked from their life with Christ. When it was recited during baptism, therefore, it was as if the united founders of the Church were guiding a worshipper's tongue.

It was briefly a tradition that those being baptised were naked when led to the large stone bath of water. Later the women were baptised separately by a deaconess, and the men by a deacon. Three times water was poured over each head, or the head and even the body were submerged three times. Most Christians believed that the number three symbolised the Father, Son and Holy Spirit, but some claimed that it referred to the three days – Friday, Saturday and Sunday – in which Christ was entombed before rising from the dead.

The newly baptised Christians were anointed with a sweet-scented oil. After dressing themselves in white garments and perhaps displaying a wreath on the head, the newcomers were ready for the final blessing. The bishop, after dipping his thumb in a bowl of scented oil, dabbed the sign of the cross on each brow while reciting the words, 'In the name of Father, Son and Holy Ghost, peace be with you.' In Rome in the third century, a baptism was valid even if it was made only in the name of Christ, and further east only God's name was usually honoured. In their white garments the newly baptised walked in procession into the crowded church. There they publicly shared in their first Holy Communion. Sometimes they swallowed a sweet concoction to which milk and honey had been added.

At one time the most appropriate day for adult baptism was Easter. Then, in a large city, hundreds of people might be baptised together. To accommodate them a separate baptistery was some-times designed: a circular or octagonal building, in the centre of which stood a baptismal bath, usually made of marble. These bap-tisteries were tall but generally small in floor area. A few are among the noblest buildings in Italy. Who can forget a visit to the baptistery at Florence, or the two older ones at Ravenna – the Catholic and the Arian, their domes alive with exquisite mosaics?

When stonemasons began to erect the handsome baptistery at Pisa in 1153, twenty years before they began the adjacent tower, the preference for a separate baptistery was in steep decline. The newer idea of dabbing water on the head of a fully dressed baby or adult person required less space and rarely led to splashing; it could be performed in the main part of the church with the whole congregation as witnesses. Some of the secrecy and solemnity of the sacrament as practised in earlier centuries disappeared. It was the eastern, or Orthodox, Church that was, and is, more eager to retain many of the early facets of baptism.

THE ACT OF FASTING

Christianity adopted fasting from a wing of Judaism: the Pharisees fasted on Monday and Thursday. Christ himself, so far as is known, did not emphasise the practice of regular fasting, though he did fast when he spent time meditating and praying in the wilderness. He attended too many weddings, suppers and banquets to be viewed as an advocate of extreme fasting. Moreover, he believed in the spirit more than the rules.

After Jesus's death, many of his serious followers chose to fast from Friday afternoon to Sunday morning, in remembrance of the forty hours during which his body lay in the tomb. During the weeks leading to Easter – the period known as Lent – the fast was expected to last for forty days, though the rules and exceptions were numerous. The command 'to fast' had a variety of meanings. In some districts, every kind of food was permitted at Lent but it had to be eaten at a single meal each day. By the year AD 700, meat was to be banned totally during Lent.

Fasting was a form of purification and self-denial. As Christ had made the supreme sacrifice, should not his followers make their own minor sacrifices in the course of the year? Fasting was believed to expel demons and even cure diseases. A few days of fasting preceded the glorious day of baptism, and no food was eaten in the hours before the Eucharist. As it was believed that Satan liked to live in a well-fed body, fasting was a way of evicting him. In a sense it did not deny the worth of the body; it stressed how important it was. The human body, wrote Cyril in his *Lectures* in the fourth century, was 'your fairest robe', a work of art, and above all 'the temple of the Holy Spirit'.

THE RISE OF THE HOLY SPIRIT

Christianity was not born with all its doctrines in place; they evolved slowly. Thus, the activities of the Holy Spirit were discussed more in the year AD 250 than in the time of Christ. In the stories of the Old

Testament, the Holy Spirit or Holy Ghost inspired prophets, giving them wisdom and understanding. In the New Testament it appeared in more dramatic forms, during the conception and birth of Jesus. The Holy Spirit also blessed him when he was baptised and gave him the power to perform miracles.

At the Jewish feast of Pentecost, the Holy Spirit appeared before the disciples – now renamed the apostles – who had assembled in Jerusalem. It was just seven weeks after the death of Christ and they were trying to carry out his command that they convert people to the faith. They had hoped to win converts in the streets, but such a polyglot crowd was present that the apostles did not possess the languages needed to address them, let alone persuade them. Here were Jews newly arrived from Arabia, the Nile and North Africa, Rome and the Greek islands and Asia Minor but speaking the languages of their adopted land. How could Christ's apostles, uneducated countrymen, possibly address them all? Suddenly, 'there came a sound from heaven as of a mighty rushing wind', and all the apostles were 'filled with the Holy Ghost'. Reportedly, all began to deliver loudly and clearly a Christian message, while speaking languages hitherto quite unknown to them. Such was the babble of foreign languages coming from the apostles' mouths that one wit said that they must have been drunk. As the news of this Pentecost happening swiftly became known, the crowds of spectators multiplied. In the end many listeners – '3000 souls' in all – repented of their sins and were baptised. It was the first mass conversion in the history of the new religion. Known as 'speaking in tongues', it became a powerful part of the Christian tradition.

The disciple Peter, who was present, believed this remarkable presence of the Holy Spirit signified that the end of the world was near, and that the sun would be 'turned into darkness'. As predicted, Jesus would return to earth, thus terminating the dreams and visions:

And it shall be in the last days, saith God,
I will pour forth of my Spirit upon all flesh;
And your sons and your daughters shall prophesy,
And your young men shall see visions,
And your old men shall dream dreams.

The concept of a powerful and disembodied spirit – a concept also familiar to the Buddhists and Hindus – was a simple way of describing a spiritual event in which God was present but unseen. The Christian leaders mentally began to place the Holy Spirit on the same throne as God, without finding the exact words to express this. They regarded God as one entity or substance existing in three persons: Father, Son and Holy Spirit. The three persons were equal. This doctrine was ultimately given the name of the Trinity, a term that did not appear in records until about AD 180, when the Greek-speaking Theophilus of Antioch used it.

Thus was solved the dilemma of how to reconcile the old Jewish tradition, which insisted that only one God existed, with the new belief that Christ reigned alongside God in heaven. To these two deities was added the Holy Spirit, making three in all. It was a long way from the concept held in old Israel. But the Christian solution of proclaiming one God consisting of three parts was ultimately not satisfactory in the eyes of many of the people of Asia Minor and Arabia. Their ultimate reaction was to worship one God and one only. His name was Allah.

5

IN THE EMPEROR'S HANDS

Major campaigns of persecution against Christians had been organised by the Roman government ever since AD 64, when Nero was emperor. A few campaigns were widespread but most centred on specific parts of the Empire and were led by provincial governors. How many Christians were executed in the space of 300 years is not recorded. How many were imprisoned cannot even be guessed at. Many defiant believers who refused to repudiate their Lord were gruesomely tortured in public. Some were women who had just given birth, some were pregnant, and some were old. Often they were first humiliated by the clipping or shaving of their hair. Stripped naked, they were then whipped and branded. Some were beheaded with a sword; others were placed in an arena with wild bulls or mad heifers, in front of a baying crowd of spectators. If somehow they managed to fend off the wild animals, they might be put back in the arena a day or two later.

Most of those who were tortured refused to abandon their beliefs. In Carthage in AD 203 the sufferings of Perpetua, aged twenty-two, and her slave Felicitas were long remembered. In the early centuries no other martyrs, except for the apostles, were more revered.

In spite of the persecution, the number of Christians grew rapidly. They believed without a shadow of a doubt that Jesus watched over them. News of this guiding and protecting God crossed seas and rivers, plains and mountains, and was passed on from person to person. The Christian religion would not have spread so far without this belief, but other factors also promoted the religion.

WHY DID THE CHRISTIANS MULTIPLY?

Christianity at first gained from its Jewish connection, spreading through the network of synagogues over a vast area. Without this network, Christianity would have grown more slowly. And in seeking converts, it had an advantage over its original partner. Except in rare periods, the Jewish rabbis did not vigorously seek new followers but the Christians did.

Part of Christianity's appeal was the down-to-earth way in which it helped the poor and the hungry, the ill and the orphaned. It gave a sense of security at a time when the welfare state was unknown and inconceivable. Another attraction for many was the Christian belief in an afterlife. On the other hand, heaven might be accessible only when Christ returned to earth, and his return was long promised and long postponed. By the year AD 300, almost three centuries having passed without that long-predicted return, scores of millions of Christians had lived their lives believing Christ was already guiding and guarding them. That in itself was a consolation. The afterlife, they thought, could only be a heightened extension of what they had already experienced. Therefore, the hope of heaven, with its diverse meanings and waiting times, was not necessarily the main appeal for the majority who decided to become Christians.

Christianity was becoming an annual cycle of feasts, processions, special dates and special numbers, each offering a fascination for new converts. From Judaism came the church's increasing fascination with the number seven. The Holy Spirit itself was believed to convey the Seven Gifts: namely, wisdom, understanding, counsel, fortitude, knowledge, piety, and fear of the Lord. These seven gifts were not the same as the Seven Virtues, which began with faith, hope and charity. Eventually, the sacraments, which included baptism, would also number seven. The Blessed Virgin Mary was assailed by Seven Sorrows, which until 1960 were commemorated annually. Not to be forgotten are the Seven Deadly Sins, while the Seven Words from the Cross are actually seven of Jesus's statements, the first being his memorable plea, 'Father, forgive them; for they know not what they do.' If the number seven had charisma, the number eight marked new beginnings. This is the reason why baptisteries were often octagonal, symbolising the sacrament of baptism as a new beginning.

It is likely that Christianity in its first centuries was also helped by an unexpected factor – the spread of epidemics. While the pagan religions rarely offered help in sicknesses, many Christians, especially women, were willing to nurse the sick and take food to their homes. Christians were valued as helpers and nurses when smallpox arrived in the years AD 165–180, causing numerous deaths, for immunity to infection was low. When measles came along some seventy years later, it was thought to be the same disease as smallpox. At the start of the measles epidemic, several thousand people died in Rome each day.

Cyprian, Bishop of Carthage, observing that measles and smallpox killed the young and the old, and the followers of Christ as well as heathens, pointed out that Christians who died of the plague had their reward in heaven, while 'those who lacked the Christian faith were, after death, doomed to receive punishment and torture'.

In nursing the sick and the dying, regardless of religion, the Christians won friends and sympathisers. But in Carthage, the city of arguments, gossip actually attributed the origins of the plague to the misbehaviour of the Christians. In other words, those who were nursing the sick may have been accused of spreading the disease. On the whole, however, Christians received much more praise than blame during the epidemics, and they coped more easily with the trauma and dislocation of illness and the approach of death.

The bishops, too, displayed an unusual confidence in their ability to cure the sick through prayer and the act of anointing. Known as unction, the practice of anointing was praised in the New Testament. The gospel of Mark records how Jesus's disciples went out in pairs to preach 'that men should repent', and during their travels they also 'anointed with oil many that were sick and healed them'. After Jesus had died, the apostle James specifically instructed the elders of his church to use the holy oil to heal the sick – 'all in the name of the Lord'. Humility, penitence and the desire for God's forgiveness were vital parts of the healing process.

Many outsiders, knowing little about Christianity, were impressed by its results. At its best it produced what could be called civilised lives: a respect for those from other lands and for parents and the old; more respect for women than was common in the Roman Empire; and a helping hand for slaves who accepted the faith.

CONSTANTINE THE LIBERATOR

The Roman leaders, whose task was to maintain the unity of a poly-glot empire and who knew the limits of what force alone could achieve, must have been secretly impressed by the Christians' ability to bring together slaves and free people, locals and foreigners, in the one congregation. Less impressive was the way Christians shunned the Romans' own longstanding gods. In AD 250 Emperor Decius ordered all citizens of the Empire to make sacrifices to the Roman gods. The most ardent Christians refused, believing they should worship only God and Christ. In Rome, Pope Fabian was bundled brutally into prison, where he died; and eight years later Pope Sixtus was arrested while conducting a memorial service in the catacombs and beheaded. Origen, a prolific writer and possibly the most impressive biblical scholar the church had so far produced, was imprisoned and tortured, dying at Tyre. Thousands of others were mutilated, wounded or killed before the decade-long attack on them was halted.

Many timid Christians promptly abandoned their church, and in public formed queues to swear the pagan oath required of them. A few bishops cooperated with the Roman authorities, disowning their creed. The question arose whether the people who had been baptised by these turncoat bishops could still truly be called Christians. If a bishop made himself illegitimate by his disloyalty to Christ, were his baptisms also invalid? Half a century later, the Christians in Carthage and the nearby countryside were to be torn apart by this question. Known as the Donatist Controversy, it was to lead to the creation of a separate branch of the church.

After about AD 260, the Christian population in the Roman Empire grew more rapidly. It multiplied in the rural areas of North Africa, one of the Empire's most productive regions, and in Rome too. Recent French excavations near Rome reveal that 11 000 people were buried in the catacombs by the start of the fourth century, and that most had been buried in the previous forty years. That many families were moving from the pagan gods to Christianity is possibly a sign that the old Roman gods were seen as unsatisfactory, having failed to reward their followers.

The soldier Diocletian became emperor in AD 284. He delayed any persecution for some years – perhaps because his wife and daughter were Christians. Then, provoked by an act of disloyalty at Antioch, he began to harry Christians for what he saw as minor and major offences. Thus, in AD 303, in farmlands in the valley of the River Medjerda in what is now Tunisia, forty-nine people celebrating the Eucharist were arrested. If farmers in the grainlands were vulnerable, so too were Christians in the cities, where religious activities were easily policed. How many churches were destroyed, and their land requisitioned, is not known, but the confiscations in some regions were alarmingly high. After twenty-one years as emperor, Diocletian resigned, but the crisis for Christianity continued under his successor.

A remarkable event was about to favour Christianity. What was unimaginable was now true. Some of the leading families in Rome and the bigger cities were attracted to Christ's teachings and to the ceremonies and sacraments of the church. The powerful military commander, Constantine, was one unexpected sympathiser. After winning a military victory against his rival Maxentius near Rome in AD 312, Constantine became the emperor of the western half of the Roman Empire. His mother was a Christian; his sister's name, Anastasia, was the Greek word for resurrection. Constantine himself, though not baptised, was said to worship Christ in a portable chapel when he was on the march with his soldiers.

At this time his Empire was hit by high taxes, inflation and heavy expenditure on the large army needed to keep barbarians at bay. It also suffered from disunity. In many regions the peasants resented the big landowners, who in turn treated peasants with disdain. The poor in the cities resented the rich, and the powerful army was not popular in many regions. Christianity, open as it was to all races in this multiracial empire, could be a force for unity. And not being militarily inclined, it was unlikely to attempt to depose an emperor.

THE NUMBER ONE RELIGION

One year after coming to power, Constantine met Licinius, the emperor of the eastern half of the Empire, to devise a policy on religions. Their Edict of Milan gave liberty to Christians, or Catholics, as they were sometimes called. The edict declared: 'that Christians and all others should have freedom to follow the kind of religion they favour; so that the God who dwells in heaven might be propitious to us and to all under our rule'. Christians who in the past ten years had seen their church property confiscated on the whim of the emperor rejoiced at the news that they would be restored. Constantine also ordered that state subsidies be paid on behalf of 'the legitimate and most holy Catholic religion' to clergymen working in North Africa. African 'madmen' who scoffed at the mainstream Christians were officially warned of punishment to come.

Now a mainstream religion, Christianity was about to become a preferred religion. Constantine resolved to suppress soothsayers and miscellaneous oracles, fortune tellers and clairvoyants; all religions were no longer equal. In AD 321 he decreed that Rome should recognise Sunday as a special day: 'All judges, city-people and craftsmen shall rest on the venerable day of the Sun.' The law courts should close rather than preside over the 'unseemly brawls' of litigants on this venerated day. Constantine pragmatically allowed farming to proceed on a Sunday: 'it often happens that this is the most suitable day for sowing grain or planting vines'.

In AD 324, after another decisive military victory, Constantine became the sole emperor, governing all the Roman colonies from the Black Sea to the Atlantic, and from the Nile to the upper Rhine. More powerful than ever, he continued to support his own religion. The punishment of death by crucifixion was abolished, a gesture of deep significance to Christians. The tax system now favoured them and their churches and other properties. The cross was depicted as a symbol on the shield of the Roman soldiers. Those Christians serving in the Roman army were allowed free time to attend church on Sundays. While the army continued for more than a century to be commanded largely by pagans, Christians were no longer at a disadvantage when they served as officers and soldiers.

Once a back-street religion, Christianity found a place in all the main streets. It opened schools, though most Romans remained illiterate. Christian manuscripts were collected and copied in large numbers, whereas it had been an offence to disseminate publicly such documents. And Christians were no longer ordered to worship the emperor as divine.

Constantine also provided Christians with their first grand buildings, notably the Basilica of St Peter and St Paul just outside Rome. One of the emperor's palaces, the Lateran palace, became the pope's, and next door was built the Lateran cathedral with its five aisles. Gifts of property and land in the provinces and Rome – and even a bathhouse and a bakery – were presented to the church. Constantine became its financial patron, and part of the wealth he donated came from the rich treasures held by pagan temples. Thus, he foreshadowed by twelve hundred years the decision by Henry VIII to nationalise the lands, buildings and wealth of the Catholic monasteries in England.

In saving the church from persecution, Constantine exposed it to a new form of interference – his own. He valued the right to intervene in any Roman institution if the tranquillity and security of the Empire was at stake. When the council of the entire church met in AD 325 at Nicaea, near the city of Byzantium, he personally attended and firmly shaped the final decisions.

Rome he did not like and he ceased even to visit it: he would start afresh building a 'New Rome'. He decided that the old city of Byzantium, founded many centuries before by Greek colonists on the very border of Europe and Asia, should become the capital of the whole Roman Empire. From 330 he began to enlarge its walls and find favoured sites on hilltops for churches, demolishing existing buildings to make way for them. The city of Constantinople, as it was now called, was the first to be planned in such a way that Christian rather than pagan temples topped the skyline. Today the city is known as Istanbul and its creator remembered as Constantine the Great.

Constantine had drawn closer to the church in spirit during his life, but part of him remained untameable. When at last he wished to be baptised, on the banks of the River Jordan, it was too late. He was not fit to travel far and was baptised where he stood. For many years he had seen himself as the protector of Christianity; and in view of his transforming of the church, he felt he was almost one of Christ's apostles. His ultimate resting place was selected with that presumption in mind; and when he died in 337 he was buried near the altar in the Church of the Holy Apostles, amidst relics of St Peter and the other apostles.

This was almost sacrilege in the eyes of some Christian leaders, and his body was removed to a mausoleum. Constantine might have conferred unmatched benefits on the church and its members, but he had not led the sacrificial life of a saint; being a fighting soldier and an emperor, he could not lead such a life. Eventually the eastern, or Orthodox, Church relented, naming him as the Thirteenth Apostle and honouring him as a saint.

Jews and Christians alternatively gained or suffered from the succession of emperors. After Constantine began to tolerate Christianity he reversed the policy towards the Jews, and they – once the favoured ones – became more the victims. Their rights were diminished. They had a fortunate respite when Julian, the nephew of Constantine, became emperor in AD 361. Reared as a Christian but still sympathetic to the old Roman gods, Julian reversed the favouritism and supported pagans and Jews. He killed many Christians who were soldiers, confiscated numerous Christian properties and denigrated the welfare network of their churches. He ruled for only a year and a half, after which the Jews were turned again from minor favourites into victims, and the Christians were supreme again.

PILGRIMS' DELIGHT

Constantine's mother, Helena, a strong Christian, was in her seventies when she decided to make a pilgrimage to Jerusalem. There she is said to have found the remains of the True Cross, a discovery that galvanised Christians' interest in that city. Not yet a busy place for pilgrims, it did not even have a resident bishop, but the building of the Basilica of the Holy Sepulchre in the AD 330s, and the chance for pilgrims to pray there, enticed more visitors from Asia Minor and western Europe. An additional enticement was the belief that when Christ returned to earth he would appear first at Jerusalem.

By the fourth century, in almost any month of the year, numerous pilgrims were on their way to Jerusalem, Bethlehem and its Church of the Nativity, and the place on the River Jordan where Jesus was said to have been baptised. Female pilgrims had their own favourite sites in Palestine: the tomb of Rachel, not far from Bethlehem, and the well at Sychar where Jesus spoke to the Samaritan women. To pray for the future and give thanks for the past were the goals of most pilgrimages.

One female pilgrim, named Egeria, spent more than three years journeying from France to Constantinople and then to the Holy Land. The Roman Empire was still strong when Egeria commenced her pilgrimage in AD 381, and in safety she visited a sequence of sacred sights, staying usually in the lodging houses or 'lodging posts' erected for travellers. Where the roadside was likely to conceal robbers, Roman soldiers accompanied the pilgrims. At every biblical halting place, the pilgrims said a prayer, read a passage from the scriptures, and heard or sang an appropriate psalm.

Occasionally, on a difficult leg of the journey, Egeria travelled by donkey or camel. She hints that strong men sometimes carried her on a litter, except where the slopes were too steep. When she caught sight of Mount Sinai, she said a prayer and then began to climb what was called the Mountain of God – the place where, according to Exodus 24, 'God's majesty came down'. On her exhausting climb Egeria welcomed the prayers of the monks who came from a nearby monastery to join her group. From the peak she had the reward of seeing the Red Sea and the Mediterranean, which she called 'the Parthenian'.

In Jerusalem, which she visited more than once, she marvelled at what was said to be the apple orchard of St John the Baptist. She also describes a rite not yet celebrated fully in Europe: the annual

February celebration known as the Feast of the Meeting of the Lord, Candlemas, and by various other titles. Joining in the procession to the Christian basilica, she felt 'the greatest joy, just as at Easter'.

St Menas, a Roman soldier, was another name on pilgrims' lips. He had been executed in Egypt in about the year AD 300, a martyr to his Christian faith. His steadfastness in the face of death caught the imagination of later generations, and a church, monastery and public baths were built in his honour. Pilgrims carried home tiny quantities of the clear water that came from the local well of St Menas; some of the pilgrims' tiny flasks or ampullae can be seen in the British Museum. They are made of thin red pottery, and display on the front an image of the saint himself and on the back a sailing ship. Though the flasks held barely enough liquid to quench the thirst of a sparrow, the water was considered holy and might have been saved to baptise relatives of the pilgrim. The flask itself was also a trophy, evidence that the owner had made the pilgrimage. That St Menas had a reputation in England is confirmed by the fact that York Cathedral annually celebrated his feast day.

His name lived on in Muslim Egypt, where he became the patron of traders who travelled the desert on camels. In World War II, when Egypt was saved from the German army, the Christian patriarch in Alexandria announced that St Menas had interceded, and in answer to prayers had turned defeat into victory.

St Gregory, Bishop of Nyssa, a town in Cappadocia in present-day Turkey, had a different view about pilgrimages. After travelling to Jerusalem with psalm-singing colleagues in a horse-drawn chariot, he decided that it was wiser to make a spiritual journey inside one's own heart and mind, rather than spending years travelling to holy places. 'For a change of scenery will not bring you closer to God,' he wrote.

6

THE GANG OF HERETICS

Arius was a fourth-century Egyptian city-preacher who drew large crowds. While he is said to have spoken gently, people heard him clearly. Impressed by his manner and his sincerity, they did not easily forget his face: 'He was very tall in stature, with downcast countenance.' Amongst his followers in Alexandria were men from the waterfront and 'seven hundred virgins', nearly all attracted from other preachers. The messages Arius delivered to his hearers in around the year AD 319 were unusual.

Challenging the heart of Christianity, he argued that Jesus, while the son of God, was not the equal of God. Of course Christ was far above any human being who had ever walked the earth, and moreover he shared in God's nature and knowledge, but Arius believed that God in his majesty and perfection was a step higher up the heavenly ladder. Looking back to the beginnings of Creation, Arius concluded that God was eternal but Christ was not. His argument undermined the Christian doctrine that the Father, Son and Holy Spirit formed a perfect trinity. He implied that Christ's power to forgive and redeem was not the same as that of God.

Arius and his opponents both used the New Testament to argue their case, citing different and competing sentences. Origen of Alexandria, the most learned theologian in his day, was seen by some as giving lukewarm and retrospective support to Arius, but many leaders of the church instinctively opposed Arius's views. The typical Christian had been taught to see Christ not only as divine but as the equal of God himself. That was one reason why Christianity was so compelling. Now Arius had dropped a bomb by questioning the exact combination of the human and the divine within Christ himself.

Arius assumed that people more easily loved and understood Christ because they saw him as human. He had mingled with tax-gatherers and prostitutes, with the shunned and the downtrodden, and Arius believed this humanity should be emphasised more than his divinity. In hindsight, the nub of the dispute seems to have been a matter of degree, but in theology and politics, positions that might be ten degrees apart can seem in the eyes of the combatants to be ninety degrees apart.

To an outsider, each side of this dispute had a valid argument. Orthodox Churchgoers believed that Christ was the equal of God, and that to argue otherwise was to demote Christ. Arius believed that God was all-important, in his words 'supremely unique': why then should Christ be called his equal?

The bishop of Alexandria summoned a synod, where the leaders heard the evidence and gravely nodded. They condemned Arius. He could no longer preach to his swelling crowds of disciples. The dispute spread far from Egypt; everyone seemed to have a view on this contentious topic. The emperor Constantine was urged to interfere, and the decision of this mighty ruler, not even a baptised Christian, to intervene in a matter of high theology was a major innovation in the history of Christianity. Until this point, Christian leaders had tried to settle their own disagreements.

In the eyes of Constantine, the continuing dispute was unseemly and a source of division in his Empire. He demanded unity in the church of which he was protector. He instructed Hosius, a bishop in Spain, to cross the seas to Alexandria and try to placate Arius and those who condemned him. The bishop failed. So in the summer of AD 325, the emperor summoned a council of the whole church to meet in Nicaea – now Izmike – which was close to Constantinople.

For the first time the bishops were provided with expense accounts, and it must have been a pleasure for them to make the long journey as the guest of the emperor. Unfortunately, they seem to have been summoned with such haste that only those in the eastern or nearer part of the Roman Empire were likely to attend. Of the 250 who were present, only five came from the west. They included two deacons sent from Rome by the pope to present his view, and bishops from Carthage and Milan, two of the leading Christian cities in the western half of the Roman Empire. It was hardly a mirror of the whole church.

What happened behind the scenes during the debate of this weighty question can never be known with certainty, but the result was that the council rejected Arius's theory. The assembled bishops declared that Christ was 'of one substance with God'. In short, Christ could be called the equal of God, to all intents and purposes. The emperor must have helped to ensure unanimity – his prestige demanded that there be unity – but unity did not exist in the hearts of those present. Nor was there unanimous rejoicing amongst those Christian leaders who, absent from the grand meeting of the council, finally received the verdict that had been slowly conveyed to them by sea or land.

It seemed that the traditionalist side had won. The council had pronounced that Christ must not be dethroned, nor his throne lowered by even one cubit. The Father, the Son and the Holy Spirit retained their perfect unity. Arius was not only defeated but in disgrace. Along with several of his powerful supporters, he was sent into exile in Asia Minor. When eventually he returned to Alexandria, he was refused permission to take part in the Eucharist by one of his main antagonists, Bishop Athanasius.

All was not lost for the wearied Arius. He retained a host of supporters, vocal and silent. When Emperor Constantine was baptised on his deathbed in AD 337, the bishop who presided was a supporter of Arius. Within a few years the new emperor, a son of Constantine, made it clear that he too was a supporter, although Arius by now was dead.

Rowan Williams, a theologian who is the head of the Church of England at the time of writing, has produced a book on Arius and the long-drawn-out controversy. He wondered at the wisdom of allowing an emperor to share spiritual authority or being granted that authority by several hundred bishops. As a church strategist, Archbishop Williams sensed how difficult it must have been for bishops holding contrary opinions to oppose, face to face, a powerful emperor who believed in imperial unity, and indeed in a show of religious unanimity.

Williams naturally had in mind Hitler and especially his allies and opponents within the Christian Church. In 1935, more than 1400 years after the defeat of Arius, the German Lutheran bishops and pastors were in a similar dilemma after Hitler won power and quickly became a dictator. Should they bow to this new German

Constantine and support his nationalist aims? Many bowed to Hitler and learned to regret it.

THE BARBARIANS AND THEIR BIBLE

The dispute about Arius refused to die, and around AD 343 the bishops were again summoned to a council, this time in Sardica, in present-day Bulgaria. This time the western bishops were the more numerous. They took the offensive, calling their opponents 'the gang of heretics', and insisting 'neither his Father ever existed without Son, nor Son without Father'. In their debates Arius's detractors relied much on the gospel of John, whereas his supporters relied on Jesus's affirmation reported in Paul's Epistle to Timothy: 'I have come down from heaven,' said Jesus, 'not to do my own will, but the will of him who sent me.' There was no doubt about it: both sides had strong cases.

The council of Sardica broke up in utter disagreement and the eastern bishops walked out. The fact that only a dozen years had passed since Constantine secured consensus on this same question suggests that imperial pressure might have played a part at that first council.

Meanwhile, the followers of Arius held their heads high. They cultivated new allies, although it must be said they were not allies of their first choice. They were Goths, people deemed to be of the second rank. In the eyes of the true children of the Roman Empire, the Goths were barbarians.

One or two centuries before the birth of Christ, the Goths and their relatives, the Vandals, had been residents of Scandinavia. Eager to move to warmer lands, and capable of fighting their way there, they crossed the Baltic and settled around the Vistula River on the plains of northern Europe. In their next move, the eastern Goths, or Ostrogoths, came south to Ukraine and the Dnieper River, from where many eventually resumed their march to still more favourable lands, streaming towards Constantinople. At about the same time, the western Goths were moving closer to France. How many Goths were on the move we do not know, but it was probably fewer than quarter of a million.

The Goths spoke their own distinctive language, with various dialects, but were not able to express their thoughts in writing until a monk, Ulfilas, provided them with an alphabet. Ulfilas was born in Cappadocia in central Turkey – not an area frequented by the Goths – but he spoke their language. Rising quickly in the church, he was befriended by an Arian bishop, and in AD 341 he became a bishop himself. Ulfilas concerned himself with the Goths now living in Thrace, a region of Europe to the west of Constantinople.

As the Goths had no bible, Ulfilas decided to provide them with one. First, he made an alphabet for the Gothic language, borrowing most of the twenty-seven letters in it from classical Greek; then he set about translating the Greek Bible. But he resolved not to translate the Book of Kings and its record of Jewish warfare, on the grounds that the Gothic people were too warlike already, without receiving further bellicose incitement from a sacred book. While living amongst the Goths in Moesia on the lower reaches of the Danube, Ulfilas carried out his vital translation, which was gratefully received. Alas, the Gothic language is now dead.

The Goths and Vandals were sympathetic to the Arian version of Christianity – the Arian heresy, as it was formally known. They preferred the simplicity of one powerful God rather than the official concept of the Trinity, with all its complications and subtleties. After the year AD 400, the Arian doctrines flourished more amongst the

Goths and Vandals than in most parts of the Roman Empire, and these happened to be the peoples who were about to invade the western half.

AUGUSTINE OF NORTH AFRICA

On the Mediterranean coast of Africa, the church possessed intense vitality, along with the controversies that often accompany vitality. Its heartland was present-day Tunisia and Algeria, especially around Carthage, then one of the largest cities of the western world. In AD 350 this area, rich in grain farms and orchards, may have had a higher proportion of Christians than anywhere else in the Empire, including Rome itself.

No African exerted more influence on Christianity than Augustine. He was born in present-day Algeria in AD 354, when North Africa was a kind of melting pot of peoples. Part of his ancestry was Berber, and he had a pagan father and a Christian mother – a moderately humble background that meant he needed a patron if he was to advance in life. Fortunately, he was highly intelligent, convivial and quick to learn, and so he easily attracted a patron. A rich man befriended him and gave him the opportunity to study philosophy.

In his religious feelings, which were slow to develop, Augustine was for nine years a follower of Mani, the third-century prophet who believed that good and evil had separate origins and separate deities, a concept generally known as dualism. Mani's followers, known as Manichaeans, practised austerity and tended to be vegetarians. Theirs was not a united sect and had various offshoots, one of which emerged near the French Pyrenees a thousand years after Mani was put to death for his unconventional opinions. Only adults could be baptised into a Manichaean sect, because only adults could know their own minds, and after baptism they promised not to engage in sexual intercourse.

Augustine shared many of these ideas but not the restraint on sex. As a young man in Carthage he ran wild, then settled down for fifteen years with his mistress, Una – a legal concubine, one historian calls her – with whom he had at least one child. When he set out for Europe for the first time, Una went with him, in a small vessel that was tossed about on the Mediterranean Sea. 'What a theatrical show the sea puts on, with its shifting colours,' wrote the astonished Augustine. He soon wished he could watch this spectacle from the safety of the shore: he was violently seasick. In the next forty-eight years he went to sea only once more – to make his return voyage to Africa.

In Rome he became a teacher. In his private life he was still a follower of Mani but was no longer satisfied with his doctrines and so was open to new influences. After moving north to Milan he experienced, at about the age of thirty-two, a religious conversion. While reading a sentence from Paul's Epistle to the Romans he had the feeling that he was naked, and then the sudden realisation that he was clothed with Christ's grace. 'The very instance I finished the sentence,' he recalled, 'light was flooding my heart with assurance, and every shadow of doubt evanesced.' He sounds uncannily like Martin Luther and John Wesley more than a thousand years later. Augustine's mother, Monica, who had long been a Christian, was overjoyed on hearing the news.

Back in Africa in AD 391, Augustine began to preach. Possessing a mastery of words, he could play music with them. He became bishop of the city of Hippo, where he spent much of his time presiding over courts, teaching the young members of his congregation and adjudicating in religious disputes. He also had time to write long manuscripts, letters and sermons, including his *Confessions* in thirteen instalments, but as he did not write Greek he was not read widely in the eastern parts of Christendom. He reflected the rift quietly widening in the Christian empire. A western Christian with brilliant and bold ideas – and his part of Africa was close to Rome – was often ignored in the east. The reverse also applied: Arius's doctrines, for example, initially won far more admirers in the eastern half of the Empire, for it was his home ground.

Augustine had an active mind and recorded much, employing several shorthand writers to take down his words, which he dictated – often late in the evening – as he strolled about the room. Among the theological concepts he shaped was predestination, a doctrine that came vividly to the fore more than a thousand years later in the writings of John Calvin of Geneva, the early Protestant. Augustine believed that God knew far in advance what would happen to all Christians during their life, and especially at its end. In essence, God infallibly predicted who would go to heaven and who to hell, whereas no bishop could foretell which members of his congregation would be saved. Augustine probably did not feel completely certain about his own fate, and that was one secret of his success as a thinker. He did not place an inflated price on his own intelligence.

Bishop Augustine held a theological view then widely held but now commonly seen as extreme in a more secular age: he believed that God and mankind in one sense were unimaginably far apart. He believed the story set out in chapter two of the Book of Genesis. Mankind since almost its very beginning in the Garden of Eden was burdened with evil, with what was called 'original sin', whereas God was the embodiment of good. Augustine preached that Christ had come to earth to relieve the burden from those who earnestly sought and deserved relief.

The bishop was therefore perturbed when a British monk named Pelagius joined the refugees escaping to North Africa from the invading Vandals. Pelagius denied the doctrine of original sin. He did not regard the shaming of Adam and Eve in the Garden of Eden after they ate the forbidden fruit as a symbolic and long-lasting misfortune. Pelagius, unlike Augustine, did not think that all the descendants of Adam and Eve must carry the burden of sin. He saw the potential for good in mankind, believing that people possessed from birth the free will to do good as well as evil. Evil deeds, he added, 'are done by us, not born with us'. Augustine, by contrast, had a gloomy view of the human race, for it was tainted and even branded by the saga of Adam and Eve.

Though Augustine lived nearly four centuries after the death of Christ, he was unconcerned that the prophecies about the Day of Judgement had not yet come to pass. He predicted that the world would first pass through strange happenings. The Jews would be converted to Christianity; Christ would appear again on earth and would judge the living and the dead, assigning the good to one place and the evil to another, where they would endure eternal punishment 'with the devil'.

For the last thirty years of his life Augustine lived in the shadow of shattering events. The once-mighty Roman Empire was collapsing from within. It had extended too far and could not raise the revenue needed to police its long borders. Too many of its soldiers were now recruited from the borderlands it was trying to police. In effect, it was attempting to defend its frontiers from the 'barbarians' by recruiting other barbarians to serve in its own regiments. Moreover, beyond the Empire's borders, vast numbers of people were on the move – Vandals, Huns, Goths – and they tended to head towards the Empire's weaker regions. Rome, not Constantinople, ruled the vulnerable areas. In AD 401, Alaric, the king of the Visigoths, invaded the peninsula of Italy, and by AD 410 had entered Rome itself. The Vandals, meanwhile, were streaming into Gaul and Spain.

These calamities seriously bruised the prestige of Christianity. Less than a century after it had become the religion of the Roman Empire, having been welcomed officially in the belief that God and Christ and the Holy Spirit would protect that empire, Christianity had seemingly failed to protect it. Prayers to St Peter and St Paul, who were buried in Rome, had not saved that city from invasion. Perhaps the old pagan Roman gods had been more loyal and effective.

In AD 429, Genseric led the Vandals in their invasion of North Africa, and one year later his forces were besieging Augustine's own city of Hippo. In that marooned city, while the siege went on around him, Augustine died at the age of seventy-five. Century after century his influence and fame grew; he was revered as a saint and as possibly the most influential Christian theologian since St Paul. Constantinople thought less of him than did Rome. His bones later became a prize for those who venerated the relics of saints, and were taken from Africa, first to the island of Sardinia. Significantly, the church of the east did not bid for his bones.

WHO YIELDS THE THRONE? CHRIST IN RAVENNA

The barbarian invaders from the far banks of the Rhine and Danube were not as barbarian as the Romans imagined. They brought with them their Arian opinions of God and Christ, but they often tolerated the mainstream Christians already living in the western Roman Empire. Ruling much of France, nearly all of the present Spain and Portugal, much of Italy and the populous central parts of the North African coast, the Ostrogoths and Visigoths and Vandals seemed likely, at one time, to make their version of Christianity the dominant one in the western half of Europe.

The Arians were not ardent missionaries, and when their military dominance faded, their religious influence suffered too. Everywhere their supporters were being converted to the traditional church. After the Goths and Vandals and their Arian creed lost control of western cities and churches, their reputation was destroyed. They were deplored by those who loved the classical Roman civilisation and mourned its passing. They were denounced by the mainstream Christians as blasphemers. Even their religious works of art were destroyed or redrawn, and the propaganda against them was strenuously maintained. 'Gothic' was a word of contempt. The 'Gothic' architecture, a later triumph of medieval Christians, was called Gothic not by its lovers but by its detractors. It was so named by the Italians because, from afar, they scorned it. But there is still an Italian city, Ravenna, where the Arian view of Christ miraculously survives, in the form of great art.

A vital naval base as far back as the time of Christ, Ravenna had replaced Rome as the capital of the western Roman Empire at the start of the fifth century. From AD 493 to 540, when it was captured by Theodoric, it was ruled by Arian monarchs and bishops. As a place of artistic importance, Ravenna is far older than Venice and Florence, present-day meccas for tourists and lovers of the high arts, but it attracts only trickles of tourists. Most of the grand buildings have gone, and the silt accumulated from flood after flood on the low coastal plain has deprived the city of its old port. Maize grows where the Roman fleets were once at anchor. And yet a shrine of early Christian art survives in the form of the wonderful mosaics created in the years of the Roman, the Byzantine and, above all, the Arian rulers.

The manufacturing process and artistic creativity behind the mosaics was sophisticated. Molten glass was poured into moulds, thus producing tiny cubes less than the width of the little finger. The glass itself was made opaque through the addition of oxide of tin, while other metallic oxides provided the colours. Rich blue, milky white and emerald green were favourites; gold and silver, being too expensive, were used only to give a dazzling background or to heighten the folds of the robes worn by Christ and the apostles. An intricate jigsaw consisting of myriad cubes was slowly pieced together by craftsmen, presumably standing on tall scaffolding. The completed mosaics, especially those inside domes or on high walls, possess a rare ability to multiply the light.

The picture of Christ in these light-filled mosaics must have seemed almost miraculous to many of the inhabitants of Ravenna, and to some of the sailors and soldiers posted to its port. In the Basilica of Sant'Apollinare Nuovo can still be seen a mosaic designed by an unknown artist around AD 520, during the reign of Emperor Theodoric. It depicts the biblical story of the loaves and the fishes, with Christ feeding the crowd of 5000 who had come to hear him teach. Against a background of glassy gold stand five men, mostly youngish with clean-shaven faces, all differing in posture. One is carrying four round, flat-topped bread loaves, another a fresh fish or perhaps two. Christ, the only one with long hair, stands in the centre, slightly taller than the rest and wearing a striped robe of purple, the imperial colour. As the other four men do not fix their eyes on the public, the eyes of Christ tend to dominate the mosaic. Calm, quiet and sensitive, he has a gentle rather than a godlike air. Is he the Jesus of the Arian creed?

Inside the dome of the small but high Arian baptistery, constructed of local bricks in about AD 500, we can see another brilliant mosaic. Christ is being baptised by John the Baptist. Tall, muscular and angular, John stands on one bank of the narrow River Jordan, and on the other bank sits a river god, of almost the same physique. A river god sitting prominently in a Christian building in what was briefly the capital city of an empire! The barbarians seem to be having their way.

Christ himself stands in the water, front on and naked, his penis concealed slightly by the river and its ripples. He appears to be about sixteen or eighteen years old, well built without being muscular, and his hair is not long compared to the later depictions of him by numerous western artists. His beardless face is relaxed, peaceful, even attractive, and shows no conspicuous sense of authority. In a circle below him stand the well-dressed and bearded apostles, all conveying a stronger air of authority, though perhaps it stems more from their experience and age. This brilliant mosaic, now fifteen hundred years old, downplays Christ, as if in sympathy with the Arian doctrine. The Christ depicted here is not godlike.

So in old Ravenna we catch a minute in time when the Roman Empire has fallen, the Arian invaders are riding in triumph, and traditional Christianity is virtually their captive. Here, and almost nowhere else in Europe, we see Christ as Arius might have seen him.

7

MONKS AND HERMITS

The great majority of early Christians lived with their families, and went to work six days of the week. They moved in the mainstream of daily life. By AD 320, however, many hermit Christians existed out of sight, and their numbers were increasing. Isolated corners of Syria attracted them; deserted Egyptian villages close to the Nile were another haven.

Many lived entirely on their own in caves or simple huts. On Sunday they might come together to worship with other hermits, before returning to the earthen floor of their homes. After a time, however, many could not stand the isolation; they felt acutely the onset of boredom and were prey to robbers and thugs. So they entered communities called monasteries, where, known as monks, they lived permanently.

Discipline was the monks' way of life. These men had usually tried to obey strict rules even when they were living on their own, and when they assembled in groups, the rules of behaviour multiplied. A monastery of even a dozen men would have been chaotic and self-defeating without rules. One vital decision was when and how to admit new members, because in years of famine or civil unrest – or evangelical fervour – numerous people must have been calling at the monastery gate seeking admission. To gain admission was to renounce and, as much as possible, forget the outside world and all its pleasures.

HOW TO LIVE IN A MONASTERY

An applicant for admission had to know the Lord's Prayer and a few psalms by heart, and he had to convince the head of the monastery that he was not a law-breaker nor someone breaking a contract with his employer in order to start a new life. His manner and personality were scrutinised. He might formally promise to give up his possessions and his first loyalty to his parents, but was he likely to keep that promise? The spirit of the monastery could be undermined if it were to admit monks who brought the selfish outside world with them.

An early list of rules was set out by an Egyptian monk named Pachomius, who founded a monastery in a half-deserted village near the River Nile in AD 323. Conscripted as a soldier under Constantine, Pachomius formally became a Christian long before his own emperor was converted. He thought that, since the outside world was a dangerous infection, the monks inside his walls should hear as little news as possible from the city of Alexandria. Rule 60, as approved by Pachomius, instructed the monks to discuss no worldly matters. When on Sunday they washed their clothes they did it in silence. Those whose task it was to bake the daily bread were not allowed the pleasure of private chatter but instead recited verses from the Bible. Other daily tasks, such as soaking reeds for the making of twine for ropes, and preparing palm leaves for the plaiting of baskets, were presumably also done in silence.

In the hall, where nearly all dined at noon, silence reigned. Sign language was used so that food could be passed along the table. Those monks who wished to undergo a regime of light fasting ate in their cells, lest the sight of plentiful food on the tables weakened their willpower. On the other hand, sick monks in the infirmary received a little wine and a broth containing a few pieces of that worldly luxury: cooked meat.

Hospitality was generously dispensed to pilgrims and to journeying monks from other monasteries. Pachomius recognised that female travellers were capable of upsetting the contentment of the monastery. If they arrived at nightfall, however, it surely 'would be mean to drive them away'. Pachomius discussed this dilemma: as women, they should be treated with even more honour than the male visitors, but also with more 'diligence'. Accordingly, they were placed in a separate guesthouse, enclosed by a wall or fence.

The words 'convent', 'monastery' and 'cloister' once had a similar meaning. 'Convent' was an alternative word for monastery, indeed for a male monastery, but eventually it became a name for female institutions. Today the word 'cloister' denotes the inner arcades and enclosed walkways of a religious building, but in the medieval era the word could embrace an entire monastery or convent. In Shakespeare's *Measure for Measure* are heard the words, 'This day my sister should the cloister enter.'

A monk could not run an outside errand without another monk to watch over him, for there was safety in pairs. The same rule was to regulate nuns as late as the 1970s. Such rules savour of a prison but the monastery was an institution whose inmates, with high expectations and devout resolutions, had entered by their own choice. Moreover, in times of famine or poverty, a monastery offered a degree of social security unusual in those centuries. It even provided a smart or casual uniform. In the nine or so monasteries presided over by Pachomius, the three thousand men wore a linen tunic or goat-skin cloak belted at the waist, a long scarf, and a hood showing the insignia of the monastery and even of the particular house where each monk lived.

A few Christians decided they could live the life of a hermit alongside a busy highway as well as in a lonely hut in the desert. Simeon Stylites, born in Cilicia near present-day Syria in about AD 390, left his monastery and resolved to build a high *stylite* – that being the Greek word for pillar – and live his life on the very top. Eventually, the pillar, extended several times, was as high as the roof of a six-storey building. Food and water and messages were sent up to him. Year after year, summer and winter, he perched there, surrounded by a wooden railing to prevent an accidental fall.

Simeon Stylites became one of the memorable sights of Asia Minor, and many centuries later the English historian Edward Gibbon spread the hermit's fame by describing his eccentric perch and what he called the invention of 'aerial penance'. In one of those celebrated volumes telling of *The Decline and Fall of the Roman Empire*, Gibbon amusingly depicted Simeon as an acrobat and a clown as much as a serious Christian.

Contrary to the impression conveyed by Gibbon, this hermit living on the top of the pillar was also a compelling and graceful preacher, delivering his message twice a day and urging his listeners to look up to heaven and 'imagine the expected kingdom'. Most of the night and morning he spent in prayer, standing up the whole time. In Constantinople, Emperor Theodosius II was said to be too readily under his influence. Generous towards local people who arrived seeking his help – and to solicit a miracle or two – Simeon Stylites at the height of his fame attracted pilgrims from as far away as Britain and Spain in the west, and Armenia and Persia in Asia Minor. In due course, a church and monastery were erected on the site, after the famous pillar was no longer inhabited.

Simeon Stylites reflected a stern, ascetic streak in Christianity. It was believed that human appetites were dangerous. The body had to be tamed, thus permitting the spirit and soul to triumph. Simeon imparted this message to those who stood admiringly below him.

While men living on top of pillars were crowd-pleasers, the groups of monks and the lonely hermits were out of sight. At first they lived only in the east, and in fact the words 'hermit' and 'monk' both come from the Greek. By AD 400, new monasteries were being planned or built all the way from Arabia and Abyssinia to France and south-west Scotland.

Western Europe had been slow to adopt the idea, and its first monastery was not opened until about AD 361, near Poitiers in present-day France. Founded by Martin, a former soldier, it was such a success that he became the bishop of Tours in AD 372. Celebrated in his day, his name was handed down to the first Protestant, Martin Luther, more than eleven hundred years later.

THE DAILY HUBBUB: TO FACE IT OR RETREAT?

The rise of hermits and monasteries was unexpected. Little in the life of Jesus anticipated groups of Christians retreating from the world. While he was said to have spent forty days and nights in the wilderness preparing himself for his new life as an evangelist, thereafter he much preferred the company of people in the towns and countryside. He loved to celebrate with them, to teach them and argue with them. While he prayed often, he had no intention of devoting most of the day to prayer and the reading of sacred works. The idea of eating in silence did not appeal to him. The idea of denying himself the companionship of women would have dismayed him.

The purpose of Christ's ministry was to take his message to the world, whereas the monk and the hermit usually wished to withdraw. Moreover, Christ's concern, when walking up and down Galilee, was that the harvest 'truly is plenteous, but the labourers are few'. As more preachers and teachers were needed to arouse the world, why allow devout men and women to enter the silence and seclusion of monasteries and convents? Their voices were needed on the roadside, in the synagogues, wherever people gathered.

One century after the first notable monastery was set up, the monks and hermits of Christendom could be counted in the thousands. Inevitably, the worthier monks were joined by a few strays and scavengers. Sometimes these misfits abandoned their monastic life and lived in the towns. In Rome, where feral monks begged for a living, observant citizens noticed disapprovingly that their clothing was coarse, their long sleeves were sloppy and their boots bulged.

Most monks were men, but more and more women – especially spinsters and widows – wished to form separate groups. They came together on weekdays to pray, and they cared for sick members of the congregation. Many learned how to read – few women were literate in the Roman Empire – so that they could read the Bible aloud to friends. On the Sabbath they provided choral music and perhaps formed a procession when pageantry was called for. They began to dress in similar but simple clothes.

It was only a small step for the more devoted of these women to live together in the same building as nuns. As women outnumbered men in most of the early Christian congregations, new nuns were not hard to recruit. Whereas in the Old Testament the childless wife was an object of pity, in Christianity the attitude differed. Some Christian leaders believed that certain young women could serve God more ably by shunning marriage. An advocate of this viewpoint was the gifted theologian Jerome, who was busily producing the Vulgate Bible, which was to be the Catholics' official text for more than a thousand years. He had once lived as a hermit, 'parched by the blazing heat of the sun', and he suggested that women should be free to create their own version of that sacrificial life. Of course, they must live in an all-female monastery, thus evading the moments when 'lust tickles the sense'.

To an unmarried woman who intended to found a convent, Jerome set out his views on female life. The status of a married woman was 'honourable' but she suffered pain, torment and servitude. Those who shunned marriage could become even more honourable in the eyes of God if they dedicated their life to him. Instead of caring for 'sons and daughters, you have a place forever in heaven,' he assured her. His advice was that she should avoid married women and spend her time with those single women whose faces were pale and 'thin from fasting'. Even then, a form of anorexia had its appeal.

How to conduct a monastery or nunnery was one of the tantalising questions for serious women and men. Basil the Great, born in Cappadocia in central Turkey in AD 330, seemed likely to become a teacher of rhetoric until he was stirred by his sister Macrina, who had founded a nunnery on her family's estate. After visiting hermits and monks living as far south as Egypt, he set up his own monastery, at first near his sister's, and used it as a base for charitable work. At about the age of forty, on becoming a bishop, his mind was still on the monasteries and how to improve them. He was to be the spiritual founder of a long line of monasteries that eventually arose in Russia and other Slavonic lands.

TO MARRY OR NOT TO MARRY?

The leaders of the Roman Empire tended to be promiscuous. Christians, reacting against them, tended to be puritanical. The early monks living in Egypt eschewed sex, and many Christians expected their bishops and priests to live chaste lives. After all, they dispensed the sacred wine and bread – the blood and body of Christ – at that important weekly sacrament. But the early Christian Church, like the synagogue, did not prohibit its bishops from entering into marriage. The question of whom they married was the more important. Obviously, a man already a priest or bishop should not marry a concubine.

Around AD 305, a decade before Constantine suddenly blessed and favoured the church, Christian leaders met at Elvira in southern Spain. The mood of the leaders, mostly Spaniards, was clear. They favoured chastity and respectability. Women must not spend a night in a cemetery, where, it was assumed, they might 'commit evil deeds'. Men who sexually abused boys were in such disgrace that they were not to be allowed the Eucharist. A deacon or priest should not contract a new marriage. Those already married were required to abstain from sex, and if henceforth they produced children they thereby ceased to be priests. These were ideals more than iron rules.

The influential Council of Nicaea, meeting in AD 325, generally repeated that Spanish call for restraint. It allowed only the lower ranks of the clergy to marry, and that rule was to be followed increasingly in the Orthodox Church, which still allows an intending cleric to marry before becoming the local priest. In such matters the Orthodox and the Protestant churches have much in common.

Any restraint on clerical behaviour was not widely enforced in the Catholic west. According to the Council of Tours, which met in

567, most bishops had wives, many of whom carried out charitable duties. In Italy many senior priests continued to marry. In France, in the century after AD 942, three bishops were actually married men with families. Wales and Ireland were for long a law to themselves. Even certain of the popes had illegitimate children.

The rules of the western Church were so often broken that some reformers argued that marriage for clergymen was the sensible compromise. Other observers, also pragmatic, disagreed. They thought that formal marriage for bishops or priests was to be avoided at all costs, because if they married they would bequeath too much of the church's wealth to their own children. Measured by the standards of St Paul and his followers, the western Church was in moral decay. Perhaps its hope of revival lay in learning from the best monasteries, which now set an example in Christian behaviour. Built on the idea of withdrawal from the world, the monasteries and their spirit were now invited to re-enter the world.

THE CALL OF THE BENEDICTINES

Benedict was perhaps the most influential churchman of his day, though at the time of his death his influence had barely begun. Coming from Norcia in central Italy, a valley-town now celebrated for many of the fungi and pork products used in Italian cooking, he moved to Rome for his education. In about AD 500, he turned his back on what he perceived as the evils of Rome and lived as a hermit in a cave near Subiaco. He was then about twenty, with the inner strength of a natural leader, but he was a reluctant leader. His first step towards leadership was to cease being a hermit.

Eventually, he took charge of a cluster of small monasteries, each holding a dozen monks. He preferred to rule by example, and continued to live a contemplative life rather than busily organise and constantly command. His last home was the monastery he founded in about AD 529 at Monte Cassino, between Rome and Naples. Not one to organise conferences, he did, once a year, discuss spiritual matters with his sister Scholastica, who ran a convent nearby. She died before him, and he in turn was buried in the same grave.

Benedict had slowly developed his own mixture of ideas about the way the monastic life should be lived. He borrowed ideas from the monks and bishops living in areas as far apart as Egypt and France. Certain rules were added by other monks, in his name, after his death. Many of his rules were similar to those drawn up for early monasteries in Egypt but more scholarly. The Benedictine liked a strong, godly and patient abbot, preferably elected by his colleagues.

Private possessions had no place in Benedict's scheme of things. He lamented that too much of the monastic week was wasted or trivialised by chatter. 'Monks should practise silence at all times, but especially in the hours of night,' decreed Benedict's rule 42. After the final religious ceremony of the day – the service called *completorium* in Latin – silence reigned in the monastery except for the occasional footsteps. Even meals were eaten in silence at well-run monasteries, for the monks had to give full attention to the public readings of scripture that went on while they ate. Each week a monk was appointed as the official reader, and before he commenced to read, a memorable prayer was spoken three times by all present: 'O Lord, open Thou my lips, and my mouth shall show forth Thy praise.' Century after century this prayer would be recited far and wide by millions of Christians. Specific hours of the weekday were also assigned for reading, and one or two of the senior brothers tried to ensure that 'no troublesome brother' was gossiping or laughing rather than reading.

Travellers were not instantly welcomed. An experienced monk was stationed at the entrance by day and even by night, because some travellers arrived long after darkness, having lost their way, 'as is always happening in a monastery'. When the doorkeeper heard a knock on the door or heard 'a poor man' call out, he was to give him a blessing or answer with the sentence, 'Thanks be to God!' If the new arrivals replied that they were pilgrims or 'servants of the faith', the senior monks hurried to the door to welcome them, first with prayer and then with acts of humility. Thus, rule 53 reminded them that even the abbot had to join in the sacred duty, washing 'the feet of all guests'.

A monastery tried to produce its own food and drink, its own clothes and leather, and to write out copies of sacred manuscripts. One of the Benedictines' unusual skills – until about AD 1100 – was as surgeons. They set up hospitals and infirmaries, planted herb gardens from which medicines were made, and became the main custodians of health in their district. As Christ had healed the sick, so too must his servants.

The first Benedictines suffered after the Lombards invaded southern Italy. Monte Cassino, the main monastery, was destroyed in AD 577 and remained derelict for about 140 years. It continued to be a target for invaders. Heavily damaged or destroyed by the Saracens and the Normans, and by the heavy armaments of World War II, it was periodically rebuilt.

Each monastery was self-governing, and independence was a source of strength as the Benedictines expanded far from Italy. They became powerful in France, Germany and Holland, where they did the ground-breaking work amongst people who were mostly Arians or pagans. In England in the Middle Ages, a total of seven of the seventeen cathedrals, including Canterbury and Winchester, were

controlled by the Benedictines. Westminster Abbey, where the English monarchs are crowned, was also Benedictine.

LIGHTING THE EDGE OF THE DARKNESS

The Benedictines did not set a firm foot in Ireland: they had no
need to, because Ireland held flourishing monasteries when most of
Europe's were struggling. In AD 560, perhaps the most northerly of
the active monasteries in the world was at Bangor, close to the Irish
Sea and the present Belfast. Founded by Comgall, its austere way of
life, its long periods of fasting, and its around-the-clock praying and
psalm-singing attracted more and more local monks until it became
the largest religious house in Ireland and perhaps even in the British
Isles.

From Ireland, monks set out to spread their message in regions
where Christianity was not yet known or was struggling to survive.
Columba left Ireland to set up a monastery and church on the island
of Iona on the west coast of Scotland, while Columbanus set out
from Bangor with twelve companions, hoping to found monasteries in France. Their journeys far from home were sometimes called
their 'voluntary exile for Christ'.

At Luxeuil in the Vosges Ranges, Columbanus founded a monastery that puzzled neighbouring abbots, who followed more the
Benedictine monastic rules and the Roman ecclesiastical practices.
For the Irish chose their Easter by a different set of calculations
to those used in Rome, and their most learned monks maintained
a knowledge of the Greek language long after the Latin liturgy
became supreme in lands west and north of Rome. Nor did the Irish
abbeys take kindly to bishops, a form of government that belonged to
Rome's traditions. As for that vital symbol, the Christian cross, they

worshipped one of their own design, a Celtic cross that has some likeness to the Coptic cross.

Western Europe for a time experienced two competing migrations of monks: the Irish travelling east to the present Scotland, England, France, Switzerland, Italy and Austria to found new monasteries, and the monks based in Rome and travelling north and west to found their own institutions in regions close to the North Sea and the southern shores of the Baltic. Thus, in AD 595, following the instructions of Pope Gregory I, Augustine crossed the English Channel and arrived in Canterbury, where he founded the Benedictine abbey that became the foremost church in England.

Early in the new century, the Irish monk Gallech or Gall, a product of Bangor, arrived as a hermit in Switzerland, where the famous monastery of St Gallen keeps alive his name. At almost the same time, his friend from Bangor, the restless Columbanus, reached the lower slopes of the distant Apennines, and in the region of Piacenza founded the Italian abbey of Bobbio. Like so many of these Irish-founded monasteries, both St Gallen and Bobbio created important libraries at a time when a few hundred handwritten manuscripts of some length constituted a treasure house of learning. Whereas the Italian library was looted by Napoleon some twelve centuries later, the Swiss library still stands in its own building, one of the most ornate in Europe.

In Europe, the period AD 400–600 is remembered for the so-called barbarian invasions. Invaders from the northern and eastern perimeters of Europe were blowing out the lights in the centres of civilization. But at the end of this period the people on the perimeter, especially those in the outlying monasteries of Ireland, were carrying back the light.

A WARNING IN THE SKY

Bede was a Benedictine monk who lived in Jarrow in the north-east of England for most of his working life. He did not travel far from Yorkshire; it is unlikely that a story of him visiting Rome is correct. Probably he did not even see the White Cliffs of Dover. Very curious about the world and scholarly in assessing what he saw and heard, Bede wrote his *History of Christianity* in his own hand in Latin, his sheepskin cloak wrapped around him. He completed it in AD 731. Conscious of his imperfections, he apologised for his 'many failings of mind and body', but his book was unusual in its emphasis on correct chronology. Following the example of Isidore of Seville, Bede made a list of what he viewed as major or significant events in the modern world, beginning with the incarnation – Christ's taking on human flesh as the son of Mary – and ending with events of Bede's lifetime. One historian judges it to be the best such book written in Europe in that era.

With a forthrightness that charms the reader, Bede's book begins simply: 'Britain, formerly known as Albion, is an island in the ocean'. He points out that its climate is different to that of Italy, Armenia or Macedonia. Indeed, at the height of summer – so Bede explains, possibly for the benefit of readers in Rome – a British person standing in the open air at midnight hardly knows whether the twilight of the previous day is ending or a new day is dawning.

He rejoiced in the climate of England and Ireland, noting that grapevines can flourish on both islands; this was actually the medieval period of global warming, which must have delighted residents of cold northern Europe. He reported that Britain had many snakes but not Ireland, and he knew why. Refusing to accept the myth that St Patrick permanently eliminated snakes in Ireland, Bede innocently explained that any snakes that were carried in a ship towards

Ireland soon 'breathe scent of its air, and die'. The book ended with a prayer to 'you, noble Jesus', and the hope that Bede may 'dwell in Your presence for ever'. In one illuminating aside, Bede refers to those 'who may hear or read this history'. Hear or read? The sequence of words, deliberately chosen, shows that most people who served as Bede's audience were illiterate and had to hear the book read aloud to them.

Bede was writing at a perilous time for Christendom. It so happened that in January AD 729, two comets appeared in the sky over England, the one being first visible just ahead of the sunrise, and the other after the sun had set. For a fortnight they could be seen like 'fiery torches', in Bede's words, and people must have been rising early to see them, for comets were the heralds of bad news and even calamity. At this time the Muslims had conquered Palestine, Syria and coastal North Africa and were advancing far into Spain. Did these comets signify that the Muslims were about to win another massive victory over Christendom? Perhaps they would next capture Italy and France and then England. Bede reported that the two comets struck terror into all English people who saw them.

8

THE RISE OF ISLAM

In the western half of Europe in AD 600, Christianity was slowly recovering from the decline of Rome and the collapse of the western Roman Empire. In the eastern half of Europe, Christianity was more powerful. Constantinople had risen high in splendour and population, its local empire on land and sea was intact, and it possessed four of the world's five leading Christian cities and their bishops, now known as patriarchs. It was also the seat of religious and regional controversy, which made it vulnerable when Islam was born.

FROM CHALCEDON TO CHINA

In the Christian east the controversy about the relative status of God and Christ would not go away. Stirred vigorously in the fourth century by Arius, the gifted preacher from Alexandria, the debate involved battalions of theologians. The defeated ideas of Arius reappeared in new garments. They were too basic to be dismissed forever. Once again the rival cities of Alexandria and Constantinople were the homes of this recurring controversy.

Bishop Nestorius, once a monk, had been the patriarch of Constantinople since AD 428. As his city was the capital of the Roman Empire, his voice was heard around most of the Mediterranean. An echo of Arius, he proposed that Christ was not the equal of God. Rather, Christ possessed two separate natures, divine and human, and they existed side by side. The implications and subtleties of such a proposition, which are puzzling to many of us, were grasped by serious churchgoers of that day. Even when they were not readily grasped, most Christians knew emotionally whose side they supported.

Nestorius was denounced as blasphemous, for he contradicted the church's prevailing view that Christ, as the equal of God, must possess solely a divine nature. The disagreement also affected the status of Mary, who was increasingly being enthroned by mainstream bishops. If Christ was not as important as previously proclaimed, neither was Mary quite so important; Nestorius implied that Mary was simply the mother of Christ, whereas the rising doctrine insisted that Mary was also the mother of God.

A council of the whole church was summoned to Ephesus in Asia Minor in June AD 431. Now in ruins, and a haunting site, it was then a major city and an appropriate place for a major conference. After grave discussions and a certain amount of political manipulation, the patriarch Nestorius was condemned. This scholar and preacher, who had been so powerful, was banished from Constantinople by the emperor. First exiled at Petra in Arabia, he was then sent to the Greater Oasis in southern Egypt, where, far from his old friends and admirers, he died.

Another council of the church met at Chalcedon in AD 451, just twenty years after the previous council had met at Ephesus. More than 500 bishops were present but only two came from Rome and the western half of Europe. In a decision combining recklessness and caution, the bishops did not fully endorse either school of argument. With the ultimate blessing of the emperor in Constantinople and of the pope in Rome, it affirmed, in a delicate compromise, that Christ had two natures, but they were united indivisibly and unchangeably and almost miraculously in the one person. Such is the doctrine officially accepted even today by the Catholic and Orthodox Churches, but it was not accepted by large numbers of bishops, priests and monks of the fifth and sixth centuries. A compromise, it offended the dedicated believers at opposite poles of the argument.

The controversy and the way it was handled did enormous harm. Successive rulers living in Constantinople had demanded cohesion and unity in their empire, but unintentionally they had promoted the opposite. It might have been wiser for them to persuade the rival Christian doctrines to co-exist rather than to be united. After all, diversity was more often a long-term source of strength for the Christian movement. Instead, under the strain of the imperial demand for unity, the Byzantine Orthodox Church faced the peril of falling apart.

Nestorius had too many enthusiastic followers for his doctrines to fade away. They formed a separate sect with their own patriarch. An inland trading town with a history of welcoming Syriac-speaking Christians, Edessa became the new sect's temporary home. Eventually making their home in Baghdad, they attracted talented Persian theologians, philosophers and physicians. At first a religion for the intellectuals as much as for the crowds, its zeal and its missionaries attracted many followers. It spread to Arabia, where one of its monks, Sergius, is said to have taught Muhammad about Christianity; and in central Asia it founded congregations at Samarkand and Herat, which then were perhaps the most easterly outposts of Christianity in the world.

Some of Nestorius's intrepid followers – maybe they were traders on the long silk route across Asia – eventually settled in Xian in western China. There a large stone tablet, erected in AD 781 in the capital of the Tang Dynasty, placed on record that a Nestorian Christian had arrived in AD 635 and was granted the notable title of Guardian of the Empire. The stone, about the size of a long bed and inscribed mainly in the Chinese language and partly in Syriac, was testament to the faith of those who travelled east rather than staying at home and submitting. In China the Nestorian Christians, under the name of the Church of the East, existed rather than triumphed; and by the eleventh century they owned meeting places and churches in only fifteen different Chinese towns. Their influence extended to the young Genghis Khan, one of whose patrons was a baptised Nestorian. Inside Europe their doctrines lived on, and flavoured part of the creed preached by Zwingli of Switzerland at the birth of Protestantism five centuries later.

A RIM OF DISCONTENT

Supporters of the traditional doctrine – unlike the Nestorians – believed in the equal standing of God and Christ. They were known as Monophysites: 'mono' of course means one, as in monopoly and monorail. Eventually, their strongholds were in the city of Alexandria and even more in rural Egypt. Their creed prevailed in the Sudan, where the Nubian king had recently become a Christian. They also dominated the ancient and isolated Christian Church in Ethiopia and were popular for a time in several trading ports of Arabia. They were powerful but not dominant in Syria, where the city of Antioch was a supporter of Nestorius. Closer to the Black Sea, their creed remained popular in the ancient Christian kingdom of Armenia and for a time in adjacent Georgia too.

Here was a huge part of the Byzantine Empire, and a few lands outside it, subscribing to a doctrine not officially approved by the capital city, Constantinople. The cleavage was political and ethnic as well as religious. Whereas classical Greek was the language of Constantinople, foreign languages such as Armenian, Syriac, Ethiopian and Coptic were prominent in the places and congregations that dissented.

Of all these lands, Egypt must have been the most dangerous source of dissent, in the eyes of Constantinople. The richest of the Roman provinces, it was at first ruled from Rome and then from Constantinople. The prolific producer of grain on the banks of the Nile and in the delta, its procession of cargo vessels fed most of the inhabitants of Constantinople. Its leading city, Alexandria, the largest in the eastern half of the Mediterranean, was being overtaken by fast-growing Constantinople. Alexandria's longstanding influence in religious matters was challenged too. In the dispute with Nestorius, Alexandria had initially won, but its victory was snatched away in AD 451 by the tactful theology embodied in the edict issued by the Council of Chalcedon. Some might even venture to say that its theology was wishy-washy. And yet no mosaic of words, even if gilded with abstractions, could satisfy both sides.

A century and a half later most Christians in Egypt were still resentful, and one sign of the resentment was a preference in the religious services and ceremonies for the native Coptic language instead of the traditional Greek. Most of the Coptic Christians, feeling oppressed by Constantinople and the official religion, were tempted to welcome a new ruler, if one should arise. By chance, at this very time, he emerged on the other side of the Red Sea, proclaiming that he had found a new religion. Its name was Islam.

THE RISE OF MUHAMMAD

Muhammad was born in Arabia in AD 570, when the peninsula was over-populated, excited by tribal feuds and encroached upon by the rival Persian Empire at one end and the Byzantine Empire at the other. When eventually the two empires went to war and weakened one another, that gave the Arabs the opportunity and breathing space they needed. Their deserts were vast but crossed by rich trade routes, and Muhammad, when young, travelled in camel caravans to distant markets. Familiar with both Christians and Jews, he absorbed many of their precepts and Biblical stories and, under the influence of religious experiences, began to form his own distinctive Islamic theology, which he first preached in public at the age of forty-six. He was old to be the founder of a major religion.

Muhammad combined intense religious views and ambitious military goals. Using armed might to gain a sure footing in central Arabia, he captured Mecca in AD 630. He died two years later. His Muslim followers, proud Arab nationalists, intent on economic as well as religious conquest, extended his victories. They tasted early success, partly because they began to advance in the footsteps and hoofmarks of a short-lived Persian conquest of many parts of Asia Minor and Egypt. Many of the regions recently ruled by the Persians were inclined to think that the Muslims were preferable. Even certain Christian sects gave a half-welcome to the incoming Muslim armies.

Omar the Arab, who had succeeded Muhammad, proved to be

a brilliant leader. Soon his lightly armed horsemen were fighting close to the shores of the Mediterranean Sea. Only three years after the death of Muhammad, they captured Beirut and Damascus, but Jerusalem was not such an easy conquest. The Muslims longed to capture it because Mohammad prized it as the home of Judaism and Christianity, and had initially instructed his followers to face in the direction of Jerusalem rather than Mecca when they prayed. The advancing Muslims surrounded the walls of the Holy City but could not break them down or penetrate them. Masters of fast-moving attacks, they were not yet accustomed to the patience required in the slow task of besieging a city until such time as its inhabitants, short of food and water, agreed to surrender.

The Byzantine forces defending Jerusalem stood firm for a year before finally surrendering. In AD 638, the Arab leader mounted on his white camel and the patriarch on his humble ass rode formally from the Mount of Olives to the heart of the city itself, the Muslim army guarding them. The terms of the takeover were not ruthless. The Church of the Holy Sepulchre, said to be the burial place of Christ, remained a Christian shrine, but later an Islamic mosque, the Dome of the Rock, was built on the vacant site of the great temple of the Jews. It was not foreseen that Jerusalem would remain in the Muslims' possession during eleven of the following thirteen centuries.

In the year that the Arabs captured Jerusalem, they also seized the ancient Christian city of Antioch and the port of Basra close to the Persian Gulf – places some 1200 kilometres apart. Four years later most of Egypt was finally captured by another small Muslim army. The capture of Alexandria, after another long siege, meant that three of the five headquarters of Christendom were in Arab control. Most of the long coast of North Africa was conquered before AD 675.

Even a few fringes of the Sahara heard the call for Muslim prayers in the silence of dawn and sunset.

The loss of North Africa, from the delta of the Nile to the present Tunisia, was a devastating blow for Christianity. That coastal strip of country, with its oases and fertile valleys, had been a vigorous Christian region. Its cities of Alexandria, Carthage and Hippo were the home of more creative and argumentative theologians than probably any other Christian region up to that time, while the Nile and nearby desert were birthplaces of the hermit's hut and monastery. While North Africa did not possess a site as sacred as Rome, it produced the minds who could argue what the sacred really meant.

It was a triumph for the small armies of Islam to capture North Africa with such ease. Egypt itself was not only a rich source of revenue after the Arabs set up their system of taxation but a source of naval strength. The Byzantine shipyards at Alexandria were taken over; more and more wooden ships were built; and the Muslim forces, previously strong on land and weak at sea, won more and more naval victories. The enemy city of Constantinople was besieged in AD 674 by Muslim ships. At the end of that century the extent of the Muslim empire was remarkable. Nothing like it had been created so speedily in the known history of the world. Ironically, the invading Arabs advanced on many fronts and were sometimes welcomed quietly by Jews, Samaritans and even the dissident Christians who resented the religious and political rule of Constantinople.

Surely Spain, the home of many martyrs and the venue for esteemed councils of the Christian Church, would defend its cathedrals, monasteries, convents, schools, charity houses, and city and rural churches? Gibraltar, the gateway to the Atlantic Ocean, fell in AD 711, and in a decisive battle near the Spanish coast the Muslims won a major victory over the ruling Visigoths. The old sources are contradictory. Some estimate that nearly 290 000 troops were involved or standing nearby, while a recent historian offers an estimate of 45 000. The Muslims, consisting mostly of African Berbers who were recent converts to Islam, pushed forward. Within ten years nearly all of the present Spain and Portugal was in Muslim control, under the name of the Emirate of Cordova, and parts of southern France were also captured. Much of this corner of Europe would not be recovered by Christian rulers for another 700 years.

The advance of Islam was not yet over. As late as AD 800, most of the major islands in the Mediterranean remained in Christian hands; but eventually the Muslim armies and navies captured Crete, Malta, Sicily, Sardinia, Minorca and Majorca, along with ports on the heel of Italy. Would Rome itself fall to the advancing Muslim forces? Now it was the headquarters of a religion rather than an army and not even protected by defensible walls. In AD 846, about 500 Muslim horsemen, having been landed at the mouth of the Tiber, went to Rome and pillaged the treasures at the sacred graves of St Peter and St Paul.

Meanwhile, in Asia Minor, the Arab armies won more territory. Persia fell, as did the present Iraq and most of eastern Turkey and Christian Armenia too. Further east, most of the present Pakistan became a province of Islam, and even Sind in India was occupied briefly. In central Asia, around the southern shores of the Caspian Sea and further east, new mosques were arising and pagan temples were turned into mosques.

In the long term, the spread of Islam into central Asia was to have an indirect effect on Europe. Asian races and tribes had periodically been advancing west towards Europe; and henceforth they carried with them the Koran, the sacred book of Islam. When eventually in 1453, Constantinople, the most populous of all Christian cities, was taken ruthlessly by Islam, it fell to the armed forces originating from central Asia.

ISLAM'S VIEW OF LIFE AND DEATH

Millions of Christians and Jews who lived in the newly occupied lands learned the hallmarks of the new religion. Islam had much in common with both, though it rightly viewed itself as unique. Like Jews and Christians the Muslims believed that only one God existed, and that he had no rivals and no equals. Islam recognised no equivalent to Christ. In its holy book, the Qur'an or Koran, 'Jesus the Nazarene' is mentioned fourteen times and depicted as a distinguished prophet, though not as wise as Muhammad. The Koran insisted that Christ could not have been the son of God. There was only one God, his name was Allah, and he was 'too exalted for anything to become a son to Him'.

Like the Christians, the Muslims warned of a Day of Judgement, with one road leading to hell and another to paradise; perhaps its paradise was more seductive and its hell more frightening than the ones pictured in most Christian minds. The road that could lead Muslims to paradise was lined with duties. One duty, if called upon, was to fight in a holy war.

In normal times, Islam demanded as much from its typical worshippers as did Christianity. They had to worship Allah five times each day, the first being at sunrise. Each year, in the holy month known as Ramadan, they abstained from food and drink between sunrise and sunset. Friday, not Sunday, was their holy day, and in the act of worshipping they were ascetic. Music was a distraction and religious art was a sacrilege. In worship they spent much time on the floor, sitting or crouching on a mat; probably they copied the prayer mat from Christian monasteries.

Islam was more like the radical wing of Protestantism – a movement that lay far in the future – than the Christianity of Rome in the seventh century. Islam had a puritanical strand, noticeable for its ban on alcohol, and a preference for simplicity in worship. Its puritanism, however, was totally abandoned in the Islamic paradise, which hinted at delights such as the Christians' heaven prohibited. A devout French scholar once made a frank comment about Muhammad's attitude to sexuality: with a 'devil-may-care' attitude, he summarily solved 'this nagging question of right sexual practice which for the Christian, especially the Catholic, is the most difficult part of morality'. Islam allowed a man – if he could financially afford the luxury – to possess several wives and several mistresses or concubines too. Less liberal than Christianity towards women, it usually insisted that they be veiled when walking in public places.

The writings of Muhammad, assembled after his death, were not as lengthy as the Christians' Bible. Coming from the pen of one man, they had more unity and did not give rise to so many theological disputes.

LIFE IN THE CONQUERED LANDS

Most Christians suffered under Muslim rule, for they and the Jews had to provide, through taxation, the revenue required by the Arab governor. Occasionally there were compulsory conversions of Christian inhabitants to Islam, but that deprived the government of tax revenue, and so a ruler sometimes decreed that new converts should still pay the old tax. When Christians decided that it was financially preferable to be a Muslim, they sometimes learned that they still had to pay the tax. This resulted in a fall in the standard of living for typical Christian and Jewish families. At times the Jews were treated more leniently because they did not believe in the Trinity, a doctrine that was the ultimate blasphemy in the eyes of Muslims.

It was forbidden for Christians to seek converts amongst the Muslims. Those Christians who were persuaded to become Muslims were not permitted to return to their former religion. Cyrus of Harran was executed in AD 770 for that unforgiveable offence. While a new Christian building could be erected, with official permission, it could not be as prominent as an adjacent mosque, and its bells had to be so gentle as not to drown the prayers coming from the mosque. Christians were forbidden to ride horses, probably because a fast horse was really a military weapon.

At times, the relations deteriorated and the Christians were compelled to wear special clothes. In Iraq and a few lands where Christians were a minority at the time of the invasion, the relations with Islam could be relatively harmonious. Spain, too, had its years of harmony; many of its Christians married Muslims, and in AD 880 a Christian king actually sent his son to be educated in the Muslim court at Zaragoza.

Most Christians accepted parts of the invaders' culture. Many Orthodox monasteries chose Arabic as their language for worship. As the centuries passed, the surviving Christian congregations resolved to conduct their religious services in Arabic but continued to recite the Lord's Prayer in Greek, Syriac or whatever was their earlier language.

By AD 700, about half of all Christians were living under the rule of Muslims. The swift conquests of the traditional Christian regions near the eastern half of the Mediterranean meant that, perhaps for the first time, most Christians lived in Europe. The pivot of Christendom was to remain in Europe for more than 1000 years.

As the centuries passed, the proportion of Muslims slowly

increased in all the lands they had seized. Muslims confiscated the grander christian churches as the need arose, and converted them to mosques. As Christian Churches faced east, their internal fittings and furnishings, and the main doors, had to be rearranged so that the new worshippers could look towards Mecca. In reshaping these churches, nearly all the mosaics and wall paintings were obliterated or removed: the loss of ecclesiastical art must have been on a colossal scale.

THE VIKING RAIDS

While the Muslims pushed back Christianity, and occupied permanently the shores of a vast stretch of the Mediterranean and the country in the interior, another enemy pushed back Christianity in the cold north of Europe. Thus, on two wide fronts the Christians were in retreat.

The Vikings in their long ships began to attack the British Isles. One of the most sacred places in England was Lindisfarne, later known as the Holy Island, and its monastery and church of St Cuthbert. In AD 793 its church was 'spattered with the blood of the priests of God' by the Vikings who came ashore. Even the altar was dug up in the hope of finding gold and silver. The early English historian Simeon of Durham pithily described the tragedy: 'They killed some, put others in fetters and took them away.' Others they 'drove out, naked and loaded with insults', while some were simply 'drowned in the sea'. Holy Island was to be raided again in AD 875.

On the coast of the German-speaking lands, Hamburg was a Christian spearhead for the converting of the Viking people. The pagan north had its own militant ideology and gave Hamburg a taste of it. In AD 848 the town was ransacked by Vikings. In due course the Vikings raided the French coast, making swift excursions to Bordeaux and Toulouse, attacking ships and harbours in the present Spain and Portugal, and even sailing into the Mediterranean Sea, where they encountered Muslim vessels.

The Vikings conquered with weapons and were in turn conquered by new ideas. Many of their leaders accepted that new idea called Christianity. Foremost was King Canute, who, eager to win more converts, sent missionaries to Denmark and Norway, and even made a pilgrimage to Rome. In becoming Christians, most Scandinavians had no choice: they obeyed their rulers.

PART TWO

9

THE BATTLE OF THE ICONS

The two churches and their priestly empires drifted apart. The pope living in Rome did not meet in person the Patriarch living in Constantinople. Rarely did they send delegations across the seas to discuss matters of common concern or disagreement. Various merchants of Venice and Genoa and other Italian cities met merchants of Constantinople frequently, but the churches they attended when their ships were in port remained separate and different.

In the eastern Church, Greek was the language of prayer, and in the western the prayers were in Latin. Attitudes to marriage and celibacy were different. In the western Church the priests could not marry, but in the east the priests and lower ranks did marry. In the typical Christian village in Asia Minor and the Balkans, a priest lived with his wife and family and all were part of the village's normal life. In contrast, in Italy and France, a priest had no wife, though he might well have a mistress. In both the east and the west, however, the bishops and the other leaders were unmarried. If an Orthodox priest was promoted to be a bishop he had to part with his wife, who usually entered a nunnery.

By the year AD 900 a few of their rituals now differed as a result of deliberate and often painful decisions. A travelling Italian merchant entering an Orthodox Church in the eastern Mediterranean found that most parts of the religious service were familiar. But he did notice that when a priest had to show humility in the presence of the Lord he lay almost prostrate before the altar. Even the emperor prostrated himself in church, whereas in Italy the priest merely genuflected. Other contrasts slowly emerged. The eastern or Orthodox concentrated on singing, and gifted composers, including Italian immigrants, wrote magnificent anthems; musical instruments were banned. Likewise, at the celebration of the Eucharist in Catholic Churches, the bread was unleavened and flat and thin, like a wafer. But in the eastern Church it was a small, high loaf made with yeast, the rising of the bread symbolising the inspiring power of the Holy Spirit.

No object so sharply illustrated the emerging contrasts as the icon. At first Christianity, like Judaism, was wary of worshipping pictures and likenesses of prophets or saints, let alone those of Christ. On the other hand a sign or symbol was allowable. Christ was sometimes symbolised as a fish or a shepherd; the church was depicted as a ship; and Jonah and the whale were symbols for Christ's death and resurrection. After some centuries, in both west and east these indirect or shorthand symbols were succeeded by forthright paintings of Christ or a saint. Here, as people stood in church, was a human face, painted on wall or ceiling or assembled as a mosaic, and looking them straight in the eye. Individuals ordered icons from the goldsmiths and other metalworkers. By the year AD 600, Christian icons abounded. Made of silver, gold, ivory or precious stones, they often showed scenes from the life of Christ. In Constantinople in the AD 690s, the latest gold coins appeared with a revolutionary image. One side was stamped with the face of a bearded, long-haired Christ, while on the other side of the coin the Emperor Justinian II stood by the Christian cross. The icons were now a vital part of Christianity and a daily object of prayer.

Did the Old Testament justify this kneeling down before a mere symbol or picture? Many Christians were reminded of the Book of Deuteronomy and its edict that people must not make 'any graven image' and must not bow down before an icon. The edict was a solemn voice from on high: 'I the Lord thy God am a jealous God.' To worship the icon was clearly a dubious practice. To value the icon simply as an aid to worship and to prayer, however, was surely a reasonable practice. So the argument began.

There are swings and fashions in theological creeds, as in cooking and clothing. The icon began to arouse criticism in the east. There the paintings and mosaics in cathedrals, churches and private homes were increasingly viewed as heretical and actually defying Christ. The Byzantine emperor and defence forces had a contrary view. During the early decades of Constantinople, the city was believed to be safe from attack because an icon or image of the mother of God was seen as protecting its walls. But it was pointed out that the Muslims, in their recent conquest of most of the Christian lands of the Mediterranean, had been careful not to display icons and other graven images. Perhaps the Muslims' victories on land and sea were partly the result of their refusal to worship images. In AD 717, once again, the Christian forces were defending Constantinople from a dangerous siege by the Muslims. Perhaps God would favour the Muslims because they obeyed his commandments.

Generals and admirals and even the emperor now had a reason for challenging the worship of icons in Constantinople and the Byzantine Empire. Bishops, too, might have their own reasons. They hoped to convert Jews and even Muslims to Christianity, and yet both religions scorned icons. Therefore, it might be easier to convert them if Christianity discarded or downplayed its reverence for icons. Moreover, in Asia Minor, the tens of millions of orthodox Christians who had recently come under Muslim rule would not be so offensive to their new rulers if their churches ceased to display icons. The opponents of icons felt they had won the argument. On the other hand, the monks especially loved their icons, and a host of the ordinary believers felt an inner peace when they could worship a simple depiction of Christ in a prominent place in their house

In the year AD 730 in Constantinople, the Emperor Leo III denounced the traditional reverence for icons and called for them to be destroyed. The patriarch disagreed and was eventually dismissed from office by a lofty tribunal. Those who persisted in openly revering icons were flogged or branded. Divided about the merit and magic of icons, villages were split in half as if by a civil war. Lives were lost; martyrs were made. On and off for 112 years, this remained an explosive topic in the Byzantine Empire.

In retrospect, this reform movement, known as iconoclasm, seems like a crusade against art, but it was not. Churches still displayed versions of paradise in mosaics on their walls, but the face of Christ was nowhere to be seen.

The death of Theophilus in AD 842 signalled the end of the destructions of icons. In the following year, on the first Sunday in Lent, the Orthodox or Byzantine Church celebrated for the first time that landmark still honoured in its calendar: the Triumph of Orthodoxy. The icons reappeared. But the question of whether it was sensible or sinful to worship them was powerful and emotional, and did not go away. Another campaign against icons was to come with the rise of Protestantism in western Europe some seven centuries later.

The icon, now restored, became more important in the eastern

Church than it ever was in the western Church. Small pictures of Christ, of Peter and the other apostles, and of favoured saints were worn as pendants, suspended from the neck by a light chain. The more expensive icons were made of gold or enamel, the simpler ones of painted wood. Larger icons might provide enough space for a short prayer such as, 'Lord, help thy servant'.

Poor families could not afford an icon, but wealthier households would display icons in several rooms. An icon might be perfumed with oil or incense and surrounded or guarded by lighted candles. Other icons fixed loosely to the wall or placed upright on a shelf might be taken down and held in the hand. The glamorous Empress Zoe could sometimes be seen tenderly speaking to a favourite icon. 'I myself,' wrote one observer, 'have often seen her, in moments of great distress, clasp the sacred object in her hands, contemplate it, talk to it as though it were indeed alive, and address it with one sweet term of endearment after another.'

PRIEST AND PATRIARCH

To most of the Byzantine Christians living in villages and small towns in, say, 1100 or 1200, the local priest was an important figure. Probably most saw him every week, though others called on him only in times of emergency. The priest had many duties. He might arrive to pray for a new house and its occupants. He might walk to the fields to bless the sowing of a crop or the planting of a vineyard. The picking of the first grapes or olives, even the threshing of the newly harvested grain, also called for his blessing. He might come to a little farmyard to bless the silkworms, or in a year of drought he might pray for rain. In villages where fishing was important he stood in the wooden boats and blessed the fishing nets.

In villages the church was an important meeting place. Young men and women came for their betrothal ceremony – their formal engagement – and later for their wedding, and the Eucharist was taken at both ceremonies. Likewise, funerals were held in the local church, after which the mourners walked to the graveyard, where the body, wrapped in a shroud, was buried in earth or clay without the protection of a coffin. The head of the corpse, usually resting on a stone pillow, faced east so that it could see the sun rise on the long-awaited morning when Christ would return to earth. The day of burial was not the end of formal mourning; other religious services might be held on the third, ninth and fortieth day after the death. While the Christian rites were dominant, a few pagan ceremonies persisted. In the twelfth century in Thessalonica, a priest often felt obliged to slaughter a dove on the tomb for the benefit of the dead person lying below.

Many people rarely entered an Orthodox Church. They looked the other way when the local priest walked by, and attended religious ceremonies only when their absence would arouse too much indignation amongst relatives, friends or employers.

Constantinople was the home of the elaborate religious ceremonies, and in splendour it outshone Rome. The emperor and the patriarch worshipped before the same altar, and sat or stood beneath the high dome of the great church, Hagia Sophia, dedicated to the Holy Wisdom of God. In status the emperor was superior, and he appointed the patriarch. On rare occasions he dismissed a patriarch; but if they disagreed on ecclesiastical matters and the disagreement became public, the patriarch was in a stronger bargaining position.

Leo VI, known as Leo the Wise or Leo the Philosopher, had time to reorganize his navy while writing vivid meditations on biblical episodes, and arguing with his patriarch. Crowned in AD 886, a youngster of no more than twenty years, Leo lost his first and second wives through natural causes, his third wife died in childbirth, and the baby – the heir to the throne – died too. The rules of the Orthodox Church prohibited frequent remarriages, and the patriarch warned the emperor that to marry a fourth time would be 'a bestial act only worthy of lower animals'. Leo's reply was that he would prefer to be a lower animal than to have no heir to the throne. He also preferred his black-eyed mistress, Zoe, and to his delight she gave birth to a son.

It was now essential that they should be married. An Orthodox priest, under some pressure, quietly performed the marriage ceremony and so made legitimate the newborn son. The patriarch was incensed. For months he debarred the emperor from entering a church.

The emperor decided to appeal to the pope in Rome. The pope, aware that rules preventing a remarriage were not so strict in his realm, decided in favour of the emperor. The patriarch, on hearing the news, was entitled to feel a surge of rage. Such disputes and entanglements did not promote harmony between the two leading cities of Christendom.

More than a century later, in 1054, a deep dispute divided Rome and Constantinople. Called the Great Schism, it hinged on that long-running, age-old disagreement about the exact relationship between Father, Son and Holy Spirit. Each church excommunicated the other. And so the two rival brands of Christianity co-existed uneasily until the approach of another enemy forced them to talk again.

MONKS OF MOUNT ATHOS

Town and monastery were not always compatible, the monastery needing quiet and solitude, the town serving as a centre of trade and conviviality. When the new city of Byzantium or Constantinople was young and growing, it gave no welcome to monks wishing to set up a monastery inside or outside its walls. The ban was relaxed, and by AD 454 an important monastery stood in a less populous corner of the city. It became celebrated because it claimed to own the sacred head of St John the Baptist. Scores of other monasteries were founded inside the city or just outside the walls; a total of at least 344 existed at one time or other in the city during its Christian era.

The most notable monasteries arose on a narrow, rugged promontory in what is now Greece. Called Mount Athos or the Holy Mountain, it is still a home for monks. The marble-white peak of Mount Athos overlooks the Aegean Sea, and along the sides of the coastal cliffs run foot tracks that linked the large monasteries to a few villages, and to many hermits' places. From a small boat following the coast there still can be seen the large-walled buildings, clinging to the steep slopes.

It is probable that refugees, escaping persecution during the decades of the iconoclastic controversy, were the earliest to live there as monks. If so, they initially lived alone or in small groups. The first of the large monasteries, the Great Laura, was opened in the AD 960s and the mountain became almost like a quarantine zone of the spirit. In 1045 a constitution, approved by the emperor, banned women from the region and even banned female animals. Soon Mount Athos became a kind of self-governing religious republic but answerable to Constantinople. Three centuries later it held almost forty monasteries, representing different homelands of the Orthodox Church – Serbian, Georgian, Russian, Greek, Byzantine, and even a monastery linked to the Italian port of Amalfi. Most monasteries were walled and fortified, for they held gold, silver and jewelled icons and ornaments as well as the valuable early-Christian manuscripts.

Not even in Italy or France was such a cluster of monasteries to be found in so small an area.

These monasteries overlooking the sea were, at times, the solvers of disputes in theology, the fountains of new ideas, and sometimes the tall walls that prevented new ideas from spreading. Emperors sometimes visited them or even dwelt there for a time. In the fourteenth century, three of the more notable men who held the office of patriarch had, when young or middle-aged, been monks at Mount Athos.

Thousands of other monasteries and convents were scattered across the empire ruled from Constantinople. Many were created by rich families with a desire to honour and pray for their own kith and kin, whether alive or dead. Some religious houses resembled, on a humbler scale, the Ford, Carnegie and other secular philanthropic foundations now widespread in the United States. Commemorating the founder's surname, they also dispensed charity and encouragement, ran orphanages and hospitals, handed food to the hungry who gathered at their doors, and supervised a library of religious manuscripts and a collection of sacred relics.

'GONE ARE THE BEGUILING PLEASURES'

Perhaps one in four Orthodox cloisters belonged to women. The head might be a member of the family that founded the convent. She upheld those rules prescribed by the founders. She maintained discipline and morale. She viewed herself as the mother and guardian, the teacher and consoler of all who lived inside the walls.

As the spiritual role of women was restricted, the female head of the convent had to invite an outside priest to conduct the Eucharist and the other religious services held regularly inside her chapel. He also officiated at the memorial services conducted at the founder's tomb. But she herself had to supervise the religious fabric and daily life of the convent. She ensured that, in the chapel, the beeswax candles were replaced and lit, that her nuns were all attending, and that the convent choir sang the psalms correctly. Over the lesser religious duties – the daily prayers and the bible readings – she could preside. She sometimes felt the loneliness of her exalted position, for many lives were in her care.

One head, having entered the convent as a teenage widow, thought that it was almost as if she were drowning, and she called out for help. Her private letters show how she longed for her spiritual adviser to visit her more frequently: 'I beg you for the sake of Christ Himself do not let me drown.' Not lacking a sense of drama, she added a last plea: 'I have written this not with ink but with my tears.'

It was a written rule that nuns must not be led into temptation. They must not directly or indirectly tempt the priest who arrived to conduct divine service. From the year AD 810 the positioning of convents and monasteries side by side was banned. Visits to convents by men were strictly regulated. One convent in Constantinople stipulated that priests who came to the convent had to be eunuchs. Even the doctor summoned to treat serious illnesses had to be either very old or a eunuch. By the year 1200 the rules were more lenient. A convent that dispensed charity at its gates had to permit its nuns to rub shoulders with the public, and sometimes with males as well as females. A nun might go out to attend a family funeral, but she could not set out on a pilgrimage.

Some nuns were widows who had arrived soon after the death of their husbands. If wealthy, they were allowed to bring a servant – female, of course. If a daughter arrived with her mother, she too was welcomed in the hope that she intended to remain for life. Theo-dora, niece of an emperor, entered a convent in 1285. She was then a twenty-five-year-old widow, with two young sons who remained outside the walls and a daughter who, she hoped, would become 'a bride of Christ'. Theodora realised how much she had sacrificed when she gave up the worldly life that she had loved: 'disregarding all delights and abandoning from my heart all the beguiling pleas-ures of this enjoyable and delightful life, I brought myself to this convent'. The consolation was being with her daughter – 'the pleas-ant and charming light of my eyes, my sweetest love, the flame of my heart, my breath and life, the hope of my old age'.

A typical convent within ten days' travelling time of a big city might include bedrooms and dormitories, kitchen and bakehouse, cellar and laundry, textile and leather workshop, orchard and garden, barn, warehouse, a relief depot and – in pride of place – a chapel and cemetery. Those nuns or servants with a meagre education would be busily tilling the garden, making wax candles, spinning and weaving wool, making or mending clothes of black cloth, and cutting and stitching leather into shoes. They made the bread and maybe the wine and cooked the meals. They waited on the table. On many occasions they were too busy to attend chapel when the wooden gong summoned all. Nuns of wealthier background, usually being literate, spent more time in reading and praying. Senior tasks fell to them, and so one looked after the financial accounts, and another managed the outside properties that provided revenue.

The dining room reflected the seriousness of their daily life. A religious text would be read aloud by a nun while the food was eaten. Silence would prevail except for that one voice. In a serious convent the more devout would deliberately cease to eat while they were still feeling slightly hungry. Others ate every morsel and, at the same time, surreptitiously kept an eye on their neighbours' plates in case a morsel of bread or flesh was not eaten. A wandering eye was against the rules: 'No one at table will be allowed to raise her eyes and look at her neighbour to see how she eats and the food set before her, and what has been served her.' The warning, from the well-known Theodora, conveys the distinct impression that some nuns, because of old age or higher status or ill health, received superior food. Here was one source of the jealousies, rivalries and upsets that seem to exist in every human institution, even those with the highest goals.

One duty of the head of a Byzantine convent was momentous. On the Day of Judgement, when the souls of the dead are judged by God, she was expected to speak on behalf of the nuns, explaining their individual faults and virtues, and so 'give an accounting' to Christ himself. That summed it up. A medieval convent or monastery, whether in the Christian east or west, was a staging house along a spiritual highway: the highway was far more important than the house.

SUNNY VLADIMIR OF KIEV

The Byzantine Church often seemed to be in trouble, but that is more an impression gained from Catholic or western sources of the late medieval period than from impartial evidence. For centuries the western Church based in Rome was more often the weaker branch of Christianity. It was also less effective in expanding. Its bishops barely noticed that the Orthodox missionaries were extending Christianity far into the interior of Eastern Europe and even towards Siberia.

In the AD 860s Basil took the Christian message to the Khazars and Moravians and Bulgars, with some success. At the same time two brothers, Cyril and Methodius, originally from the port of Thessalonica, were busy amongst the Slavonic peoples. Their language and that of their church was Greek, but it was not intelligible in most of those parts of eastern and central Europe where they preached. So they translated the vital Christian liturgies and documents into the Slavonic language, even devising an alphabet to aid their work. They were virtually the founders of Slavonic literature. It has to be said that the Orthodox Church in Constantinople viewed Greek as a precious language for which barbarian Slavs were not fitted.

By AD 988, Russia and the nearby lands were on their slow way towards Christianity. Prince Vladimir, sometimes known as Sunny Vladimir, ruled the important state of Kiev, astride the overland trade route from the Baltic to the Black Sea, and his conversion was a triumph for Christianity. At one time he had toyed with the idea of becoming a Jew but the beauty and majesty of the religious services conducted by the Orthodox Church captured him. Once he was converted, his loyal subjects had to follow him, and they were baptised in the Dnieper River. Living, moving water, it fulfilled the Christian tradition initiated by the River Jordan, far away.

Half a century passed, and the cathedral of St Sophia was built in Kiev. For two centuries it was more important than any church in Moscow. Part of Kiev's influence came from the monasteries founded nearby by Antony, a monk from Mount Athos. At last Christianity was moving slowly eastwards, and eventually a chain of Orthodox Churches extended all the way from the Ural Mountains to the Pacific Ocean.

10

BEHIND FRENCH MONASTERY WALLS

In the year 1000, Christ's Second Coming, though long delayed, was widely expected. A religious awakening was at work. Monasteries multiplied, and convents too, and they often displayed an intensity of purpose. More and more religious hermits tried to live lonely and spartan lives, the mountains of central Italy and forests of France being favoured retreats.

Rome was not so easily awakened. The pope was not elected on his merits but as a result of plots by Italian landowners or threats by German emperors. The results were predictable. A saintly man had no prospect of being elected. If by chance he was elected, his life was likely to be short. In 1012 it was sobering to look back on recent Papal misfortunes. In the space of 140 years, six popes had been murdered. One, Leo V, was killed by the man who succeeded him as pope. Another, John XII, elected to that great office at the age of eighteen, died in the arms of a married woman nine years later. Amidst these sensations were occasional decades in which the reigning pope lived a life of quiet decency, so far as is known.

While Rome was recovering from a long period of ignominy, France was about to become the engine of Christendom. The energy came not only from cathedral towns but also from the monasteries of Cluny, Cîteaux and Clairvaux, which stood in isolation in central and eastern France. Their rural isolation was intentional: seductive cities had to be kept at a distance. These French places of piety and learning housed monks who specialised in theology, and others who experimented in farming and vine-growing. Here the idea of a monastery took on a new life. Here, too, an extraordinary monument was being built, surrounded by trees and fields.

'SUCH WAS CLUNY'S FAME'

The Cluny Abbey was founded in about AD 910 by Duke William the Pious of Aquitaine. Situated near Mâcon in Burgundy, the abbey began to attract devout young men from noble as well as humble families, and it elected strong leaders who, once in office, rarely accepted higher honours in the ecclesiastical world beyond. At a time when most monasteries were small, Cluny became very large. The mother of many other monasteries, it tried to regulate and control them. Known as Cluniacs, its monks were a strict brand of that old Italian order, the Benedictines.

Increasingly, the name given to a Benedictine monastery was 'abbey', and its head was called the abbot. The Abbot of Cluny became a rare leader in Christendom, being subject only to the pope. Within his own order he was extremely powerful. He could decree anything so long as it was in harmony with the law of God and the Benedictines' own rules; but in important matters he was expected to seek advice. When a new abbot had to be appointed, the monks made the final decision. They were careful not to elect a monk who, though highly talented and experienced, was 'puffed up with the malignant spirit of pride'. Once in office the new abbot appointed the more senior officers. They included the monk in charge of the novices, the cellarer who bought or stored provisions, and the monks in charge of guarding the entrance gate, or running the guesthouse, or caring for the sick.

A monk's day was filled with duties. The first service, held in the dead of night, usually commenced at 2 a.m. but one hour later in summer. On regular duty was a timekeeper, with his water clock and hourglass, for the recording of time in the abbey was complicated. Daylight was divided into twelve equal portions or hours, and therefore a summer hour was much longer than a winter hour.

Children as young as seven were admitted to the Cluniac monasteries, and many spent their whole lives inside their walls. The very young entrants tended to come from landed families and brought with them the promise of money for their upkeep and education – they had to be taught to read and write. The celebrated Bede entered a Benedictine monastery in England as a small child, while Matilda, a daughter of Emperor Otto I, entered at the age of eleven. The young were conscripts. In the opinion of some critics, their presence weakened the tone of the serious monasteries. By the 1190s, the pope decreed that children entering a monastery must not take the final lifelong vow until they were young adults and they knew their own minds. In contrast, the adults who deliberately chose to enter a monastery knew that they would have to obey its rules for the remainder of their lives.

At Cluny the monks lived well. Early in the afternoon they received a main meal of cooked food and a small ration of wine, which on special occasions was enriched with honey, cinnamon and cloves. In season, cooked beans were served daily, along with a plate of eggs, fish or cheese. On days of fasting the monks had smaller helpings of food. Some monasteries insisted that their monks should labour in the open air in summertime, for the crops had to be harvested, the hay cut, the grapes picked and the wine made. Monks doing hard physical work needed more food than those who studied and penned manuscripts during the day.

The monks cared for the hungry who called at Cluny's gates and also helped poor people living nearby. At times the food given away had to be rationed or the monks themselves would have starved. For those beggars who called at the gate, the monastery kitchens regularly baked a dozen very large pies and gave out bread and hot soup. At the sister abbey of Beaulieu, food was given to the poor on three nights a week, and room was set aside for a maximum of thirteen poor people to spend a night under shelter. Some of those able-bodied people who called regularly at Beaulieu for food and shelter were expected to perform work in return.

Eventually, the monastery at Cluny became a nightly haven for wealthier travellers and pilgrims, those on horseback usually receiving preference, being people of distinction. By the early 1100s, Cluny was providing stables for the horses, and forty-five beds for visiting men and another thirty for the women. It employed so many servants and purchased so many supplies that it became the nucleus of a town.

Cluny set up branches or priories in many lands. Likewise, old monasteries in Italy remodelled themselves in the spirit of Cluny, and even St Benedict's original homes at Subiaco and Monte Cassino were influenced. Ravenna, once the capital of Italy, was the setting for another Cluniac monastery. By the middle of the twelfth century about a thousand brother monasteries in many parts of Europe were under the protection or control of the abbot of Cluny. A favourite of wealthy French families, and therefore the recipient of large donations of land, livestock, manuscripts and other assets,

Cluny's wealth and amenities grew. Eventually, in Paris, its abbot could stay in the monastery's town house, the Hôtel de Cluny, now a museum. While property and possessions were deemed a curse to the individual monk, they were almost a necessity for a large monastery, especially if it helped the sick and poor.

Such was Cluny's fame that visitors regularly came to take part in a form of divine service that was long, elaborate and full of colour. A new Romanesque church, the Basilica of St Peter and St Paul, was designed to hold the growing congregation and to provide space for the long religious processions; by 1088 the stonemasons and carpenters were busy. Forty years of work lay ahead of them.

To travellers, the soaring walls and the three towers, their spires capped by crosses, were inspiring. As the basilica was more than one tenth of a mile in length, it could have spanned the arena of a modern Olympic stadium. It called for majestic opening ceremonies. The high altar was consecrated by Pope Urban II, who was once a prior there, while Pope Innocent II made the long journey to consecrate the completed church.

It was a reflection of the upsurge in monasticism that such a grand building arose not in Paris, Rome or Constantinople but in the quiet countryside of Burgundy. The largest church in Europe and Asia Minor, it was to remain so until the new St Peter's Basilica was erected in Rome some four centuries later. Alas, most of the Cluny church has vanished, except the impressive octagonal tower holding the bells.

IN THE STEPS OF THE HERMITS

From Cluny's network of monasteries, numerous hermits set out. They hoped to find God in the loneliness of a forest or rocky headland.

One such hermit was St Romuald, who came from a wealthy and noble family. At first a monk, he became discontented with daily life at the Cluniac Abbey of Sant'Apollinare in Classe, near the marshes of Ravenna and the Adriatic Sea. Believing that a self-sacrificing way of life had been part of the early Christian Church, he set out to find it. Living and praying in isolation, he went to the Pyrenees before finally settling in the Tuscan hills. About 1022, he founded his own monastery called Camaldoli. From this stiff spiritual training camp, monks went into the mountains to build an isolated hut and live in silence. Each possessed only one cloak, even in winter, and, owning no shoes, they walked barefoot on the mountain slopes. It was observed that most were skinny and unkempt, but they would have replied that a hermit who cared one jot about his personal appearance was a victim of vanity. A most dangerous vice, vanity was suicidal in spiritual terms.

Over the course of the centuries, a few of the Camaldoli monks, ceasing to be so single-minded, widened their interests to botany. A peculiarity of the botanical history of Australia is that one of its best known eucalypts, the massive river red gum, takes its official name from a Camaldoli monastery. Seeds of the river red gum tree had been shipped as curiosities to Naples, and a specimen – observed in a private garden next to a Camaldoli monastery – was first described and named by a leading Neopolitan botanist in 1832. It is still formally known as the Camaldoli gum or *Eucalyptus camaldulensis*.

Another hermit was Peter Damian. He came, like the founder of the Camaldoli order, from the Cluniac abbey on the marshes near Ravenna, and after living a hermit's life he founded his own monastery at Fonte Avellana in the Apennines. The home monastery stood on the lower ground and the huts and caves of the hermits were in the colder, higher ground. His rules were strict. Bread, salt and water formed the monks' main menu for about half the week. Flagellation was seen as a healthy practice that curbed pride and tamed the body.

Every few decades, a handful of monks tried to relive what they believed were the palmy days of Christianity. Thus, the Carthusians were founded by Bruno of Cologne in 1084. Their name came from the place where their first retreat was built: La Grande Chartreuse, which lay in the mountains near Grenoble. The Carthusians later became known for the rich liqueur made by their monks. That famous after-dinner drink, chartreuse, conveys the impression of self-indulgence but the early Carthusians were not exponents of the long-drawn-out dinner. They dined as a community only on Sundays and feast days, and most meals, consisting of bread and salt and fresh water, were consumed privately in their own cells.

In their willingness to go without food for many hours they were unlikely to win the hearts of a first-class chef. At one time they wore hair shirts: their body had to feel discomfort. Intense in their commitment to privacy and silence, they spent hours each day in their own little cells, which they left only to attend the religious services spaced through the day and night.

In England these Carthusian monasteries were called Charterhouses – a word that seemed close enough to the original French name. A public school founded in London on the site of their monastery is still called Charterhouse. Within four centuries the Carthusian monasteries had spread across northern Europe and exceeded 200 in number. Some admitted women.

THE RISE OF THE WHITE CISTERCIANS

Saint Robert, of noble birth like so many of the prominent French monks, entered an abbey near Troyes at the age of fifteen. A natural leader, magnetic and practical, he was placed in charge of one monastery and then another. In trouble, people looked to him. In 1074 his help was sought by seven hermits, and at Molesme he created a simple institution especially for them. At first it was an energetic and evangelical haven, but the habit of working each day in the fields fell away. The monastery's discipline and devotion were undermined. It was time for another breakaway. Eventually, Robert led his more faithful followers to a swampy, marshy patch of wilderness, not far from Dijon. Their new home was called Cîteaux – its Latin name was Cistercium – and the monks were called Cistercians. Building huts, they settled down to live the simple monastic life and remained frugal, even after a new monastery was built for them by a French nobleman. Recruits who thought of joining them sometimes preferred to live in other monasteries, their stomachs full and their eyes cheered by the tall candles and brilliant vestments.

Stephen Harding, an Englishman of 'pleasing countenance', born and schooled at Sherborne in Dorsetshire, had made the pilgrimage to Rome as a young man, and while returning on foot through France he decided to become a monk. He was abbot of the swamp-surrounded monastery at Cîteaux when he and his colleagues resolved to admit nuns. Their first convent was formed in the French diocese of Langres, and eventually they possessed more convents than monasteries. He was also the abbot when, in 1112, there arrived another group of dissatisfied Benedictine monks. The young leader of the newcomers, Bernard, was accompanied by male relatives. Three years later Bernard was placed in charge of an infant Cistercian abbey at Clairvaux, near the famous market town of Troyes. There, as Bernard of Clairvaux, he created one of the most talked-about institutions in France.

In appearance, Bernard of Clairvaux was tall, spare and even gaunt. He suffered from a recurring illness. A gastric ailment made him lose his food, and even when in chapel he was troubled. He was to become a celebrity, though hardly one in a thousand Christians of his era knew what he actually looked like. But those who read Dante's *Inferno* could glimpse Bernard's face, for that long poem described his eyes and cheeks as filled with joy.

Bernard attracted recruits and knew how to organise them. Young men and old joined the rush to become 'white monks', white cloth being the mark of the Cistercians. The saintliness of his life inside the monastery – when he was present – and his shining sincerity when on the road appealed to those who met him or heard him. At the same time he had the ability to cut himself off completely while he was praying or considering some dilemma. It is said that for a whole day he went along the shores of Lake Geneva with companions, and saw nothing of the beauty of the distant mountains and did not see the water. When at the end of the day the lake was mentioned he replied, 'Which lake?'

The Day of Judgement, when all would have to give an account of their spiritual and secular lives, was foremost in his thoughts. He declared it urgent that people prepare mentally and spiritually for their own deaths. Meeting a young scholar who was so absorbed in his manuscripts that he neglected his spiritual life, Bernard said to him, with thunder in his voice, 'What will you answer at that dread tribunal?' Bernard was a mixture of the mystic, the unworldly and the practical. Popes, kings and princes wished to be advised by him. He was never a bishop: he had no need to be.

He more than anybody created the momentum for the second crusade against the Turks. On the other hand, he did not believe that Jews should be persecuted. On such matters his brethren did not argue with him, unless he gave the signal that an argument was called for. He was quietly overpowering. His inner confidence and self-possession, he believed, came from constant prayer and contemplation: God had made him what he was.

The Cistercian monks favoured whatever was simple. They worshipped – it is said – with the light from one candle. When stained glass was first used to decorate and illuminate French cathedrals, the Cistercians were not impressed. Instead their monasteries had an elegant simplicity, and even after they fell into ruins centuries later the simplicity was captivating. The style of architecture was matched by the religious manuscripts that their monks produced by hand. They did not usually adorn the written pages with the charming miniature paintings and the decorated capital letters often found in the finest religious manuscripts.

They fired the imagination of the young. They recruited monks and nuns from a cross-section of society, including builders and other artisans and peasants. For about a century they attracted intellectuals. As their generosity was well known, they also attracted a certain kind of wandering monk. Really a professional tourist, living off the monasteries that lay on his route, he arrived about sunset and stayed three or four days – until the welcome first given him became lukewarm. It was noticed that he might suddenly disclose his decision to depart just after the abbot invited him to lend a hand in bringing in the harvest or sawing trees in the forest.

The aim of Cistercians was to avoid the temptations of the busy world. Their choice of solitude was also influenced by the wish to take up uncultivated lands, forests and swamps and make them fit for grasslands or crops. In the wildernesses they selected as the sites of new monasteries, manual labour was essential if they were to earn their daily bread. Toil and sweat, they said, were food for the soul. England offered them untamed valleys and slopes, and there tourists can marvel at the remains of their abbeys – maybe the roof no more, but the walls of light-coloured stone still enchanting. In 1798 the young poet William Wordsworth, visiting on foot the ruins of Tintern Abbey, two and a half centuries after it was dissolved by Henry VIII, wrote one of his most-loved English poems. In his 'Lines Composed A Few Miles Above Tintern Abbey', he happily described 'the wild secluded scene' and the 'lofty cliffs' overlooking the running river. He also admired the cottages and green farms and orchards enclosed by rough hedges. Naturally, he did not realise that the cleared acres had been covered by forest when the first monks had arrived from France.

The Vallumbrosian monks on the high slopes near Florence had admitted lay brothers, and the Cistercians copied them. In their larger monasteries they eventually employed as many as 300 lay brothers, most of whom came from humble homes. The brothers lived in separate quarters with their own dining room, dormitory and infirmary, and they worshipped in a separate part of the church or abbey, usually the western half of the nave. They were easily recognised by visitors, for they wore special clothes and, unlike the monks, grew beards.

There came a time when the lay brothers, not the monks, did most of the hard labour. As they were not taught how to read and write, they had virtually no chance of being ordained as priests. Their status was firmly defined as workers, but increasingly they claimed the right to be well fed.

The existence of a brawny workforce eventually allowed most of the monks to return to their religious duties, thus undermining the original purpose of the Cistercian order. The lay brothers, however, were a law unto themselves. In the view of the Abbess of Bingham, who lived in the heart of the booming Rhineland wine region, the

Cistercians attracted lay brothers who thought more of material comfort than of religion: the brothers 'love perversity rather than uprightness and perform their duties with the noise of temerity'. They sometimes showed the resoluteness of a trade union. Official attempts to reduce their daily allowance of beer or wine could provoke a display of disobedience.

Visitors to these monasteries were impressed by the presence of one of the latest inventions – the waterwheel. It was a vital labour-saving machine before the eighteenth century, when the steam engine was developed in the British Isles. In many monasteries a running stream turned the large wooden wheel that supplied the motive power for such tasks as the grinding of wheat and the tanning of leather.

Clever farmers, they set an example for villagers in their vicinity. As they grew the wool from which their clothes were woven, they took pains to improve the breeds of sheep and cattle; and when England was the leading wool exporter in Europe, the Cistercians' own flocks produced some of the finest wool. In Yorkshire, at Fountains Abbey alone, they owned 18 000 sheep. The breeding of sheep was fully justified because the sheepskin, when treated, provided the parchment onto which religious manuscripts were copied.

In Burgundy, the home abbey of Cîteaux produced the wine that is still famous, Clos de Vougeot. Further east, along the Rhine Valley, the abbey at Eberbach was perhaps the first vineyard to build terraces before planting vines. Some abbeys grew nothing but grapes, selling the casks of wine to the cities and buying grain and cloth in return. To specialise in producing wine on the monastery's own lands was justified partly because it was the practice, later abandoned, to serve ordinary people with wine as well as bread at Eucharist or Holy

Communion. Even more wine was consumed in the monastery. St Benedict, whose rules remained influential, had patiently explained that 'in our day' it is simply impossible to expect the average monk to give up his wine.

The danger for the winemakers was that they became absorbed in their product. Some monks were so befuddled that they hardly knew Sunday from Saturday. As St Benedict in rule 40 delicately explained: 'wine can make even the wise to go astray'.

The Cistercians were not alone in promoting farming and economic welfare. Other monasteries situated near the sea erected navigational signs. Near Lynn in England, a tall cross served as a landmark for sailors. At Tynemouth, a lighthouse lit by burning coals was kept alight by monks in a tower, and during fogs they rang a bell to warn ships how near was the coast. It was easier for monks to keep an all-night vigil because they were accustomed to sit up late to perform devotions. On the coast of County Wexford in the thirteenth century a tower was built, partly with help from monks, to guide and warn ships exposed to 'the dangers of the sea' and to the 'waves of the deep'. Ships passing some of these landmarks dipped their sails, it was said, out of respect to the monks.

THE WHISPERING GALLERY

In little more than half a century after the founding of the first Cistercian abbey, another 250 were created. By the year 1200 more than 500 existed, and a century later they numbered more than 700. Though France remained their stronghold, the abbeys stretched from Ireland and Portugal in the west – the king of Portugal, Alfonso I, was a regular donor – to Poland and Hungary in the east and Sicily in the south.

Simplicity and austerity were the Cistercians' ideals, but in the far-flung abbeys those ideals were not always maintained as the centuries passed. The Alcobaça Monastery in Portugal – a gift from Alfonso – contained a kitchen so magnificent that the eighteenth-century English traveller William Beckford could not wait to describe it. Down the centre of its vaulted hall, 'not less than sixty feet in diameter, ran a brisk rivulet of clearest water, flowing through pierced wooden reservoirs, containing every sort and size of the finest river-fish. On one side, loads of game and venison were heaped up; on the other, vegetables and fruit of endless variety. Beyond a long line of stoves extended a row of ovens, and close to them hillocks of wheaten flour whiter than snow, rocks of sugar, jars of purest oil, and pastry in vast abundance, which a numerous tribe of lay brothers and their attendants were rolling out and puffing up into a hundred different shapes, singing all the while as blithely as larks in a corn-field.'

With so many monasteries separated by long journeys, how could the head office control them? In Cîteaux an annual conference usually commenced on 13 September or Holy Cross Day. It was a way of meeting a challenge that the giants of international capitalism were to face more than six centuries later: how to manage all the scattered offices.

Each year the Cistercian abbots arrived from far and near to join in the making of new rules, and to be admonished, if necessary. Even those travelling from the nearer regions might spend five or six weeks on the road, after which came the long journey homewards. The assembly, known as the general chapter, also served as a place where news and rumours were exchanged. Abbots and their little entourages brought the latest news that they had received by word of mouth: perhaps a military victory in Spain against the Muslims, or the coming of a plague to Prague. One historian has called these regular assembles 'an emporium of news – a whispering galley of Europe'.

The strain on kitchens and accommodation must have been acute, because a visiting abbot usually arrived with a secretary and a servant. But a few abbots living far away began to wonder whether so many weeks of travel were really worthwhile. It became the custom for abbots from faraway Scotland, Ireland, Syria or Greece to attend the conference in only one year in every four.

The decisions made at the Cistercians' annual assembles were not always obeyed. A resolution forbidding the installing of stained-glass windows had to be renewed, for it had been widely ignored. Many abbeys flouted a new rule that boys under the age of eighteen could not be accepted as novices or trainee monks. In 1201, more than forty years later, the rule had to be announced afresh, presumably because noble families living nearby had insisted that their younger sons be admitted early. The annual conference proved its worth and was copied by Cluny.

The Cistercians in their heyday were one of the triumphs of Christendom. Intent on simplicity at a time when some rivals were tempted by luxury, they believed in the spirit of Christianity more than in its letter. By their skill in agriculture they taught European families how to farm their small allotments more effectively and so keep famine away. Their smelters and forges, especially in Burgundy and the present Czech Republic, were among the best in Europe. But like many religious institutions they were eventually impaled on their own success.

Many of their monks became easygoing. After a hearty meal some dozed in the abbey, the recited prayers competing with their snores. Centuries later in France a new kind of Cistercian came into being.

They were the Trappists, celebrated for their silence. Their brave aim was to recover, through silence and prayer, the simplicity that had been lost.

11

GRENADIERS OF GOD

While the early medieval church often seemed almost static and oppressed by its long past, it was quietly changing. Several reforms were dramatic, and initiated by women, who were more central than at any previous time in the history of the church.

For ten centuries Jesus was usually depicted as a young hero, preaching or performing miracles. Sometimes he was painted as the king of kings and the supreme judge. He was rarely shown nailed to the cross, for that was considered demeaning for one who commanded such majesty, and unfair to Christianity itself. A new attitude towards him can be glimpsed in a German carving, commissioned in about AD 969 by Gero, the Archbishop of Cologne. Carved from oak, it shows a near-naked Jesus, nailed to the wooden cross, strong-faced but thin and gaunt. His muscles are stretched tight, his stomach distended and his knees bulging. Captive and humiliated, his eyes are closed. In little more than one century this grim depiction of the crucified Christ was to become widespread.

The wooden cross and the dying Christ, increasingly displayed in churches, posted a message about imminent death and the terrors of hell. The era itself carried dark strands of pessimism. It was widely believed that not one heathen would be saved, nor would large numbers of dutiful and professing Christians. According to St Anselm, the north Italian priest who became Archbishop of Canterbury, most of those destined for heaven were monks.

THE DISCOVERY OF PURGATORY

The early Christians had not thought of hell so often – paradise was for them. But in the few centuries before 1000, hell was a frequent topic for sermons and for artists. While virtuous Christians who had sought forgiveness might eventually join God in heaven, evil and unrepentant people – and even those who called themselves Christians – were probably destined for hell. A place of 'unquenchable fire', it was mentioned rarely but vividly by Christ himself.

Between hell and heaven the contrast was enormous. But what if a person missed selection by the narrowest margin? What if the sins of the dead person were minor but still deserving of correction? A third place was needed to accommodate the dead, and so purgatory was proposed. Though the concept had been in circulation for centuries, and was emphasised by earlier leaders such as Augustine and Gregory the Great, it did not quickly become a widely accepted truth. The word 'purgatory' is now known to have entered European speech between 1170 and 1180, being detected first in the writings of a Cistercian and a Benedictine monk and also those of a secular teacher. Purgatory was clearly defined at the Council of Lyons in 1274. Not as emphatic as heaven or hell, purgatory did not become a frequent subject in painting and sculpture for another 250 years or more.

Purgatory was the stern waiting room for heaven, where past sins would be purged, sometimes by fire, so that the purified soul was ready to enter the heavenly kingdom. The time in purgatory might be long, but the concept gave hope to many Christians. They knew that they could achieve ultimate salvation.

Once the concept of purgatory was officially accepted, the church amplified the idea. It taught that the sufferings of those in purgatory and the time spent there could be lessened by Christians who were still alive. The habit of praying for the dead was long established, but now the living relatives and friends, or even complete strangers, could pray with more certainty. Kind acts could be performed on behalf of the dead, and money or even land could be given to monasteries and churches in the hope of lessening the time in purgatory. This brought comfort to numerous living Christians who, in turn, were comforted by the thought that when they died, a family member or dear friend would pray for them.

The idea of purgatory was a revolution. The dead who had lived normal lives, a mixture of the good and the bad, were now offered a new assurance. Someone now dead and in purgatory might be aided by the prayers of those still living. The idea of purgatory linked the living and the dead by the act of prayer, so that they formed a vast, living and united Christian community.

The church began to sell pardons, which promised to shorten a soul's time spent in purgatory. Grieving men and women rushed to buy the pardons on behalf of their beloved dead, but radical theologians had their doubts. Should the simple payment of a sum of money have the power to shorten a soul's suffering? Since the sale of the pardons provided the church with a handsome revenue, it was a practice not easily abandoned.

Other questions about purgatory, rather more fanciful, were also a cause of debate. St Peter held the keys of heaven, but who held the key to the exit door of purgatory? A saintly woman from Namur in Flanders was said to hold it. A Cistercian, she was quite blind when she died in 1246. Sanctified, she became the one to whom many Christians prayed, when they remembered those poor souls locked away to suffer. Her prestige was a sign of the quiet feminising of a corner of Christian doctrine in the Middle Ages.

Perhaps prayer was practised more often by the ordinary inhabitant of Europe during this period. Several innovations possibly increased the habit of praying. One was the firm belief in the existence of purgatory. The other was the growing cult of the Blessed Virgin Mary, the super saint who was increasingly known as 'The Mother of God'.

IN HONOUR OF MARY

In the church nearly all the key players, from God and Christ and the apostles all the way down to the village priest, were men. And yet some of the Christian virtues –, humility, hope, faith and charity – were believed to be exemplified more fully in the lives of women than of men. Moreover, many of the eastern religions, such as the Egyptian cult of Isis, had worshipped a goddess. Perhaps the absence of women in the Christian hierarchy should be remedied, for most congregations consisted of more women than men.

In the first century the cult of Christ's mother, the Blessed Virgin Mary, was virtually unknown, and later it was more attractive to the eastern Church than to the west. Nevertheless, by AD 431 the veneration of Mary was sufficiently widespread for the Council of Ephesus to grant her the title of Mother of God. In AD 533 the Council of Constantinople declared that she was perpetually a virgin. In that same century, her 'assumption' – the belief that on her death she had gone bodily to heaven – was officially proclaimed. Time passed, and Mary's own conception was celebrated as a feast day, even though belief in her sinless or 'immaculate' conception did not become an official doctrine for another twelve centuries.

By now she was prayed to, more and more. In AD 863 her own celebration, the Feast of Our Lady, was pronounced by the pope to be equal to the feasts of Christmas and Easter.

The venerating of the Blessed Virgin Mary reached new heights in the twelfth century. The prayer 'Hail Mary' or 'Ave Maria' became popular: 'Hail Mary, full of grace: the Lord is with thee; Blessed art thou among women, and blessed is the fruit of thy womb, Jesus.' Eventually, inside or outside churches across Europe, the bell rang three times when the Ave Maria had to be recited. As time went on, the Ave Maria was recited morning, noon and evening. The prayer led slowly to the widespread use of the rosary, a string of beads or semi-precious stones or even precious jewels that guided the memory of those reciting the Lord's Prayer, the Ave Maria and the Gloria, so that the words were recited in the correct sequence.

Meanwhile, artists took pleasure in painting Mary as she tenderly cradled the baby Jesus in her arms. In keeping with the new fascination with the crucifixion, Mary was also depicted nursing her son's lifeless body as soon as it was released from the cross. Michelangelo, in his famous sculpture, the 'Pietà', powerfully conveyed her grief as she performed this duty.

The ancient 'Song of Solomon' was seen by many priests, monks and nuns as an allegory of Mary expressing her love of Jesus. Of the verses read aloud from the Old Testament, the 'Song of Solomon' became almost the favourite. Likewise, in prayers, Mary was the favoured intermediary through whom the ear of God could be reached. By the end of the twelfth century she was known as the Lady of Flowers. It was said that when her tomb was opened and only her shroud was found – her body had gone to heaven – the shroud gave off a flowery fragrance. Preachers said that her perfume mingled together the scent of the violet, the flower of humility, the scent of the rose, the flower of love, and the scent of the lily, the flower of chastity. The Blessed Virgin was often painted holding a lily.

The popes endorsed the increasing reverence for Christ's mother. As a universal saint she was under the patronage of the pope, unlike a multitude of local saints who were known in one corner of only one district. When new churches were built, there was almost a craze to honour her. By the fifteenth century the River Thames, from source to estuary, resonated with her name. An English boys' school, now famous, was called 'the College of the Blessed Mary of Eton', but Blessed Mary later disappeared from its name. In the heart of London, the cathedral of Southwark was called St Mary Overie – meaning Mary over the river. Downstream, on the Isle of Dogs, stood a Mary chapel at which people prayed for mariners setting out on voyages or missing at sea.

To a miller sitting beside his flour mill near the Rhine, to a washerwoman rinsing her clothes on the banks of the Seine, one question arose when they were low in spirits or fearful of the future: to whom should they pray for help? The Blessed Virgin Mary was chosen. As the most special woman she was more likely to hear their prayers, and more likely to respond to them sympathetically in her own voice. The effect was to make Christianity a very complex structure. Arius of Alexandria in the fourth century had complained that the threesome of God, Christ and the Holy Spirit was dethroning God; and now the Blessed Virgin Mary was very close to them, and occupying fourth place in the minds of most worshippers. Her title was now the crowned Queen of Heaven.

In the sixth century, another female saint – Mary Magdalene – was rising to prominence. Unfortunately, the evidence in the gospels about her is tantalisingly meagre. It was understood that Jesus cast seven devils out of her, that she had been present at the crucifixion, and that on Easter morning she had been the first to speak to the risen Christ. Longing to know more about her, Christians began to play a guessing game. What if several other of the women Jesus encountered in the gospels were really Mary Magdalene? Was the unknown woman who washed his feet in the house of Simon none other than Mary? And might not Mary of Bethany, at whose house Jesus was so warmly welcomed, really be the same Mary Magdalene? Filling in the gaps by imaginative means, ingenious people slowly built up a composite picture of a well-born but sinful woman who, through penitence and devotion, became almost the female disciple of Christ.

In the early thirteenth century a Dominican monk, Jacobus de Voragine, composed the *Golden Legend*, one of the most popular religious books of the era: indeed, so popular that about 1000 manuscript copies survive, not to speak of the hundreds of printed copies, in many European languages, produced soon after the advent of printing. Drawing on the composite portrait, Jacobus spoke lyrically of Christ's relationship with Mary Magdalene.

'This,' he wrote, 'was the Magdalene upon whom Jesus conferred such great graces and to whom he showed so many marks of love. He cast seven devils out of her, set her totally afire with love of him, counted her among his closest familiars, was her guest, had her do the housekeeping on his travels, and kindly took her side at all times. He defended her when the Pharisees said she was unclean, when her sister implied that she was lazy, when Judas called her wasteful. Seeing her weep, he could not contain his tears.'

This intensely devout portrait had first been granted validity by Gregory the Great in the late sixth century, and the feast day of Mary Magdalene was religiously kept from the eighth century onwards. Today this composite Mary is no longer accepted as true by the Catholic Church, but the veneration once given to her is yet another sign of the higher standing of female Christians at this time.

THE MYSTERY OF BREAD AND WINE

In 1215, after a meeting of bishops in the Lateran Palace in Rome, Pope Innocent III made a vital statement about that sacrament known variously to us as Holy Communion, the Lord's supper, mass or the Eucharist. The consecrated morsel of bread that the worshippers solemnly consumed was now declared to be the actual body of Christ, and the wine that the priests consumed, along with the bread, was declared to be the actual blood of Christ. This doctrine, known as transubstantiation, was to be a vital cause of dissent when Protestants emerged three centuries later. In the English language this word is awkward and abstract when first heard, and its meaning is not instantly clear. The word is also cumbersome – it has eighteen letters, including four Ts – but the idea behind the word was vivid and enriching to a Christian living at the time.

The new doctrine made the bishops and priests more important, for they presided over the ceremony of consecration, at which the bread and wine instantly became the 'whole substance' of the body and blood of Jesus. The same decree insisted that the wine, the very blood of Christ, should be swallowed only by the presiding priests. The ordinary people who had previously been handed both the bread and the wine were in a sense downgraded. Large numbers of people had previously evaded the ceremony. Now they were instructed to take part in the Eucharist and to confess their sins to a priest at least once a year.

The emphasis on the miraculous nature of the Eucharist or mass affected the layout of the church building. The ceremony now was partly concealed from the congregation. Here was a new theatre to which the people themselves were not fully admitted. While the newer cathedrals conveyed an overwhelming sense of space, especially on a bright summer Sunday, the space at the holiest part of the church was partitioned. The altar and seats of the clergy – the inner sanctuary of the church – were now obscured by a screen of wood or metal or an ornate latticework. This separation of congregation from priests probably increased the mystery and solemnity of the ceremony. The screen remains in place in Orthodox Churches, but long since gave way in Catholic Churches to the altar rail, a low wooden fence that prevented the ordinary worshippers taking Holy Communion from coming closer to the altar. Even the rail has now gone.

THE NEW FEAST OF CORPUS CHRISTI

In a few Catholic parts of the world, a public pageant still takes place on the second Thursday after Pentecost or Whitsunday. The Thursday was chosen because that was the day of Christ's Last Supper, and this particular time of the year happily coincides with spring in the northern hemisphere. In late-medieval times this pageant was a highlight for millions of Christians. For some it was more important, more magical, than Christmas Eve. It was called the Feast of Corpus Christi, meaning the body of Christ.

An alpine Swiss village called Kippel stands beside a stream running down a deep valley. For generations many of its sons have moved to Rome to serve the pope in his Swiss Guards. On the chosen Thursday morning each spring, the quiet in the village is disturbed only by the distant cow bells, and everything is closed except for the large church. As more people arrive than can find seats, they stand amongst the tombstones and tiny flowerbeds of the small surrounding cemetery, while a bodyguard of old soldiers wearing fur-topped hats and known as the 'Grenadiers of God' stand at attention by the church door. When the service in the church is concluded the procession begins, a brass band playing a solemn hymn. It moves through the narrow streets of the village, the women wearing national dress and each carrying a Bible and some also holding a sprig of rosemary.

The priest leads the procession, walking beneath a canopy held up by four men of the village, and the young girls who have just taken their first Eucharist, and who are dressed like brides, walk behind him. Here and there the procession halts, the music ceases, and the ornate vessel holding the Host – the consecrated bread that is believed to be the actual body of Christ – is raised high. The church bells are rung, and the procession resumes.

In most Catholic countries the same ceremony is now held on the Sunday following Trinity Sunday. In Italian villages can be seen the same canopy for the priest, the same procession in which the village policeman usually joins, and – if the wildflowers are plentiful in the nearby mountains – a few walkers carry a basket from which they scatter flowers on the road, thus making a white carpet. If the village is too small to support a brass band, several women tug a loudspeaker mounted on wheels so that recorded music can be amplified.

A Belgian nun first proposed this mightiest of medieval pageants. Juliana of Mont-Cornillon, an Augustinian nun who lived near Liège, had experienced repeated visions of a full moon in all its brilliance. The moon, however, was not symmetrical, for a small slice had been excised from it. The nun pondered the oddity and decided that the moon was the church and that the gap represented something vital. What was absent, she concluded, was an outdoor pageant that celebrated the Eucharist or the Lord's supper and publicised its importance. From her visions arose the feast of Corpus Christi.

Her own bishop adopted the idea in 1246, and later a visiting German dignitary saw the celebration and praised it. The new Dominicans welcomed the idea, for they were diligent teachers and knew that such pageants impressed ordinary folk and therefore taught them a message. Pope Urban IV, coming from Troyes in nearby France and familiar with the new pageant, decided in 1264 to make it an annual pageant of the whole church. A miracle at the central Italian town of Bolsena in the previous year spurred or confirmed his decision to proclaim this as a feast day. It was understood that in Bolsena a visiting Bohemian priest celebrating mass had not fully believed in the new doctrine of transubstantiation, but his mind was changed when, as he officiated at the altar, he saw real blood colour his hands and spill onto the white cloth below him.

In the twenty-first century most people in the western world show instant respect for concepts that seem to have a rational foundation, though some of these concepts are later disproved. In contrast most medieval people tended to marvel at myths, mysteries and rumours, and instantly assured themselves that they were true. According to one specialist in medieval science, one of the charms of that period was the way in which the miraculous delighted the learned and the unlearned. The rumour about a female pope fitted into that era.

In the thirteenth century a Dominican author told the story of a female scholar of high distinction who, centuries earlier, had been elected as Pope Joan. The year of her election was not known to him, but the absence of such a vital detail did not seem to undermine his story. At about the same time another account of this mysterious papal election was written by a former papal chaplain, Martin of Troppau, who died in 1278. He even assigned a year, AD 855, to Joan's election as pope. According to his version, Pope Joan had successfully disguised herself as a man during her brilliant early career. Her gender was revealed only when, leading a procession in Rome, she gave birth to a child and then died beside the road. The child survived, some said, and became the bishop of Ostia.

Other stories about Pope Joan were circulating. It was believed that her face, carved in stone, could be seen in the decorations on Siena Cathedral. Later, in central Europe, the rebellious Bohemian theologian John Hus referred to Pope Joan as if she had actually lived. Several Catholic feminists like to think that she did exist but was never acknowledged by the all-male hierarchy in Rome. So far there is no convincing evidence that a female pope reigned, and yet the stories and rumours, in emphasising the high potential of women, fitted in with the deepening veneration for the Blessed Virgin Mary.

THE PERSECUTION OF THE CATHARS

In earlier centuries the followers of Mani believed that good and evil were separate deities. In Spain the disciples of Priscilla held a similar idea. The belief gained followers in Bulgaria, Macedonia and Croatia – regions which became Christian in the eighth century – and by 1200 a similar set of beliefs was preached in western Europe by the Cathars.

In the Rhineland, Flanders, Champagne and the Loire Valley, the Cathars were powerful, and Cologne on the Rhine and Orleans in western France became their strongholds. The Cathar movement spread to the south of France, where the name Albigenses was often given to them, the town of Albi being a haven.

While believing in an afterlife, Cathars did not regard Jesus as a keeper of the gate. In their opinion, he had not been crucified and therefore had not risen from the dead. On various occasions the more militant Cathars destroyed Christian crosses and even pulled down the altars inside churches, for they thought that the mass was pointless. They believed that not only did God exist, but so, too, did his rival, a god of evil. Thus, the evil Satan had created creatures such as snakes and wolves, flies and lizards, and he also created the hailstorm and the thunderstorm. A separate force, he was more malicious and resourceful than most Christians were willing to believe.

In fear of persecution, thousands of Cathars had gathered in the French region of Languedoc. Cut off from Paris and the north by the mountainous Massif Central, this isolated region favoured its own Occitan language and its own political regime. Here, noble families even supplied some of the Cathars' teachers and holy men: they were known as Perfects, were indispensable to the life of the sect, and were willing to face death as martyrs.

French bishops, priests and especially the new religious order called Dominicans were indignant at the growth of the Cathars. Today their level of indignation is not easily grasped. In medieval Europe, however, a major heresy was like a barrel of poison about to be emptied into the town's wells of water. It was understood that God would cease to protect and defend a town where such a heresy was rife.

Rome and its secular allies were slow to attack this expanding heresy with vigour, but finally in 1208 it acted. Many Cathars were tried, found guilty of heresy and burned alive. A few were lynched by angry crowds. Others were imprisoned or deprived of their land. Those Cathar heretics who decided to confess their guilt had to wear, as punishment, a yellow or saffron cross, sewn onto the back of their outer garments. Many were compelled to go on pilgrimages, mostly to local shrines, but a few others wearing their yellow cross had to walk all the way to the distant Spanish shrine of St James of Compostela.

The crusade against the Cathars seemed to be victorious by the 1220s, but nearly one century later they were still winning converts in the mountains and slopes of the south of France. We know a lot about them because the church sent inquisitors to those villages where they flourished. So there remains a record of how a small cross-section of ordinary people spent their lives and what they thought about the religious questions of the day.

INSIDE A MOUNTAIN VILLAGE

Montaillou was a village in the Pyrenees mountains, close to the present French–Spanish border. A castle stood on the top of the high hill, the people's huts and houses and tiny farms were scattered along the slopes, and further down stood the Romanesque parish church. The district had no carts, partly because the ground was too steep. The climate was too cold for growing grapes and olives, and so wine and olive oil and salt too were carried from the lowlands on the backs of mules.

The tiny patches of farmland around the village grew grain, flax, hemp and turnips: the grain was ground into flour at the local mill, and the bread baked at home was the main food. Each little house included a stable where sheep lived in winter before being guided in spring to the higher country, where their milk was made into cheese. The village houses were so small, and the winter so cold, that people normally slept two or three to a bed. As jars of water, balanced on cushions perched on the heads of women, had to be carried some distance from a spring to most of the houses, the washing of hair, hands and feet was not common. Across Europe, thousands of villages must have similarly suffered from their own mix of disadvantages.

Being isolated, the village was a welcome haven for the surviving Cathar leaders, who, compared to the local Catholic priest, were sufficiently holy in their lives to win many admirers. In Montaillou the village priest was the village rooster, for he quietly conducted a series of sexual affairs with unmarried women and widows. He implied that the church's teaching was not primarily against him sleeping with a woman but against him taking her as a wife. Like many priests and friars he was widely criticised because he relied on the daily work of the villagers to pay for his shelter, clothes and meals. One-eighth of their annual harvest had to be paid as a tithe or tax to the local church, and those who refused to pay were excommunicated. While the excluded villagers were permitted on Sunday to stand inside the church during the first part of the religious service, they had to leave before the mass began and wait outside in wind or rain. Such expulsions were resented by many villagers, for they pointed out that they or their ancestors had financed the church. 'We built it, we bought and put in it everything that was necessary,' said one man indignantly.

In surrounding villages not more than half of the people went to church on Sunday, and some left early without hearing the sermon – if there was a sermon. One quarryman who claimed that the world – contrary to the Christian belief – would not come to an end on the Day of Judgement offered a clever excuse for his heresy: 'Because of my work in the stone quarries, I have to leave Mass very early and I do not have time to hear the sermons.' Cathars were, in proportion to their numbers, more regular attenders at mass than were the local Catholics; regular attendance helped to camouflage their real beliefs.

Religious topics were discussed privately when Cathars met but their discussions were in secret, for they feared prison and even the sentence of death. For the same reason the visiting perfects sometimes wore hoods when they met around the kitchen tables of families who were fellow believers. When staying for the night they slept in a concealed place in the ceiling. Shepherds were amongst their sympathisers, and a few became true Cathars. The smiling shepherd Pierre Maury learned much about the faith when he walked beside a Cathar 'goodman' who rode a mule and quietly talked as he rode. It was common for Cathars to spread their message in this way, because no stranger could then overhear their heretical ideas and have them arrested.

The lives of goodmen were said by some villagers to be exemplary: 'They do not lie: they do not cheat.' If goodmen found valuable possessions on the roadside they would not even pick them up, because they knew that they belonged to others. One woman vowed that the Cathars alone 'keep the Roman faith which was kept by the Apostles'.

Most villagers wondered about heaven and tried to picture it. Could it accommodate all the people entitled to go there? One peasant replied that if a huge house were built and it stretched all the way from the town of Toulouse to a specific mountain pass in the Pyrenees, it would still not be as large as heaven. The Cathars and the

Catholics placed the same importance on the art of dying correctly. They shared with all Christians the deep fear of dying alone without receiving the last rites. Usually the Catholics sent for a priest, and as he carried the last sacrament to the dying person, a bell was rung ahead of his footsteps. The more devout Cathars, if expecting death, sent for one of their own 'goodmen', who likewise offered them forgiveness just before they died.

Here and there lived people who were neither Catholics nor Cathars. One summer day, the villagers and the priest were standing under the elm in the churchyard and chatting about their pleasing harvest when one of the talkers exclaimed, 'thank God it turned out all right'. To the astonishment of the priest, another villager replied that it was not God but nature that provided the abundant harvest. So spoke the doubter. How many doubters and atheists lived in medieval Europe we will never know.

12

THE MAGIC OF GLASS AND PAINT

If these were really the dark ages, the new church buildings were their light. Soon after the year 1050, plans were eagerly made in many parts of Europe to build massive cathedrals and basilicas and the most ornate of chapels. Amongst the early triumphs was St Mark's Basilica in Venice. The chapel of the doge or ruler, and not the cathedral of Venice, it was designed by a Greek architect in the Byzantine style. It was remarkable for its light. Today, many of the window spaces have been blocked, almost conveying the dimly lit appearance of a cave, except on those grand occasions when it is brilliantly lit with electricity and candles.

In the next century came grand cathedrals that made most churches in Venice seem like those of a small seaport. The Romanesque cathedrals at Florence and Pisa are now two of the world's goals for tourists. The treasure captured from Muslim ships in the Sicilian port of Palermo helped to finance the cathedral at Pisa. Alongside arose the elegant campanile now known as the Leaning Tower, which was commenced in 1173. It proclaimed the growing importance of tuneful bells, of enormous size, in beckoning people to church.

THE RISE OF THE GOTHIC CATHEDRAL

While Italy favoured the Romanesque, France was more adventurous and flew high with the Gothic. The first cathedral in the new style was commenced in the 1140s in the French town of Sens; but the eastern end of the rival cathedral in St Denis, a suburb of Paris, was completed first. The height and shape of these Gothic cathedrals surprised most travellers. Their windows were a jigsaw of small pieces of stained glass, of a brilliance that on a sunny day filled visitors with delight. The walls held far more glass than any previous building in the western world. Distinctive, too, at the top of the tall windows, were the pointed arches that probably were borrowed from Islamic buildings in Syria and Turkey during the First Crusade. Possibly some builders and stonemasons in Asia Minor were enticed to come west with the returning crusaders.

Astonishing was the sense of space inside the new Gothic cathedral. Here was a maximum of space enclosed by seemingly delicate walls, though they consisted of a mass of stones. Each cathedral called for its own quarry in which the stones were cut roughly and then smoothed and shaped.

It is not surprising that the generation that built so many large fortified castles in Europe showed its mastery of stonemasonry by building the first Gothic cathedrals. Castles, once built of earth and timber, were increasingly built of stone so that they could withstand a long siege. The new form of warfare required few soldiers: the strong castle was itself a gigantic soldier. The skills of quarrying, carting, cutting and lifting heavy blocks of stone were vital for

building huge churches as well as solid castles. Year after year, sometimes for more than half a century, as many as 150 labourers were
at work together, often pulling on the thick ropes that hauled each
block of stone from a nearby quarry. Another team erected the high
wooden scaffolding on which the stonemasons stood while building
walls and roof. Yet another in the nearby forests sawed the tall trees
that supplied the timber.

The standard of living of many families had to be sacrificed while
these cathedrals were being built. Taxes had to be collected. Men
who might otherwise be building cottages, flour mills or stone-lined
cellars were diverted to these ecclesiastical tasks. Sometimes the
monks joined in the work, though few initially possessed the practical skills required.

Why did many bishops and princes of this time demand such
spacious churches? They built, in part, out of rivalry. They wanted
to be the best. They built spectacularly in order to glorify God,
and their spires and arched windows pointed straight to heaven.
There were also ceremonial reasons for a large church, for it provided the space inside for grand processions. Moreover, many men
and women were entering religious orders, and so a larger building
was often needed to house members of an expanding monastery as
well as those visitors who came to worship on Sundays and other
holy days. The magnificent building helped to make their visit a
day to remember, and caught the imagination of passing travellers,
especially pilgrims.

High engineering skill was provided by the architects and builders.
Their flying buttresses coped ingeniously with the outward thrust of
the towering walls. Their groin vaulting, with the four corner points
carrying the weight, consisted of building-stones and bricks, which
gave the strong support once performed by timber. The cathedral

in Speyer, Germany, was a bold pioneer of the groin vault. Stone instead of timber was a boon. The traditional cathedral had been capped by a wooden ceiling; and when lightning struck the roof it could set fire to the wood. In a congested town the fire could easily spread to the adjacent cottages and shops with their thatched roofs. In contrast, the ribbed vaulting of stone was more practical as an arch, and majestic too.

The 'Gothic of Royal France' was dominant between 1140 and 1200. Its triumphs were seen in Sens, St Denis, Noyon, Laon, Paris and Chartres. Early in the next century came Reims with its naturalistic foliage carved in stone, and Amiens with a style of architecture that influenced the German town of Cologne. Begun in 1248, Cologne Cathedral's eastern or choir end was completed after seventy-four years. Frustrations and delays were frequent. Designed to be the tallest and largest of all the Gothic cathedrals, it did not attain its present grandeur until the nineteenth century. Between 1878 and 1880 two mighty medieval cathedrals were at last completed, Rouen first and then Cologne, and they were briefly the two tallest buildings in the world at the very moment when the first American skyscrapers were planned.

While Gothic was the dominant style in much of Europe, experiments went on. Monks and friars who travelled far were surprised to see Germany's hall churches with one high roof covering the nave or centre and the aisles as well. The emphasis on loftiness was seen in Scandinavia's steep-roofed stave churches, where wood remained the prime material and carpenters were more important than stonemasons. The walls consisted of timber planks standing upright. The frame of the building itself was timber and the roof usually consisted of those small wooden tiles called shingles. But in Norwegian ports such as Trondheim and Stavanger the cathedrals were of stone, with something very English in the architecture. Trondheim owed much to Lincoln Cathedral, then the tallest building in Europe.

GLASS OF MOSSY GREEN AND SMOKY AMBER

The newest Romanesque and Gothic churches contained more windows, and they tended to be larger windows. Larger windows meant less space for the walls. As these walls internally had displayed biblical scenes painted by hand, where now could the bible stories be depicted? The windows replaced the walls as potential galleries for religious art. Stained glass began to challenge the painted wall. The earliest surviving windows of true stained glass are a set of four, created in about 1100 at Augsburg in south Germany.

The craft of painting or staining glass began to flourish. At first the Cistercians, the advocates of simplicity, rejected stained glass in the windows of their churches, but eventually they were converted. The preacher could point to the brilliant scenes and the faces in the windows and deliver his message about the Last Supper or the Resurrection. If the daylight streamed in from the appropriate angle, the glass dispensed a brilliance unequalled in that era. Even the clothes of a queen, expensively dressed, did not quite match the brilliance of a window of stained glass, subdivided into many small panels rich in colour.

In the years between 1203 and 1240, the new Chartres Cathedral with its 176 windows was filled with coloured glass, a task performed by at least nine master designers. One very large window displaying the Life of Christ covered 23 square metres. From these dazzling decades of the first half of the thirteenth century, the surviving glass includes the windows in the choir clerestory at Troyes in central France, the rose window of Lausanne Cathedral in Switzerland, the Jesse tree window in the Cathedral of Freiburg im Breisgau in south-west Germany, and the theological windows in Canterbury Cathedral. Italy was slow to adopt stained glass. Its earliest known examples were created in Assisi in the 1230s by German craftsmen who had worked on a Franciscan church in their homeland.

Artisans learned to manufacture stained glass that was apt for each particular part of the church. In the cathedral of Chartres the intense blues were stunning in the westerly sun. When the sun began to set, however, these dark blues lost their brilliance, and the ruby colour began to command the attention of worshippers standing below. With new architecture and construction methods, more light was admitted to the church. On some sunny days the effect of the brighter light inside was to diminish the contrast with the intensity of light outside the church and that in turn affected the play of light on the windows.

Metallic oxides provided new colours for the glass. In the early 1300s there appeared moss-green and violet and smoky amber. Another invention was a vivid yellow, produced by applying a solution of silver to the glass when it was still under the influence of the glassmakers' fire. The glassmakers actually supplied the colour for the early windows: it was embedded in the glass. The painter and stainer came later, rising to prominence when the small pieces of coloured glass had to tell a more detailed story or tell it more dramatically.

Much of the magic of medieval stained glass comes from age itself. Time and weather, and the outside smoke coming from wood and coal fires in the town and the inside smoke drifting from candles and lamp oil have mellowed the glass. The light itself is often enhanced by bubbles and other imperfections in the glass. Even the pitmarks on the surface of the coloured glass, rather than displeasing the eye, flirt charmingly with the natural light.

THE ILLUMINATED ALPHABET

As the church was the bastion of literacy it required more reading matter than did any other institution. Every book had to be written by hand. On any weekday, in the monasteries scattered between Northern Ireland and the shores of the Baltic and Adriatic, a few thousand scribes were at work, pen in hand, painstakingly copying a version of a handwritten work laid out before them. The Vulgate Bible had to be copied, though not many copies of the full work were called for. More in demand were excerpts from scriptures and theological works: the selected epistles of St Paul, the psalms set out in a book called the Psalter, or a book of the Old Testament with a commentary on chosen verses. These were the ecclesiastical *Reader's Digests* of the day.

Handwritten books had a long life: the pages were not easily torn. The costliest books were written on the surface of vellum, a word that is similar to veal. The pages, made from the skin of a calf, lamb or goat, were known as parchment. A book of 200 written pages required the skins of some eighty lambs. It is said that the cost of this parchment exceeded the cost of the clerk or scribe.

The strongest demand was for the books that could be used year after year in conducting religious services. They were religious everyday books, not too large. Bishops who had to conduct ceremonies and pronounce blessings used a handwritten book called the *Pontifical*. A handwritten choirbook guided those singers who had to chant together during religious services; often in large print, these books were placed on a wooden reading stand, around which the singers would gather to read musical notes and words on the open page. As each book was written to order, it could suit the distinctive needs of the Franciscans or Carthusians, or the preferences of a certain district where local saints were esteemed. Thus, a prayer book would be in Latin but would also hold a few prayers written in French or Flemish or another native tongue. Those who ordered these books could specify what additional items must be included. One work now preserved in the Art Gallery of Ballarat, on the far side of the world from the Italian workshop where it was written in about 1451, includes a set of rules for 'finding the new moon'. The date of the new moon determined when Easter would fall in a given year.

Most of these manuscripts were commissioned by churches or monasteries, but some were written for members of devout families who could afford the high price of a personal copy. After 1250 came an increasing call for these devotional manuscripts, known as Books of Hours. They contained a long calendar listing the landmarks of the Christian year and the special day of each saint. Women especially liked these books, which combined a series of prayers and a diary of the whole religious year.

Sacred works, these manuscripts by their very nature called for the neatest, most elegant script a clerk could produce with his sharp pen. Then came the artist to provide the illustrations. While many pages were unadorned, large numbers carried magnificent hand-painted illustrations in dazzling colour. The border of the page might be decorated with flowers, thistles, pea pods and entwined leaves. In a book created expressly for a Carthusian monastery at Limbourg in Holland, a tiny monkey is playing the bagpipes, another is blowing bubbles and a third is dancing with a pig. A dazzling parrot is easily perched in a corner of such pages. Amidst these zoological gardens stand occasionally a capital, say O or D or P, serving as a porthole through which can be seen in miniature the face of a saint or apostle depicted with startling clarity.

Certain pages resembled a medieval window of stained glass with their vivid colours in wine-red, apricot, rich brown, mauve, lilac, blue, green and burnished gold. Whoever reads the Book of Hours, created in Florence in about 1495, can only marvel at that city washed in a kind of blue moonlight. In the imagination of the painter, centuries that were far apart were mixed up in a very folksy way. Thus, on the banks of the Arno can be seen King David kneeling in prayer alongside that invention unknown in his reign, a huge wooden waterwheel. Propelled by the fast flow of the river, the wheel is rotating the grinding stones of a tall grain mill or paper mill.

It was the same invention, the waterwheel, that was to help terminate the era of parchment. From the twelfth century in Spain, and from the fourteenth century in Italy, waterwheels driven by mountain streams were the basis of the new paper mills, where the item called paper was produced from old rags and lengths of rope and from flax and hemp. Paper, while not so beautiful, was cheaper than parchment and vellum. To the growing supply of cheap but strong paper was added, in about 1450, the innovation of printing with movable type. A revolution was on the way. The new printing press and the new paper were to shake up Christianity in the most unexpected way. The monk who more than any other exploited the printing press and the stacks of new paper was himself a revolutionary, a German named Martin Luther.

THE KEYS TO THE PAINTINGS

Today the works of art in the cathedrals, galleries and palaces of Italy attract connoisseurs of the arts and general tourists from every part of the globe. In 1500 the district's inhabitants – for they were the main 'tourists' – came primarily to see the religious messages vividly expressed in the paintings. Christ and the apostles were then the heroes, whereas today the famous painters and sculptors are the heroes or, better still, the geniuses. In 1500 there was only one genius and his name was Christ.

Most of those tourists who, today, glory in the works of medieval and Renaissance artists, whether displayed in Rome or Paris, Washington or London, miss something vital in these sacred paintings that they crowd together to see. They miss the messages expressed by symbols and signs. An illiterate peasant of 1500, knowing the sign language, could well have discerned in these paintings so rich in symbolism as much as a fine-arts graduate of our era. Many of the messages lay in the detail. Here is a painting of the archangel Gabriel appearing before the pregnant Mary, soon to be the mother of Jesus. How can we be sure that it is Mary? The archangel carries a lily. Who is that woman with an ointment box at her feet? She is Mary Magdalene, who was with Jesus near the end of his life.

The churches were the main art galleries of that era but no artistic guidebooks or earphones were available for visitors and worshippers. The religious painting had to speak without the aid of interpreters. How could it be otherwise? It was pointless to place captions on religious paintings because most people could not read.

Just as today's footballers can be identified by the team colours they wear, so the heroes of Christianity could be identified by the clothes they wore, or by the symbols placed in their hands or at their feet. The painting of the baby Jesus by Giovanni Tiepolo might well puzzle visitors to the National Gallery of Art in Washington, for in the infant's left hand is a plump goldfinch. To the true believers, however, the goldfinch was the herald of the fate of Jesus, who was to be decked with a crown of thorns before he was killed. As almost everyone knew in that era, when most people were peasants and farm labourers, the goldfinch ate thorns and thistles.

In many paintings, St Peter, dressed in bright yellow, carried a set of keys – the keys to the kingdom of heaven. Or he carried a fish, for he went fishing for human souls in the hope of capturing and converting them. St Mark was often shown in company with a lion; and when he became the patron saint of Venice the lion went with him as a symbol. St Paul was often shown with a sword, the instrument by which he was beheaded. St Scholastica, the twin sister of St Benedict and the female saint of the Benedictines, was usually painted with a lily in her hand and a dove at her feet. Her brother, at the moment of her death, was said to have seen a dove conveying her soul to heaven.

And who is that gaunt figure dressed in a camel skin and carrying a lamb? That must be St John the Baptist. Who is that man dressed in Augustinian black and showing a star on the left-hand side of his cloak? He is the Adriatic-Italian saint, Nicholas of Tolentino. A star on the forehead, in contrast, usually signified St Dominic, because on the day of his baptism in northern Spain a star is said to have shone on his tiny forehead. St Francis of Assisi was usually shown in bare feet and with stigmata or Christ-like wounds on his hands and feet. Perhaps a friendly wolf was with him, reminding worshippers of that day in the nearby town of Gubbio where reportedly he had negotiated a truce and formally shaken hands with the paw of a wild wolf.

The colours of the religious robes and other garments depicted in the paintings were also a vital clue, for the Christian Church was more and more the exponent of colour and rich decorations. Innocent III, enthroned as pope before he was forty, turned his mind in the 1190s to the colours used in the numerous religious ceremonies. He set down the nucleus of the present system of colours selected to mark each event of the Christian year. White, red, green, purple or violet, and black were the main colours. An informed worshipper entering a church in Paris or Lisbon knew the colour of the robe the priests would be wearing on a feast day of an apostle. On the other hand, the Orthodox Church refrained from such precision, though it preferred white garments for Easter and funerals.

THE RISE OF THE UNIVERSITIES

Universities were largely creatures of the church. Irrespective of whether they were formed by bishops or by informal groups of teachers and scholars, they were soon under the control of the church – except in the eastern Mediterranean. They obeyed its precepts; they promoted its goals. They were spurred by and preceded by the schools attached to monasteries and cathedrals; the monks and friars were often the main scholars inside them. The early universities of western Europe were in Italian towns. Perhaps the first was in the southern Italian port of Salerno and was essentially a medical school. By the eleventh century it was the finest in Europe and relied much on Greek and Arabic physicians, whose writings at that time were being translated into Latin. The students learned to dissect bodies, but those of pigs rather than human beings. Some remedies taught at Salerno would now be called modern, for they encouraged the habit of bathing in warm springs and a preference for a sensible diet and regular exercise: 'After breakfast walk a mile.'

The most influential of the early universities was at Bologna in north Italy, with steep hills on one side and the wide plain of the River Po on the other. It first specialised in canon or church law and in civil law. Foreigners, especially men in their twenties and thirties, heard of its success and made the long journey by land and sometimes by sea to study there. As its fame spread, it attracted many Spanish students, for whom a special college was founded in

1364, by which time Bologna's university had been flourishing for two centuries.

Paris was the first serious rival to Bologna. Its university was under the supervision of Notre Dame Cathedral, and its specialty was theology and other fields of more abstract thought. Soon four departments or faculties – law, medicine, arts and the all-powerful theology – were established in Paris's university. In Spain the most famous university, Salamanca, was founded in 1243. By then the English river town of Oxford possessed a university that rivalled Paris in theology. Like the Catholic Church, the university was an international institution, and its students and teachers came from many lands: the common language of Latin made such movements easy. At first the spoken word, not the book or manuscript, was the essence of university teaching. Its lecture was the equivalent of the church's sermon. The role of the university was to teach, argue and reason within a Christian framework; and initially it was inconceivable that science, technology and utilitarian pursuits would come to dominate its courses and degrees.

Central Europe was slower to imitate these places of high learning, but the founding of universities in Prague in 1348 and in Cracow sixteen years later were intellectual landmarks. The university was to become a hallmark of Christian civilisation. In the sixteenth century the Protestant Reformation – that violent shaking-up of the Catholic Church – was to be initiated by graduates of the universities, but in the most recent century perhaps no institution has done more to promote an alternative or secular view of the world.

13

A STAR ABOVE ASSISI

The ocean of Christendom could be placid for long periods, but sometimes the winds and currents were swift. The first decades of the thirteenth century experienced swift seas.

That revolutionary mystic from the mountains of Calabria, Joachim of Fiore, had travelled as a young pilgrim to the Holy Land. Returning home and joining the Cistercians, he became a preacher, and then in 1177 the reluctant abbot of a monastery. His interest was more in studying, contemplating and prophesying than in running a monastery. Popes actually encouraged him in his mental explorations, not quite knowing how far his brilliant mind was deviating from mainstream Christianity. Joachim believed there would arise a golden age, not in heaven but on earth.

Joachim divided human history into three stages. In the first, presided over by the Old Testament, mankind tended to admire earthly and material pursuits. After the birth of Christ emerged a second stage in which mankind was torn between the spiritual and the material. That stage would last only for forty-two generations, and its ending in about the year 1260 would be heralded by violence and even chaos. Then would dawn stage three, the golden age. Heaven would descend to earth. Thereafter people would be truly spiritual, goodness and charity would prevail, and poverty would fade away. At the same time the Jews would become Christians, and the birds – rejuvenated – would fly ever higher. In such a paradise of good behaviour, the clergy might no longer be needed.

Here, hidden in the far south of Italy, was a monk making predictions that could never be accepted by a Christian civilisation in which clergymen were so important. In the ultimate utopia predicted by Joachim himself, even Christ would have a less active role. Joachim's ideas – understood or misunderstood – had little effect during the few years remaining to him: already he was approaching the age of seventy. Soon after his death in 1202, several of his ideas were condemned by the Second Lateran Council. Later they were attacked by the theologian Thomas Aquinas. But all the time the ideas were creeping through keyholes and open windows, and surprising people who heard them for the first time. Dante the poet was influenced by the scribbling monk. So too was Christopher Columbus when, landing in the dazzling world of the Americas, he wondered whether this was Joachim's third stage of history already come into being.

While Joachim was stirring the air, another Italian was finding his wings. Both expressed bold ideas while living in what is seen, by many, as a medieval intellectual prison. Whereas Joachim of Fiore is now viewed as a herald of Marx and Engels and utopian communism, Francis of Assisi – a teenager when Joachim was old – is now viewed as a herald of the green crusade of the twentieth century.

FRANCESCO DISCOVERS A NEW LIFE

In the year 1200, Western Europe's population and its cities were growing, though most people lived on the land. Cloth and wool merchants were becoming minor magnates in the larger cities, and a new species of merchant was arising to deal in money: namely, the early bankers. England and north-western Europe were the main growers, spinners and weavers of wool, but much of their cloth was bought by Italian merchants and carried home for the final part of the manufacturing process. The mineral alum was vital for dyeing the cloth – it enabled the colour to cling to the cloth – and the powerful wool town of Florence almost went to war with rival Volterra over the ownership of an alum mine.

The wool industry financed the childhood home of perhaps the most famous Christian since Christ himself. Francesco di Pietro di Bernardone, later called St Francis of Assisi, was born in the central Italian town of Assisi, probably in 1181. His father was a merchant who specialised in cloth. It sounds an old-fashioned trade but in Europe it was a vital part of long-distance commerce, and the processing of cloth was more important than the making of automobiles is nearly eight centuries later.

His father travelled to the trade fairs of Champagne in France, the largest fairs in Europe, where untreated cloth could be bought in large quantities. Possibly on one such journey he met Pica, the French woman who became his wife. Little is known of Pica, but often it was the mother who shaped the personality of those who kept Christianity alive or gave it new life. Understandably, their first son was given the name of Francesco, with its strong French connotation. The son, however, grew up to disown the fashion industry that sustained his father. That this dashing young man sometimes dressed himself in rags instead of stylish clothes caused a stir after he became a dedicated Christian. But so much about him caused a stir.

Francis's conversion did not come quickly. One of the soldiers of the hill town of Assisi in its conflict against Perugia, he became a prisoner of war for a year. At the age of twenty he was still seen as worldly. Later he had a vision in which he believed that he was in the presence of Christ. Another vision he experienced while in a cave, for this was hermit country, and in the hills many cave-dwellers were alert for any signals from Christ. He came to see poverty as his rightful life and believed that the devout Christian should befriend the poor. Making a pilgrimage to Rome, he dressed like a beggar and sought alms outside St Peter's. It is fair to say that the passages in the New Testament emphasising the virtues of poverty were not recited as frequently in churches as their frequency in the four gospels might have demanded. But Christ's words, such as those in Matthew's sixth chapter, were unmistakeable: 'Do not lay up for ourselves treasures on earth, where moth and rust consume and where thieves break in and steal, but lay up for yourselves treasures in heaven.' It was easy for Francis, from memory, to finish off that passage: 'where your treasure is, there will your heart be also.'

Leprosy was widespread in medieval Europe, and lepers lived on the plain outside the walls of Assisi; most people turned the other way when they met lepers on the road. One day Francis resolved to kiss a leper on the face, though the skin was repulsive. The distasteful task, to his surprise, gave him joy. He felt 'a sweetness of soul and of heart'.

Believing that Christ was instructing him, Francis was alert for any message that might come. Outside the walls of Assisi stood the crumbling chapel of San Damiano, and Francis was visiting it when, from the crucifix standing on the altar, he thought he heard a voice commanding him to repair the dilapidated building and make it fit again for worshippers. Needing money for such a project, he knew where to find it. From his father's house he borrowed or stole bales of new cloth, tied them to the back of a horse and travelled to the nearby town of Foligno. Its fine church, with a southerly facade completed less than ten years previously, was adorned with carved exotica including monsters and, of all things, a small Islamic star and crescent.

In a nearby street, Francis sold the cloth and the horse, and with the money in hand he prepared to organise repairs to the derelict chapel near Assisi. His father, angered by what he regarded as an act of theft, took action. The bishop, informed of the episode, tried to rebuke Francis, who deflected the rebuke in his disarming way and kept the money.

With the aid of his illicit funds, Francis began to repair the chapel, sometimes using a mason's trowel and even climbing the scaffolding. He then turned his hand to the nearby Benedictine oratory of Porziuncola, where another chapel was dilapidated. In this phase of his life – he was in his mid-twenties – he was almost a builder and developer on a small scale.

In one of these chapels he experienced another transforming day. A priest was reading aloud from the Latin version of the gospel of Matthew, and Francis sensed that it was as if Christ's words had been written especially for him. He heard the advice to take to the road, travelling lightly, carrying 'no gold, nor silver, nor money', and not even sandals or a stick. Now a traveller, he began to preach to those willing to listen. He wished to live the kind of simple daily life that Christ might have lived if he had been born in Assisi. Whether Christ lived as frugal a life as the one now chosen by Francis is doubtful.

Francis gathered a dozen disciples. In Rome, about 100 kilometres away, he received the pope's blessing to carry on his mission. As he was not even a monk, the blessing must have seemed extraordinary to those who heard about it. With his followers he returned to Assisi, where the Porziuncola chapel was loaned to him by the Benedictines in return for a basket of carp. It became his home, but his duty was to be always on the move.

Intent on visiting the Holy Land, he set out in 1212, but his ship was wrecked near the Adriatic coast and he returned home. A voyage to North Africa to convert the Moors from Islam was thwarted by his own sickness, but in other expeditions he did reach southern France and Egypt. Most of his short working life, however, was spent along the steep slopes, valleys and plains of central Italy.

Several paintings of him show a longish and sombre face, frank eyes and a dark clipped beard. In other portraits the face is kindly and even cheerful. Dressed in a hood and a dark robe, with a rope belt hanging from the waist, he was usually depicted in bare feet. At times he would play or pretend to play a stringed instrument with his long fingers and sing his own words – often in the French language – in praise of the Lord. His voice, important for an outdoor preacher, was sonorous, sweet and clear.

GOD'S MINSTREL

Francis of Assisi went on long journeys, accompanied by at least one 'brother'. After halting to preach a short sermon he would walk to the next village or crossroads and repeat the message again. In his travels he usually slept on the bare ground but one evening – he must have been ill – he was persuaded to place his head on a pillow filled with feathers, but not for long. Once, after accepting a tunic as a gift, and observing that its cloth was temptingly soft and smooth, he instructed a companion to stitch cords on the inside so that the tunic was no longer comfortable.

He deliberately imposed hardships on his body. The succession of pain and pleasure must have been similar to those experienced by a hard-working athlete, and he explained that the experience placed him in the presence of God. He ate simple wholesome bread and drank water, and when he was offered a small portion of cooked food he diluted his potential pleasure in tasting it by lightly sprinkling ashes on the food. Any spice in his meal he weakened by dashing a little cold water on it. He gladly shared his food with those who were hungry: to share it was for him a privilege.

The sheer simplicity of his life earned public respect, for this was an era when wealthier priests and even bishops ate and drank copiously, dressed stylishly, rode fine horses, and kept at least one eye open for the affections of attractive women. Admittedly, on Francis's own travels, he too was tempted by women. If his feelings were aroused, he did everything he could to curb them. After one such temptation, he deliberately walked waist-deep into a ditch of snow and shivered there. As a biographer fancifully recorded, Francis covered himself in snow so that he might 'preserve his white robe of chastity from the fire of lust'. Of course there are layers of myth and propaganda guarding and embellishing his life, but most of the landmarks and achievements are not easily disputed.

As his reputation grew, Francis received the kind of idolisation that is now focussed on a pop star. On rural roads, admirers tried to cut a thread from his ragged garment as a keepsake. On the outskirts of villages his arrival was preceded by the delighted cry that he was coming. As he modelled himself on Jesus he preferred to preach from the New Testament. In his collected writings and speeches,

164 quotations come from the New Testament but only thirty-two from the Old – a most unusual ratio. The best sermon was brief, he explained, 'for the words which the Lord spoke on earth were brief'. Much later, a variety of Franciscan preachers became celebrated for their acting skills. St Bernardino of Siena, who was born half a century after St Francis died, could mimic the buzzing of a bee or make other sounds so vividly as to arouse his audience and imprint on them his message.

Countless young men – and older ones too – longed to join the leader. The numbers became almost unmanageable. In 1209 Francis possessed twelve disciples, but ten years later that had grown to 2000 or more, and within a few decades his followers numbered 39000 and were scattered in many lands. Not called monks and not called priests, they were simply friars.

At the first Franciscan settlement in Assisi, he had insisted that all meals be eaten while seated on the ground. A table and chair would have smacked of luxury. At night the friars slept on the bare earth, with just a little straw as a mattress and 'a few poor coverlets, almost completely worn out and coming to pieces'. Instructed to earn their own living, or to work amongst the people, most performed work on farms. They were prohibited from receiving money: food and shelter formed their payment. For much of the year they slept in the open air – under hedges, against a wall that protected them at least from the wind, or in makeshift shelters they built with scavenged timber. In colder weather they crowded onto church porches or slept in barns, within sound of the penned cattle, sheep or goats.

Most Franciscans tried to follow the biblical text: 'Take no thought for the morrow'. Personal possessions – other than the simple necessities – were prohibited. 'The brothers shall possess nothing,' Francis commanded. He reminded his followers that 'the Lord made

Himself poor in this world for us'. His strict instruction was to be 'poor in goods, but exalted in virtues'.

Francis was rebelling against a new wave of wealth and worldliness, for banking and trade were flourishing more during his lifetime than at any time for almost 1000 years. New coinages – then a rare event – appeared when Francis was young, and in 1202 the republic of Venice, a haven of commerce, first issued the silver coin called the matapan or grosso, which depicted Christ enthroned in glory. Between 1232 and 1284 several Italian republics were to mint gold coins of high value, including the florin from Florence – the florin was a play on the town's name – and the Venetian ducat, which was probably the best-known gold coin in Europe when Shakespeare, three centuries later, wrote his play *The Merchant of Venice*. Francis warned his followers that a shining coin was a moral menace. In 1221, contrary to his father's view, he decreed that coins were no more useful than pebbles.

THE POOR CLARES

Francis's most admired recruit appeared in 1212. Named Clare, she had heard him preach in the cathedral and was captivated. About twelve years younger than he was, she came from a noble household in the town. She was determined to be one of his disciples but the dilemma was how to accommodate this eager, well-bred woman in an all-male fraternity. With the consent of the Bishop of Assisi, she was admitted to the local Benedictine monastery as a so-called Black Nun. At first her rich parents knew nothing of this plan; she had simply run away.

Clare readily accepted the life of poverty that Francis prescribed for all his followers. Her fine clothes were replaced by coarse cloth, and Francis himself formally cut her long hair. It was perhaps one of the more sensual moments of his self-disciplined life. Not liking the monastery, for she was a follower of St Francis and nobody else, Clare was allowed to settle in the chapel of San Damiano, now repaired. With a younger sister and a few like-minded friends, she became the leader of the Poor Ladies of San Damiano, known later as the Poor Clares.

Setting a spartan example, and fasting for three days in each week, she slept on a bed of vine twigs with only a stone for a pillow. As this rough life harmed her health, she finally accepted the stern command from Francis that she sleep regularly on a straw mattress and eat a little more bread. Her fame spread. In imitation of her piety, new groups of Franciscan women arose in such towns as Lucca, Siena and even Bordeaux in France.

As many married men and women wished to become Franciscans, a third order called the Penitents was formed to organise them. As they lived at home and met formally only once a month, they did not require a monastery or convent. Most were illiterate but eager to learn. 'Let those who cannot read', wrote Francis, have the gospel frequently read aloud to them. Members were to eat no meat on four days of the week, were not to be spectators at games and pageants, and were not to carry swords. Such rules must have chased away many who had joined in a rush of enthusiasm.

SISTER LARKS AND BROTHER FISHES

Francis of Assisi could charm a bird off its perch. In an era when working animals and domesticated birds were treated harshly, he felt an affinity with them. Larks and their drab colours were his favourites. He thought that the larks by implication warned the friars and monks not to wear 'coloured and fancy clothing'. Larks were also humble, which was a religious virtue, and their days were spent mainly 'in the heavens'. Larks seemed to wear a hood or cowl, which suggests that those whom Francis especially liked were the crested larks or the calandra larks, which displayed a black collar. In his eyes, a lark was both cheerful and frugal; she goes 'cheerfully along the road to find herself some corn, and even if she finds it among the dung of beasts she takes it out and eats it'. When horses, oxen and asses were the main means of transport, lumps of animal manure littered the roads, and they contained a few grains that the animals had not digested. Here was food for a hungry bird.

To Francis the larks were his brothers and sisters. He prayed that one day a law might protect them from being trapped and caged. On Christmas Day he hoped that every city and village would honour the larks, and feed them by scattering grain on the roads. Preaching to the birds at Bevagna – a central Italian town still admired for its medieval piazza – Francis formally greeted them as 'my brother birds'. He invited them to praise their Creator, 'who has given you feathers for clothing, wings for flight, and all that you have need of'. In expressing affection for the birds, he was seen by bystanders as an utter eccentric. Perhaps no one in Europe was quite like him.

The hill town of Gubbio, close to Assisi, is said to have witnessed several of his miracles. There he healed the paralysed hands of a girl. More memorably, he befriended a wolf that had been terrorising the neighbourhood. Gravely, Francis made a pact of friendship by clasping the wolf's paws – as if to seal the deal with a gentlemanly handshake. A painting in the National Gallery in London captures that scene and the wonder it inspired.

St Antony of Padua – not yet known by that name – travelled from Portugal to Italy as a very young man, and joined one of the

Franciscan preaching teams. In the 1220s he visited Rimini, the former Roman port on the Adriatic, where he tried to convert 'a great multitude of heretics'. He preached and preached but they were not moved. One day he walked to the mouth of the river, just below the Roman bridge that still stands, and decided to address the sea. If the people would not listen to him, surely the fish would. Lo and behold, according to the ever-popular fourteenth-century book *Little Flowers of St Francis*, the fishes of the sea and river mouth dramatically appeared, holding their heads out of the water and listening to him preaching. Arranging themselves in perfect order, with the small fishes at the front, they bowed their heads 'as a token of reverence'. The inhabitants of Rimini, hearing of this strange spectacle, came down to the lapping sea and marvelled.

A hallmark of the early Franciscans was the fanciful idea that birds and animals, like human beings, were capable of assembling themselves in precise regimental formations when moved by the Holy Spirit. A painting in the Santa Croce church in Florence, completed a few years after the death of Francis, depicts him as a dark-robed saint, earnestly addressing some birds. Thin long-beaked creatures, they listen to him attentively while standing in neat rows of six. In the next panel of the painting are Muslims, also arranged six to a row, listening to him preach, for this was an era of Christian crusading in the hope of winning their souls.

The mood of the twenty-first century is not fully impressed with such miracles; but to most medieval people they showed how God performed his wonders. Indeed, the twenty-first century is more impressed with Francis's compassion towards nature than with his miracles. At the same time, nature was not his main parish; the people were his mission. In his view they alone had the prospect of shaping their lives by trying to live like Christ.

The Muslims and their fate were of more concern to Francis than larks. In 1219, with ten or twelve brothers, he made his last attempt to join a crusade in the hope of converting thousands of Muslims. His ship departed from Ancona and its triumphal Roman arch on the foreshore, passed the high rounded headland, glided along the Adriatic, and probably called at Crete and Cyprus before reaching the crusader port of Acre. Francis then travelled on to Egypt, where the Sultan, surrounded by his army, treated him kindly. Francis responded by trying to convert the Sultan to Christ, a hopeless task. Reaching Italy on his homeward journey, he called at Bologna, by then a celebrated university town, where to his dismay he learned that a building had been set aside for those Franciscan friars who wished to study. The larks did not study and Jesus did not study: why should the friars set aside years for study?

The reins were slipping through his hands. Safely home in Assisi, he did not wish to be the organiser of the regiments of recruits that arrived, but novelty still attracted him. He initiated the practice of placing in churches at Christmas a small crib in which a baby lay.

THE LAST DAYS OF FRANCIS

Before Francis reached his mid-forties, his body was failing. He still wished to preach and would set out riding an ass, but he did not go far. Not only weak, he was also becoming blind.

The intuition that he would soon die made him all the more precious in the eyes of his followers. Towards his end a remarkable happening increased his fame. There reportedly appeared on his body a strange pattern of scars and wounds, reminiscent of Christ after his crucifixion. Apparently caused by nails, the wounds were visible on his sides, hands and feet. Called 'the stigmata', they were hailed as a sign that he was uniquely blessed by Christ. Early in the twentieth century, similar marks were to appear on the body of an Italian provincial priest, Father Pio, whose town was later to be a focus for buses crammed with pilgrims.

In the last full year of his life, Francis spent two months in the company of St Clare in the familiar church of San Damiano, where he composed the 'Canticle of the Creatures', and its praise of Mother Earth, Brothers Sun and Wind, and Sisters Moon and Water. After visiting other towns he became weak. Barely able to walk, he was carried home on a stretcher to Assisi for the last time. He was wearing his sackcloth cap, knowing that death was near.

He spent his last days at the scene of his conversion, in a huddle of huts on the plain below Assisi. There he asked for bread and blessed it, giving a portion to each of the friars who were clustered around him, and placing his hand on their heads in turn. During these farewells he felt deep joy. At his request, passages of St John's gospel were read aloud to him, and once again he heard the words: 'Jesus knowing that his hour was come that he should depart out of this world unto the Father'. He died on 3 October 1226, in the stillness of evening; it was enthusiastically told that his favourite larks, reportedly congregating nearby, took to the sky and began to wheel around and around him in neat formation, as if waving farewell.

Francis wished to be buried naked in the earth and then forgotten, but his body was too important to be forgotten. Soon after his death, his devoted supporter, Cardinal Ugolino, was elected pope. As Gregory IX he travelled to Assisi and proclaimed Francis a saint. Preaching on a text that was popular in medieval times – 'He was as the morning star in the midst of a cloud' – the pope entered the crypt of the new shrine or basilica just being erected and said mass in the presence of St Francis's body, recently removed there. It was strange, to some Franciscans, that one of the costliest shrines in Italy should be erected in honour of a saint who had praised poverty and practised frugality.

His followers were now in many countries. In Hungary their miserable clothes were stolen and they had to smear them with cow dung to make them less tempting to thieves and bullies. In one Spanish town they camped in the cemetery. The first expedition to Germany failed – the friars did not know the German language. In Morocco some became martyrs. In other lands, including Italy and France, they already were astonishingly successful. In England, where they were noticed walking barefoot even in winter, they made their mark before Francis died and set up simple religious houses in London, Oxford, Cambridge, Canterbury and Northampton.

The perils of spiritual success, so feared by St Francis, were already visible. Elias of Cortona, a friend of Francis, became the Minister General in 1232 and had little time for frugality and no inclination to make deep personal sacrifices. He kept gaudily clad servants, and employed his own cook to prepared tasty dishes – he was possibly an invalid – and ate them apart from the other brothers. Much time he spent lying on a couch or sitting, in winter, in front of a fire. The ascetic Francis had rolled in the snow, but Elias dozed by the fire. Francis in his last years, being frail, rode an ass, but Elias in his later years rode a horse and sat on a saddle.

Certain of the specific wishes and aims of Francis were not carried out after his death. He thought learning was a hazard and books and manuscripts were dangerous because they fostered pride, but soon one of the strongholds of the Franciscan order was in the new universities. His followers originally did manual work or cared for the lepers and the sick. But these were not glamorous tasks and tended to fall from favour. St Francis saw great virtues in poverty but some of his leading followers became the friends or the chaplains of the rich and persuaded them to leave their money to the Franciscans. The order became powerful and wealthy and – Francis would have been astonished – trained and encouraged its own administrators and organisers who eventually became cardinals and popes.

Instead of working in the countryside and preaching in the unroofed spaces of the villages, many Franciscans liked to accept invitations to preach in the big parish churches or to erect their own buildings in large towns that were already well served by churches. While a hard core of friars adhered to the old frugal way of life, and were soon busy as preachers in remote India and China, another group helped to make the Franciscans a wealthy and fashionable institution. Every so often the frugal, spiritual reformers won victories: all Franciscans in 1310 were ordered not to eat meat – unless they were frail or ill and needed to gain nourishment. The battle between the two ideologies went on. A version of the battle was to be repeated centuries later in the first two or three generations of the Wesleyan and other new Protestant churches.

THE DOMINICANS

While Francis was setting Italy alight, another glow could be seen at Bologna, on the northern side of the mountains. The glow was lit by the Spaniard, Dominic. He was about a dozen years older than St Francis, with whom he had much in common. Both had a rare ability to attract and inspire disciples. Both came from the wealthier corner of society but were acutely aware of the pitfalls of wealth and knew the New Testament warning that it was not easy for a rich man or woman to enter the kingdom of heaven.

The rise of Dominic was not as speedy and glamorous as that of

Francis. His real name was Domingo de Guzmán. His home was in the far north of Spain, near Burgos, and he was of noble birth. Much of the vitality of medieval Christianity came from those parts of the Spanish peninsula that had recently been under Muslim rule or were close to the frontiers of Muslim rule.

Dominic was about twenty-one when a famine struck the district. He sold his books – a handsome book was expensive, for it was written and illustrated by hand – and gave the money to the hungry. In Osma he joined a monastery, under the Augustinian rules, and his talent was recognised by the local bishop, Diego de Azevedo. Together they made a long tour, eventually meeting the pope, who dissuaded them from travelling to distant lands to win over the heathen. The pope pointed out that tens of thousands of the heathen and a hidden host of heretics lived almost within sight of the mountains of northern Spain. Surely they should be converted first.

Moving to what is now southern France, Dominic tried to convert those obstinate and brave heretics, the Albigenses; it was hard work. In 1207 – he was then in his late thirties – he made preaching his special goal. Repudiating those Catholic priests who preferred fine clothes and a comfortable way of life, he decided that the evangelists should dress frugally and walk in bare feet. When the active crusade began against the heretics, he organised a convent for women who had been saved from the heresy. He was already a fine organiser, and lovable or likeable in the eyes of most of those whom he organised.

In Rome in 1216 he was granted permission to set up a religious order, entrusted with the special goal of preaching. His first base was Toulouse, previously a stronghold of the Cathars. His sixteen followers spread out, enlisted more men ready to dedicate their lives to Christ, and established more religious houses than Dominic could possibly inspect. In one tour – beginning in Rome, embracing

France and Spain, and made entirely on foot – he is said to have walked 6000 kilometres.

Within five years of the founding of the order, Dominicans were active in Paris and Rome, Poland and Bohemia. Another of their houses was about to open in Oxford, for they resolved to be active in the new universities. In London their centre gave its name to an inner neighbourhood still known as Blackfriars. Called variously the Friar Preachers or the Black Friars, they were known formally as the Order of Preachers.

Preaching tended to be lacklustre in most towns and villages, and the sermon was largely out of favour; in contrast, most Dominicans knew how to hold an audience. Increasingly, they were invited to mount the pulpit in parish churches and to take confessions from worshippers. Their black mantle and white cloak were easily recognised in the streets. Their poverty and sincerity won respect. As they usually begged for their own food, they could not be accused of living off the fat of the land or the sweat of the poor.

In 1220 Dominic presided over the first meeting of the general chapter of his Order. A kind of parliament, it met in Bologna, where, one year later, he was to die. He and his Dominicans had sympathy with the democratic process favoured by a few of the monastic orders. In effect, the local Dominican houses and convents elected representatives to attend a provincial assembly, which in turn elected delegates to the general chapter, which in turn selected, by vote, the master general or head. For a long period their choice of leaders and their eye for talent were notable, and several popes and numerous eminent scholars were to come from this Order.

Thomas Aquinas, born in Italy four years after the death of Dominic, accelerated the Dominicans' drive for intellectual dominance. He was eventually acclaimed as perhaps the finest theologian for some 800 years, and the patron of all Catholic universities, but his learned opinions were not accepted universally. For a time, his works were banned in the houses of the rival Franciscans.

In certain circles, the popularity of the Dominicans waned after the Inquisition began to stamp out heresies. The Dominicans, being preachers and theologians, knew exactly what a heresy was. The most feared of the heresy hunters was the Dominican priest Tomás de Torquemada, who became Spain's Grand Inquisitor two and a half centuries after the death of Dominic. It is somewhat unfair that the Spanish Inquisition and its Christian strongmen have become the symbols of intolerance, for we forget that intolerance is normal, not abnormal, in the recorded history of truths held to be precious.

THE BEGGING FRIARS

The Franciscans and Dominicans were known as 'mendicants': in other words they were beggars. The public knew them as 'friars', a derivation from the Latin word *frater*, meaning a brother. People in the streets and highways of most parts of western Europe began to identify the costumes of the new mendicant orders. The Franciscans wore a grey robe and grey mantle or cape, though later they turned to the now familiar brown. The Dominicans or Black Friars wore a black mantle and a white robe. The Carmelites or White Friars wore white on top and brown below. The most recent of the large mendicant orders, the Austin Friars or Hermits, were founded in 1256, less than half a century after the birth of the Franciscan order.

Whereas a monk was rarely seen in the street of the nearest town, the friar became ubiquitous. The colour scheme of his garments was like a standing advertisement and was eventually seen in every continent. Understandably, the early European settlers in Australia and

New Guinea, after discovering several species of honeyeater with a bare head and contrasting body, christened it the friar bird.

Francis and Dominic had commenced their religious life in the long era of the monastery, an institution that initially tried to retreat from the world so that its members could be closer to Christ. They ended their life as founders of institutions that belonged more to the hurrying world. Their friars did not pray behind locked gates but prayed in the city squares and at the crossroads. They acquired no wealth, for they were married to poverty. At first they relied on the kindness or sense of duty of the populace for their daily food. Francis sometimes imagined his friars as resembling 'the fowl of the air'. In the words of the gospel of Matthew, they did not sow and reap grain, they did not 'gather food into barns', and yet their 'heavenly Father' fed them. Later, both the Franciscans and Dominicans became owners of houses, convents, orphanages, asylums, schools and churches on a large scale. Their move away from a hand-to-mouth existence to permanent organisation was almost inevitable, and was a penalty for their early success. Their new form of Christianity would shake much of the world.

The commercial towns were favoured by the new mendicant orders. The friars preferred a street to the solitude and loneliness favoured by the monasteries. In the crowded streets of thriving towns such as Florence, Ghent and Genoa were to be found the Franciscans and Dominicans, the Augustinians and Carmelites. When they first arrived, the towns already had numerous churches, and so the new orders had to build their own churches in roadside fields outside the wall or on vacant land between the inner and outer walls; that was where the Franciscans built in Bologna. The advantage of the towns was that the mendicant preacher could reach the ears of a larger and more influential audience. If he were persuasive, he could also hope to improve morals that were in need of improvement, for the town was seen as the home of immorality and vice, while the countryside was simpler and more homely.

It is easy to underplay the importance of the friars. The Reformation and the birth of Protestantism tend to dominate the recorded history of the years 1200 to 1700, thus overshadowing the rise of Franciscans and Dominicans. The friars, however, were part of an earlier religious upheaval that affected a larger part of Europe than did the early Calvinists and Lutherans. And when in the 1490s the new sea routes to Asia and the Americas were opened, the Franciscans and Dominicans often were the first to step ashore.

14

THE CRUSADERS

In France in 1095, Pope Urban II made a momentous decision. He was about to organise one of the boldest and most remarkable ventures in the history of the world – a mass pilgrimage or crusade. The implications of his decision are still felt in the Middle East.

Originally a monk at Cluny, the pope had returned in papal splendour to consecrate the huge abbey. His other mission in France was to address the synod of Clermont in November. There his vision centred on distant Jerusalem and how to recapture it. His scheme was ingenious. For all those Christians willing to join in a crusade to free the Holy Land from Islam, he resolved to offer rewards in heaven – or along the road to heaven. Those who went as pilgrims to pray, and those who went as soldiers, would equally be forgiven their lifelong sins. Wisely he attached strings to his promise. The reward would go only to those who set out 'to free the Church of God at Jerusalem out of pure devotion and not out of love for glory or gain'. This conditional clause was soon forgotten by most of the crusaders, if ever it was clear to them.

Remarkably, paupers as well as rich men were encouraged to take part in this pilgrimage. Surely the monasteries and other Christian houses along the way would help poor travellers making such a worthy journey. For the rich crusaders the incentives were later raised even higher. Their families and property would be protected by the church in their absence.

A STAMPEDE TOWARDS JERUSALEM

Jerusalem – it was fervently hoped – would be rescued and saved by the crusaders pouring out of western Europe. It was assumed that the forces of Islam would be driven back and that Jerusalem, once recaptured, would be held forever. Henceforth, it would be open permanently to Christian pilgrims, who, inspired by their experience, would return to their homes and be preachers of the gospel.

The earliest season suited for commencing the crusade was the spring, which was still three or four months away. It was hoped that, in the warmer days, some crusaders, both civilian and military, would travel overland. Others would travel by ship. The ship-owners of Genoa, Venice and other Mediterranean ports must have cheered when they heard the pope's promise, for this might prove to be one of the largest sea excursions ever planned. The news of the crusade was infectious. France was particularly infected. French and German princes, dukes, knights and other lesser landowners planned to raise armies, hoping to annex for themselves the lands they captured from the Seljuq Turks.

The pope himself authorised the annexations. Militarily it seemed sensible. The new Christian states would form a buffer zone protecting the Holy City of Jerusalem. Indeed, the air of holiness was mixed with a sense of adventure and a desire to punish old enemies, and a simple hunger for wealth.

For this opening crusade the evangelists rallied an army of volunteers. Peter the Hermit, a long-faced Frenchman from Amiens, spoke fervently of the Second Coming and the need to liberate Jerusalem in readiness for the day when Christ returned. Surely on the day of his return, Christ would set foot first in Jerusalem, the city in which he had been crucified. Like the Pied Piper, Peter the Hermit was followed by a growing army of volunteer crusaders, including women and children, and a host of men ranging from minor nobles and major landlords to carters and peasants. Preaching in Cologne at Easter in 1096 he enlisted crowds of Germans to follow him.

Perhaps 20 000 were already members of Peter's crusade when the onset of spring enabled them to set out. The overland procession went past Belgrade and Sofia, and so towards Constantinople. On fine days it covered about 40 kilometres, such a fast pace that many dropped down exhausted beside the road, or halted in order to rest blistered feet or to cope with what can best be called travel sickness. Peter the Hermit, riding his donkey, was with them, exhorting them, praying for them, and promising them a glimpse of paradise.

The emperor of Constantinople must have been astonished when this amateur cavalcade approached his territory. First he had to feed them: otherwise they would have been like a plague of locusts as they traversed the miles of farmlands. He was only too happy to ferry them across the narrow Bosphorus to the shores of Asia. This was only the beginning, for trained armies of crusaders were about to arrive from northern Europe by sea and land.

Eventually assembling outside the walls of Constantinople, the professional armies and their sympathisers and onlookers were at last ready to advance, some readier than others. The long road to

Jerusalem lay ahead. Mainly under French leaders, the armed cru-saders captured Antioch in 1098 and, a year later, Jerusalem, where they reportedly killed up to 50000 Muslims and Jews. Four separate colonies – but usually described as kingdoms or principalities – were established by western European noblemen near the Asian shores of the Mediterranean. One of these Latin kingdoms ruled over Jerusalem itself.

The Seljuq Turks seemed defeated but were not. When they regained the initiative and captured the crusaders' city of Edessa in 1144, and the news reached western Europe, the pope organised a second crusade. Led by kings, it was defeated at Damascus. In 1187 the Turks finally recaptured Jerusalem, ending the crusaders' occu-pation, which had lasted for eighty-eight years.

THE CRAZY FOURTH CRUSADE

It was originally expected that the crusades against Islam would unite Christendom. In the end they accentuated the religious rift between Catholic and Orthodox Christians. They also deepened the commercial rivalry between the Christian republics of Genoa and Venice, and therefore strained their bonds as fellow Catholics. Increasingly, the crusades were an evangelical backdrop to the com-mercial rivalry in what is now seen as a crucial phase in the growth of capitalism.

The rivalry of Venice and Genoa was partly the result of Italy's geography. As the major ports at the respective heads of the deep Mediterranean gulfs extending northwards, they served the trade routes that crossed the Alps into northern Europe. Genoa was on the west side of Italy and her galleys vied with neighbouring Pisa's in trying to control the seas extending towards France and Spain and north-west Africa. Sometimes in foreign ports, even at the Golden Horn, the Pisan and Genoan sailors fought one another with knives.

In contrast, Venice was on the eastern side of Italy and her galleys controlled much of the Adriatic, the Aegean, the eastern Mediterranean and the narrow straits leading to Constantinople and the Black Sea. Constantinople increasingly agreed to allow much of its commerce to be carried in Venetian galleys. It had no alternative because it lacked naval power. So Venetian vessels were arriving regularly, not only from their home port but also from Byzantine ports in the eastern Mediterranean and Black Sea. Constantinople, that huge port standing at the crossways of Asia and Europe, even set aside a Venetian suburb where resident Venetian officials adjudicated in disputes between their own sailors and merchants, and Venetian chaplains regularly conducted religious services, using the Latin language and rites. The peace was shattered on 12 March 1171. The Byzantine emperor ordered that Venetians living in his city be arrested. From the bloodshed and death a few managed to escape, though their ship was pursued for days by the enemy. Four years later the grievances were partly remedied and Venetian merchants returned to Constantinople.

Venice waited until the year 1204 before taking its revenge. The revenge was on other commercial cities as well as on Constantinople. In commerce there was now a three-pronged rivalry between the Catholic cities of Venice, Genoa and Pisa, while the Byzantines and the Muslims were rivals of everyone else. The Venetians were temporarily the strongest. They organised the fourth crusade, supplying more ships than the crusaders and accompanying pilgrims could fill.

Intermittently, the rulers of Constantinople had pleaded with the pope to organise military help against the threatening Muslims. This time they received more help than they sought. In 1204 a Venetian fleet, consisting of troop galleys and supply galleys, sailed safely through the Dardanelles and reached the walls of the mighty city. An army of some 30 000 was ready to fight its way ashore. Storming the fortifications, they massacred many of the inhabitants, and burned, pillaged and wrecked buildings. Amongst the loot shipped away were four noble bronze horses that had adorned the city's hippodrome, where chariot races and civil pageants took place. The bronze horses now stand in the open air in Venice, outside St Mark's church, in sight and sound of the sea.

The Venetians were initially content to occupy Constantinople and Athens and the Adriatic port of Zara, which lies in the present Croatia. The rewards of this naval conquest were high, both for merchants and for priests. A Venetian became the patriarch of the Orthodox Church – in effect, the pope of the east. In the wonderful old church he conducted religious services, speaking Latin in place of the familiar Greek. He also crowned as the new emperor a French nobleman, Baldwin, the Count of Flanders. It seemed appropriate because the French had contributed most of the fighting forces to most of the crusades. Remarkably, the pope, waiting in Rome for news of the latest crusade, had little influence on this Italian triumph in the city of his rivals; he was too far away.

Many western Christians felt ashamed at the way in which Constantinople and its priests and people had been humiliated. They later learned that the Orthodox Christians, largely as a result of these events, disliked the Catholic Christians even more than the Muslims. It later became known that Franciscan friars, working as missionaries in Asia Minor, did their best to apologise for the insults inflicted by fellow Christians. The friars explained that the sacking of Constantinople was the work of 'laymen', sinners and those who had been, or were about to be, excommunicated. The sacking was the regrettable behaviour of people who were beyond the control of the pope. On the contrary, Pope Innocent III, who had blessed this latest crusade, actually rejoiced when he learned that the Greek-speaking patriarch in Constantinople had just been deposed: 'By the just judgement of God,' he said, 'the kingdom of the Greeks is translated from the proud to the humble.' The humble awaited their chance. In 1261 they recaptured their own city, hailing Genoa as their special friend, and holding on to their city for nearly two centuries.

THE CRUSADES: A POST MORTEM

The crusades form one of the barometers of the way we view the past. They are such exciting, tragic events that they tend to colour the picture of Christianity that is widely held today. In fact the crusades became as much commercial as Christian ventures, and the financiers and shippers reaped the rewards. In addition, the crusades are now seen as one of the most disastrous episodes in the history of Christianity, and a cause of the present rift between a small militant branch of Islam, on the one hand, and the western near-Christian world on the other. Several European leaders have publicly apologised for their own country's militant role in the crusades. Though apologies are a slightly debased form of currency when they are coined and paid centuries after the event by people who were not participants, they are Christian in spirit.

Most western historians once viewed the crusades more favourably. They noticed not only the violence but the heroic deeds and the idealism of tens of thousands of crusaders, and of those Christians who stayed at home. 'Humanity is the richer because of the crusades,' wrote one distinguished British scholar at the start of the twentieth century. 'The ages were not dark in which Christianity could gather itself together in a common cause, and carry the flags of its faith to the grave of its Redeemer.' No longer do well-informed citizens of the western world seem to remember one significant fact. From the seventh to the tenth centuries, the forces of Islam had captured more than half of all the Christian territories in Europe and Asia Minor. The crusades, poorly coordinated, recaptured only a fraction of what had been lost. Whether the casualties, civilian and military, of the Muslim conquest were larger than those of the Christian reconquest is not known.

And yet the violence of the crusades, extending over two centuries, reflected no credit on Christianity, in the eyes of many thoughtful citizens of the second half of the twentieth century. The sheer length of the crusading era causes much of the present-day unease or guilt. Why were they so prolonged? Clearly religious ardour was one powerful reason. The Christians – and their enemies – believed that they were fighting for a holy goal. Another reason for the prolonging of the crusades – the tyranny of distance – had nothing to do with Christianity. The Christian forces from western Europe, having won early victories that enabled them to set up kingdoms on the far side of the Mediterranean, had difficulty in supplying those distant kingdoms or colonies with volunteer soldiers, war-horses, arms and reinforcements either by land or sea. Western Europe's first valuable overseas possessions, their supply lines were long and costly.

The Christian invaders had difficulty in manning their new Asian kingdoms with a sufficient number of men and cavalry horses. The crusades therefore had to be continued, at massive cost in people and supplies, simply to retain Jerusalem and the other towns, forts and rural lands that had been conquered in the first crusade. The crusaders were like the emperor Napoleon and his French forces fighting in faraway Russia in 1812, or like the British defending remote Singapore and Malaysia in 1942: they were fighting too far from home. After the first capture of Jerusalem in 1099, the crusades became an expensive attempt to retain by force what had been won by force. Each new crusade, so glamorous when launched, was usually more a defensive war.

For Christians, the sites of Jerusalem, Jericho, Bethlehem, Nazareth and the Sea of Galilee were central to the life of Christ. His whole life had been spent in that tiny region. Here were the scenes of his preaching, his miracles, his death, his empty tomb. To abandon the hope of visiting those sacred places was almost unthinkable for a serious Christian, whether a bishop or a peasant. To abandon Jerusalem after it had been captured was almost seen as blasphemy, a denial of one's own religious faith. Rather than abandon the crusades, the incentive to participate in them was increased. On the eve of what was called the fourth crusade, Innocent III decided to offer the same religious incentives to stay-at-home Christians who donated money as were offered by his predecessors to soldiers and civilians who actually embarked on a crusade.

The loss of Constantinople to the Turks in 1453 did not finally crush the hopes of crusaders. In Rome, in the space of twenty years, a new crusade was devised and provisionally financed, though it was not pursued. Its aim was to recapture Constantinople. In fact another crusade, quite unforeseen, was about to commence. Its aim was to convert the people of the Americas and Asia.

15

ROME, AVIGNON AND THE GOLDEN HORN

The big political entity in Europe was the Holy Roman Empire. It was more a supervised alliance than an empire, and the emperor himself was elected. Possessing no army in its own name, it could not always rely on the support of the armies of the kings and princes who made up the Empire. In area and potential power, however, the Empire was impressive.

If fitted onto a map of present-day Europe, the Holy Roman Empire was vast. In 1330 it embraced most of Germany, much of Austria and the present Czechoslovakia, all of Switzerland, the present Holland and Belgium, parts of eastern France, and much of Italy. The Empire extended like a patchwork carpet from the Baltic and the North Sea to the Mediterranean. It included such southern ports as Marseilles and Genoa but not Venice, which was a maritime empire in its own right.

Rome itself lay about 200 kilometres outside the southern border of the Holy Roman Empire and so did not belong to it. Rome was the capital of its own little empire, the Papal States, which extended to the Adriatic shores and almost in sight of Venice. Italy was divided into many republics and kingdoms, the largest being the Kingdom of Naples, which dominated southern Italy and also owned the Greek island of Corfu. Italy was celebrated more for its prosperous cities than its mighty states. Milan, Venice, Florence and Naples were among the ten largest cities in Europe. Rome stood far down the list of such cities.

Most of Eastern Europe lay outside the Holy Roman Empire. In the east lay three large kingdoms – Hungary, Poland and Lithuania – which extended to the Black Sea. Russia was not yet strong nor united. Much of the land now held by the three Baltic nations was in the possession of the Teutonic Knights. On the shores of the Baltic Sea, Denmark was larger than it is today, owning part of the present Sweden, while the kingdom of Sweden owned the more liveable regions of the present Finland. Norway had its empire too. While recently it had lost control of the Scottish Hebrides and its sacred monastery of Iona, it retained the Orkneys and the Shetlands.

England already owned a small empire but it did not yet extend to the north. It did not govern Scotland and did not completely control Ireland. On the other hand, the large duchy of Aquitaine, in the south west corner of the present France, belonged by marriage to the English monarch. Even the port of Calais, from 1347, belonged to England, and remained her possession for more than 200 years. Despite these intrusions by the English and her armies, France was a large piece in the jigsaw of states of north-western Europe. Paris was probably the largest city of western Europe.

Spain showed few signs that it would ever be united. In the Spanish peninsula, most territory belonged to the kingdom of Castile, while smaller areas belonged to Portugal, Aragon, Navarre and Granada. The Muslims, once dominant in Spain, were in slow retreat.

In 1330 they clung to the small southern state of Granada, which extended some 300 kilometres along the shore of the Mediterranean Sea, eastwards from Gibraltar. On the opposite shore, the long coastline of North Africa was also Muslim. Indeed, the approaches to the Strait of Gibraltar and the Atlantic Ocean were guarded on both the European and North African coasts by Muslims.

Europe did not have one dominating kingdom. No ruler held a real hope of controlling, in his lifetime, more than one-quarter of Europe. In theory that should have strengthened the popes, giving them more independence. But their independence was in jeopardy. Soon there would be two, even three popes.

A HAND WITH TEN FINGERS

The Catholic Church and its activities pervaded most of Europe: today, no cultural, religious or educational institution is comparable. It was not only a church but also an early version of the welfare state. It conducted hospitals for the old and orphanages for the young; hospices for the sick of all ages; places for the lepers; and hostels or inns where pilgrims could buy a cheap bed and meal. In times of famine the church was often the largest supplier of daily bread and other essentials such as salt. Monasteries built capacious barns in which grain and hay could be stored, and the monks and nuns handed bread and even beer to the poor on certain days of the week.

To fulfil these duties the various branches of the church had to collect taxes on a large scale. These tithes or taxes – representing one-tenth of the produce of the soil – were paid to the church by landowners. The Catholic Church also possessed an array of farmlands, being the largest landowner in Europe and owner of innumerable properties in the cities and large towns, including the most costly buildings, the cathedrals and churches. It conducted directly or indirectly most of the universities in Europe and owned nearly all the large libraries, having produced most of the books in its monasteries. It was the main patron of the arts. It was the main educator of the young, though most children attended no school.

Nearly all economic activities were regulated or guided by the church. The merchant who imported leather and grain, the brewer who paid his employees, the banker who exchanged his purse of foreign coins, and the monastery that sold land – all had to inquire: what is a fair price? A person was answerable to God for every trans-action. Some theologians made their reputation by adjudicating on these fine points. Popes sometimes pronounced on them. Usury – the receiving of interest on money loaned – was a special sin. The Old Testament warned about its dangers, and the gospel according to Luke memorably reported that Christ held radical views. 'But woe to you that are rich,' Christ said. That message was not honey for a merchant's tongue. On the lending of money or commodities he said sternly: 'and lend, expecting nothing in return'. These warnings were given to a crowd that included people from seaports, the home of merchants.

While the church in medieval times repeated such warnings, they were utterly impractical to merchants whose very existence as long-distance traders depended on selling wool, wine or grain for much more than they had paid for it. Trade and finance were not eas-ily adjudicated by the church and its ally, the civil authorities. And yet Europe and the Mediterranean world relied more and more on trade, especially in years of famine and glut.

Penalties for un-Christian behaviour were set down. They were enough to make a good Christian wring his hands or blaspheme.

A guilty merchant or landholder could no longer take part in the Eucharist. Some medieval theologians said he must not even enter a church. When he died he was forbidden the normal privilege of being buried in or near the church. Prayers could not be said for his soul by his parish clergymen. The same laws applied to bishops, abbots and priests. Some owned private wealth and added to it by lending sums for a fee. If a priest was found guilty of usury, he might be suspended or defrocked. As early as AD 325, the Council of Nicaea had warned priests about the moral dangers of usury.

The medieval church was like a hand with ten fingers. It extended its rewards and punishments into every corner of daily and nightly life. As the pope was entrusted with the governing and supervising of this massive institution, his death and the election of his successor were momentous events.

THE HERMIT POPE

Peter, the child of Italian peasants, was number eleven in a family of twelve. He was one of those young men who, after deciding to dedicate their lives to Christianity, preferred the lonely ways of the hermit to the collective life of the monastery. Originally a Benedictine, he did not easily fit in with a group and the communal way of life, and did not like Rome, so he retreated to the mountains that formed the spine of central Italy. Occupying a cave, eating simple food and wearing humble clothes, he prayed or contemplated for much of the night and day.

While the hermits formed a fast-growing occupation, not all relished the lonely life. Some needed a spiritual guide, and some needed the occasional support and stimulus of a religious community. Eventually, at Monte Morrone, Peter helped muster the surrounding hermits into a new community or order that was eventually called the Celestines, a name also conferred on a sky-blue colour. At the new monastery in the Abruzzi mountains, near Sulmona, he developed into a quietly inspiring leader. Naturally, his gift as an organiser was a willingness to delegate. He still preferred a lonely cave to a busy monastery.

Meanwhile, in 1292 it was time to elect a pope. For just over a century the cardinals, as members of the Sacred College, had elected the new pope when the position became vacant. Rarely more than twenty in number, they themselves had been selected by recent popes, and so they belonged to an inner circle with similar interests. But their views about candidates for any vacancy were not necessarily the same, and they were also influenced by powerful monarchs and outside prelates who demanded a say in the appointment, which caused long delays. The procedure was finally adopted of turning the key in the door of an apartment and locking the cardinals in until they had reached a decision.

Peter the Hermit, now more than eighty years old, and not to be seen at any gathering of the mighty, was absent from the shortlist of names that were first considered for the vacancy. After two years of deadlock, however, a final decision was urgent. Through the influence of Charles II, King of Naples, it was resolved that Peter was just the man. Papal messengers found their way to the cave of this slightly dishevelled hermit and persuaded him to accept the nomination as pope. In July 1294 he was ready to be enthroned.

To the disappointment of many, he was not to be crowned in Rome. Instead, a town was chosen in hermit terrain in the flat-topped hills to the east. L'Aquila, barely half a century old, was within sight of the dominating mountain called the Gran Sasso. Much of its income came from the small flocks of sheep in the surrounding hills and valleys, and from the newly clipped wool washed in the fountain of the ninety-nine spouts – still to be seen on the outskirts of the town. L'Aquila was hardly the place for the grandest ceremony in Europe but it did possess a handsome basilica, Santa Maria di Collemaggio, with its freshly built walls resembling a chessboard of red and white marble. There the new pope was crowned in the presence of cardinals and a few of his fellow hermits, dressed in black. A vast concourse of people surrounded the church, hailing the hermit who, it was hoped, would restore innocence and simplicity to the papacy.

Pope Celestine V, who mentally was not always dwelling in the clouds, accepted the opportunity to promote his own group, now known as the Poor Hermits of Celestine. Eventually, their monasteries extended from Italy to the Netherlands and Bohemia, numbering more than 200. Meanwhile, tired and old, he could not adjust himself to the regulated life of the pope and the incessant demands on his attention. He quickly came to regret the decision to be enthroned, as did those who enthroned him, for he was not as malleable as they had anticipated. He was that rarity, a pope who decided to abdicate. He stepped down – or was pulled down – after only five months in office. He did not live much longer.

Peter was buried in the basilica at L'Aquila, within sight of the late-season snow on the mountain tops. More than seven centuries later, lying in his coffin, embalmed and in ceremonial dress, he was disturbed by the severe earthquake of April 2009. So his remains were carried from the half-destroyed church to a safer place, in the presence of the reigning pope and the television cameras: an unimaginable intrusion on the privacy of a hermit.

WHEN ROME WAS MOVED TO FRANCE

Rome and its surroundings were sometimes in anarchy. The district was a cockpit of intrigue and disputation. The reigning pope had many reasons for leaving that city whenever possible.

In 1304 Pope Benedict XI died in the hill town of Perugia in central Italy. The cardinals assembled in the same city to elect his successor, but after eleven months of disagreement they still couldn't reach a decision. In the end, a French name was selected. The new Pope Clement V was the archbishop of Bordeaux, but he was not even a cardinal and, of course, not present at Perugia. Crowned in the French city of Lyons, and somewhat under the influence of the French king, he was not attracted to the idea of leading the church from the palace in the unstable town of Rome and the turbulent peninsula of Italy.

In effect the king of France seized the papacy. Instead of moving to Rome, the new pope simply agreed, in 1309, to live in the town of Avignon in southern France. Hardly a very important town, it was at least in the Rhône Valley, one of the vital waterways and trade routes of Europe. In some ways Avignon was more central than Rome, for in recent centuries the Christian empire over which the pope presided was expanding in northern Europe but not in the Mediterranean. As for the argument that France was seizing the papacy, it could be explained in reply that Avignon was not actually ruled by the king of France.

Clement V did not try to create a stately town in the hope of rivalling Rome. He did not believe that Avignon should be the permanent home of the pope, for he hoped that Rome and the countryside around it would become less incendiary. Meanwhile, content to live in the Dominican monastery in Avignon, he had no need for a new palace. The bishop of Avignon became the next pope, and so he did not have to move his residence. Eventually, on the cathedral rock overlooking the river, the building of a papal palace was commenced. More commanding than the town's cathedral, it was a combined palace, fortress and monastery. In sight were dozens of churches and religious houses, their bells carried far by the wind that so often blew along the Rhône Valley – the author Rabelais called it 'the city of bells'. The crenelated wall around the town was completed in 1368, by which time the papacy actually owned both the town and the countryside. It remained a papal possession for more than four centuries, being finally snatched away during the French Revolutionary Wars.

In a typical half-century most of the cardinals had been Italians, but in the decades when the popes reigned in Avignon a new kind of face appeared. By 1331, seventeen of the twenty cardinals were French. When vacancies occurred, even more French cardinals were created; and not surprisingly, when they assembled at Avignon, they elected their fellow countrymen as popes – seven in all. In turn the popes selected more Frenchmen as cardinals. In the space of seventy years they elected 112 Frenchmen as cardinals – mostly from Languedoc in southern France – and only twenty-two cardinals from the remainder of Europe. There had often been criticism of the way in which cardinals and popes were elected, especially of the temptation to elect one's own relatives to these high offices; but Avignon displayed a relatively novel form of preference, and this quickened the demands for reform.

The French takeover of the papacy weakened its prestige. No person did more than Catherine of Siena, a Dominican nun just turned thirty years of age, to persuade diverse churchmen that the pope really belonged to Rome. In that city St Peter had been buried, and each successive pope was obliged to carry on St Peter's mission.

Likewise, most of the popes who lived contentedly in Avignon sensed or believed that Italy was the rightful home of the papacy. Indeed, about two-thirds of papal revenue now went into hiring mercenary soldiers so that they could gain the initiative, mostly in central Italy. Eventually, the papacy became more powerful in Italy and regained Bologna and Verona and important towns that it had lost. So the pope was tempted and beckoned to return to a Rome made more secure.

Pope Urban V, a decent and even saintly man, decided in 1377 to return to Rome. It was a sad day for Avignon when, with pomp and ceremony, he departed from the papal palace. Boarding a river boat, he sailed downstream to the Mediterranean coast, from where he was conveyed by galley to Italy. As soon as he approached the outskirts of Rome in October 1377, many residents of the city, long bereft of their pope, welcomed him with open arms. For the papacy in effect was a huge service industry, and the pope wherever he lived was a magnet for endless processions of pilgrims. For seventy years, in the absence of the pope, Rome had attracted fewer pilgrims, and little inns and hostels, eating houses and street vendors, and even horse-stables, hay merchants and blacksmiths, had lost income. The collection boxes at the churches were no longer so full of coins, the sale of candles slumped, and the sellers of souvenirs who sat outside the church doors felt the pinch. Now, into this dilapidated city came the pope, long awaited. Alas, in the following year he died.

His successor was an Italian. An unwise choice, he provoked those who had elected him. In the end most of the cardinals disowned him. It was easier, however, to elect a new or parallel pope than to depose the existing pope. So the bishop of that French-speaking town, Geneva, was elected. Naturally, he resolved to live not in Rome but in the papal palace in Avignon. Known as the anti-pope he received the support of France, Spain, Scotland, Savoy, the kingdom of Naples and therefore the south of Italy and Sicily too. Meanwhile, the pope in Rome had the support of most Italian- and German-speaking states, as well as Hungary, Poland and England.

In effect, Christendom was divided into three: an eastern Church and a western Church, which was itself divided into two. For nearly thirty years the new schism was a blow to the prestige of a church that valued unity and in earlier centuries had worked hard to maintain it. The presence of rival popes in western Europe undermined the idea that the pope was the supreme authority whose word was not to be challenged.

Another influence was also undermining religious authority, initially in its heartland – Rome, Florence and central Italy – but thereafter in Paris, Flanders, London and dozens of other places. The Renaissance was underway. A rebirth of the secular and pre-Christian spirit of classical Greece and Rome, it encouraged a worship of beauty and shape, a new attitude to painting and sculpture, a questioning of traditional morality, and a celebrating of the joys of this world rather than the world to come. The small educated section of European society – even the papacy – was especially affected.

WYCLIFFE'S CHALLENGE

Into this vacuum of religious leadership stepped protesters and stirrers, the most influential of whom lived north of the Alps. One was Gerhard Groote, a member of a wealthy Dutch family who pursued studies in at least four universities extending from Aachen to Prague, and in at least four major disciplines from medicine to theology. He briefly enjoyed an indulgent life before falling under the influence of the Carthusian monks. After two years in a monastery, he made his home base in Utrecht and set out as a preacher. That he attacked the morals of many of the clergy won him disciples amongst the people but not the favour of his bishop, who prohibited him from preaching. Groote appealed to Rome but his appeal was not yet answered when he died in 1384. He left behind two influential groups: the Brethren of the Common Life and the Sisters of the Common Life, the sisters already having possession of the home in Deventer in which he lived when young and wealthy.

A more vigorous stirrer was John Wycliffe, a scholarly priest born in Yorkshire. Fluent in Latin and English, he was one of the best-known faces around Oxford, where he was briefly Master of Balliol and for long a resident of Queen's College. He also had friends – though not sufficient – in high places in London. He might have ascended those high places, becoming at least a bishop, but for his independence of thought. He did not fit neatly into any hierarchy nor into the regular offices of the church. He spent little time at the succession of parishes of which he was the rector. His flock heard his words, second-hand. He was almost one of those lax priests criticised by his own pen.

As the years went by, Wycliffe denounced almost everything that could reasonably – and even unreasonably – be denounced. He criticised the monasteries and the large and small properties they accumulated. He disliked their long dining tables, amply provided with food and wine, and the fertile farmlands and the large flocks that they owned. He deplored the sexual licence of many of the priests and monks, and even the nuns. Those priests who did not seduce women, he implied, were tempted to indulge in sodomy.

He criticised the ceremonies inside the grand cathedrals and humble chapels and churches in England. Even the Eucharist became his target. How, he asked, could the thousands of Christians who took part in the Eucharist and solemnly ate the wafer of bread baked in a nearby oven actually believe that, before their eyes, it had been miraculously converted into a piece of flesh from the body of Christ? The mysteries of the church – the blessings, the holy water, the incense – he saw as achieving no miracles. Why did the holy water, he mischievously asked, not cure sores on the human skin if it were really so holy? Even the power to forgive sins should not, in his opinion, be the monopoly of the church. When a priest heard confessions in private from members of his flock, he was claiming a power to forgive that only Christ possessed. His was a challenge to the Christian Church and its legitimacy. His solution was for the church to return to the simplicity that, he believed, had once pervaded it.

Wycliffe mocked the cycle of Christian festivals and the long street processions. He likened Corpus Christi, the pageant beloved in late-medieval times, to 'a miracle with a hen's egg'. He deplored the church's attitude to warfare, and regretted the priestly promises that persuaded the Christian soldiers of England, decade after decade, to fight the Christian soldiers of France. Wycliffe had valid reason to regret the war. In 1377, even as he spoke, the French warships were raiding a stretch of English coast between Rye and Plymouth.

Masses of men and women who did their best to live a Christian life exulted in the ceremonies, paintings, incense and choral music of the church; they had little time for Wycliffe. High authorities were also perturbed by his views. But Wycliffe had a few friends in high places, and he largely escaped public censure. Only after several of his doctrines were condemned – by the pope in 1377 and by his own university in 1381 – was he punished. Even then his punishment was light: he was simply banished to a rural parish.

As the New Testament was available only in Latin, he sponsored a brave scheme to translate it into English, though he did little of the painstaking work himself. After his death his followers continued to translate the bible from Latin into English. As printeries did not yet exist, the new gospels were slowly written out in clear handwriting and the copies circulated, usually in some secrecy. In 1407 the unauthorised Wycliffe Bible was virtually banned.

Many of his followers were nicknamed Lollards. The word, possibly of Middle Dutch origin, had originally mocked those people who mumbled their prayers. The mumbling Lollards were now to be found in London, Coventry, villages in the Chilterns, in north England and even in Scotland. Most Lollards were not poor, and many were craftsmen. Viewed by the government as rebels, many went into hiding.

Wycliffe's message, dangerous in England, reached central Europe by an unusual route. It so happened that in the era of rival popes, the powerful king of Bohemia had usually stood on the same side as France and Avignon, but now he entered into an alliance with England, and it was thought that perhaps the alliance should be cemented by a royal marriage. It was therefore proposed that the young Richard II, not yet old enough to rule as king of England, should marry Anne, the teenage sister of King Wenceslas, who ruled Bohemia. Anne's great-uncle, the Duke of Tetschen, travelled across Europe to England to sign the new treaty, to be followed by Anne, who reached Dover in December 1381, one week before Christmas Day. The marriage and coronation took place in the following month.

The marriage between London and Prague had unexpected effects. As many Bohemian students now visited England to study, they picked up the new heresy propagated by John Wycliffe, now an old man, and carried it home. The stir he was causing in England was soon echoed in what is now the Czech Republic, whether along the river towns or in the foothills of the Tatra Mountains.

A generation later, Wycliffe's writings had an influence on a young priest of Bohemia named John Hus. His family were peasants, but he was able to climb the ladder available for bright boys wishing to be priests or monks. In the esteemed Bethlehem Chapel in Prague, he made a reputation as a preacher in the Czech language when only in his mid-twenties, and he also translated Wycliffe's denunciations into Czech. In the spirit of his English master, Hus attacked the emphasis on pilgrimages. He ridiculed the miracle said to have happened at Wilsnack, thus converting that small German town into a place of pilgrimage. At first a favourite of the archbishop of Prague, Hus went too far. He remained popular with masses of people but not with the church's leaders. Finally, he was excommunicated. But was the pope who drove him out the legitimate pope?

A BLAZE IN BOHEMIA

There were two popes and neither wished to abdicate. To heal the disastrous rift a council of the church, consisting of a variety of leaders and theologians, was summoned. It met at Pisa in 1409, and its first step was to depose the rival popes in Rome and Avignon and to elect a new all-dominant pope. Named Alexander V, he did not solve the divisions. In Constance, five years later, another council of the church had to be summoned.

That Constance was chosen as the site of one of the most important councils in the history of Christianity now may seem puzzling. While it is no longer an important town, and its medieval church is not even a cathedral, it was very influential in 1415. Ruled by its bishop, who was an elector of the Holy Roman Empire, it covered a large area in which monasteries could be counted by the hundreds. Moreover, it lay on the shores of the second-largest alpine lake in Europe, at a time when transport and travel on water was cheaper than on land, and it flanked the Rhine. Significantly, also, Constance was not in Italy, France or Spain, each of which was the home of one of the three rival popes.

To the streets clustered around the old cathedral in Constance came a cavalcade of cardinals, bishops, diplomats, masters of theology, abbots, monks and priests. In the opinion of some historians it was the largest assembly so far seen in the history of the church. Nearly all those present were determined to restore unity to a divided church, but first they had to claim high authority for themselves. Otherwise, the rival popes could not be deposed. Here, in April 1415, the Council announced that it 'holds its power direct from Christ'. It affirmed that 'everyone, no matter his rank or office, even if it be papal, is bound to obey' its own rulings. Armed with such power the Council deposed one pope on 29 May. Five weeks later a second pope abdicated. There remained only the pope or anti-pope who belonged to the Avignon line of succession, and even he had to find shelter in a Gibraltar-like fortress at the town of Peñiscola, a high Spanish rock overlooking the Mediterranean Sea. At last, he was deposed; the papal throne was free; and a member of the long-powerful Colonna family of Rome was elected in November 1417 under the name of Martin V.

Rome was again the official home of the pope – the only pope. For nearly four more centuries, Avignon remained one of the papal territories but ceased to be influential. During all that period and beyond, no Frenchman was to hold the office of pope.

The Great Schism had ended. In lasting so long, however, it had gravely weakened the authority of the papacy. Thus, when those talented reformer-priests such as Wycliffe and Hus disputed the authority of the pope, they were merely repeating the strategy of those cardinals and bishops who, by allowing three rival popes to exist, had indirectly proved that no pope possessed divinely given authority.

There remains to be read the last page of the story of Hus. When the church council met in Constance in 1414, one of its fears was the potential rebellion in Bohemia. Hus, viewed as a firebrand, was summoned from Prague, a journey of more than 500 kilometres through forests and farmlands. He reached Constance, having been assured that he could travel home again after he had been cross-examined.

In the end that promise was broken. It was partly Hus's own determination that imperilled him, though he was also betrayed. Banned from saying mass and from preaching, he resolved to disobey while in Constance itself. The dignitaries assembled in their bright robes decided to imprison him. It is remarkable how many real or improvised prisons existed in this lakeside town; in turn, Hus was locked away in a Dominican prison, the bishop's castle and a Franciscan convent. Prisons did not weaken his faith. He knew his own mind and believed that he knew the mind of Christ. The church council, deliberating at Constance, was determined to uphold its authority. It had refused to be cowed by the rival popes, therefore it must stand up to a defiant priest. It resolved that he should die – unless he disowned his faith. In the Franciscan convent he was questioned and lectured for the last time by the church leaders, the Bishop of Salisbury amongst them. Hus refused to recant. In July 1415 he willingly faced death in the flames.

A few centuries later the town of Constance was to become that rarity, a Protestant place of pilgrimage. There the Czech Republic still maintains a museum. A monument marks the spot where Hus was burned, but in summer it can be almost hidden by the shrubs tended by eager town-gardeners.

A MIGHTY CITY FALLS

Long before the birth of John Hus, the Ottoman Turks were advancing towards Constantinople from the direction of the Turkish uplands. Originally from central Asia, relative newcomers to the Mediterranean, they advanced slowly, in stages. Their first celebrated leader was Osman. Born in 1258 in the town called Sogut in the present Turkey – a town where mosques were replacing the Orthodox Churches – Osman assembled an army that was skilled in guerrilla tactics. He set out to occupy strategic places closer to the Mediterranean. When he died in 1326 at the age of sixty-eight his forces were in the possession of the biblical city of Ephesus, within sight of the Mediterranean and in control of Bursa, within easy walking distance of Constantinople.

It was only a matter of years before almost the whole of the present Turkey was controlled by the Ottomans. From their forts overlooking the eastern and then the western shores of the Dardanelles, they watched the galleys glide past with grain and other goods bound to and from Constantinople and the ports of the Black Sea. Rarely did they interfere with this commerce. They were patient, knowing that a carpet was laid out, ready for them to approach the walls of the famous city.

Constantinople was now a rich trading city like the modern Hong Kong and Singapore rather than, as once it was, the capital of a vast empire. Almost a puppet port of the Ottomans, it paid them a tribute or tax for the right to exist. It even hired Turkish soldiers to serve as some of its defenders. Meanwhile, the Ottoman troops simply bypassed it on their advance into Europe. By 1400 they held the present Bulgaria and long stretches of the shores of the Black Sea. They advanced into Serbia, winning the decisive battle at Kosovo in 1395. They encircled Mount Athos and its lines of monastery walls and eventually decided to occupy it. They already held much of the Adriatic coastline facing Italy, and with a favourable wind they could reach Italy in a day and a night. Indeed, the Ottoman sultan – a title he adopted in 1393 – now ruled a territory in Europe that was probably as large as France.

In the space of 1000 years Constantinople had survived many sieges except the one initiated by its own fickle Christian allies in the year 1204. The city had defeated Bulgarians coming from Europe and Muslims coming from Asia Minor. This largest Christian city in the world surely could withstand the Muslims. Fortified by geography and human ingenuity, this 'New Rome' stood on seven hills, and possessed the advantage conferred by high ground. A triangle of a city, it was surrounded on two sides by the sea and coastal walls, and on the third or landward side by a high wall and a moat. Reservoirs and cisterns of fresh water and storehouses of grain ensured that it would not suffer from thirst and hunger, if it were besieged. An enemy besieging Constantinople was itself likely to run out of food and water before the city ran short.

The city and the small empire it now ruled urgently needed a naval ally. Perhaps the pope would enlist one. To a conference, opened in the Italian town of Ferrara in 1438, came the emperor himself and his powerful delegation from the Byzantine Church. The two churches agreed that they should cooperate against the Muslim Turks, but even in a cathedral they did not see eye to eye. At the end of the conference the Latin mass was celebrated but not the Greek.

Their alliance led to the launching of a new crusade. The Christian army reached the Black Sea and was defeated. The emperor now hoped he might rely on fellow Christians possessing a strong navy. Italy's leading naval power was no longer Venice but the republic of Genoa, and it had long been permitted – as a sign of friendship – to occupy the walled port of Pera, on a promontory just a few kilometres across the narrow sea from Constantinople. Surely, if the Ottoman Turks began to attack, the Genoese would oppose them. In May 1453 the Genoese stood by and watched the Muslim ships preparing to blockade and then attack the Christian city. Commerce, to Genoa, was as important as religion. The Crusades are looked on as simply religious wars between Christians and Muslims, but they were also trade wars between Christian rivals.

In May 1453 the Ottomans besieged Constantinople. The walls, mighty to contemplate from the sea, were not strong enough. The emperor himself and thousands of soldiers and civilians were killed or gravely wounded by the all-conquering Turks. After scores of thousands of people had fled, the city was almost deserted. It was, up to that time, one of the biggest and quickest depopulations of a large city in the history of the world.

The news of the Christians' collapse and retreat, when eventually it reached Rome, was devastating. It can almost be likened to the astonishment when the world heard that Muslim pilots had deliberately flown their aircraft into the twin towers in New York on 11 September 2001. A city that seemed unassailable was shown to be defenceless. The loss of life in Constantinople in 1453 was infinitely higher than the loss of life in New York, and yet these cities were symbols of dynamic institutions, the one of Christianity and the other of democratic capitalism, and so the successful assaults on them were humiliating. In Italy a cardinal, on hearing of the fall of

Constantinople, declared that 'one of the two lights of Christendom has been extinguished'.

During most of the centuries of Christian history there was only one vital western city, Rome, but a total of four vital eastern cities – Jerusalem, Alexandria, Antioch and Constantinople, each with its patriarch. Now, for the first time, these eastern cities were all in the Muslims' hands.

The fall of Constantinople – renamed as Istanbul in the twentieth century – was a mark of the deepening peril facing the pope and his western world. Here was a new crusade, and it was coming from Islam. In the following forty years the Ottomans captured most of Albania and Bosnia and the remainder of Serbia. They captured Athens and the rest of Greece and parts of the present Ukraine. All these had been Christian lands. In 1480 they even captured the Italian port of Otranto, which was only a day's horse-ride from the old Appian Way leading straight to Rome.

Meanwhile, in 1454 the Ottoman rulers appointed a patriarch of the Orthodox Church and expected him to be a puppet and an assistant bureaucrat. In Constantinople he was the judge in divorces, and in financial disputes between Orthodox Christians. In due course the Orthodox Christians, Armenian Christians and Jews were summoned back to their old city, for it had to be rebuilt and its trade rekindled.

The Orthodox Church – still the main seat of Christianity in a large area of south-eastern Europe, Asia Minor and Russia – was seriously hurt by the Ottoman conquests. It was allowed to exist: it was not allowed to flourish. Traditionally, the emperor was the head of the church, for he was seen by his subjects as God's 'representative on earth'. Constantinople now had no emperor and a tame patriarch. In the seventeenth century, fifty-four different men held the office of patriarch.

The spectacular Christian Church of St Sophia became a mosque. Four minarets, one at each corner, marked the building's conversion to an Islamic temple. Other churches, one by one, were confiscated from the Christians, so that a former patriarch who returned to the city in 1568 saw that his own church had become a mosque, 'and he wept bitterly'.

The Orthodox Christians could live where they wished in the Ottoman Empire and attend their own church, if the building was not taxed out of existence. Forced personally to pay a high annual tax, they carried the tax receipt wherever they went, for it was their passport. Easily identified, they wore special clothes and carried no firearms. In various parts of the Ottoman Empire, especially in the Balkans, Christian boys from the age of seven to about twenty were conscripted and sent away for training, and most did not see their home again. They became Muslims, dressed in uniform, learned the Turkish language, and served as janissaries in the Ottoman Army. A few were to occupy the highest civilian and military posts in the capital city. Curiously, Christian boys living in Constantinople, Egypt, Hungary and the Greek-speaking islands of Rhodes and Chios – and all Muslim boys – were usually exempt from this call-up.

The incentives to become a Muslim were high. In every generation Christian families took the step.

MOUNT ATHOS

The spiritual powerhouse of the city, indeed the Empire, had for long been the monasteries clustered by the sea cliffs at Mount Athos. Ceasing to be dynamic, they were lucky to remain at all. In 1568 Sultan Selim II began to confiscate all the land and property of the Christian monasteries in the Ottoman Empire. In answer to this form of nationalisation, the monasteries gained permission to buy back their land and buildings from the Ottoman Government if they could raise the revenue. Mount Athos was traditionally so important in the life of the eastern or Byzantine Church that well-wishers raised the money, mostly from the Christian states of Wallachia, along the Danube River, and Moldavia on the Dniester River.

Russia was becoming the hub of the Orthodox Church. By 1600, for the first time, Moscow had its own patriarch, whose potential influence far exceeded that of the patriarch in Constantinople. As Russia became more powerful and extended its empire further east, the Orthodox Church spread too, eventually reaching central Asia, eastern Siberia and Alaska.

16

THE PILGRIMS' PATHS

To be a pilgrim became almost a craving during the Middle Ages. For serious pilgrims it was more than a journey and a holiday. They believed that their arrival at a sacred site, far from home, would bring them closer than they had ever been to the presence of Christ. It might also win them a pardon for their sins and reduce the time they would spend in purgatory.

A pilgrimage was usually planned years ahead. Most of those who hoped to be pilgrims did not achieve their dream. They lacked the money and time. The daily demands of work and the duties of family detained them at home. Even so, the number of Christian pilgrims travelling in Europe and the Middle East multiplied – until the coming of the plague known as the Black Death in 1348.

For ambitious travellers, Jerusalem was usually the most enticing of all the places of pilgrimage; but during many periods it was not in Christian hands, and even when open to travellers it called for an expensive journey by sea or land. Rome, the burial place of St Peter and St Paul, was the pilgrims' second choice, but it was too far away for most northern Europeans. A nearer place of pilgrimage was usually chosen.

More shrines arose – shrines for the notable personages or local saints whose names and resting places were known only within a radius of two or three days' travel. For the English and Irish, the tomb of St Thomas Becket in the cathedral at Canterbury was a special shrine, and the medieval poet Geoffrey Chaucer mentally accompanied his pilgrims there. Mont-Saint-Michel on the coast of France, Tiegem in Flanders, Trier on the River Moselle, and Monte Gargano near the Adriatic coast of Italy were amongst the shrines that became spiritually fashionable. In France, on a stony hill overlooking the marshes near Arles, was a Benedictine abbey. About the year 1016 its monks were granted the valuable privilege of conferring pardons for sins on those who made the pilgrimage. As more travellers walked up the rocky slopes to the church, the monastery became richer and grander.

In the German-speaking lands, Cologne belatedly became the longed-for goal of pilgrims. It was the home of the remains of the Magi or the three wise men, later promoted to kings, who had followed the star to Bethlehem and reportedly presented themselves to the infant Christ. Their bones were in precious containers on view in the new city of Constantinople in the year AD 490. Later they were taken to Milan and enshrined there; and in 1162, as part of plunder taken by the Emperor Frederick Barbarossa, they were enshrined yet again in Cologne in western Germany. Their presence made Cologne a unique place of pilgrimage, for the three had been the very first pilgrims in the history of Christianity.

The millions of Germans – peasants and weavers, boatmen and woodcutters, women and children – who in the course of the centuries stood in front of the shrine devoted to the three kings must have had an overwhelming feeling of being close to the events recorded in Bethlehem more than a millennium earlier. The New Testament had a phrase for this sense of wonder: 'touching the hem of the garment'.

Another centre of pilgrimage was Einsiedeln, which nestles amongst flat-topped hills some 50 kilometres from Zurich. It attracted pilgrims because it was once the home of St Meinrad, a French-born hermit who lived in the forest. After his murder in AD 861, two birds – for birds were often the companions of hermits – pointed out the fleeing murderers, who were then arrested. The simple shrine in his honour was replaced by a Benedictine abbey, now huge and baroque, and a town sprang up nearby. It is still a bustling place of pilgrimage, especially on Sunday mornings when crowds of pilgrims enter the town's winding streets in air-conditioned buses and alight to see the black Madonna in the abbey.

Einsiedeln's abbey was once a resting place on the most arduous of the main pilgrim routes: Der Jacobsweg, leading from Germany through Switzerland to France and finally on to Spain. Once in Spain, the pilgrims walked towards the remote Atlantic coast and a wave-splashed promontory. Only a few days' journey away stood the church of Santiago de Compostela, where the bones of the apostle St James – known as Santiago in the Spanish language – were believed to be buried. In the eyes of most Europeans living north of the Alps, Santiago de Compostela was the most revered shrine. Long-distance travellers probably arrived there for the first time in the 900s, and we know that a French bishop arrived in 951, followed much later by an exotic Armenian who was living as a hermit in Italy. The traffic, at first a trickle, became a stream as the centuries passed. In 1478 the pope declared that it was equal to Jerusalem and Rome as a place of pilgrimage, and it remains a favourite for modern pilgrims willing to walk.

It was inevitable that Assisi would also become a goal for pilgrims. Nobody could compete with St Francis for spiritual glamour in the century after his death. In Italy, in the fullness of time, Assisi was to be challenged by Loreto, which in 1294 experienced the miracle of miracles. Here, an old stone house was said to have arrived mysteriously by air, landing gently in a wood. It was understood that this humble dwelling had flown from Nazareth, being the house where Mary had been born and brought up, and the home of Jesus's childhood. From the wood, the house flew off again, coming to rest on a nearby hilltop. There it was garnished by a handsome shrine. Today the Holy House, encased in white marble, stands inside a grand cathedral, which can be seen from the decks of ships on the Adriatic, or from the train carrying the multitudes towards the hill of Loreto.

JOURNEY OF HOPE

For the devout, a pilgrimage was the hope of a lifetime. Even for the less devout, a journey at a certain time of their life was mixed with the possibility that their devotion to Christ might be awakened. Numerous men, grateful that their lives had been saved during a plague or in a storm at sea, vowed to make a pilgrimage to a distant shrine, even to Jerusalem. Their families might hear the news of the proposed pilgrimage with disbelief or dismay. Who would do the daily work, and who would provide the daily bread, while the breadwinner was away? Sometimes a wife was eager to be a pilgrim – more eager than her husband. Often a man who was determined to go publicly showed his intention by ceasing to shave. The beard he grew would not be cut off until he had finally reached the sacred destination. Some had to break their promises. In 1412 an English priest explained that his hope of reaching the Lord's sepulchre in Jerusalem was frustrated by 'the leprosy with which he has since been smitten', and by his lack of money.

Other Christians, finally concluding that they would never make a pilgrimage, left money in their wills so that their son, daughter or a steadfast friend could journey on their behalf. In the rich Baltic port of Lübeck, in the years before 1363, the destination mentioned most often in a collection of sixty wills and testaments is Compostela, which is named nineteen times. Another sixteen name nearby Aachen, the home of Charlemagne, but only six name Rome, which was too far away. Everywhere, the local saints attracted pilgrims because their shrines were near. On the anniversary day of a minor saint, almost every able-bodied woman and man in the nearby villages – and even children – would make the walk to the local shrine and back again. Beggars joined in, confident that they would receive food from pilgrims eager to show kindness on such a holy day.

Many went on their journey as an act of thanksgiving. Others hoped to receive forgiveness, for they believed that the Holy Spirit presided at very sacred places. Others went as a punishment. Priests were sent on a pilgrimage by an ecclesiastical court because they were guilty of offences against the church. Pilgrimages were a kind of reform school. Many offenders, irrespective of whether they were priests or nuns or merchants, were compelled to travel in their bare feet or to pay for an expensive candle to be lit at their destination. Some had to give alms to the poor they met along the way. One convicted murderer, ordered to visit a distant shrine by the Bishop of Orleans in the ninth century, went in bare feet and wore conspicuous iron rings on his arms and body as a sign of his guilt. Others carried a letter from the bishop signifying that they had sinned. The letter had the advantage that it served as a passport.

Depending on the calibre and mood of individuals in the group, and the obstacles met along the way, a pilgrimage could be either the most uplifting spiritual experience of a person's life or an indulgent pagan excursion. The scholarly priest Erasmus was to write an essay mocking the 'religious pilgrimage'.

A town possessing a shrine or holy relics was on the tourist map. Good fortune fell on towns that became stopping places along the pilgrims' way. Rich pilgrims and the servants who went with them brought revenue to local shops, taverns and food stalls, and to makers of boots, dresses and tunics. Pilgrims who arrived on horseback paid sellers of hay and chaff, for their horses had to be fed and groomed. Some traders earned so much, by selling goods or exchanging foreign currency, that they were eventually regulated by the town authorities. Avaricious traders were endangering the tourist traffic, it was rightly said. In 1517, Hildesheim, a German town on the pilgrims' route to Aachen, stipulated what was a fair rate of exchange for a Hungarian penny – a popular coin along that route. Rome especially gained from pilgrims, for at one time they had to stay in the town for fifteen days in order to receive a certain forgiveness of sins. Under the name of 'plenary indulgences', additional incentives were extended to pilgrims who visited Rome in the jubilee year of 1300, and again in 1350 and 1400. The multiplying array of papal indulgences, offered to pilgrims and to donors of money to other worthy causes, was to propel the Protestant breakaway from Rome in the era of Martin Luther.

The typical pilgrims brought back their souvenirs, perhaps a real or metallic cockleshell, sold by hawkers along the road from the coast to Compostela, or a palm frond from Jerusalem. As a palm branch was too cumbersome to be carried all the way home, it was carefully wound around the walking stick or staff that nearly every pilgrim carried. Returning pilgrims resembled today's backpackers who, at the end of a period of travel, display on their hat or shirt the badges of metal bought in towns along the way. Some pilgrims were almost weighed down by souvenirs. We read about such a pilgrim in *The Vision of Piers Plowman*: 'on his hat were perched a hundred tiny phials, as well as tokens of shells from Galicia'.

A TOY FOR PALM SUNDAY

Many Christians, century after century, could share in a pilgrimage without even travelling. On the Sunday preceding Good Friday, known as Palm Sunday, millions of European adults and children imagined that they were visitors to Jerusalem. In their mind's eye, they watched Christ's arrival on a donkey. A day of jubilation before the gloom of Good Friday, it was marked by the placing of branches of palms or other foliage on the road as a welcome to Christ. In northern Europe, where a palm tree was virtually unknown, limbs were sawn from a pine tree or oak in order to decorate the roadway or church. They were seen as a safeguard against evil, if the Devil displayed his wily ways.

The ceremony or procession of Palm Sunday was old, though often reshaped. It was recognised in Jerusalem in the fourth century, and early in the medieval period it appeared in western Europe. Often the procession began in one church and then moved to another, where the palms were blessed. The procession then resumed, returning to the first church.

In many towns of northern Europe a memorable event on Palm Sunday was the entry into the church of a little trolley on which stood a donkey carved from wood. The donkey, running on four wheels, was pulled or pushed along by an attendant; and an image of

Jesus, his face carefully painted on wood, sat on the donkey. On the trolley or moving platform were painted a few green branches of a palm tree, thus evoking the familiar scene from the New Testament. Jesus and his donkey excited little children, for such an expensive toy was unknown except in the richest households.

One of these donkeys can be seen in the Barfüsserkirche in the Swiss town of Basel. It was carved from wood by a craftsman living near Lake Constance in about the year 1500. Similar toys, richly painted, had been used in churches as early as AD 980. The kind of object that a child loved to touch and pat, it would not be readily abandoned by the new churches of the Reformation. In England it was permitted, then banned, and again permitted, being finally banned by the new Queen Elizabeth in 1559.

Medieval Europe operated a pilgrimage in reverse. While thousands of Europeans each year went as pilgrims to see the holy places, pieces of those places were acquired and carried back as relics to European towns. The traffic in relics, on a vast scale, had been going on for centuries. From Jerusalem, Bethlehem, Antioch, Alexandria and a hundred places in Asia Minor and North Africa, pilgrims carried home perhaps a tiny bone reportedly from the bodies of saints, threads or even sleeves of the clothes they had once worn, soil from the edge of their tombs, or seeds of the flowers growing nearby. In Dublin and Venice, Warsaw and Moscow, the bones, mounted on silks or surrounded by jewels, were placed in prominent positions in churches, abbeys and shrines, there to become the goal of new pilgrimages.

Rome, the skilled pageant-maker, knew how to welcome a sacred relic carried from afar. Even in 1462 there was an art called show business and Rome was its capital. The skull of the apostle St Andrew had been acquired from the Byzantine world, and now all was in readiness for its arrival. In an open field not far from Rome, Pope Pius II formally received it in the presence of a vast crowd of worshippers and held it high for all to see. Briefly he explained: 'This mouth often spoke to Christ, these cheeks Jesus surely often kissed.' Henceforth, declared the pope, this relic would serve as 'our Advocate in Heaven'. Such an advocate was urgently needed, for the pope intended to organise another military campaign against the Turks.

The next day, the head of St Andrew was to be carried in a procession along the three kilometres of roadway to Rome. Its arrival had long been advertised, and those who had come to Rome for that long awaited day were promised, as a reward, an indulgence that wiped away part of their sins. Waiting in the city was a throng of Germans and Hungarians and other long-distance pilgrims, and masses of Italians, together forming the largest crowd seen in the city in living memory. But that night the wind blew from the south and the falling rain could be heard all night, converting the surface of most streets into mud. Surely the procession must be postponed. Next morning the sky was blue and the summer sun shone, and the pope, feeling as if a miracle had descended, called on the procession to proceed.

The pope travelled beneath a slow-moving canopy with the head of St Andrew in his hand, while the cardinals carried the branches of palm trees. Meanwhile, other officials marched in pairs with lighted candles in their hands, and children dressed as angels played musical instruments. The procession of long robes could be heard rustling and brushing the wet ground, except in those places where carpets had been hurriedly laid, or aromatic herbs and flowers had been scattered by waiting spectators. On all sides were the reverent faces of the onlookers. 'The crowds,' wrote the pope, 'were so closely packed that if you had thrown a grain of wheat it would hardly have fallen on the ground.' And so the head of St Andrew reached St Peter's, where it became one of the most valued relics.

PART THREE

17

THE HERALDS OF CHRISTENDOM

In 1500 there were signs that human hands would grasp the Catholic Church and shake it. The gigantic hands would not be those of the pope, his cardinals and bishops. They would come from the church's own rank and file.

That the church was in danger was beyond dispute. In 1463 Pope Pius II, addressing his cardinals, made the startling claim: 'We have no credit. The priesthood is an object of scorn. People say that we live in luxury, amass wealth, are slaves to ambition, ride on the fattest mules and the most spirited horses.' The reference to dashing horses was almost the equivalent, today, of accusing church leaders of driving fast sports cars. The pope went on to express his regret that the cardinals, beneath their red hats, were often seen as proud officials whose cheeks were 'puffed out' with pride. He could see some truth in these criticisms.

The pope was rallying the faithful. He was entitled to demand higher standards. And yet how can one fairly and impartially judge a huge institution that, for all its conspicuous failings, continued to fulfil its duties in so many places and inspire so many worthwhile lives? At the end of the fifteenth century, on the eve of the Protestant Reformation, it was continuing to produce brilliant theologians and the usual procession of saints. It is safe to say that in Europe more intellectual activity, whether religious or secular, was taking place in the Catholic Church than in all other institutions added together. Many of the impressive sea explorers in the emerging age of global exploration saw themselves as missionaries as well as commercial entrepreneurs. A quarter century years after Christopher Columbus found the new world, the church that was supposed to be decaying had its missionaries at work in remote places and numerous volunteers eager to join them.

Francis of Paolo, who lived in Calabria when that part of southern Italy was ruled by the King of Naples, was one who showed that the much-lamented church still possessed vigour – as well as torpor – even in out-of-way places. His parents were said to have been poor, but this is not quite certain since they must have possessed enough money to take their small son on a pilgrimage to Rome and Assisi. After spending time with the Franciscans, Francis became a hermit first in a cave and then on a coastal rock and finally on firm mainland soil. He founded his own order, somewhat on the model of the Franciscans, and attracted frugal followers, who swore that for the remainder of their lives they would eat no meat, fish, eggs, milk, butter or cheese.

Francis of Paolo was apparently capable of sometimes foreseeing momentous events. He is said to have predicted that the Muslim Turks would capture the southern Italian port of Otranto, which they did within his lifetime. Miracles were also attributed to him. He is said to have crossed the Straits of Messina in a boat that he had instantly devised, his cloak serving as the sail and his wooden staff as the mast.

Louis XI of France, afflicted with apoplexy, feared death and sent for the celebrated Italian monk. With some prompting from the pope, Francis of Paolo answered the call and travelled to France. He brought with him a culinary gift, an Italian pear. As he was known as 'the good Christian', this pear was eventually christened 'Bon Chrétien', though in the English-speaking world it is now known as a Bartlett or William pear.

Francis of Paolo became a saintly hero and monasteries were built by the kings of France in his honour. Other monasteries arose in Germany, Italy and Spain, so that ultimately they exceeded 450 in number, without even counting those that belonged to the female branch of his order.

It was a sign of the vitality within Catholicism that this humble Calabrian monk, even in his late eighties, could attract followers in so many lands. He died in 1507, the year when Luther – soon to shake the church – became a monk. Four centuries later, the name of Francis of Paolo was virtually emblazoned on the coasts and reefs of the world, for he was named the patron of seafarers.

A LIGHT FROM ROTTERDAM

Desiderius Erasmus, a Dutchman born near Rotterdam, owned two of those hands that began to shake Christendom. His background reflected some of the travails of the church. His father was a priest and he himself was illegitimate. He did not enter a monastery of his own free will: like thousands of other priests of his generation, he was given no choice of career. In compensation, the church was the most wide-ranging of all careers and callings available in Europe.

Becoming an Augustinian monk in Holland in 1492 – just four months before Columbus sailed from Spain to discover the New

World – Erasmus was eager to visit other universities and absorb their intellectual excitement. At the University of Paris he taught several young Englishmen, and they invited him to their homeland, where he met talented scholars with whom he debated, and vivacious young ladies with whom he sometimes frolicked. He observed that the English ladies 'are divinely pretty, and *too* good-natured'. They were generous with their kisses: 'They kiss you when you come, they kiss you when you go, they kiss you at intervening opportunities, and their lips are soft, warm and delicious.' His English friends admired him, hoping to keep him in their country. So he was appointed as priest of a village church in southern England, and was permitted to keep the income, even though he delegated his duties to a deputy. Leaving England and travelling over the Alps, he learned much in Rome and Turin – he became a doctor there – but his home was in the north. His first two stays in England had been brief but he was to live there again from 1509 to 1514.

His mental energy and the range of his learning were impressive. He wrote in Latin as if it were his native language, and began to learn classical Greek when few scholars in western Europe were fluent in it. At first he said that Greek 'is nearly killing me', but he finally mastered it, thereby gaining access to long-forgotten Greek versions of sections of the New Testament. He was probably the first to teach Greek at Oxford. In theology he had read as widely, by the age of forty, as almost any other European. He also discovered humour. He saw it in the monasteries and even in archbishops' words and deeds. He had sufficient prestige to decry the church and escape rebuke.

Remarkably, the church allowed him a rare measure of independence: from January 1517 he was permitted to wear clothes that were not the formal robes of his Augustine religious order. Nor was he required to shave the top of his head in the style normally observed by priests and monks. Instead, he wore his hair long and swept back, the better to frame his clean-shaven face, with its strong nose and wide, sensitive mouth. He liked a touch of extravagance, and the portrait of him by Hans Holbein shows ornate rings on two fingers of his left hand. Erasmus was not one to prefer the monk's cold cell and simple food and drink. He liked his wine – burgundy was a favourite.

The town where he eventually chose to live was Basel. Possessing the only university in Switzerland, it was a centre of Europe's latest and most dynamic technology: the art of printing with movable type. Amongst the printing workshops of the town was one conducted by Johannes Froben, which Erasmus began to employ for his major works. The two men became dear friends.

From this printery in March 1516 came one of the most influential books of the century: Erasmus's edited version of the New Testament. In several vital places and many minor places he contradicted the Vulgate Bible, long used by the Catholic Church but possibly altered by long-dead clerks who were careless in transcribing sentences from one manuscript to another. Erasmus's new version, while not as accurate and scholarly as he had hoped, undermined crucial passages in the all-powerful Vulgate Bible. For example, he found evidence that John the Baptist had called on people to 'repent', whereas the Catholic Bible used the phrase 'do penance'. These rival interpretations were an ocean apart: one called for a complete change of heart in a sinner, while the other stipulated a punishment that, once accepted, ended the matter. Here, from the pen of perhaps the greatest scholar of the age, was the implication that Christ's word itself could be open to conflicting interpretations.

Erasmus believed that his new translation, compared to the official

Vulgate Bible, brought clarity in place of obscurity. He thought that his translation, if read closely, told a Christian even more than if he had sat on the shores of Galilee and listened in person to Jesus's teachings. Now, through this new version, 'Christ lives, breathes and speaks to us today.' It was his lament that most of the Christians he came across were 'wretchedly enslaved by blindness and ignorance'. In short, they were ignorant of the God whom they worshipped.

Other radical ideas stirred in his ever-active mind. He thought that the regular attending of church was not absolutely essential, and that money given to a monastery or shrine would be more effective if given to 'Christ's living temple', the poor. He concluded that certain Christians doctrines, such as the existence of a place called purgatory, had little biblical justification. He worried about the tendency to judge people by their outer rather than their inner conformity to Christ's commandments. 'Who is truly Christian?' inquired Erasmus in his work *The Education of a Christian Prince*. 'It is rather the man who has embraced Christ in the innermost feelings of his heart, and who emulates him by his pious deeds.'

Erasmus was not easily labelled. He showed that it was possible to be a priest and at the same time a member of the celebrity circuit. He was perhaps the first scholar to make a living from the sale of his books. He was a kind of Einstein of his age, one whom scholars longed to meet and princes and abbots tried to entice to their courts and monasteries. At the same time, he did not have the sacrificial qualities, the courage to the point of rashness, of the true religious reformer. Like many advanced thinkers, Erasmus had stepped out far enough for his own peace of mind. The day would soon come when other theologians would snatch from him and ignite attitudes and ideas that he himself had not viewed as so inflammable.

Erasmus died in 1536 at Basel, by then a Protestant town, and was buried in the local cathedral, which sits on a cliff above the fast-flowing Rhine. His memorial names him simply as Erasmus of Rotterdam. Inside the cathedral, sombre and brownish, can be read gold lettering that calls him a servant of Christ and the most learned of scholars: *'Incomparabilem in omni'*. In essence, he was without equal in the many fields of learning.

THE RISE OF MARTIN LUTHER

In the space of at least 1000 years, most of the notable Christian reformers came from comfortable and relatively prosperous homes. Martin Luther, the son of a copper miner, seems at first sight to be an exception, but his father, like many experienced German miners, was not only prosperous but a man of status, being proficient in a highly skilled craft. From his hometown of Eisleben, young Martin set out to study. His choice was limited. At that time Berlin had no university; Hamburg had none; Frankfurt had none. Luther attended Erfurt, one of the few universities in the northern part of continental Germany.

By the age of twenty-four, Luther was a monk in a small religious order, the Austin Friars. He was not glamorous, and one portrait by Lucas Cranach shows a strong face with a lumpy nose and small, knowing eyes. But he was scholarly as well as earthy and became the young star of his monastery. By the age of thirty he held the chair of biblical theology – one of the most influential of chairs – at the new University of Wittenberg, and was the kind of outspoken and enthusiastic teacher who captivated students. He was also the head of his monastery and the preacher at the town's parish church.

In his late twenties he made the long journey to Rome, the most coveted of all pilgrimages and an exciting event for which there is no parallel today. Though people now travel far more widely than in Luther's time, there is no single pilgrimage – whether to the World Cup in football or to the Parthenon in Athens – that is today the goal of almost everyone. To cross the Alps on foot, following a road or track, was itself an event to be talked about interminably once a pilgrim returned home. As the journey was known to be full of hazards, moral as well as physical, the monks travelled in pairs. But on many evenings they were pampered tourists, for they were welcomed by roadside monasteries, some of which gave generous hospitality.

Luther is thought to have crossed into Italy by way of the Brenner Pass in the winter of 1510–11. On reaching Rome he was full of elation. He marvelled at the holy places spread across the straggling city, including the walls of the present basilica slowly rising above the spot where St Peter himself was buried. In some churches he saw, enclosed in jewelled splendour, the fragments of bones and other holy relics of the apostles and saints. Outward display, however, did not impress him. That Michelangelo at that very time was painting the ceiling of the Sistine Chapel did not excite him.

In the first days of his visit Luther almost ran from church to church in order to see as much as possible. He descended a catacomb so that he could feel the presence of the martyrs buried there. He attempted to experience the celebration of the mass at the church of St John Lateran, until the crowd inside proved too dense to admit him. On his knees he ascended the steps of the Santa Scala and prayed as he made his way; but the story that he had a vision – a religious awakening – when he reached the top step is unlikely to be true. The story was not heard in his lifetime and came later from his son.

What Luther saw in Rome also perturbed him. He was vexed to hear priests gabbling or mumbling their way through the sacred ceremonies, as if they begrudged the time taken from their personal amusements. The congregations he knew in north Germany displayed a devotion that he rarely observed in Rome and other Italian towns. Many churches in Rome, he noticed, were in grave disrepair. Outside, in the streets, the sight of prostitutes touting for clients distressed him. One high-minded resident of Rome informed him with regret that the Holy City was far from holy: 'If there is a hell, then Rome stands upon it.' Years later, after Luther had formally parted from the Catholic Church, he was to emphasise the defects of the papal city. At the time, however, the joy he felt at simply being present in the heart of Christendom must have outweighed the disappointments. The vivacity of the Italian people also captivated him.

Luther knew that Rome was not the only blot in the Christian world. He saw enough of the monasteries in Germany to know that they harboured a certain amount of lasciviousness, gluttony and drunkenness. In one monastery that he visited, each monk normally consumed two pots of beer and 'a quart of wine' for supper, and gingerbread 'to make him take to his liquor kindly'. After such steady drinking there were monks so red in the face that they 'came to look like fiery angels'.

Luther sensed that something was lacking in his own religious life. Anxiously, he searched the Bible for the answer. He was to become almost obsessed with the problems of sin and penitence – his own as well as that of the other clergy.

The church's way of dealing with penitent sinners followed a recognised formula. A sinner desiring forgiveness confessed his sin to a priest, and the priest promised absolution, provided the sinner completed an appropriate penance. Maybe the priest would order the reciting of prayers, maybe the performance of a virtuous action, maybe the payment of money. A humble and contrite heart was expected to accompany the penance, but this was difficult to detect and was all too often forgotten.

In his early days in the monastery Luther often felt oppressed by his own sinfulness, and despaired of ever earning God's forgiveness and his own salvation. Now his reading of the New Testament brought him the comforting belief that the key to salvation lay not in good works, a virtuous life and the observance of ritual, but in one's personal relationship with God. Christians, he concluded, were incapable of earning salvation by their own efforts. Forgiveness and salvation were gifts from God for those who loved him and trusted in his mercy. Luther called this belief 'justification by faith'; and since his own faith was strong and true, the belief brought him peace of mind.

THE SALE OF FORGIVENESS

For many decades the church had been awarding or even selling a kind of pardon – also called an indulgence – but lately the sales had soared. The church's traditional idea of granting forgiveness seemed to be degenerating into the practice of selling forgiveness, thereby exonerating Christians from sins committed in the past and still to be committed in the future. Indulgences could also be bought on behalf of the dead. Thus, a dead relative or dead friend would spend less time or suffer less punishment in purgatory – that painful region where dead Christians expiated their sins before they were declared fit to enter heaven.

The practice of conferring an indulgence, when the emphasis was on personal penitence rather than on the payment of money, could be defended by theologians. But what if its real purpose was simply to raise money for the church or for the local rulers? The prince of

Saxony, where Luther lived, sold indulgences in order to finance and construct a costly bridge over the River Elbe at the town of Torgau. Christians who bought this particular indulgence were permitted, during the season of Lent, to eat cheese, butter and milk – foods normally forbidden at that time of year. Of the money so raised, half went to the Vatican and half to finance the bridge.

Pope Leo X then devised a bolder sale. In 1515 he issued a 'bull' or pronouncement offering indulgences in order to finance the new St Peter's Church in Rome. Prince Albert, who was also the archbishop of the Rhine-river town of Mainz, appointed agents to grant these indulgences, usually in return for a gift of money. One agent was Johann Tetzel, a Dominican friar, who entered German towns with the ringing of church bells and gave persuasive sermons. Many came to hear him and to take part in the transactions that followed. The sum they paid was graduated according to the income of the payer. Thus, a bishop paid twenty-five Rhenish gold guilders, while those earning rather low incomes might pay half a gold coin. This seemed hard on the very poor but they were offered a bargain. They were permitted to earn their pardon through prayer and fasting, for Prince Albert of Mainz insisted that 'the kingdom of heaven should be open to the poor as much as the rich'. A contrite heart, and a willingness to pray and to confess one's sins were sufficient for the poor! On the other hand, a rich donor was told that he could evade these demeaning rituals and instead pay handsomely for his dead mother or father to be spared the punishments of purgatory.

The exact financial arrangements of Prince Albert of Mainz were not known to Luther, and perhaps not fully understood in Rome. In fact part of the money so raised was to go the rich German bankers, the Fugger family, in repayment of a loan. More importantly, Luther thought that the pope would not approve of Tetzel's theology. The pope, wrote Luther, 'would prefer to have St Peter's Basilica collapse into ruins' rather than accept money raised by what really was a churchman's barefaced promise to sell forgiveness.

Tetzel did not enter Saxony, which was Luther's home. This made it easier for Luther to criticise him publicly, for he had no wish to undermine a fundraising scheme if it was backed by his own prince. While Luther was in some ways a saintly monk, he was also a politician. He had to be.

It was Tetzel's theology – more than his salesman's skills – that angered Luther. As most priests actually welcomed Tetzel to their pulpit, Luther was further incensed. In February 1517 he delivered his first attack on them: 'Oh, the dangers of our time! Oh, the snoring clergy!' In October, Luther resolved to intensify his criticism of the sale of certain kinds of indulgences in north Germany. While they were enticingly advertised as a shortcut to heaven, there were, in Luther's view, no such secret corridors for either the rich or the poor.

Luther prepared a closely argued document consisting of ninety-five theses or objections. Strictly speaking, they formed not ninety-five separate points but a general argument, each sentence of which was numbered. On the evening of All Saints' Day in 1517, he nailed his document, like a poster, to the outside of the big door of the Castle Church at Wittenberg. To fix them to the door was less an act of rebellion than a call for debate.

The town of Wittenberg with its small, new university was hardly the place in which to turn the Catholic world upside down. But it had its own sphere of influence. Already students came, mostly on foot, from as far south as Salzburg and as far north as the Baltic ports of Lübeck and Danzig. When the following summer vacation began, they carried home Luther's message by word of mouth or in pamphlets.

Most of Luther's arguments were courteous and restrained. Every now and then he showed a sign of losing his temper. He thought it was outrageous that a Christian should be informed that it was worthier to buy a pardon from the church than 'to give to the poor or to lend to the needy'. He pointed out, in thesis number 75, how preposterous it was that a human sin could be forgiven in return for the purchase of a pardon, almost across the counter as it were. And what if the sin was enormous? Luther thought it absurd to pretend that, once 'a coin tinkles in the collection-box', such a soul might be released from painful purgatory.

Luther must have expected a vigorous debate. In some monasteries in the district, he was accused of playing with fire. Obstinate, he refused to stamp out the flames. His ninety-five theses had not mentioned by name Johann Tetzel, the Dominican, but now Luther openly denounced him. In turn, Prince Albert, the archbishop of Mainz, reported to Rome the verbal crusade initiated by 'the rash monk of Wittenberg'. Luther, however, was deaf to rebukes from Rome. Moreover, Luther's own ruler stood by him. Many students decided that the university where Luther taught was the place for them, and it soon became one of the larger universities in Germany. Luther, busier and busier with his writings and sermons, half-resented his growing fame and the workload imposed on him. In May 1520, he was to suggest that fame had been sent by Satan to interrupt his work.

Half of the Christian world was now hearing or reading versions of what Luther said. His pamphlets and tracts were printed in Basel, Strasbourg and other important towns. Froben, who was Erasmus's publisher, printed 600 copies of Luther's latest criticisms and sent them overland to France and Spain. In monasteries where these arguments raged, some monks thought that Luther's arguments resembled those that had led Hus, the Bohemian heretic, to his humiliating death more than a century previously. One rumour insisted that Luther himself came from Bohemia and had been indoctrinated there.

It was now clear that Luther was not just a theologian but also a nationalist. Some of his writings in 1520 made a powerful appeal to Germans as distinct from the whole Christian world. One of his accusations was that Rome was robbing Germany: 'Poor Germans that we are – we have been deceived!' Luther declared that 'the glorious Teutonic people should cease to be the puppet of the Roman pontiff'.

Pope Leo X, slow to act decisively against Luther, at last threatened to excommunicate him. On 8 October 1520 the printed works of Luther were formally burned by the public executioner in the market square of Louvain, a university town. They were set alight again in the open air at the German river port of Cologne. Another burning of his works in Mainz, just upstream, was thwarted when a witness vowed that the books on fire had not even been written by Luther. In the following month, in a meadow outside Wittenberg, Luther's supporters, with loyal students to the fore, retaliated by burning the papal documents that denounced him. Luther was no longer careful in what he said. God himself, he informed the pope from afar, 'condemns you today to the fire, amen'. On 3 January 1521 Luther was formally excommunicated.

Luther had begun his challenge by respecting the pope but no longer did he accept him as the supreme head of the church. He now argued that Peter, the source of the pope's authority, had been only one of the twelve apostles, and was not a Christ-like figure. He no longer believed that the pope had power over heaven, hell and purgatory; he eventually ceased to believe in purgatory. Nor could the pope take away sin. In essence, to enthrone the pope, as Catholics did, was to diminish the role of God himself.

The key phrase in Luther's protest was 'justification by faith', a phrase that has slipped from public understanding. The word 'justify', once spiritual, has come down to earth and is now assertive. It is now used mainly in such personal ways as: 'I justify my behaviour; I am justified in saying this'. In its original meaning, however, it was humbling. To be justified meant to be pardoned – not by one's own good deeds but by God's generosity.

JOURNEY TO WORMS

Luther was summoned to appear in person before the imperial assembly or the Reichstag of the Holy Roman Empire. Though confined to the major rulers of central and western Europe, it was the foremost international political gathering of that era. Of the rulers who met together, most came from German-speaking lands. That they met regularly was remarkable. The Holy Roman Emperor, the boyish Charles V, was to preside personally at this meeting convened at the town of Worms on the River Rhine, and though Luther was only one item on the agenda, his personal appearance was a sign of the commotion his preaching had caused.

The town of Wittenberg helped to finance Luther's journey, providing a wagon and horses, while the university gave him a living allowance. He invited three travelling companions, who along the road could debate those biblical questions that were always in his mind. The wagon left Wittenberg on Tuesday 2 April 1521 – almost as soon as the Easter celebrations were over. From Leipzig the wagon proceeded to Weimar and so to Luther's old university town of Erfurt. As the wagon approached the town, peasants paused in their work in the fields, and students lined the road, easily recognising Luther in his monk's clothing. On the following day he preached the Sunday sermon in the Augustinian chapel that he knew so well, and the audience was so crammed, inside and out, that some feared the building would collapse. After a crack appeared in the portico, Luther wittily assured his listeners that it was the Devil at work, trying to halt his journey.

Towards the end of the journey Luther looked worn and pale. He sensed danger. He remembered the history of protests against the papacy. Almost a century before, Hus had travelled from Prague to Constance to face his accusers, having been enticed by the promise of a safe journey, but instead he was condemned to death. On the last night of the journey, Luther was met at the roadside inn at Oppenheim by Martin Bucer, a former Dominican priest, who warned his friend not to proceed to the seat of judgement because his life was in peril. Rejecting the warning, Luther entered Worms the next morning, seated on the wagon. The riverside town was already packed with the mighty – the emperor, ruling princes, ambassadors, archbishops, bishops and abbots. Luther, next day, visited a barber, for he had allowed his hair to hang below his ears.

As the elected Holy Roman Emperor and the head of the House of Habsburg, Charles V had a duty to curb the spread of Lutheranism and tame the monk who stood before him. This was the year of his twenty-first birthday, and he had already held high office for two years and would hold it for more than three decades. He now ruled Spain, the new Spanish colonies in the Americas and North Africa, the present Netherlands and Belgium, portions of the present France and Germany and the islands of Sicily and Sardinia.

Austria was also part of his realm. Until this vast domain was divided amongst two separate rulers in 1558, it constituted the most far-reaching empire a European had ever ruled.

Escorted into the assembly hall, Luther bowed his head. He had no wish to be seen as proud. Allowed to speak only if questioned, he was under intense strain and sweating heavily. A list of his writings and criticisms, which had been printed at Basel in the one edition, was publicly read aloud. Luther was asked whether he was the author. The question was asked in Latin and then in German, and Luther replied in each language. Requesting time in which to consider, his request was churlishly granted. Should he disown several or all of his own writings or accept full responsibility? Here was his chance to retreat. In a letter written that evening to a friend in Vienna, he explained that he would not alter one comma of what he had written. 'Truly with the help of Christ', he wrote, 'I will not revoke even a dot in all eternity'.

On the following afternoon the assembly met in a larger hall. Luther was dangerously defiant. Making his plea in Latin, he defended his beliefs. They were based on the Bible and his conscience. His final words, in German, were: 'God help me, amen!' Perhaps he could be persuaded in private to alter his views. Discussion went on for several days but all arguments were rejected.

Luther fortunately had one resolute protector: Frederick III, the Elector of Saxony. Not one of the most powerful rulers in Europe, he was willing to challenge or defy the Holy Roman Emperor. Theologically, Frederick III and the protesting monk were not soulmates, but he knew that his independence as a ruler within Germany would suffer if he bowed and gave in. It was he who had wisely insisted that Luther be tried on German soil and not in Rome.

The risk of total condemnation, imprisonment or death hung over

Luther. He left Worms on 26 April, before the assembly had come to its final decision to condemn him and before it had resolved to publish a papal bull of condemnation signed in January but not yet released. A week later, for his own safety, he was kidnapped by a party of horsemen acting on behalf of Frederick and escorted to the castle at Wartburg. For a time his whereabouts was unknown, and his loyal supporters even wondered whether he was dead. He was very much alive, and month after month he wrote and wrote, beginning at last his translation of the New Testament into German.

Luther needed public support, but in lands that remained Catholic only the brave gave him support. He hoped for friendly words from Erasmus; and at first the mighty scholar seemed sympathetic, sensing that Luther was a bolder and earthier version of himself on many religious matters. But Erasmus did not share Luther's burning desire to transform the world. He had helped to launch a giant rocket but now saw that the rocket was soaring out of control.

LUTHER'S HIDDEN STRONGHOLDS

Luther composed a hymn, vivid with military references, proclaiming that a 'safe stronghold is our God'. Other strongholds were rebellious German states whose rulers were supporters of Luther. A less predictable stronghold was Allah and his Ottoman army and navy. Muslim armies and navies were advancing further and further along the shores of the Mediterranean Sea and overland in central Europe. At the very time when Luther had been preparing his first declaration of defiance, news of unexpected victories by the Ottoman Turks were reaching him. In 1516 they captured Syria and took over Jerusalem from other Muslim occupiers. In the following year they captured much of Egypt. In 1522, one year after Luther met his accusers in Worms, the Turks captured the island of Rhodes – the home of the Knights of St John. In 1526 the Turks gained indirect control of the rich Adriatic port of Ragusa, near the main sea lanes to Venice. Three years later, they approached the city of Vienna and besieged it. The persistent advance of the Muslims provided breathing space for Luther at the time when he most needed it. Catholic rulers faced the dilemma: should they attack the Lutheran strongholds or should they form an alliance and attack the encroaching Turks? For his part Luther viewed Rome as more offensive, ideologically, than Islam.

For a decade or more the internal and external events in Europe and Asia Minor seemed to be favouring Luther and his protests. The two foremost Catholic emperors were divided. Catholic Spain fought Catholic France in four different wars between 1521 and 1544. They included that extraordinary episode, the invasion and looting of Rome and the killing of some 4000 of its residents. The looters and killers were mainly Catholic troops who, indignant that they had not been paid, mutinied against their Catholic leader, Charles V of Spain.

Meanwhile, Luther introduced reforms slowly and patiently into the religious services he conducted. He believed that at Holy Communion the people should be given the sacrament of both the wine and the bread. Late in 1522, more than a year after his return from Worms, he allowed the chalice of 'blood' to be passed to the people in turn. For centuries Holy Communion had been celebrated every day. In March 1523 it became a weekly sacrament in Wittenberg. The German language was not introduced at once. The temptation to destroy the religious images in which Catholicism rejoiced was resisted. After a mob of enthusiasts had mutilated stone statues and the rich altar ornaments in several Wittenberg chapels, Luther tried to restrain them from further acts of religious vandalism.

THE PEASANTS AND THE PRINTERS

Once the supreme religious authority was challenged, what principle would be challenged next? By tearing down one important house Luther was inviting protesters to pull down another. The excitement of pulling down structures, especially those that once had been unassailable, could easily become a fever. In the winter of 1524–25, in parts of south Germany, peasants and small farmers rebelled against harsh living conditions; and they coupled their demand for economic reform with a demand for religious reform. At first the peasants' leaders thought that they were almost on the same wave length as Luther, for they now saw the church as a brotherhood and Christianity as embodying the spirit of love.

At Memmingen in March 1525, peasants drew up plans that shocked their wealthy neighbours. They wanted to appoint their own pastors. They wished to pay to the church a lower proportion of the grain they produced at their annual harvest, and they wished to pay a lower rent to their own landlord. They wanted more access to the open countryside: to firewood, which was their only fuel in winter, and to the streams where they could catch fish. The demand for fishing rights was cautious, for they did not seek the right to fish in manmade ponds on private property. One ancient right of the landlord they especially opposed: he had the right, after his tenants died, to choose for himself the most valuable of their movable possessions.

The justice of most of these demands, known as the Twelve Articles, was accepted by Luther. But he did not support peasants who insisted that they should achieve these demands by rebellion. Least of all did he support those more radical peasants who called for common ownership of property. In refusing to support the radicals the whole way, he was promptly labelled as the friend of princes and rich landowners. Here were signs that the Reformation, having reformed so much, was in danger of undermining itself. Suddenly he was in danger of losing a precious layer of his popularity. That is the fate of many of those who are on the winning side during the first stages of a strong revolution.

Amongst the converts to Lutheranism were numerous tradesmen. Many were printers, exponents of a craft that had recently been carried in slow steps from China to the Rhine Valley and there adapted and improved. The new printing presses spread Luther's message. In one day the compositor and printer could do as much work as maybe 500 monks and their quill pens. In contrast, if Luther had happened to rebel against the church in the era of handwriting, his message would only have spread slowly.

Luther's Wittenberg was briefly the spearhead of a technology that was beginning to reshape the world. In 1524, the year he produced his translation of the New Testament in the German language, more than half of the books published in Germany were printed there. Another force spreading his message was the German people's delight that he spoke and wrote in their language. The pamphlets that fluttered from the printing houses, and the passages of the newly translated Bible, were read aloud in the German language to those who either could not read them or could not afford to buy them. The hymns he composed were also in everyday German, and the congregations learned them by heart and sang them eagerly. The marriage of religion, the native tongue and nationalism was one of the marks of the new Reformation.

Those who called at the printeries could eventually buy a copy of the Lutheran creed, which they began to read or recite each morning and evening:

I believe that God has created me and all other creatures, and has given me, and preserves for me, body and soul, eyes, ears, and all my limbs, my reason and all my senses; and that daily he bestows on me clothes and shoes, meat and drink, house and home, wife and child, fields and cattle, and all my goods; and supplies in abundance all needs and necessities of my body and life; and protects me from all perils, and guards and defends me from all evil. And this he does out of pure fatherly and divine goodness and mercy, without any merit or worthiness in me. For all which I am bound to thank him and praise him, and, moreover, to serve and obey him.

18

A SWISS SWORD-CARRIER

Luther had astonishing success in his own German-speaking region near the Rhine and the Elbe. But his gospel was not likely to survive if it was confined to one segment of Europe. He needed allies elsewhere, and one of his first was Ulrich Zwingli, a priest and theologian who was almost the same age as Luther.

'THE VESSEL I AM'

Zwingli came from that corner of Switzerland which was close to the borders of the present Germany and Austria. The village's name, Wildhaus, hints at its isolation. It lay between the mountain range called Toggenburg and the fast-flowing Rhine, which was only a day's walk away. The village lived on the produce of its flocks and herds, sending its butter and cheese by packhorse to the towns in the valley. The Zwinglis owned land, and Ulrich's grandfather once drove cattle across the Alps to Italy.

The three-storey house in which Zwingli was born is like a wooden box in the hollow of the valley. Still standing, it breathes simplicity with its heavy floorboards, wooden walls, and the steep stairs leading to the uppermost storey. Irregular stones form the floor of the kitchen, while the wooden beams of the ceiling have been blackened by smoke rising from the stove. A small forest of firewood must have been burned in the kitchen stove over the last five and a half centuries. On Sunday mornings a congregation, mostly of the old, still meets near Zwingli's old house, and inside their church they face a painted text in German: 'Wherever would we be if we lost the word of God?'

At an early age, Ulrich Zwingli was sent down to the valley to receive his education, thereafter seeing less and less of his parents and mountain village. He commenced his serious theological studies at the University of Vienna, walking there and back, and almost dying of cold on the return journey. In 1506, at the age of twenty-two, he became the vicar in the town of Glarus, where he continued to read widely, studying Hebrew and Greek as well as Latin. Living only a couple of days' walk from Basel and its printeries, he travelled there in 1516 and met Erasmus. After reading Erasmus's New Testament, his way of preaching was transformed: 'I never mounted the pulpit without taking personally to heart the Gospel for the day and explaining it with reference to Scripture alone,' he recalled.

Zwingli was physically and emotionally adventurous. Twice he accompanied Swiss mercenary troops as their chaplain to Italy, and was present on battlefields. He also had an affair with a barber's daughter that caused him guilt. At the age of thirty-two, he was transferred to Einsiedeln, a small monastery town that was almost the Canterbury of Switzerland – the goal for countless pilgrims who were not able to afford a journey as far as Rome. Some, after hearing Zwingli, said they had never heard vital passages of the New

Testament explained with such insight. One wrote his thanks for 'such a fine, intelligent, serious, Spirit-filled and evangelical sermon as you preached at Whitsuntide a year and a half ago'.

On the strength of his rising reputation Zwingli was invited to the wealthy lakeside town of Zurich, where in 1519 he became the special preacher at the twin-towered Grossmünster. During his first summer there, a plague arrived, knocking on half the doors. Perhaps 2000 of the 7000 inhabitants died. Zwingli visited the sick until he caught the sickness. He survived but his brother Andrew died. On hearing of the death, Zwingli 'wept like a woman', but he saw the death as part of God's will. On recovering he wrote a hymn – soon popular – proclaiming that people were like fragile plates. It was for God to decide whether each plate should be broken or remain intact.

Thy vessel I am,
To make or to break.

Zwingli and his band of religious radicals amplified Luther's protests. Zwingli criticised the idea of fasting – so central to Catholic ideals – and the compulsory eating of fish rather than meat in the season of Lent. Where, he asked his congregation, did the Bible actually claim that those Christians who fasted would be rewarded? He challenged the veneration accorded to the saints: why pray to them instead of to Christ? Why, he asked, should Swiss people go on pilgrimages when they would be enriched more by studying the Bible at home than by walking to nearby Einsiedeln, let alone to Rome. A Franciscan monk, arriving from Avignon on a donkey, debated several contentious topics with Zwingli and was defeated – at least in the opinion of the officials of Zurich.

One of the largest towns at the foot of the European Alps, Zurich was a self-governing republic, a fact of importance in propelling Zwingli's crusade. He was a member of the town council and that gave him more influence. By the mid-1520s, Zurich was the showplace of the religious reformation in Europe, and more radical than Wittenberg or Strasbourg.

The Bible was Zwingli's court of appeal. While he knew that priests were not allowed to marry, he observed that the Bible itself did not specifically prohibit them from marrying. He understood that nearly all of Christ's apostles were married, and he knew that the Greek Orthodox clergymen could marry. In 1522 he quietly married, or began to live with, a youngish widow named Anna Reinhart. The bishop of Constance, though approached, had not given permission for their marriage. At last, in April 1524, Ulrich and Anna were publicly and formally married – just fourteen weeks before the birth of the first of their four children. A year later Luther himself discarded his monk's clothes and married Catherine von Bora, who had been a Cistercian nun. Members of that religious order, which was more than 400 years old, must have shuddered when they heard that one of their nuns had married the Devil himself.

To traditional Catholics these marriages were amongst the most scandalous events of the Reformation. More shocks awaited them. As the Bible denounced the worship of idols and graven images, Zwingli and his close advisers ordered in 1524 that the paintings and statues of Christ and the Madonna and saints be removed from the churches in Zurich. In the spacious church where Zwingli regularly presided, the organ was removed, and its rich sound and the voices of the male choir were heard no more. The crucial ceremony – the mass – was altered and Zwingli no longer turned his back formally on the worshippers when he consecrated the wine and bread. It was at least several hundred years since the central ceremonies of the Catholic service on

Sundays had been so dismantled and remade. From 1525 in Zurich the sermon was always preached in German, and at some length. In the same year the call for the closure of all local monasteries and convents became louder, and they were shut down.

In essence this religious reformation was a rebellion, and Zwingli for a time was its leader. The whole authority of the traditional church, whether of pope or local bishops, was under attack. Rome receded from sight. In its place stood the opened Bible.

A financial quarrel with Rome drove Zurich further along the road of rebellion. The various Swiss governments or cantons were providers of mercenary soldiers for the rulers of Europe, especially of Italy. Fighting for their pay and also for loot, they were amongst the most esteemed fighters in Europe. It so happened that Zurich had signed a military contract to provide 1500 men to fight on behalf of Pope Leo X, who was determined to recapture the northern Italian towns of Parma and Piacenza. When the four months of fighting were over and the Swiss soldiers tramped home, Rome refused to pay the full sum contracted, pointing out that Zurich had ceased to be a faithful Catholic town and had taken up 'the abominable Lutheran heresy'. To the merchants and leaders of Zurich, a contract was an obligation, and the pope had violated it.

Zurich alone could not defend Zwingli and his rebellion. Fighting Swiss allies were needed and were found in the lowlands, where Basel and Berne but not Geneva were becoming Protestant. At the same time thousands of Swiss people, loyal Catholics, were hostile to religious reform. Many rural inhabitants were eager to defend the church they loved and all its ceremonies, music, liturgy, pageantry, pilgrimages, processions and traditions. As the smart Swiss trading towns were in favour of religious change, that was an additional reason for the farming villages to be wary or suspicious.

A PEACE TABLE IN MARBURG

Ten years after Luther had made his stand at the big church door of Wittenberg, the rebellion he led was not yet victorious. Germany itself was divided, with some northern princes – especially those of Saxony and Hesse, Brunswick-Lüneburg, and Mecklenburg – favouring Luther and offering him protection, but various Catholic princes opposing him. Moreover, the rebel theologians were themselves divided, and on occasions criticised one another as fiercely as they attacked their common enemy in Rome.

If only the main Protestant leaders could be brought together face to face, might they decide to agree? Luther's church in Germany was only 600 kilometres, as the crow flies, from Zwingli's church in Zurich, and the two leaders spoke the same language. Perhaps fervent prayers and the descent of the Holy Spirit would unite the rival leaders if they met. The prospects of arranging a meeting increased after Philip, who was the ruler of Hesse and a strong Lutheran, set aside the thousands of florins needed to bring the leaders safely to his castle town of Marburg. There was a further motive for creating unity among the Protestants. The emperors of France and Spain seemed likely to send an invading force to the German-speaking lands, but they might hesitate if the political and spiritual leaders of the Reformation were united.

Zwingli consented to travel to the peace table or what was called the Marburg Colloquy. The town authorities of Zurich were asked for their approval. Reluctantly they gave it, for they feared that during the journey Zwingli might be captured or killed. Quietly he slipped out of Zurich with a colleague, after sunset one evening in September 1529. Calling first at Basel – now converted to Protantism – he was joined by that city's religious leader, John Oecolampadius, a former priest who had recently married. The journey down the Rhine, in the company of Swiss merchants on their way to a trade fair, gave the leaders an opportunity for religious discussions. At the Protestant city of Strasbourg, they were joined by two theologians, including the talented Martin Bucer. So the party, consisting of former Catholic priests, travelled slowly to the north-east, traversing one German princedom after the other and finally reaching the border of Hesse where forty horsemen escorted them safely to Marburg. Two days later Luther and his colleagues arrived from the opposite direction.

The rival reformers first conferred at 6 o'clock on the morning of 2 October 1529. Forthright words soon flowed. Luther later apolo-gised to Zwingli for his outspoken sentences, saying that he was only human: 'after all, I am flesh and blood'. The rulers of Hesse and Wurtemburg assumed or saw that, despite the tensions, the rival Protestant leaders agreed on almost everything.

One topic was beyond all hope of compromises; and even the genial Martin Bucer – 'that chatterbox', in the words of Luther – could not repair the rift. It centred on that central ceremony and sacrament of the Christian Church. Catholics believed that, dur-ing the consecration by the priest at the altar, the bread and wine prepared for the congregation became the actual body and blood of Christ. Luther had ceased to believe in this miraculous change but could not bring himself totally to reject the physical presence of Christ in the ceremony. He believed that although the bread and wine on the altar remained the same everyday commodities stored in a kitchen, somehow, by the power of God, the body and blood of Christ were present in the 'unchanged bread and wine'. For Zwingli, there was no physical presence of Christ in the bread and wine. They were simply the symbols of Christ's Last Supper, a thanks-giving taken in remembrance of him – nothing more.

Remarkably, Zwingli and Luther did not entirely disagree. They agreed that the people waiting reverently in church should now take not just the bread but also the wine, whereas in more recent centuries the Catholic priests had ceased to offer them the consecrated wine. Today, to agnostic outsiders, such intense disputes about the consecrated bread and wine seem of passing significance, but that is how many disputes appear after the centuries glide away. To Christians this disagreement based on Christ's last supper at Jerusalem was almost a matter of life and death, of eternal life or eternal death.

A frustrating event in the history of Christianity, the Marburg conference merely confirmed the existing differences. In the very process of rebelling, the leaders themselves had become strong and almost unshakeable in their new views. Zwingli said that Luther was 'foolish and obstinate'. Who now, replied Luther, is the obstinate one?

Zwingli finally arrived home on 19 October after an absence of nearly seven weeks. Most members of his Swiss congregation must have rejoiced that, on the one topic of grave contention, he had reached no agreement with Luther, and that he was true to what he had taught them.

At home, Zwingli and his town were in conflict with those nearby districts that remained staunchly Catholic. In October 1531 the Catholic armies, drawn mainly from Schwyz, Zug and Uri, which was itself the domain of the legendary William Tell, were ready to wage war against Zwingli. These part-time Catholic soldiers lived near the steep shores of the elbow-shaped Lake Lucerne, a place of exquisite beauty. They were boatmen, farmers, woodsmen, townsmen, herdsmen and the mercenary soldiers who had once been hired out to foreign monarchs. Now their army prepared to attack the smaller Zurich army that was camped not far from the lake of Zug.

Zwingli himself travelled with his soldiers, and another twenty or more chaplains or pastors went with him. Relatives, too, were fighting on his side: his wife's sons, his wife's brother, and her son-in-law and brother-in-law, all of whom were killed that afternoon. Witnesses differed on whether Zwingli was actually fighting or was consoling and praying when the battle commenced, but certainly he was wearing an iron helmet. Struck in the head and leg by lances, he was so gravely wounded that he was offered the last Catholic rites by the victors. His Catholic captors did not immediately realise who he was. At last, his face recognised by the light of a torch, he was killed instantly. When the jubilant word went around that he was amongst the dead, an old Catholic priest from nearby Zug – presently a chaplain on the enemy side – arrived to look at Zwingli's face. They had been colleagues together before the Reformation, and the Catholic priest remembered those more harmonious times; and with some compassion he said: 'May God pardon your sins.'

Zwingli's doctrines continued to prevail in Zurich and many other towns and villages, while the Catholic faith prevailed along most of the shoreline of Lake Lucerne and in the mountains and the valleys beyond. There, even today you can walk up winding roads or foot-tracks and come to villages with only a few inhabitants but still maintaining a Catholic Church and school.

THE WORD MARCHES ON

In the month of Zwingli's death, perhaps fewer than 5 per cent of the people of Europe were Protestants, to use the new name for the reforming churches. Primarily a German-speaking protest, it initially made slow headway in the Netherlands and England, but won quicker victories in Scandinavia, to which Protestant pamphlets had been carried by German merchants, university students, and sympathetic monks and priests. Congregations of Lutherans appeared in Hungary, Poland, Bohemia and other parts of central and eastern Europe. Some met in Catholic Churches, where the priest, while keeping his formal loyalty to the pope, began to preach Luther's message. Others were breakaway congregations in cities or in those rural areas where the large landowners, attracted to the new message, could afford to pay Lutheran pastors and build chapels.

Nothing did more to spread the message than the printing of the Bible and the new hymns and prayers in native languages. Knowing in the twenty-first century how the birth of the website and the internet have quickened the exchange of ideas, we can easily appreciate how the printing press created a similar momentum.

19

A TEMPEST ACROSS ENGLAND

It was not easy to predict whether Luther's message could be preached openly in English churches. So much depended on the beliefs and opinions of the reigning monarch, Henry VIII. Strong-willed and ambitious, a conservative Catholic, he commanded high loyalty from his people. One historian wittily called him 'the gigantic maypole' around whom all England danced. Initially, however, the maypole held no space around which the religious reformers could openly dance.

When first making his name, Luther was opposed by Henry VIII. In 1521 the king wrote a book on the sacraments, setting out the papal view and opposing Luther's. For his valuable work as cheer-leader, the king received from Pope Leo X the honour that is still claimed by his successor on the throne of England: the title of 'Defender of the Faith'. But after 1529, Henry VIII gradually ceased to be the defender of the Catholic faith. Diplomatic needs – the quest for the best military and diplomatic ally on the continent – as well as personal ambitions made him pursue goals that were not supported by the pope. The king especially wanted a male heir to the throne. In 1533, having no son, he cast off his wife, Catherine of Aragon, and married her lady-in-waiting, Anne Boleyn. In his search for a healthy infant son he was to be married to a succession of women.

As the pope would not sanction the divorce and remarriage, his authority had to be challenged. Henry VIII issued such a challenge with the aid of sympathetic English bishops and theologians. The dispute with the pope had only one solution: Henry VIII was excommunicated. With the approval of the English parliament, summoned after a long absence, Henry VIII made himself the 'supreme head of the church' in England. Bit by bit he tore away the possessions and rights of the pope. He abolished the traditional right of the pope to collect the first year's income of each new English bishop; he abolished the right of bishops to take their grievances to the pope. In any case, the king himself now appointed bishops, without consultation. In 1535, England began to imitate Zurich and abolish all small monasteries: they had outlived their purpose, the king announced. The big monasteries were the next to fall.

More than 8000 monks, nuns and friars living in the monasteries were dispersed. Those under the age of twenty-four, their vows not being binding, were simply sent away. Many of the older ones received a pension. Many became parish clergymen; several became bishops; while a few abbots who courageously tried to defend their monasteries against the king's soldiers were hanged. The monasteries had employed an army of labourers, cooks, housemaids, gardeners, shepherds, handymen and other paid servants, most of whom now served the new owners of these monastic lands. The beggars who had waited regularly for food at the monastery gates and doors had to find new patrons.

These sweeping changes in England were carried out with surprisingly little 'rage and animosity against the Catholic religion', as was observed two centuries later by David Hume, the historian and philosopher. The fabric of the old Catholic realm in England was pulled apart quietly rather than aggressively. In effect the monasteries, nearly 400 of them, became the property of King Henry VIII, who retained them, gave them to his favourites or sold them.

Through all these escapades and adventures, Henry VIII insisted that he remained, all along, a loyal Catholic. The religious services held in his new Church of England remained essentially Catholic, and for years he personally upheld most of the Catholic doctrines against criticism by the new Lutheran converts. The pope – so the king claimed – was the enemy, while the great and venerable church founded in Rome remained his friend. But having dissolved and confiscated the Catholic monasteries, the king took further measures. In 1536, in what was called a 'royal injunction', the priests were told to discourage that ancient and often happy practice of setting out on a pilgrimage, perhaps to Canterbury or even to Compostela in northwest Spain. They were instructed not to venerate the relics of saints, once so revered. Increasingly, the king was becoming sympathetic to the Protestants, so long as they were not too radical. He did not go as far as Luther in reforming the church, but in 1540 he did marry a Lutheran princess, Anne of Cleves, a town near the lower Rhine.

TYNDALE: MAN OF MANY MANSIONS

When Henry VIII had come to the throne, the language of religion and scholarship in his land was overwhelmingly Latin, and on Sunday morning the Latin words and chants could be heard right across London. At the two English universities, Latin was the language of serious discourse, and when Erasmus was lecturing he is said to have spoken no English. Nearly all the new books published in England were printed in Latin, and the volumes in the library at Oxford University were nearly all in Latin.

William Tyndale, originally from the cloth industry of Gloucestershire, did much to reverse this trend. After spending his childhood in sight of the hills on the Welsh border, he went to Magdalen College in Oxford and then to Cambridge, proving himself to be an able student. Resolving to translate the Old Testament into English, he had beside him the familiar Catholic Bible called the Vulgate, and Erasmus's new translation, both of which were in Latin. He also relied, soon after it appeared, on Luther's translation of the New Testament into German, for he was becoming intensely sympathetic to Luther's theology. Probably he was busy with these diligent studies when, at the age of thirty, he sailed away to Germany, never to see England again.

In the summer of 1525 – a year after reaching Germany – he was completing his translation in the riverside town of Cologne, and was almost ready to supervise the printing of the New Testament in the English language. He had in mind to print 3000 copies – a considerable number and very costly. The local workshop had almost completed the printing of the gospel of Matthew, and had reached chapter twenty-two – and its twelfth verse – when he and his assistant, an English friar, realised the danger. In this Catholic city the printing of an unusual bible was likely to be condemned as heresy. The whole operation had proceeded in secrecy up to this point. But spies had now discovered what was happening in the printery. Tyndale and his assistant decided to escape, carrying with them the piles of printed pages not yet bound. They loaded their cargo at the wharf and sailed upstream, landing at Worms, the city where Luther had faced the Holy Roman Emperor four years previously. There, another workshop completed the printing of the four gospels and the Acts of the Apostles, the pages of which were bound together to form a large book. It contained 700 pages of narrative but no notes of explanation such as those Luther had added to the margins of the pages of his German translation.

A smaller version of the New Testament, easier to carry and conceal, was also produced. In size it was no bigger than a modern hymn book, and its typeface was small. Only one known copy of this printing remains. It was kept at the Bristol Baptist College until 1994, when the British Library bought it for one million pounds. Even this volume is not quite complete – its title page is missing – but we know with certainty that it did not disclose the name of the translator. Tyndale knew it was too risky to claim authorship of a book that, if inspected in England or Rome, might lead to his death.

As a translator, Tyndale wrote the kind of English spoken by the common people rather than by the aristocracy. Those who first turned to the pages of his New Testament probably came across, for the first time in print, such phrases as 'the salt of the earth'. It was a slightly altered form of a phrase used in Tyndale's youth in rural Gloucestershire. Many of the memorable sayings and sentences of present-day English came from his pen. He first wrote the words, still heard each Christmas, that there were 'shepherds abiding in the field'. It was his translation that gave us such quaint phrases as 'the birds of the air, the fish of the sea'. He gave his own flavour and cadence to Christ's commands: 'Seek and ye shall find', 'Let there be light' and 'No man can serve two masters'. His quiet emotions stirred his readers as they read or heard the Bible in their own language for the first time.

Sometimes he bequeathed to us a happy mishap. 'In my Father's house are many mansions,' wrote Tyndale. The word *mansione* had been in the Vulgate Bible and originally signified a dwelling, but it was also coming to signify a grand place or mansion. By virtue of his choice of images, he gave to that sentence of the New Testament, which was to be read aloud in the fullness of time at millions of funerals, a mixture of majesty and mystery. The mystery was to be erased in modern times by revisionists earnestly reworking the English Bible. Now the sentence is often translated, correctly but dully, into the bland statement that in our Father's house are many rooms. The new translation almost turns heaven into a boarding house.

Tyndale's Bible became one of the glories of the English language. A more celebrated version, the authorised or King James Bible, was printed nearly three-quarters of a century later, but it consists overwhelmingly of the prose of Tyndale. Even Shakespeare, two generations later, did not contribute much more than Tyndale to the health, vigour and cadence of English.

The first copies of the Tyndale Bible, freshly printed in Worms, had to be smuggled in boats or barges down the Rhine, transferred to sailing ships in the North Sea, and so shipped to the nearer harbours of England, which was still a Catholic country, for Henry VIII had not yet broken from the pope. Sets of printed pages, bound or unbound, reached England concealed in new bales of cloth. They were at first sold in 1526 by London booksellers under the counter. English readers inquired who had translated and produced this remarkable work. Suspicion fell on Tyndale but he was safely on the continent.

More printed copies of the English Bible came from an edition printed in Antwerp. The English government opposed this secret intruder and ordered that any copy found should be burned. Most, however, were in private hands and, being treasured, were hidden away after each reading.

Occasionally, readers who were discovered with the book were apprehended and severely punished, but the traffic of new copies across the North Sea did not cease. In 1530 in England ten people were prosecuted merely for hearing the new book read aloud to them. Several others were executed because they owned, distributed or provocatively quoted a Tyndale Bible. The persecution of heretics, whether Protestant or Catholic, remained normal in England; one brave Catholic victim in 1534 was Elizabeth Barton, known as 'the Holy Maid of Kent'.

Tyndale dared not return to England, and even in the Lowlands he was in danger. Steadfastly he revised and polished his first volume and, continuing to work on his translation of the Old Testament, was about halfway through that formidable task when his end came. In 1536 near Brussels he was found and identified by Catholic authorities and sentenced to death.

THE TREACLE AND OTHER BIBLES

In England two years later the government resolved to place one Bible in every parish church. It seems such an elementary decision, but throughout Europe and the Middle East, most churches possessed no complete Bible, only an official selection of extracts. The chosen translation was not Tyndale's but Miles Coverdale's. He had been a member of the Augustinian Friars – related to Martin Luther's religious order – before becoming a reformer. His new Bible, a mosaic, relied on Tyndale's version in the English language, Erasmus's two versions in Greek and in Latin, and the Vulgate in Latin. It was a kind of Christian pudding with mostly borrowed ingredients.

The first attempt to print it was made in Catholic Paris, at the printery of Francis Regnault, who had access to fine printing paper and a handsome typeface. News of this private venture became known to French officials, who saw it as an heretical bible. On 17 December 1538, they confiscated everything. Coverdale and his London backer, Richard Grafton, a wealthy grocer, feared for their lives and hurriedly returned to England. They expected their precious pages to be burned in public or at least tossed into the River Seine. Instead, they were sold to a haberdasher who intended to make use of the printed sheets of paper, perhaps for wrapping up his wares.

Eventually, Coverdale thought it was safe to return to France. He located the house of the haberdasher and acquired the printed sheets that were undamaged, having being stored in four big vats. Most of the printed sheets and even the French printers – some say – were hurriedly escorted to England, where the work of printing continued. In the summer of 1539 the first complete copies were available. English readers were impressed by the title page and its artwork – probably by the celebrated Hans Holbein – depicting the king handing out copies of the book with God's blessing. The kind of book that was too large and heavy to be carried by a child, it was called the Great Bible. Book collectors, in a more secular age, were to christen this edition the 'Treacle Bible', for it treated in a distinctive way the well-known passage in Jeremiah 8, verse 22. Normally expressed in English as 'no more balm in Gilead', it was here rendered as 'no more treacle in Gilead'. In fact Coverdale was not being quaint: treacle then denoted a medicine used to cure poisonous bites and general maladies rather than the by-product of a sugar refinery.

Perhaps never before had every church in the same populous land been given the opportunity to acquire a copy of the Bible. Of course, many of the village churches could not afford it, and most members of the congregation could not read it, and many of the parish priests could not decipher the longer words. But in numerous churches it took its place, pages always open, a foretaste of a day when the word of God would be freely open for public discussion. In 1541 a proclamation was printed, ordering that the Great Bible be read aloud in all English churches, but the private owning and reading of the Bible was limited by law. The only females who could read it were defined as noble or gentle women, while such males as apprentices, journeymen, labourers, skilled tradesmen and others were prohibited 'under pain of fines and imprisonment'. Even this bible was banned in 1546.

With the king interfering so readily in England's religious life, the death of a monarch was a destabilising event. Henry VIII was succeeded by his children: first by his son, Edward VI, in 1547; then, six years later, by his daughter, Mary, a devoted Catholic. Her loyalty to the pope was confirmed when she married a powerful Catholic monarch, Philip II of Spain. In England, she altered many of the rules and preferences that her Protestant predecessors had imposed. Priests who had been allowed to marry were ordered to resign from the church or divorce their wives. A few monasteries were revived, and Westminster Abbey again became the home of monks. Catholic practices crept back or appeared openly. High officials who had been in favour were imprisoned. Cranmer, who had been archbishop for twenty years and was now a prisoner in his own country, was humiliated by being forced to confess his religious and political sins to two resident Spanish friars. In England, at least 270 Protestants, mostly shopkeepers and tradesmen, and women as well as men, were burned at the stake for their religious defiance. And after a new monarch ascended the throne it was the Catholics who became the persecuted ones.

THE STREAMS OF REFUGEES

When governments changed hands and a new religion was imposed on the people, many of the clergymen who belonged to the old faith tried to become refugees; at least those who were wealthy enough to travel. If they were sensible, they left as soon as the new leader took office. When Mary I accepted the English throne in 1553 and commenced what would be a five-year reign of Catholicism, plans to escape were drawn up by thousands of Englishman and foreigners. David Whitehead, an English dissenter, and John Laski, a Polish nobleman now active as a Protestant pastor, were leaders of the 175 passengers who, in two vessels, prepared to escape down the River Thames.

Laski, highly intelligent and argumentative, was so many times a refugee that it was almost his occupation. When his uncle was the primate of Poland, he had lived in Rome in a most favoured residence, and had spent ten months in Basel as a guest in Erasmus's house. Becoming a Protestant, he led a congregation in Germany before moving to London, where in 1550 he became pastor of a church given over by the government to European refugees – the old church of the Augustinian Friars. There, as in Germany, he conducted it on Presbyterian lines, with senior laymen taking part in the governing of the congregation and in policing its members' morals and beliefs. Perhaps he was the first influential Presbyterian in the British Isles.

He and many in his congregation had so much to lose from a new reign in England that they were ready to move when Mary became the monarch. Where could they find a haven? North Germany and the Baltic were the likely choices, and the two refugee ships crossed the North Sea just before the winter storms began. Laski and Whitehead reached Elsinore, but the Danish authorities, while Lutheran, decided that some of the refugees might be radicals and refused to allow the ships to land. Likewise, along the southern shores of the Baltic Sea, Lübeck and Rostock said 'no', and Danzig allowed only a few passengers ashore. Back in the North Sea, the wealthy Protestant port of Emden finally welcomed them.

Frankfurt was another haven for Calvinists. Sufficient exiles lived there to form an English-speaking congregation, and a message was sent to Emden inviting Whitehead to be their preacher. Tinged by Catholicism, he still allowed 'lights and crosses' to be prominent in the church services he conducted; and so he had to give way to Robert Horne, another exiled divine who had recently been the dean of Durham Cathedral. Eventually, Horne went to Strasbourg, the home of more refugees.

At the end of 1558, news from London reached these refugee cities that Mary of England was dead and that a moderate Protestant, Elizabeth I – the third child of Henry VIII – had replaced her devout Catholic sister. The married priests returned to the churches, and the English rather than the Latin Bible was read aloud on Sundays. The monks vanished from Westminster Abbey, and England's links with the papacy were cut after being so recently renewed.

Many refugees moved back to England, but even in their homeland they did not fit in. Offered the plum post of Archbishop of Canterbury, David Whitehead refused, explaining that as an evangelical he did not approve of bishops. While some of the reformers had no wish to be a bishop, others rejoiced when invited. Horne, after returning from the refugee havens of Frankfurt and Strasbourg, became Bishop of Winchester. He used his authority there, and at Oxford and Cambridge, to destroy ornaments and symbols that he regarded as too papal. Paintings deemed unduly superstitious were thrown out, stained-glass windows that offended him were smashed, and priestly caps and capes were tossed into the cellars. A tabernacle at the eastern end of the chapel of New College, Oxford, a fine work of art, gave way to painted walls on which were inscribed simple texts from the Bible. It had been the custom of congregations to turn to the east at the reciting or singing of the 'Gloria Patri', but under Bishop Horne's stern eye such papal reverence for the most sacred point of the compass was dismissed. Even the singing sometimes became ragged because the costly organ was played no more. These destructive acts occurred more in England and Switzerland than in Lutheran Germany.

Now that the fine arts are favoured more than religion in some circles in the western world, such vandalism is often, in retrospect, condemned strongly by scholars. But in many churches and cathedrals in the sixteenth century, the worshippers rejoiced that the Catholic ornaments and messages had been deleted in order to emphasise the simpler Protestant essentials. Such upheavals, and the ensuing succession of winners and losers, were frequent in certain kingdoms and republics during the first century of the Protestants.

20

JOHN CALVIN'S REALM

John Calvin came one generation after Luther. As he first lived in the cathedral town of Noyon, some 100 kilometres north of Paris, his early life was spent in closer proximity to London than to Geneva, with which his fame is now associated. His original name was Jean Chauvin, which he first converted to Calvinus, the Latinising of names being in vogue, and later to plain Calvin. After studying at Paris University he learned law in Orleans and then classical Greek in Bourges, increasingly coming under the influence of scholarly Protestants.

Grave and intense by disposition, and orderly in his ways of working and thinking, Calvin began to study the Bible closely and write about his insights. Edging towards Luther's ideas, at a time when they were arousing hostility as well as curiosity in Paris, he walked out of France with his unfinished manuscripts and travelled up the Rhine to Switzerland. He was barely twenty-seven years old when the first edition of his religious work, the *Institutes*, was published in Basel in 1536. It was written in Latin, the language of international discourse, and the few copies printed were sold in the space of twelve months. Some reached France and were read voraciously. Wisely he did not publish the book under his own name. It might have condemned him to a term in prison if he returned to France.

In 1536, in exile from his homeland, he arrived in Geneva, a city state recently liberated from the Duchy of Savoy. Protestants were taking it over: the cathedral of St Peter's was theirs, the mass was replaced by a simpler form of Holy Communion, and the Catholic bishop had departed. Pastors and magistrates were for a time marching in step, but the reformation was not yet complete. Calvin, against his inclinations, agreed to stay as a city preacher and theologian. It was as if God, stretching down his hand from heaven, had seized him. In turn he, in company with Guillaume Farel, seized the people of Geneva, sometimes by the neck but usually by persuasion, and set out to make their city the most godly city in Europe. After two years the good citizens had had enough. Farel and Calvin were expelled.

Calvin retreated to another Protestant citadel, Strasbourg. Years before he arrived, the riverside town was alive with theological discussion, experiments in ways of worship and an enthusiasm for hymns. On Sundays, the various churches held their services – with a sermon – at 5 a.m. and 7 a.m. An hour later in the cathedral, within walking distance of the other churches, there was another service with a sermon. And so the morning of almost continual worship went on. Calvin preached to the French-speaking congregation and fell somewhat under the spell of Martin Bucer, a much-older pastor who had been a central figure in the failed attempt to reconcile Luther and Zwingli at Marburg. Calvin also fell under the spell of Idelette, a widow. Once an Anabaptist, she now accepted Calvin's views, and they married.

In 1541 Calvin was invited to return to Geneva, where the strict reformers were again in power. There he became more and more influential in specifying what was the correct conduct and, with the aid of a tribunal, in imposing adherence to it on citizens. By 1555 he was the dominant man in the tiny republic. The training ground in the new theology, it sent hundreds of well-taught pastors to serve in France and other lands.

Calvin had to revise his book, for his own views were changing in the light of his experiences in Strasbourg and Geneva. He translated it from Latin into French in about 1545 for the sake of his country-men, 'multitudes of whom I perceived to be hungering and thirsting after Christ'. In his opinion most Christians in France had scant knowledge of the Bible, and he hoped that his book, along with close and constant reading of the Bible, would inspire them. He also hoped it would inspire the Catholic king, whom he addressed in all editions as 'his most Christian majesty, the most mighty and illustri-ous monarch'.

Finally ending up as two volumes, Calvin's notable book carries the forbidding title of *Institutes of the Christian Religion*. Filling nearly 1300 closely printed pages in the modern English translation, it covers almost every Christian theme relevant to his era. What an arguer he was. Pondering over a mass of detail, he was barely inter-ested in a proposition that could be confined to one point rather than four, and he set out his erudite arguments with an air of lofty authority.

His views on predestination were to become notorious. He pro-claimed that God decided in advance what would happen to the soul of every man and woman. Therefore, many people, no matter how earnestly they might appear to be living their lives, were doomed from the outset. There was no court of appeal, no banner of 'equal opportunity. It was like a race in which the result was 'fixed' and predetermined.

Calvin insisted that individuals had no intrinsic claim to God's mercy; God alone decided. People are not created as equal, wrote Calvin, 'but some are preordained to eternal life, others to eternal damnation'. He conceded that such apparent unfairness was 'incomprehensible' to many Christians. In essence the doctrine stressed the might and wisdom of God and, by contrast, the frailty and ignorance of human beings.

Today Calvin's name is stained by this theory but for centuries before his birth it had been a mainstream Christian doctrine. The writings of St Paul – and particularly the eighth chapter of his Epistle to the Romans – gave support to this idea that was so essential to Calvinism. Calvin's views also rested on the words of the great St Augustine, who lived in North Africa more than 1000 years earlier, and the blessing given by the Council of Orange, meeting in the warm south of France in AD 529. Nor was Calvin alone amongst the Protestant reformers in preaching this doctrine. Luther and Zwingli supported it, as did Bucer; indeed, he influenced Calvin, who, when young, had not yet accepted it firmly.

The idea of predestination was almost elementary to many true believers. Since God knew everything in advance, he already knew which men or women would answer his call and which would not. It was pointless and even impertinent, said Augustine and Calvin, to inquire any further about God, 'whose judgements were inscrutable and whose ways past finding out'.

Today, in a more secular and egalitarian era, it is difficult for many people to think favourably of such a remote and unimaginably powerful god. Moreover, in Calvin's version the doctrine seems cruel because he himself decreed in his godlike manner that many persons were doomed to 'eternal damnation' from birth, and not even their striving for a most virtuous life might alter God's final verdict. The doctrine tended, amongst groups of serious Christians in the sixteenth century, to give rise to confidence more than despair as their life matured. In the Church of England in 1563, one of the thirty-nine articles – the foundation stones of the faith – proclaimed this doctrine as 'full of sweet, pleasant and unspeakable comfort to godly persons'. If God was primarily seen as loving and merciful, the doctrine could easily be attractive. For the young, however, it could be an emotional millstone.

Calvin is wrapped in surprises when his books are opened for the first time by new readers in the twenty-first century. Many evangelical Protestants today do not believe in angels but Calvin saw them everywhere. They existed in huge numbers, he vowed, and each true living Christian was assigned one angel to guard him. Angels – with the exception of those who misbehaved – performed many of God's tasks. On hearing of Christians in distress, they hurried to their aid with lightning speed. They also took their revenge, and Calvin praised the angel who, according to the Book of Isaiah, slew 185 000 Assyrian soldiers during the one night. Calvin thought that angels were 'mysterious subjects' with no bodily shape, and their physical appearance would not be known until they were finally seen on the Day of Judgement.

Angels were needed, a myriad of them, in order to fend off Satan, for he was 'the most daring, the most powerful, the most crafty, the most indefatigable' of enemies. Mischievous and depraved, he stirred hatred and caused wars but had no influence on people who placed their trust in Christ. Calvin declared that in the end Satan would be 'dispossessed by Christ'. Calvin's views on the wide realm of theology were expressed in Geneva in thousands of weekday and Sunday

sermons – he delivered 174 different sermons from the Book of Eze-
kiel alone – and in myriad letters, which made his collected works
run to fifty-nine volumes in the German edition.

On the life that the Christians should lead, Calvin was a talking
encyclopedia. He offered secular as well as religious advice to his
followers. One of his three arguments for honouring Sunday was
that servants and labourers, and especially those who were under
the authority of others, should enjoy a day completely free from
work. That day of rest, he insisted, was more valuable to servants
than their employers.

Fasting at the time of Lent, he insisted, was sensible, but was
also hazardous because it could give Christians a false sense of pride
at the very time when they should be showing humility. To attend
church regularly was also important, but it would be foolish to pretend that God would be more willing to listen to prayers offered
inside than outside a church – he called this a fad that had arisen in
recent centuries. To sing psalms was appropriate but the words did
not count for 'one iota' unless they were sung from the heart.

Calvin hoped that Christians would pray often. But to expect their
prayers to receive an early and pleasing response from God Almighty
was almost an act of blasphemy. God answered the prayers in his
own way, in his own time, for he was not like a shopkeeper or entertainer, eager to serve his clients. Calvin insisted that people should
pray for others. If instead they prayed for themselves, they did not
even know what was best for themselves. Thus, if they prayed to be
saved from hardships, God might well ignore them, instead seeing a
long-term gain if they walked uphill rather than downhill.

Calvin sometimes sounds arrogant, but humility sits alongside his
magisterial dignity. He ends the final and much-revised edition of
his major book with the message: 'Farewell, kind reader: if you derive

any benefit from my labours, aid me with your prayers to our heavenly Father.'

Calvin, though his Swiss realm was tiny in area, was one of the most influential men in the history of the world. He had become the unofficial leader of Protestantism after Luther's death in 1546, and for the remaining eighteen years of his life he continued to issue his carefully weighed words of hope and caution. He did not wish to be famous after death. Maintaining his opposition to the Catholic practice of making pilgrimages, and fearing that his grave might become a shrine for long-distance pilgrims, he expressed in advance his wish that his exact burial place in Geneva be not known.

Geneva was the engine house of the Reformation. It was still the mecca for dissenting clergymen, theologians, students and Bible-translators, expelled from their own land or fearful for their lives if they remained. A stronghold of printers, it published religious books in numerous languages, including the Geneva Bible in 1560. It was one of the first to display, instead of a solid mass of words, each chapter divided into separate verses, each verse numbered, and the whole set out with plenty of white space instead of a dark ocean of type. Not too heavy, not too expensive, easily carried by its readers to church and studied at home, this book was a bestseller in Britain for half a century.

Critics with a sense of fun called it the Breeches Bible. The reference was to Adam and Eve and their adventures in the Garden of Eden. The typical modern English Bible tells how Adam and Eve, being naked, 'sewed fig leaves together, and made themselves aprons'. In contrast the Geneva Bible reported that they made themselves 'breeches'.

PSALMS – THE POP SONGS OF GENEVA

Jersey in the Channel Islands was predominantly Calvinist in 1564, the year of John Calvin's death. Its religious services were said to be virtually a replica of those conducted in Geneva and a long line of towns in central and western Europe, and Scotland and England too. Most of the people entering the church were clothed in black, in memory of Christ's death. Women sat on one side of the church, men on the other. The men wore their hats inside the church but took them off at crucial parts of the service, such as the praying aloud, the reciting of the confession, and the reading and singing of the psalms. To take off one's hat was what Calvin called a gesture 'of humility'. The gesture was again made during that hushed moment when the minister read or recited aloud the biblical text on which he would base his long sermon. Once that text had been announced, the black hats were returned to the heads. The pulpit – there was no altar – was the centrepiece of the church.

Even the Holy Communion – celebrated just four times annually, the first being at Easter and the last being on the Sunday after Christmas – was celebrated in front of the pulpit. For communion the members of the congregation sat on benches around a simple table, almost as if they were imitating the disciples at Christ's Last Supper; when people in one group had received from the clergyman the bread and the wine, in remembrance of Christ, they gave up their seat at the table to the next group in waiting.

A list of Calvinist instructions guided people's conduct. To buy food for the poor, money was collected as people left the church, the coins being placed in pots held at the door by the church officials. If the poor were numerous, the officials called on the wealthier Calvinists and requested additional gifts of corn or money.

Every family was expected to thank God before each meal was

eaten, and to meet for household prayers each morning and evening. Everyone was expected to attend church on Sunday, while on weekdays some of the popular pastimes were banned. People were not allowed to play skittles, or dance, or indulge in caressing and kissing, at least in public. At night at low tide, when edible sand-eels were speared and then collected in buckets, this was traditionally a pretext for young couples to visit the beach and kiss and cavort in the darkness – until a Jersey law of 1598 intervened: 'All women and girls are forbidden to go sand-eeling except in the company of their husbands, fathers or employers'. It was not easy to enforce strict rules after the first wave of religious fervour had ebbed.

To John Calvin, as to the Catholics, the psalms were vital. In Geneva and in France he insisted that they be sung by the people in French and not in Latin, so that they could fully be understood. He and a few colleagues translated them from Latin into French, converting them from prose into verse and adding new tunes. When the *Geneva Psalter*, consisting of psalms in verse, was published in 1562, it was such a bestseller that in the space of three years, forty-six editions were printed. Calvin, unlike Luther, insisted that no musical instrument or choir should accompany the singing of the congregation. The idea seems austere but foreign visitors who entered his great church in Geneva and heard hundreds of people singing together were almost transfixed by their sincerity and power.

In the Spanish Netherlands – the present Belgium – the Catholics ruled. Therefore, Calvinists often met in the fields, beyond the supervision of the town's inspectors. Sometimes they met on a weekday evening in shops and private houses – if the authorities were lax. Occasionally in the streets the passers-by could hear the singing of the Calvinist version of the psalms. Even Catholics were heard to sing them privately with enthusiasm, for in their churches the priest and the choir monopolised the singing, leaving little scope for the individual worshipper.

In the northern part of the Spanish Netherlands the people broke away from Spain and formed the United Provinces – the present Holland. After Calvinist congregations took over the Catholic cathedrals and churches in the 1580s, the singing of psalms and their attractive tunes became a centrepiece. As most people were illiterate, an official known as the precentor would stand in front and sing the words of the psalm, a line at a time or even a short verse at a time, after which the congregation would imitate him: this practice was called 'lining out'. If the teacher was effective, and the tunes were popular, the regular attenders soon learned dozens of psalms by heart. In Scotland, however, the tunes were not allowed to dominate for fear that they would divert attention from the words. Early in the seventeenth century a total of just twelve tunes, called Common Tunes, was approved, and between them they had to accompany all the psalms that were sung in church.

When, about this time, the first Puritans settled in North America, they sang no hymns except the psalms. As newcomers to the congregations had to learn the words by rote, aided by the technique of 'lining out', the singing could be exceedingly slow. In the space of half a century, various congregations selected their own pace of singing and even embellished certain words or verses. Here was a simple democracy at work, with no choirmaster, choir, organist or violinist to challenge the people's pace or performance. Significantly, the first book printed in the English language in the Americas was the *Bay Book Psalms*, published at Cambridge near Boston in 1640.

The singing of psalms by all the worshippers was a major Protestant reform and even spread to some Anglican congregations in England. It was therefore a target for Archbishop Laud when he tried to restore certain Catholic rituals in England. A new Anglican vicar whom he sent to the parish of Isleworth announced in 1640 that he hoped to 'root out the Puritans there'. Accordingly, he encouraged his congregation to bow towards the altar, fully aware that most Puritans did not believe in bowing. He also made them listen to the playing of the organ, knowing that they preferred to sing a psalm to a simple tune or chant – a mode of singing he derided as the chanting of 'the unlearned'. In trying to defy him they were standing up for the new principle affirming that every Christian was entitled to sing.

JOHN KNOX AND THE PRESBYTERIANS

When Geneva was the asylum for many religious refugees, its English-speaking congregation was presided over by a dynamic preacher, almost as logical as Calvin and fiery as well. In his early forties, John Knox was of shortish and solid build with blue eyes, a ridge-like nose and a face that ended in a beard like a hanging garden. Originally a Catholic priest in his native Scotland and later a Protestant pastor, Knox had suffered the misfortune of being captured near St Andrews and shipped away to France, where he become a slave in the galleys on the Loire. Released after a year and a half, his health not completely recovered, he resumed his preaching and was appointed as one of the six royal chaplains in England. But after Mary I became Queen of England in 1553 and restored the Catholic religion, Knox retreated to Europe and became a pastor in English-speaking congregations. At last, in 1559, he returned to Scotland, where the struggle between Catholics and Calvinists was far from resolved. It would be determined by the monarchs of Scotland, England and France, by the relative military power of the trio, by wealthy noblemen and landowners in Scotland, and by Scottish clergymen and worshippers. The most influential among all these powerbrokers was John Knox. That Calvinism and the form of government known as Presbyterian would be the ultimate victor was far from certain when Knox died in Scotland 1572.

Initially, Calvinism itself was autocratic and aristocratic in spirit. Calvin proclaimed that people were unequal. He insisted that equality of opportunity had no place in the only life that mattered – the spiritual life. Similarly, his disciple and colleague John Knox was well known for his view of half the human race. In his work *The Monstrous Regiment of Women*, Knox proclaimed an opinion widely held at the time: that women were unfit to take high office. Knox was attracted to that opinion partly because, in the month when he wrote, the separate thrones of France, Scotland and England were held by women, each of whom was a Catholic.

While not democrats, Calvin and Knox were sympathetic to experiments in self-government, so long as they protected their own doctrines and disciples. They opposed a state or town controlling the church unless their friends were in charge of the state or town; and they were somewhat inclined to the opinion that all ordained clergymen should be equal rather than be divided into a strict hierarchy. In places as far apart as Scotland and Hungary, Calvinist churches experienced a wide variety of governing structures in the period 1550–1650, but only in Hungary did they retain bishops.

Most of the followers of John Knox were known as Presbyterians; the presbyters in the early era of the Christian Church were those members of a congregation who actually governed it. Originally, this formula came from the Jewish synagogue, which possessed its board of elders. In setting up a similar scheme, Knox and his colleagues felt reassured that they were harking back to a representative form of government that prevailed in the early Christian Churches – before the pope became the supreme head. Knox was also imitating the mode of government prevailing in those independent refugee churches that flourished all the way from London to Geneva. In essence the new Calvinist churches gave weight to the Geneva principle that power came from the congregation of the devout. Typically, the members of each church elected a small group of elders, who, together with the local clergyman, guided the congregations. The people or their representatives, the elders, also selected the minister, who, once in office, shared with the elders the duty of disciplining those members of the congregation who broke the church's numerous rules. This Presbyterian form of government could not be called very democratic, but it was more democratic than anything that was attainable in the state-controlled Lutheran and Anglican churches or in the distinctive Catholic Church with its stepladder of authority rising to the papacy itself.

CALVIN SPREADS HIS WINGS

Luther's creed did not so readily attract peoples who spoke languages other than German. In contrast the words of Calvin flew from land to land, entering royal courts, country estates, merchant's counting houses and the huts and cottages of peasants. In Italy the royal household of Ferrara, a wealthy town on the northern plain, was sympathetic: Calvin himself had visited it before Geneva absorbed his energies. Even the Orthodox Church toyed with Calvinism when Cyril Lucar, a native of Crete, was its patriarch in Constantinople.

In some German principalities and in Bohemia and Hungary, Calvinist chapels arose in town and countryside. In the Grand Duchy of Lithuania most of the senators and the magnate families were

Calvinists and Lutherans. In Poland, which today is the most stead-fastly Catholic country in Europe, the Calvinists and Lutherans multiplied quickly; in one large Polish region half of the nobility temporarily became Protestant, and most were followers of Calvin. But the Polish loyalties to Rome were so strengthened by the arrival of the first Jesuits, the most assiduous of priests, that in 1632, the year of the death of Sigismund III, Poland again was overwhelmingly a Catholic kingdom.

The Calvinists' burning desire was to convert France – the strong-est and most populous country in Europe. To do so they first had to convert the royal family, and at times they almost did. The king had long been powerful in religious matters. He appointed the bishops, and the pope merely gave his formal approval. The king, in return for money, selected noblemen and other wealthy landholders as bish-ops, and it was said, with some exaggeration, that 'bishoprics were sold like cinnamon and pepper'. In various ways the king gained revenue from the Catholic Church, and did not have quite the same temptation as English or German rulers to dissolve the monasteries and confiscate other properties.

Well-born preachers, personally selected by Calvin in Geneva, arrived in France to set up congregations; and as they spoke French, they won converts with ease. Known in France as Huguenots, they multiplied in the south and south-west, where the Atlantic seaport of La Rochelle and the nearby region of Cognac were strongholds. Soon embracing about one in every ten French people and even stronger amongst the nobility, they became almost too strong to be banned. Even the royal family included Huguenots and sympathis-ers. Civil war broke out in the danger spots. Many of the Huguenot towns in self-defence needed their own garrisons to survive. Conces-sions were made. In 1562, formally permitted to exist, Huguenots could hold divine service under strict rules in specified places. Many loyal Catholics understandably resented even this concession. More blood flowed, for which each side was responsible, while blaming the other.

In Paris on the night of 23 August 1572, the Huguenots were attacked. Catherine de Medici – Queen Mother of France and niece of an earlier pope – gave the signal to attack. The first casualty was the esteemed Admiral de Coligny, whose mutilated body was flung from a window. Cautious estimates of those fatally wounded in Paris and many small towns exceeded 5000. Called the massacre of St Bartholomew's Day, it was the most dramatic episode, so far, in the running war between the Catholic majority and the strong Protestant minority. Later a truce would be negotiated at Nantes in 1598, granting the Huguenots civil rights, the protection of the law and limited rights of public worship: an unusual but fragile experiment in religious toleration.

Meanwhile, in 1572 the news of the massacre on St Bartholomew's Day reached Edinburgh. John Knox, now frail but not old, was shocked. He had preached regularly to Huguenot congregations, especially in the port of Dieppe, when he was living in exile, and now his mind recalled all the enthusiastic, alert faces arranged in front of him at each divine service. Carefully, he mounted the pulpit of St Giles in Edinburgh and delivered a lament for the dead. It was his second-last sermon: he died that year.

BATTLELINES AND BELLS

The fights between Catholic and Protestant accentuated previous battlelines and divisions drawn across Europe. They reflected the battlelines of geography, separating the north and south of the

Alps. They reflected the rising political awareness of the German-speaking peoples and their reluctance to pay heavy taxes to Rome. They reflected contests between the trading fleets of the Atlantic and those of the Mediterranean Sea, and the contest for political and commercial supremacy between the old Mediterranean maritime powers and the North Sea powers of England and Holland. The political, economic and religious were intertwined.

The Reformation was also a replay of theological battles between old Rome and new evangelists with new messages. In the medieval church, most reformers had been handled with skill. Rome had granted a surprising degree of independence to new religious groups, such as the first Franciscans three centuries earlier and the first Jesuits, who were exact contemporaries of Calvin. Perhaps the first Protestants, if responded to earlier, could have been persuaded to remain in the Catholic Church.

For centuries, the outward unity in Christendom had been noticed even in the little events of daily life. The sounds and sights of Sunday were similar in towns and villages extending all the way from Ireland to Sicily and Hungary. In the densely settled regions of Europe a Sunday traveller could walk 30 miles through the countryside and hear the pealing of church bells nearby or far away. In bell-making the Europeans were masters, and huge sums were spent in casting bells in workshops in towns, carrying them in carts to distant Catholic Churches and installing them in steeples or belfries. And now, for the first time, the sound of these bells – once joyful – annoyed tens of thousands of the more evangelical Protestants. Many Calvinists complained that the bells spread a Catholic sound and message. In London, John and Cecily Eaton, while visiting the house of a neighbourhood butcher, heard the church bells ringing and responded with scorn: 'What a clampering of bells is here!'

The rift widened, partly because it was more than a simple religious rift. Even the diplomats of the rival governments ceased to negotiate. Thus, Elizabeth I, on becoming Queen of England in 1558, appointed an ambassador to the Catholic republic of Venice, and naturally she arranged for a full-time Anglican chaplain to accompany him. However, the pope insisted that if a religious service were to be held inside the building occupied by the English embassy in Venice, it must follow the Catholic liturgy. Elizabeth replied by demanding that the Protestant rituals be followed in the Catholic chapel inside the Venetian embassy in London. The desire to retaliate was intensified.

The important diplomatic ties between England and Spain suffered through a similar deadlock. The two kingdoms failed to resolve the question of which religious service, Protestant or Catholic, should take place in the respective chapels inside the embassies. Spain objected to any heretical religious ceremony taking place anywhere on its soil — even in a foreign embassy. In 1568, England withdrew its ambassador from Spain. The split became wider. For some decades, not one of the new Protestant countries sent a resident ambassador to the various Catholic courts in the peninsula of Italy.

21

TRENT: THE ENDLESS MEETING

If only Luther could meet the pope, if only the wound could be healed. While Luther was alive, attempt after attempt was made. A grand conference or council of the whole church was contemplated, at first in one city and then another. But it was as if the bleak winds that blew across the Alps kept Wittenberg and Rome permanently in their separate worlds. At last in 1545 the wind dropped. One of the far-reaching conferences in the history of Christianity set out to adjudicate between the increasingly Protestant north and the solidly Catholic south.

The meeting place was the town and riverport of Trent or Trento in northern Italy. Guarded by high escarpments, and standing on a road between the north and south of Europe, it was near the Brenner Pass, where in World War II the German and Italian leaders, Hitler and Mussolini, held a momentous meeting. Trent linked the separate regions that spoke German or Italian. Most of its 8000 inhabitants were Italian but the town lay more in the German sphere of influence, being a free city within the Holy Roman Empire.

The bishops of Trent traditionally were German. Bishop Cristoforo Madruzzo, with his distinctively Italian names, informed the council that he had first learned the Lord's Prayer 'in the German language', his mother's tongue. A bishop at the age of twenty-six, and now a cardinal, he relished the red velvet dress that signified he was the ruler of the town as well as its churches. Tall and pale-faced, he knew how to entertain in the banqueting hall of his magnificent palace. His welcoming dinner to the first guests consisted of seventy-four different dishes and a befuddling variety of wines.

Invitations had been issued eighteen months in advance. Who could tell how many bishops and theologians would come, along with their retinues of secretaries and servants? A crowd of Italians arrived first, followed by four Frenchmen and two Spanish bishops. Trent became busier as supplies of food for the foreign visitors and hay for their horses were brought in by oxen-cart or boat. Herds and flocks were walked long distances to the town in order to supply the butchers with meat. Hundreds of guards were enlisted so that the arriving bishops could make the last stage of their journey in safety.

The Council formally opened on 13 December 1545 with the celebration of mass in the Romanesque cathedral. Four archbishops – from Ireland, Sweden, Sicily and France – were joined in the procession by twenty-one bishops, mostly Italians and Spaniards. Alas, only one bishop came from the German-speaking lands whose religious disputes were the very reason for the calling of the council. The heads of the two main branches of the Franciscan Order, longtime rivals, were welcomed, and their presence was a sign that even rifts within the Catholic Church might be healed. Three cardinals came from Rome, but where was the pope? In the course of meetings spread over many years, three successive popes were reigning in Rome, but none came to Trent. Moreover, those Swiss reformers who were invited did not come. Lutherans did not appear until the sixth year, and their stay was brief.

At the inaugural mass the popular preacher spoke of many things, including the Turks, whom he called 'the scourge of God'. He hoped the conference would 'effect the reunion of Germany with the Roman church'. For the emperor the main item for discussion was how to rouse – even from the Lutherans – help in fighting the Turks.

The meetings were adjourned for long periods. In the autumn of 1547, an epidemic struck Trent and the council temporarily retreated south to Bologna. A dispute between the pope and Charles V, the same emperor who had looked down on Luther at the Diet of Worms, led to another postponement that lasted for ten years. Once again the divines and theologians met at Trent to debate and fast, or debate and feast, depending on the religious calendar.

Several churchmen departed because they did not like the climate. It was humid and steamy in summer, and the winter was so severe that the Sicilians and southern Italians had to be furnished with earthenware stoves and firewood. Shivering bishops even ordered fur coats from Venice. In the second-last year of the deliberations, the Bishop of Bergamo withdrew after complaining that the cold air impaired his eyes. For the final session, which closed in December 1563, more than 200 bishops were present.

The council extended over eighteen years, though it was actually in session for a total of only four and a half years. It failed in its primary aim to reverse the Reformation but it also achieved some victories. The absence of Protestants enabled the Catholics to concentrate on their own dilemmas. Courageously, they confessed that their church needed reform, and they set about it. While they reasserted the spiritual authority of their own Latin Bible, the Vulgate, they recommended its revision, and slowly it was revised. They spoke out against those bishops who, often or always absent from their own domain, neglected their worshippers. The parish priests, too, were rebuked for delegated the preaching of sermons to the Franciscans, Dominicans and other wandering friars. The time had come for the local priest to preach again. The council resolved that its bishops should create local seminaries and seriously train priests, many of whom possessed scant knowledge of the Bible and an eccentric knowledge of their church's own doctrines.

Trent reaffirmed the role of the saints, the importance of statues and images and holy relics, and the existence of purgatory. It reaffirmed that a clergyman should not marry. The churchmen who assembled at Trent, refusing to reject every Protestant reform, resolved that the sale of indulgences – a cause of Luther's revolt – must be halted. On the mass, the centrepiece of the church, the French bishops tended to agree with the Protestants, who allowed members of the congregation to sip from the chalice of wine as well as to eat the wafer of bread. The French bishops, outnumbered, lost the debate.

It was Pope Pius IV who had to make the final decision on whether all the recommendations should be adopted. One year after the Council of Trent was dissolved, he endorsed its work and began to implement it. After four years, Rome published a new catechism – a kind of theological handbook – and a breviary on the conducting of the mass. The new guide or breviary set out systematically what the priest must perform and the words he must recite each day: the prayers, psalms, lesson and hymns. As a further step towards equipping cardinals, bishops and theologians for public debate, the complete works of St Thomas Aquinas – the wise man of the church and virtually its court of appeal – were published in 1570. The new version of the Catholic Bible had to wait until 1590.

A new burst of energy was visible amongst the popes. Gregory XIII, who earlier was a church lawyer and judge and one of the pope's delegates at Trent, began a thirteen-year reign in 1572. Ten years later he instituted, in place of the old Roman calendar, the Gregorian calendar that is now universally in use in the secular world. Gregory's calendar was adopted quickly in Catholic lands but slowly in Protestant and Orthodox lands, so that for many decades – and even centuries – one city would be celebrating Sunday while a nearby city would be at its weekday work. England, for example, did not adopt the Gregorian calendar until 1752, at which time the year leaped forward ten days. His successor, Sixtus V, whose five-year reign ended in 1590, was also impressive. It was he who reshaped the College of Cardinals, limiting it to seventy members. This limit on the size of the college that elected each pope would persist for nearly four centuries. One result was the improved quality of the popes. 'There have been a few ineffective Popes since the Council of Trent,' writes one long-time watcher of the Holy See, 'but none who could be called evil.'

The idea of calling another advisory council of the church faded away. The authority of the pope was thereby confirmed and rein-forced. The church's wisdom and sanctity lay mainly with him, not with an international council of bishops and learned theologians. Another version of the Council of Trent was to not be seen in Chris-tendom for three centuries.

CARMELITES AND CAPUCHINS

Catholics gained from the Protestant Reformation. It is difficult to assess the quality of life of those millions of people who remained Catholics in Europe or the soaring numbers who by 1600 were new

Catholics living outside Europe, but the life of the church and its adherents in many regions was quickened.

The Protestant reformers seem, in retrospect, to dominate the sixteenth century, but dozens of notable Catholics were their rivals. Who now, except a few followers of all the saints, has heard of Alessandra Lucrezia Romola? Later known as St Catherine de' Ricci, she must have been fourteen years old when in 1535 she entered a Dominican convent at Prato, near Florence. An excellent administrator, she was also celebrated for her trances, which usually lasted from noon on Thursday to 4 p.m. on Friday. She attracted so many pilgrims that her fellow nuns prayed that she would be less famous.

Even more celebrated was Teresa of Avila, who was born in Spain two years before Luther made his stand. A Carmelite nun, she had *mystical* experiences before that word came into vogue; she would describe how she learned to pray persistently, how she gained a deeper communion with God – 'May you be blessed forever!' – and how she slowly learned that cultivating the art of prayer was like irrigating and cultivating a garden in dry terrain – an exercise in patience and persistence. The first woman to be made a 'doctor of the church', she wrote at length about the private and personal side of Christianity with a charm, intimacy and homeliness that Luther and Calvin could not match.

Soon after Luther began to preach, the Capuchin monks, with their beards, the pointed cowl on their heads, and their sandals, were becoming a familiar sight in many Italian towns. A breakaway from the Franciscans, they tried to revive the ideals of St Francis of Assisi. Determined to share in the lives of the people, they were admired for their charitable work after a plague struck the hill town of Camerino near the Adriatic Coast of Italy in 1523. Their first rules, drawn up six years later, were more austere than those of the other branches of the Franciscan orders then in existence. In some ways these Capuchins, with their attack on poverty, were forerunners of the Liberation Theologians, who flourished in South America more than four centuries later.

Persuasive preachers, the Capuchins imitated St Francis in their desire to attract the sympathies of the men mending the streets and the women picking the olives. It was a blow to their standing when their third leader, Bernardino Ochino, a brilliant preacher, began to spread a Lutheran message. Captivated by the Protestants, and fearing punishment in his homeland, he discarded his pointed hood and in 1542 made his way – a preacher in exile – to minister to Italian Protestants in places as far apart as Geneva, London and the Polish town of Cracow. Meanwhile, all other Capuchins, seemingly contaminated and utterly out of favour in the Vatican, were banned from preaching in public for a short time and prevented, for three decades or more, from extending their work beyond Italy.

Once given the freedom to extend their work they were adventurous missionaries, and were seen in Isfahan in Persia and other places in Asia Minor, on the pirate-infested coast of North Africa, where they rescued prisoners working in the galleys, and in north Brazil, where they rivalled the success of the Jesuits, another remarkable product of this Catholic awakening. French Capuchins, working amongst Muslims in the eastern Mediterranean, were recalled to France in 1630, when it was feared, rightly or wrongly, that they and other friars were becoming too sympathetic to the infidels.

Like many other religious groups, the Capuchins later befriended the rich as well as the powerless. Today, those tourists who, visiting Vienna, wish to see the tombs of Emperor Franz Josef and also the Archduke Ferdinand and his wife – memorably assassinated at Sarajevo in 1914 – learn that they are in the care of the Capuchins.

FILIPPO OF THE ORATORY

The new vitality of the Catholic Church was visible in Rome, not a rich seedbed of saints. Philip Neri was a Florentine who had come under the influence of the Dominicans before moving to Rome at about the age of eighteen. Befriending young men who worked for the Florentine banks that did business in Rome, he also enjoyed an argument or joke with pilgrims and other strangers, many of whom he met in Rome's streets or squares. He soon became a quiet friend of many of the poor and sick of that city. His humility and good cheer attracted them: it was unexpected in one who seemed like an aristocrat. A London disciple, two and a half centuries after Neri's death, thought he must have been in manner rather like the well-dressed English clubmen he knew: 'emphatically a modern gentleman of scrupulous courtesy, sportive gaiety, acquainted with what was going on in the world, taking a real interest in it'.

Unusual religious experiences – accompanied by a rapid palpitation of his heart – so altered his outlook that he thought of going to India as a missionary, but he was persuaded that Rome's streets held numerous beggars and a variety of distressed people who needed his love and help.

Realising that many patients discharged from the hospitals were too weak to resume hard physical work, Neri cared for them. He made his home at the hospital of San Girolamo della Carità, where much of his day was spent in religious duties, especially in hearing confessions. In the evenings he conducted an unusual form of entertainment and devotion that grew so popular he built a hall or oratory to house it. Initially, the typical evening combined a musical soiree, prayers and hymns with a discussion on a Christian theme. Later it took the form of a musical performance in two acts, one performed before and one after the lecture. Often the theme was biblical, and singers told the story.

Neri's hall, known as the Oratory, was the birthplace of the musical art form called the 'oratorio'. The earliest surviving oratorio, performed at Rome in 1606, included ballet dancers as well as soloists. Later a chorus appeared, and by the time of Bach and Handel it had become a vital part of the oratorio. Curiously, this innovation from priestly Rome was to become a form of music dear to Protestants.

Eventually, Philip Neri moved from the hospital to his own church in Rome, where he had formed a religious order called the Congregation of the Oratory. His urban monasteries – and they began to multiply – were open to lay brothers as well as experienced priests, but did not enrol very young men. There was no ban on members owning private possessions, they did not have to live in dormitories if they preferred their own rooms, and being people with some wealth they bought their own clothes and books, and paid for their meals. They did not employ servants, and the Oratorians themselves, even their elected head, took turns to wait at the dining tables. Their ornamental churches, grand but not huge, arose in many Italian and French towns.

The founder of the Congregation of the Oratory lived until 1595, when he was in his eightieth year. In Rome his death aroused more emotion and public sadness than could the death of a pope. The Oratorians expanded quickly into France and, two centuries later, were part of one of the most remarkable events in the religious history of England. The Reverend John Henry Newman, the most prized convert ever enticed from the Anglican to the Catholic Church, and later a cardinal, founded a branch of the Oratory near Birmingham in 1849 and made it his home.

THE BAROQUE AND ITS PEARLS

Catholics traditionally admired pageantry, theatre, grandeur and mystery. Their church services, when performed at their highest levels, were one of the cultural achievements of western civilisation. Here the performing and visual arts competed for eyes and ears in many of the finest buildings to be found in the world. The Catholics' own reformation, a response to the Protestant Reformation, fostered these arts even more than previously. A new architecture, first displayed in a Roman church by Carlo Maderno, a young architect from Lake Garda in north Italy, became the favourite style amongst Catholics in western Europe and the pioneering provinces in Latin America. Probably named after the baroque pearl, which was handsome but irregular, the baroque churches and palaces had grandeur, colour and a sense of the dramatic.

Internally and externally, space was needed for baroque buildings to display themselves, for display was their aim. Statues clambered for places outside and inside the building. Paintings of biblical scenes filled every lofty space inside, and the gilded interiors of the domes resembled a newfound goldmine. Gold was plentiful now, for on the far side of the Atlantic the Spanish owned many of the richest mines the world had seen. The baroque style was taken up by painters, too. In the Spanish Netherlands, Peter Paul Rubens painted buxom women whose breasts and thighs blossomed across his canvases. Protestant by birth, he became a Catholic and painted four masterpieces for the Gothic cathedral in Antwerp.

One and a half centuries after the close of the Council of Trent, new buildings in the baroque style still aroused wonder. Europeans longed to see the rising facade of the cathedral in Granada, the colonnade at the piazza of St Peter's in Rome, the palace of the French monarch at Versailles, and the church of Santa Maria della

Salute that seems to float on the sea surrounding Venice. Few Europeans, however, had the chance to visit the startling facade of the new cathedral at Lima in Peru. Even Protestant bishops paid architects to build almost classical varieties of the baroque, though their designs were relatively restrained. The contrast is evident between the baroque of St Paul's Cathedral in London and that of the flamboyant Catholic Church of Les Invalides in Paris, both of which were completed in 1675. The baroque not only transformed the appearance of the churches but also shaped the music heard inside them – music at which Monteverdi, Vivaldi and Handel excelled.

The Protestantism of Zwingli and Calvin was essentially the religion of the book. Now it had to compete with a religion that, more than ever before, enthroned architecture, painting, sculpture and music.

22

TO THE ENDS OF THE EARTH

In 1492, Christopher Columbus sailed from Spain on one of the landmark voyages in the history of the world. He hoped that he would discover a field for Christian missionaries as well as enormous wealth for Spain. He hoped, too, that he would find places described in the Bible.

About eighty men were crammed into his three ships when, on 12 October 1492, they saw a nearby coastline on which stood inhabitants who were naked. Columbus guessed that they were Indians, and that the land was India or close to it. As the three ships were unfurling green flags displaying the Christian cross, he formally took possession of the coast on behalf of the king and queen of Spain and christened it San Salvador. 'To this island,' he wrote, 'I gave the name in honour of our Blessed Lord.' A fortnight later he reached Cuba, which he thought was part of the Asian mainland.

At this time Spain was probably the most fervent of all the Christian countries, and Columbus, though an Italian, imbibed its fervour. Eager to confer Christian-sounding names on many of the islands that he discovered, he named the Virgin Islands after St Ursula, who had been a martyr in Cologne, named Antigua after Santa Maria de la Antigua, who was venerated in the cathedral at Seville, and named the island of Montserrat in honour of a celebrated Benedictine monastery near Barcelona, all in the space of one week.

Columbus's second expedition from Spain, consisting of seventeen tiny ships, carried priests and friars, and two Franciscan laymen who were from the present Belgium, then a Spanish possession. Columbus privately was excited by the thought that he might be about to rediscover the land from which the Magi had come with their gifts for the baby Jesus at Bethlehem. As his ship approached Cuba in October 1495, Columbus announced: 'Gentlemen, I wish to bring us to a place whence departed one of the three magi who came to adore Christ, which place is called Sheba.' On landing, the Spaniards asked the name of the place, and the people replied 'Sobo', to which Columbus responded with delight. He suggested that it was really Sheba but that the native inhabitants simply did not know how to pronounce it correctly. The excitement of rediscovering the land of the Magi must have been intense. If the island was Sheba, then gold and frankincense – the gifts of the Magi – must surely be discovered there. It was only one of many disappointments for Columbus that the biblical sites he expected to find did not eventuate.

Columbus felt closer to the Franciscans than to any other friars. When he returned to the Spanish port of Cadiz at the end of his second voyage, he dressed himself in the grey cloak of a Franciscan. So dressed, he proceeded towards Seville, staying with a parish priest on the way; he wore the same cloak when, a few months later, he met the king and queen of Spain. The royal family saw the opening of the Americas – they still imagined it to be India – as a Christian as well as a commercial adventure, and instructed Columbus that the

American people should be converted 'to our holy Catholic faith' and be encouraged to take the holy sacrament. As the church financed none of these voyages of exploration into the Atlantic and beyond, it was a junior partner in practical terms but a vital partner in the eyes of the royal family and Columbus.

Beginning his third voyage to the West Indies in 1498, Columbus sailed in the name of the Holy Trinity, but it was noted that the ship conveyed more miners – described as panners of gold – than friars and priests. Touching South America on this same voyage, Columbus found the mouth of the Orinoco River and marvelled at the flow of water. Still insisting that this tropical region was part of Asia, he convinced himself that the river flowed all the way from the Garden of Eden, where Adam and Eve had first lived.

The long eastern coastline of the American continent was soon explored by other captains, accompanied by friars who knew their Bible. When a Portuguese navigator, Pedro Alvares Cabral, found Brazil's north east coast he called it the Land of the Holy Cross. The Spanish found Florida in 1513, naming it in honour of Easter Sunday. Far to the north, the estuary of the Gulf of St Lawrence was discovered by Jacques Cartier, who had sailed from St Malo in France with two ships manned by only sixty-one sailors, several of whom were lads. Cartier erected a tall wooden cross, 30 feet high, to mark the entrance to the St Lawrence estuary, which he jubilantly believed would lead him to the Northwest Passage – the missing seaway to the Pacific Ocean and China. Of course, many places in the Americas were named for worldly reasons, Brazil being named after the valuable brazilwood, and Argentina named in the hope of mining silver there. The Christianising of the map was resumed. In California were adopted the names of San Francisco or St Francis and Los Angeles; in Chile they chose Santiago, the name of the apostle; and in Brazil the largest city bears the name of another apostle, São Paulo.

THE 15 000 CHAPELS AND CHURCHES

Christians had to be recruited to carry the Bible to the new lands. In 1508, Pope Julius II gave the Spanish monarch the right to appoint all the bishops, priests and friars who were to set out for the huge part of the Americas to be ruled by Spain. As Seville was the Spanish port that welcomed ships bringing home silver and other American commodities, it was the archbishop of Seville who sent three bishops to Puerto Rico, Hispaniola and Cuba. At first the bishop of Cuba also presided over a corner of what is now the United States mainland. Those who worked in the mission fields were already there, coping as best they could with foreign languages and customs and tropical diseases.

Wherever the Spanish explored or settled they were usually accompanied by Franciscans and Dominicans, driven by a sense of urgency. As the world might be about to end, the native 'Indians' must be converted to Christianity as soon as possible so that they could enjoy the prospect of eternal life. Soon the friars had permission to carry out all the normal duties of the priests: baptising infants and adults, celebrating mass, hearing confession and forgiving sins, and blessing marriages.

It was a triumph for the barefooted disciples of St Francis that as many as 1000 people were baptised at the same time. In Mexico the Franciscans claimed to have won more than one million converts by the year 1533. As only sixty or so Christian workers were busy in Mexico, their harvest was astonishing. The Dominicans and Augustinians came ashore too, and multiplied the converts. Rarely in the history of Christianity had so many been converted by so few. Not that all the converts quite understood what Christianity signified.

The ease with which Amerindians accepted Christianity delighted the friars in their long robes but puzzled many Spanish laymen. But most of the new Christians, like many medieval converts in Europe, continued to believe in their old religion as well as the new. Behind the baroque facade of such a fabulous cathedral as that commenced in Mexico City in 1573 were the old shrines of other gods. In Peru in the mid-seventeenth century, in a time of Christian diligence, official raids in a small area found 9056 idols in the possession of Peruvians; they were collected and destroyed. In various towns 'Christians' passed through the doorway of their church to worship in the special dresses of their old pagan religion. A new church about to be erected might be placed on the site of a pagan shrine, thus combining the old religion and the new. A South American woman who kept a pagan idol at home could be seen fervently fingering her Christian rosary in the street before returning home to embrace an idol of her old religion.

As in Europe, Christian priests noted that long-standing members of their congregation, eager to know whether a certain day would be lucky or unlucky for them, consulted a pagan priest from their former religion. The Mexican pagan priest was more experienced than the new Spanish priest in such matters.

Many of the new American converts were more pious than the arriving soldiers, merchants and farmers who had been baptised in their native Spain or Portugal, and whose culture had inherited hundreds of years of Christian precepts. To Brazil and the West Indies the European settlers imported slaves from West Africa, and the Spanish overseas economy and its sugar and coffee plantations depended increasingly on forced labour. Missionaries, in the name of the pope, were the only defenders of the Amerindians and their rights. Franciscans and Dominicans gave sermons against the practice of slavery. It took courage, for they must have seen anger on the faces of the slave-owners who listened to them. In 1537 Pope Paul III issued a bull, *Sublimis Deus*, against the owning of slaves. Five years later a Spanish law banned the maltreatment of labourers in 'the Indies'. It seemed that nothing could halt the slave trade.

Latin America was learning to rival Spain in the expensive art of architecture. By 1650 the little Mexican city of Puebla was a minor wonder of the western hemisphere. Standing on a fertile plateau some 2400 metres above the level of the sea, and looking upwards to three snow-tipped volcanoes, it possessed a tall cathedral that was extravagantly decorated with marble and gold and onyx, all of which were mined nearby. Except at Advent and Lent, when only the organ and bassoon were played, the worshippers heard a capable choir and orchestra, conducted usually by musicians who were themselves composers. A collection of printed ecclesiastical music was at their call, while the city itself held 5000 volumes – the largest library in the Americas. In the same city were another thirty church buildings, some of them sumptuous, a sign of rivalry between the various Spanish religious orders. In the following 150 years the Spanish were to build another 15 000 churches in what they called 'the Indies'.

Spain had one other success in religious activity – the Philippines. A cluster of 7000 islands, named after King Philip of Spain, it was supplied annually by a ship that sailed west from Mexico. In the century after the first Spanish friars landed in 1565, a chain of churches was built across many of the islands. In the following 300 years it was to be Christianity's only permanent success in that vast Asiatic area lying east of the Ural Mountains and the Persian Gulf.

Meanwhile, the dividing of the New World in 1494 into two

spheres of influence by Pope Alexander VI, formerly of Spain, had granted Brazil, Africa and Asia to the Portuguese and the Americas to Spain.

At least the pope gave the Portuguese a vital start in the first European era of overseas colonising. Their population was smaller than Spain's, and their Catholic Church was less dynamic; wisely, they enlisted churchmen from Spain.

The Portuguese explored the territory east of the Cape of Good Hope, often with the aid of pilots who knew the coastline and its trading cities, mostly dominated by Muslim merchants and vessels. In the space of fifteen years the Portuguese captured a long line of strategic harbours spanning the Indian Ocean. They built a port at Mozambique in Africa, captured Hormuz at the mouth of the Persian Gulf and Goa in western India from the Muslims, and Malacca in the Malay Peninsula – a hub of the spice trade. In the process of Portugal's expansion, the coastline of the Indian Ocean – unlike the Americas – did not acquire a long list of Christian saint names because large areas had long been mapped.

THE JESUITS SET SAIL

Ignatius de Loyola, a Spaniard of noble birth, possessed slightly auburn hair, a tanned face and a pointed chin. Wounded in the right leg while serving as a soldier in Spain in 1521, he became a dedicated Christian at about the same time that Luther and Zwingli were making a stir. Not lacking money, he sailed to Jaffa as a pilgrim, and in Jerusalem visited the holy place under the guidance of a Franciscan. He must have been the only celebrated Christian of the Reformation era who had the privilege of visiting the site of Christ's death. A mystic, he was to come to the conviction, though he did not utter it, that Jerusalem was not of ultimate importance because God was everywhere. He advised the young to look for God wherever they were, not only when they were in church but 'in all they see, taste and hear, in all their actions, since His Divine Majesty is truly in all things by his presence, power and essence'.

In his thirties Loyola began another life as a Christian scholar, studying for three years at universities in his native Spain and then for seven years at the University of Paris, where he gathered a circle of like-minded young men who made a vow to be chaste and poor so long as they lived, and to make a pilgrimage to Jerusalem if possible. They went to Italy, hoping to be pilgrims, but warfare blocked the sea route from Venice to Palestine.

Their little Society of Jesus, formed in Paris in 1534, was blessed by the pope six years later. Loyola, elected for life as their leader or 'general', was a superb organiser and his tiny office in Rome became the world hub for his Jesuit priests. Within fifteen years his men were in such scattered outposts as Brazil, India, Ethiopia and the Congo, where fortunately the emperor was a Christian.

The Jesuit assigned to India was Francis Xavier, who was a northern Spaniard – indeed, he was a Basque. From Italy he went to Lisbon, where he commenced the voyage to India. There Xavier displayed charm, empathy and an ability to communicate even in a language that he was just learning.

Beginning his Christian crusade in 1542 amongst the pearl-fishing people on the Indian coast, he moved here and there, meeting those Moluccans who were called headhunters. A turning point in his life was a meeting in the Malay port of Malacca with a Japanese named Anjiro, who decided to be baptised as a Christian. In 1549 they sailed together in a Portuguese merchant ship to Kagoshima, almost the most southerly port in Japan.

Xavier learned the language. Within two years his teaching had won perhaps 2000 Christian followers, and they in turn won more; years after his departure the tally reached 150 000: a warning bell to those Japanese who rejoiced in their traditional culture. It was realised that the converts' loyalty to Christ lowered their loyalty to their god-emperor in Japan. The Japanese Christians ceased to be tolerated. In the 1630s Christianity was totally banned in Japan, and so strong was the demand for cultural seclusion that Japanese individuals, even sailors, were forbidden to travel abroad. Xavier's legacy was almost wiped out, except in Nagasaki, where it survived perilously.

Francis Xavier did not again see his homeland. He died in 1552, while visiting the island of Sancian near China, and his remains were taken to Goa, where today their presence in the cathedral attracts numerous worshippers. He is said by admirers to have converted 700 000 Asians in all, but the real number, though probably smaller, gave inspiration to Catholics in Europe.

The port of Macao in southern China became another Catholic base, with its own bishop answerable to Goa. Northern China was even more important. Finally, a few Jesuits reached Beijing, where Matteo Ricci, an Italian, had success by mixing Christianity with Chinese ancestor-worship. The Chinese emperor smiled on the Jesuits, for they were skilled in mathematics and astrology. Of the new religion, however, Confucian scholars were suspicious. They wondered whether the Christian emphasis on heaven was not quite ethical and indeed an 'ignoble' form of self-interest.

In Europe the Jesuits, hearing of the exploits of their colleagues in faraway Asia, were entitled to feel proud. The achievements of Francis Xavier were noble and his journeys were remarkable, but in his first months in Asia he had possibly gained a little by following in the footsteps of others.

Long before the Portuguese reached the west coast of India, Christians and Jews had been living there. In this Malabar Coast, with its chains of sand dunes alongside densely settled farmlands, Christian Churches could be seen. The priests – they were married – vowed that the apostle Thomas, nearly 1500 years ago, had landed on their coast and spread the story of the resurrection of his friend, Jesus Christ. It is almost certain that Christians had been living near Cochin and Goa since at least AD 500, and they still conducted their Christian liturgy in the Semitic language known as Eastern Syriac.

Others would argue that the Jesuits gained little from the fact that other Christians had preceded them in Asia. Earlier Christians had proved how difficult it was to succeed, whether in India or China. The story of John of Montecorvino, an Italian Franciscan, is revealing. He set out for India in 1291, met the Christians who said they owed their religion to St Thomas, and then travelled to northern China. Welcomed by the Mongol rulers in Beijing, the new capital city of China, he set to work to build a small cathedral inside the city with its earthen walls. Later he added a tower from which the ringing of three large bells invited the Chinese to worship in the company of a choir of Chinese boys singing the psalms. By translating the New Testament he won at least a few thousand converts.

It was the happiest of days when, out of the blue, a German Franciscan arrived from Cologne: the first fellow European Christian John had met for more than a decade. Moreover, he learned the good news that an elderly Italian, John of Tolentino, who had served the Christian king of Armenia, was leading a small party of clergy towards Beijing. They did not arrive; later it was learned that they had been killed by Muslims on the way. The church in Beijing faded away, and no Christian was present to welcome the Jesuits on their arrival several centuries later.

ATLANTIC PILGRIMS

On the Atlantic coast of North America most of the early European visitors were explorers, fishermen, fur traders, merchants and would-be landholders. In 1620 fewer than 1000 people lived in the first British colony, Virginia, when it began to export tobacco grown by black indentured servants and black slaves. Soon Europeans settled the fringes of the region stretching from Long Island to Massachusetts Bay. One influential group came primarily for religious freedom. Arriving in the small square-rigged sailing ship *Mayflower*, they went ashore at Cape Cod in November 1620. Some passengers were French and English religious refugees who had been living in Leiden, Holland, and others were puritanical or far-from-puritanical English emigrants.

They were followed by shiploads of other migrants, sometimes entire congregations complete with pastors, who settled in a variety of coastal regions, set up their own church-dominated government, built their own houses and fenced their own farms. These little towns tended to be split by grave religious disputes, after which the losers moved out to found new towns, some crossing to the Connecticut Valley.

By 1660 maybe 30000 Protestants – mainly Congregationalists or other kinds of Calvinists – had settled in the vast areas known as New England. Far to the south, Maryland was initially favoured by Catholics, New Amsterdam (now the city of New York) was the home mainly of Dutch and French Protestants, and Virginia of the Anglicans. These colonies, extending far along the Atlantic coast, attracted the first large group of Protestant missionaries to be seen in the whole of the New World, whether in the Americas or Asia, and by the 1670s a small crowd of Amerindians were being taught the principles of Christianity and agriculture in fourteen separate farm-settlements in east Massachusetts. Europeans and the native Indian tribes sometimes shook hands and rubbed noses, but sometimes fought, with heavy casualties.

THE URSULINES REACH CANADA

Men were the early missionaries across the seas. In the Catholic Church, at home and far from home, only men could conduct divine service and that most pivotal of ceremonies, the Eucharist. But surely there must also be a place for women. The Ursulines found a place. They were probably the first female missionaries to succeed conspicuously in the New World.

Named after St Ursula, who died at Cologne on the Rhine, the Ursulines began their work in the north Italian town of Brescia in 1535. Their founder, Angela Merici, at first a helper with the Franciscans, saw spiritual needs that were not being met, and decided that women could meet them. Her original Ursulines consisted of two groups: experienced widows and young virgins. The old taught the young how to teach children, run hospitals and orphanages, and care for the poor.

Effective in north Italy, they founded their first French convent in 1592 in Avignon, and in another French town they engaged in what was seen as an unfeminine activity – they virtually preached in public. Enthusiastically, they conducted a limited form of religious service and sang vespers on feast days and Sundays, and 'everyone flocked to the chapel' – until 1623, when the bishop intervened.

To the new French colony on the St Lawrence River in Canada the Jesuits beckoned them. Leading the venture was Marie Guyard, a forty-year-old married woman who, after bringing up her son in

France, had become an Ursuline nun. In 1639 she crossed the Atlantic, accompanied by nuns and nurses, and taught the daughters of French colonists together with native children entrusted to her care. Compiling a dictionary in one Amerindian language and a prayer book and catechism in another, she became a fluent spokeswoman for the Amerindians. At the inducement of French merchants the Amerindians began to trade beaver skins in return for alcohol, and often the effects were devastating. They needed protection, and Marie tried to become one of their protectors.

THE POOR HEATHEN

In Europe the thought that Jesus was unknown to hundreds of millions of foreigners had spurred an urgent desire to convert them. Meanwhile, the foreigners had to be given a common name. Sometimes they were simply called savages, which was derived from the Latin word signifying woodland or a state of nature, but the other names were 'pagan' or 'heathen', which was a Germanic word.

In the *Book of Common Prayer* a sentence in the second psalm was translated as 'Why do the heathen so furiously rage together'. The name heathen was simple and short. Nearly everyone knew what it meant – at first it meant anybody who was not a Jew, not a Christian and not a Muslim. The word had many variations. A man might be called a heathenly fellow or a heathenist and a woman might be called a heatheness, while a Christian who relapsed was seen as reverting to heathenhood or heathendom or even heathenry. Sensitive clergymen sometimes spelled the words with a capital H; the young John Wesley, when living in Savannah, was to refer to them as 'the poor Heathens'.

Reginald Heber, the first Anglican bishop of Calcutta, described a host of such people – Indians or Sri Lankans – in a well known hymn:

The savage in his blindness
Bows down to wood and stone

Later, having second thoughts, he changed the word 'savage' to 'heathen'. Naturally, Chinese and Indians had their own words for European Christians, and some were derogatory at their inception or became so with long usage.

Whether the Christian missionaries were better than the heathens can be debated. On the whole they probably were, most having been hand-picked. If hand-picked groups of heathens and savages had been sent to Holland or Poland in 1600, they too would often have been impressive. Most Christian workers in overseas lands – but far from all – showed their spirit in the lives they lived. Most showed compassion; most maintained their faith in the face of personal and natural disasters; most tried to speak the truth as they knew it. They tried to be patient more often than impatient. They usually tried to forgive their enemies. Of course there were countless exceptions.

Most Christian missionaries denounced cruelty and violence. But it was not an easy message to deliver when, in the same district, their fellow Portuguese and Spanish merchants, soldiers and officials might demonstrate the opposite set of qualities. And yet the Christian missionaries would not have survived in many regions without the military backing and worldliness of their countrymen.

Now that the west – and especially its intellectual leaders – has lost some of its sense of superiority and its confidence in its way of life, and lost some of its interest in religion, Christian missionaries have tended to fall from favour. It is widely assumed that they should have stayed at home and left the native peoples to follow their traditional life. They are now widely rebuked because they disturbed or helped to destroy a variety of cultures. Sometimes it was done willingly, sometimes thoughtlessly and sometimes reluctantly. The accusation has to be accepted. But it is easy to over-praise many of these vanquished and vanished cultures after their violence has been forgotten.

Missionaries would have lived longer if they had remained as priests and friars in Europe. Tropical disease was a common killer in the mission fields, and massacre was a prospect. They might have been physically more comfortable if they had remained in a Spanish monastery rather than travelled to the steamy tropics. Moreover, the long voyage to Central America or India, and perhaps the further journey to an inland town, was likely to be a permanent parting from friends, family and native land.

23

A REFORMATION UNTANGLED

How can we sum up the century and a half of religious turbulence that marked the rise of the Protestants? How can we pluck conclusions from countless armed and unarmed disputes, from the printing of a deluge of fiery pamphlets, the burning of rebels and the sanctifying of others, and the overturning of the daily religious life of millions of people, many of whom silently resented the changes they were forced to accept?

The gap between our era and theirs, between the respective attitudes to life and death, is now wide. Death was of intense interest to people at that time. It came when they were younger and it came quickly or suddenly, usually with pain; and mentally, they were more prepared for it. We have trouble understanding their absorption in death and their interest in religion, just as they would be puzzled by our fascination with material affairs such as money, and even with foreign travel when no real pilgrimage was in mind.

At the same time they combined a deep interest in religion with an easygoing attitude to some of the stricter religious rules. For example, they swore and blasphemed. Blasphemy was the habit of speaking about God, Christ or the saints in a lighthearted or even disrespectful way. Moses had demanded that we do not 'take the name of the Lord thy God in vain'. The ancient Hebrews banned swearing because the person who swore was showing public contempt for God or was trivialising sacred themes.

Christians adopted the same precept but not wholeheartedly. Indeed, in AD 818, in the present Germany, the Council of Aachen restored the death penalty for serious blasphemy, but when Geoffrey Chaucer wrote his story of a band of English pilgrims, his *Canterbury Tales*, he described clergymen swearing aloud, and other pilgrims casually employing such phrases as 'Sweet Mother of Christ, be quiet!' Some swear words were disguised, but nearly everyone knew what they meant. Thus, 'sblood' meant God's blood, and the word 'bloody' was a variation on the same phrase. The oath 'zounds' meant to swear by Christ's wounds.

The typical person knew that swear words had a lubricating or soothing effect. Whether they swore often or occasionally can no longer be known. But in this time of religious puritanism, Queen Elizabeth I and King James I, who were successively the formal heads of the Church of England, swore heavily, as did William Shakespeare, the playwright – until a ban was placed on blasphemy in London's playhouses. In essence it was a mottled Reformation.

A FEW SPROUTS OF DEMOCRACY

The Reformation sowed some of the seeds of modern democracy, without an awareness of how and when those seeds would sprout. Whereas the Catholic tradition was based on hierarchy – on the authority of popes, cardinals and bishops – the Protestant emphasis was on reading the Bible and on the individual's personal relationship with God. All baptised Christians of a certain age could be their own priest, and they needed no middleman in the form of a priest or bishop in order to approach God.

Luther called this 'the priesthood of all believers', and its democratic spirit coloured, at least to a light shade, most of the Protestant sects that came after him. Moreover, various isolated Calvinist, Lutheran, Baptist, Unitarian, Presbyterian and other congregations ran their own churches and selected their own clergymen, especially when they were living in exile in London, Geneva, Amsterdam, Frankfurt or other foreign cities. This form of organisation depended on small governing committees composed of leading members of the church and the clergyman himself.

Protestantism, once the Bible was freely available in a homeland language, tended to foster that debate and discussion, which are the core of democracy. After all, the Bible was a cluster of books open to many interpretations. Worshippers, often in a humble way, debated theological questions privately among themselves and sometimes came to their own conclusions. In the words of one discerning theologian, Protestantism tended quietly to promote democracy because it rested on the belief that 'unspecialised folk can grasp great thinking'.

Those experiments in decision-making and self-government within the churches, though practised rarely in some Protestant parts of Europe, were to have startling effects in the long term, especially in the United States. In their slow-moving potential they were as democratic as almost any event or institution experienced in Europe since the reign of the ancient Greek city-states.

The Reformation discouraged Latin, which was the international language of that day, and fostered a glorious era for English, German and several other national languages. In that sense the Protestants promoted nationalism, just as nationalism itself had tended to promoted Protestantism. The religious changes also fostered education. Luther, Zwingli and Calvin – each was the product of a university – believed that everyone should learn to read, and the one book they had to read was the Bible. In 1530, Luther observed the long-needed advance in education in his own Saxony. 'I am deeply moved', he wrote when he realised that so many Germans were learning to read the Bible.

To compete with Lutherans, Calvinists and other breakaway churches, the Catholics here and there began to promote education more vigorously. More than any one Protestant group, the Jesuits fostered education and often succeeded. In the following three centuries perhaps no Catholic country attained the level of literacy of Scotland, Holland, Prussia and a few other Protestant countries. The arrival of popular democracy in the second half of the nineteenth century depended on the spread of literacy.

Finally, the Reformation fostered an appeal to history. Many of the arguments could be solved only by a study of the early Christians and their beliefs and way of life. Even difficult questions – in what language Jesus spoke to his disciples, for example – became matters of great concern and at first yielded strange answers. In the seventeenth century, a Jesuit in Vienna, Melchior Inchofer, argued that Jesus must have spoken Latin. In the twentieth century, Inchofer's argument was paraphrased by a notable biblical scholar with a sly smile: 'The Lord cannot have used any other language upon earth, since this is the language of the saints in heaven.'

WOMEN AND MEN: WHO WERE THE LOSERS?

Did women gain from the first phase of the Reformation? Initially they did not. In medieval Europe, the Virgin Mary had become central to Christian faith and symbolism, and in biblical paintings on the walls and in the brightly coloured windows of medieval churches she was seen as breathing a quiet spiritual authority in a very human way. Convents and nunneries had flourished in Catholic countries, and women presided over them. Likewise, Catholicism revered saints, of whom many were women. In medieval Christianity certain celibate women had been ranked highly; now their status was lowered in the Protestant regions of Europe. There the daily work, if well done, was praised as a vocation almost as noble as the priesthood. Luther thought that a woman who raised her children and taught them Christian ways was more deserving of praise than one who left home to go on a pilgrimage.

In one notorious activity during the Reformation women were especially singled out. They were more likely than men to be denounced as witches. Three in four of those who were sentenced to death as witches were women, and in charges brought against them other women had a part. The accusations of witchcraft often arose from domestic quarrels and disputes and were spurred by religious differences: indeed, witches seemed to be more numerous in places of religious conflict.

Long before the Reformation arrived, witches had occasionally been tried and convicted, but between 1580 and 1640 the search for them sometimes became a frenzy. Witches were said to fall under the influence of Satan, to take part in his clever warfare against individual Christians and thereby divert their attention from the Second Coming of Christ. After trials in religious or secular courts, about 40 000 or 50 000 witches were executed.

The present Germany was the home of about one in every three Europeans convicted of witchcraft, but there the Lutherans were less likely than Calvinists to lead the hunt. Of the Catholic lands,

Spain, Ireland and southern Italy rarely tried witches, but eastern France and Switzerland were troubled by them. The authorities in the Calvinist Netherlands were at first hostile to witches, but after 1590 they rarely persecuted them. The infectious fear of witches was not often found in Russia and other Orthodox countries.

WARFARE AND TOLERATION

The century and a quarter after the launching of the Reformation was a period of heightened warfare in much of Europe. The Wars of Religion is a popular and old label for that period. Religious feelings gave an intensity to many of the wars; they also discouraged the idea of compromising during the negotiations for peace. But it is unwise to think of the Reformation as the decisive and defining factor in these wars. The period of violence began with wars between Catholic monarchs, whose disputes were not about religion. In fact the Catholic kings at first were too intent on fighting their own wars to devote much energy to the suppression of the new Protestant movement at the opportune time.

This long period of intermittent warfare was also affected by new weapons. The cannon and the musket made fighting more deadly. Reigning monarchs were becoming more powerful, and they, more than the religious reformers, planned, financed and directed most of these wars. Modern students of warfare, as distinct from students of religion, do not see these wars in Europe as primarily caused by religious hostility: religion might well have been 'a cloak for other motives'. If they are still to be called the Wars of Religion, it would be appropriate to call World War II, with its atheistic background and massive casualties, 'the wars of irreligion'. The simplified labelling of great events conceals more than it enlightens.

The Reformation displayed intense religious rivalries and even hatreds amongst Christians. In the long term, however, it did more than almost any other event in the last 2000 years to soften that hatred and intolerance. The rise of religious toleration, however, was slow and unpredictable. When Protestantism was born, it demanded for its doctrines the same allegiance that Catholics demanded in the lands they governed. Religion was not a matter of choice but compulsion. In the year 1550, Calvinists demanded complete loyalty and unanimity in Geneva, for they were the rulers. Lutherans demanded it in Saxony and Sweden, and Anglicans in England. Rulers demanded social and religious unity partly because they believed it made their country more secure. It was generally agreed that a kingdom or a republic would be an easy target for its enemies if it lacked religious cohesion.

The Catholic Church, faced with the rebellion known as the Reformation, continued to demand uniformity and obedience. In 1559 it issued for the first time an *Index of Prohibited Books*. As religion spanned nearly every intellectual activity, a religious leader had no hesitation in intervening in science as well as theology. Thus, Giordano Bruno had argued that the number of physical worlds was not one but a multitude. He added to his enemies by saying that the stars had souls. As punishment for his heresies, he was burned to death in 1600. Galileo Galilei, a mathematical scholar and the inventor of the finest telescope the world had seen, publicly gave his support to the theory that the earth was not the hub of the solar system. Galileo was a Christian and his views were actually tolerated for years, though they were opposed by official Vatican doctrines. Almost certainly he would have retained his liberty but for the fact that in Rome two of his patrons sided with the Spaniards in political intrigues. In 1633, on the longest day of the year, he was compelled to kneel in Rome and seek forgiveness for his heresy. Amidst the instances of suppression were numerous episodes in which controversial theologians and scientists cautiously went about their work, undisturbed.

The simple fact, now puzzling to us, was that toleration itself was not a goal in the Christian world, nor the Islamic, Hindu, Buddhist, Chinese or Aztec and Inca worlds. A high level of religious toleration is almost a modern invention. A few centuries ago it was almost unthinkable. Then it was important to hold the correct religious views rather than hold the freedom to reject them. The right to disobey the government and the Church, the right to be free in matters of conscience, was a precept that slowly emerged after the acute tensions aroused by the Reformation. Today the western trend is to devalue the merits of religion and to enthrone the virtues of toleration. In western civilisation we view religious deviance or heresy as a minor matter because religion is no longer seen as all-important.

THE FRAGILE RIGHT TO WORSHIP IN PUBLIC

Poland, a Catholic kingdom fragmented by the Reformation, thought it saw a solution to fierce religious rivalry. By the Confederation of Warsaw in January 1573, Poland agreed to tolerate a swathe of religions. It approved not only Catholics but also Lutherans, Calvinists, Polish Unitarians, the Orthodox, and miscellaneous sects and groups, so long as they lived in peace. Soon the Jews received certain liberties, and were even permitted their own little parliament. This monumental concept of all-round toleration in Poland, then a populous kingdom, did not last.

Holland launched the boldest experiment in religious freedom. It was tolerant, if measured by the intolerant standards of the time.

Religious freedom was promised, more or less, by article 13 of the Treaty of Utrecht of 1579, and was achieved partly through a laxity in enforcing the law against minor sects and groups. The Catholics were not tolerated but they survived in considerable numbers, especially in the provinces to the east, where their priests, though sometimes fined, quietly performed their duties. Refugees from other parts of Europe travelled by sea or land to Holland. When France in 1685 destroyed all Protestant churches, its ports lost many merchants, craftsmen and clergymen, for whom Holland was their first choice as a place of refuge.

Nothing did more to give religious toleration a fair name than Holland's prosperity. It attracted persecuted religious groups as migrants, many of whom were Huguenot merchants and skilled craftsmen. Holland, less than a century after breaking free from Catholic Spain, was the most prosperous country in Europe and the home of a remarkable chain of trading posts that extended from the West Indies and New York – then called New Amsterdam – to ports as distant as Cape Town in South Africa, and Jakarta and Malacca in South-East Asia.

In Rotterdam and in Amsterdam, by now the largest Jewish city in western Europe, several synagogues flourished, many of their members having been expelled from Portugal. Many had long tried to live a double life in Portugal, clinging privately to a version of their ancient religion but also attending Christian Churches. They also had a tendency to drift away from both religions – from the one because it was forced on them, and from the other because they had long ceased to have both the guidance of a rabbi and a clear knowledge of Jewish rituals. Once in Holland many revived their faith, although a few broke away from everything that was spiritual. Uriel da Costa, after bravely writing a book praising the voice of reason and even attacking the sacred Torah, was excommunicated. He committed suicide in 1640.

Seventeen years later another of those Portuguese Jews, who were known as the Marranos, stirred up trouble. Juan da Prado, recently arrived, was a free-thinker who asked why his fellow Jews should be allowed to view themselves as God's chosen people? For his forthright sayings he too was excommunicated but not punished by the Dutch civic authorities. Baruch Spinoza, a child of Marrano parents who had settled happily into the Jewish community in Amsterdam, knew of these dramas. Only eight when the first Marrano was expelled from the synagogue, he was following the same rebellious path by the time he was twenty. A deist, he believed that God did not interfere in the running of the world. Natural laws, he explained to those who would listen, made the world go round – he had studied physics and astronomy. In protest at what was taught by the rabbis, he ceased to take his place in the synagogue on Saturdays. In counter-protest the rabbis expelled him on 27 July 1656. Five years later Spinoza wrote his rebellious *Short Treatise on God.*

He was probably the first well-known 'semi-atheist' to announce himself in a Christian land in the modern era. An unbeliever was expected to be a rebel in almost everything and wicked in all his ways, but here was a virtuous one. He lived the good life and made his living in a useful way. In The Hague he worked in one of the new scientific trades in which the Dutch excelled – grinding lenses.

It took courage to be a Spinoza or even one of his supporters. If a handful of scholars agreed with his writings, they did not say so in public. For more than a century in Europe his name was largely shunned – until a few poets and philosophers, especially in Germany, acknowledged his talents. Wilhelm Goethe, soon to be the most celebrated literary man and all-round scholar in Europe, was an open admirer of Spinoza.

At the very time when Spinoza was about to be expelled from his synagogue, a rabbi in the same city was expressing his views. Israel ben Menasseh, born in Lisbon in 1604, was a mere teenager when he accepted a senior office in an Amsterdam synagogue called Neveh Shalom. The speaker of several languages, he was intellectually so quick and so personable that in Amsterdam even Christians eagerly listened to him on the wide range of topics open to such a polymath.

Menasseh hoped that England might welcome back Jews, for they had long been excluded. Visiting London in a deputation with other influential Dutch Jews in 1655, he persuasively pleaded with Oliver Cromwell, now the ruler of the new republic, to permit them to open synagogues, their own cemetery and merchant houses too. They promised in return to be loyal and useful citizens and – a slightly ambiguous promise – to proclaim 'the Great and Glorious Name of the Lord'.

Cromwell shared that widespread Christian desire to convert the Jews. If Christ's Second Coming was in sight, the Christians had to act quickly. Practical in economic matters, Cromwell realised that a strong economy was essential and that an inflow of heretics could strengthen it. To lose skilled people, even to Britain's own colonies in North America, was a financial loss to the motherland. In January 1655 he publicly regretted that 'many of our brethren forsook their native countries to seek their bread from strangers, and to live in howling wildernesses'. To bring back such citizens from North America, or entice Jews from Holland, which was now a colonial competitor, could be beneficial.

So Jews were permitted to live in London and at least one English colony, Surinam, in tropical America. It was an unusual concession from a leader who was wary of allowing freedom of conscience to Catholics living just across the sea in Ireland. Even at home Cromwell persecuted Unitarians because – like Jews – they did not believe in the divinity of Christ.

Governments were not always consistent in expelling heretics. A person of influence known to hold heretical views was usually ignored so long as he did not parade those views. William Byrd, an English composer, continued to produce his sacred music for Catholic patrons in England. Lord Baltimore, a convert to Catholicism, wished to set up a haven for Catholics as well as Protestants on the shores of Chesapeake Bay, and his request had been granted by Cromwell's predecessor as ruler, King Charles I. Maryland was named not after the Blessed Virgin Mary but the wife of Charles I. In 1634 the first British settlers landed, and fifteen years later a local law gave freedom to all Christian denominations, though not formally to the Jews. For a short time Maryland and Rhode Island were possibly the most tolerant places in the English-speaking world.

Prussia, small in area but powerful in its fighting forces, was one of the few other beacons of tolerance: perhaps we should call it half-tolerance. The royal family of Prussia was Calvinist, though most of its citizens were Lutheran, and it welcomed the 20 000 refugees arriving from France in the three decades preceding the year 1700. The hope was that the two Protestant sects would live in harmony. The king's toleration, however, was not extended to the pulpit, where the rival pastors were instructed not to fire theological arrows at each other. Not many Catholics lived in Prussia, which solved some of his problems.

Poland, Holland, Maryland, England and Prussia, and perhaps one or two others, did not seem to be very tolerant by modern standards, nor was France's two-religions policy, created in 1585. But those countries began, in fits and starts, to create those higher standards by which their era is now judged unfavourably. So far as we can see, the founders of the Reformation had no firm intention of sponsoring a new era of religious toleration, but that was the foundation stone they tentatively or accidentally laid.

PART FOUR

24

PILGRIM BUNYAN AND QUAKER FOX

The Reformation produced powerful sects. Some rose quickly in a European city or province. Others rose and then seemed to be waning, but their influence soared after crossing the Atlantic to North America.

The splintering sects known as Baptists, looked down upon by most rulers in Europe, eventually produced powerful leaders in the United States. Abraham Lincoln, the most famous of American presidents in the last two centuries, had belonged to a Baptist sect during a childhood spent amongst struggling farmers. Two recent presidents – Jimmy Carter and Bill Clinton – were active members of Baptist churches.

WHO SHOULD BE BAPTISED?

In Europe the early Baptists were known usually as Anabaptists, a name that savoured of anarchy but really denoted people who were rebaptised. The early Anabaptists ran swiftly ahead of the mainstream reformers. At Wittenberg they insisted that Luther did not go far enough in reforming religion. In Moravia one believed in common ownership of property, and in far western Germany another believed in polygamy. At Zurich they lamented that Zwingli, who in the opinion of Catholics appeared to be a most revolutionary priest, merely dipped his toes in the radical waters instead of swimming naked against the current. The Anabaptists believed that they were the only reformers who were really returning to Christianity as it was in the years of St Paul. For them baptism was the central ceremony, and of such significance that it was wasted on infants.

Baptists revived a debate that had risen and fallen for more than 1000 years. In nearly every such debate the urgent questions were alike: who should be baptised or initiated into the Christian Church, what the appropriate age for baptism was, where the ceremony should be conducted, and whether a bishop or priest or even a layman should preside. For centuries the Catholics had baptised infants, but they had also baptised converts who might be twenty years or even seventy years old. But after the Christian Church grew dominant throughout Europe, and virtually everyone was nominally a Catholic from the day of birth, the baptising of infants rather than adults became almost universal. The act of baptising, performed by bishop or priest, usually consisted of pouring or sprinkling water over the head of the infant held in his arms. Almost everyone standing around the baptismal font was moved by the solemn words proclaiming that the baby was thereby baptised 'in the name of the Father, Son and Holy Spirit, Amen'. If the baby was only a few days old and almost certainly about to die, the ceremony was poignant to many witnesses.

The importance of the ceremony was clear to Catholics. If a baby was not baptised, its soul went straight to purgatory or limbo, where it remained; no longer is limbo a part of the Catholic faith. If the baby was baptised, it was thereby made free from original and inherited sin. If it died soon after the baptism, it went straight to heaven.

To the Anabaptists of the sixteenth century, this old Catholic sacrament of baptism was misplaced. Baptism was too important to be administered in this way. Babies and infants were incapable of understanding it, and even a fifteen-year-old was too young. The ceremony and sacrament therefore should be confined to adults, who could publicly affirm that they themselves had genuine faith. Adults also understood the serious sacrifices that would be demanded of them if they dedicated the rest of their life to Christ.

To be a real Christian, one had to be born again, and baptism was the ceremony confirming that rebirth. Baptism was a sacred pledge, so the Anabaptists insisted. Adults who had been baptised as babies now had to be baptised again, if they were worthy. On the other hand, Luther, Zwingli and Calvin held to the orthodox Catholic ideas on baptism. All infants should be baptised. If they died when very young it was a relief to their parents to know that, through the act of baptism, their souls had been saved and that they were regular members of Christ's flock.

In 1525, on the advice of Zwingli, the civic leaders of Zurich insisted that all children should be baptised, preferably as early as possible. Parents who disobeyed were to be expelled from the republic. Most Anabaptists did not bow to such threats. In their ranks were former priests and monks who, having made the brave decision to break with Rome, were willing to make other brave decisions. They wished to be baptised again, arguing that their baptism as infants was meaningless. So a wave of adult baptisms took place in the shallow lakes and streams in the lowlands of Switzerland, an

Anabaptist pastor officiating. Sometimes the person was immersed totally; sometimes only the head was sprinkled.

For Zwingli it was hard enough to win the first round of the Reformation and convince the civic leaders and former priests and monks and nuns that the theology he preached was soundly based. The reformation in Zurich and the nearby hills and valleys would be endangered if he surrendered to extremists. So he and his followers retaliated. They threatened death to those Anabaptists who continued to preach and baptise. In January 1527 Zwingli approved of the tribunal that tried a leading Anabaptist. Felix Manz, a former Catholic priest who had been one of Zwingli's earliest supporters, was condemned to death. To carry out the penalty a wooden hurdle – the kind used to erect a makeshift pen for sheep and goats – was fetched from a farm. Manz, his arms and legs tied to the hurdle, was thrown into the ice-cold river. His death was certain.

Anabaptists were seen as a danger to the whole Reformation. Many middle-roaders would have preferred the pope than these wild reformers, bursting with religious fervour, and arguing with each other as well as everyone else. In some cities the Anabaptist leaders were sentenced to long terms in prison, or whipped, or executed. Many evaded capture and arrived at Augsburg, Strasbourg and other safe towns and spread their word. Moravia was another favourite place of retreat, for the seed of dissent had been sown there by John Hus in the previous century.

We tend to define each religious sect according to its specific beliefs but the sheer intensity of belief was another defining character. Some were distinguished by their willingness to die rather than abandon just one of their beliefs. Their fervour increased the prospect that they would splinter into small groups rather than sacrifice a point of principle. Not one minor principle could be sacrificed. They had to be true to the Christ they believed in.

One group of Anabaptists was prominent in the peasants' revolution in south Germany as early as 1525. Another group came under the leadership of Menno Simons, who had originally trained as a Franciscan priest. Named after him, the Mennonites survived persecution and became numerous in the Netherlands. The young painter Rembrandt was a member and employed his knowledge of the Bible in many sketches and paintings. From those Mennonites who emigrated to North America, the exclusive Amish sect was formed. From Mennonites who settled as farmers on the River Vistula near the Baltic coast were descended members of their sect who farmed in Russia until repressed by the Soviet Union.

English Protestants, seeking refuge in Holland, had come under the influence of the Mennonites. When they returned to England as moderates they adopted some of the Anabaptist ideas. They also demanded the right to control their own churches, electing a committee of elders free from government interference. Probably the first London church that was definitely Baptist met in Newgate Street in the city in 1612.

The Baptists in England split over the question of whether salvation was available to everyone or to just a few. While many Baptists believed in the hope of universal salvation, one congregation, formed in the 1630s in Southwark, insisted that only a few were predestined to be saved. Called Particular or Calvinistic Baptists, they formed a separate organisation because their beliefs stood on the opposite sides of what to them was a wide and uncrossable river. The two sects did not merge, under the name of the Baptist Union of Great Britain and Ireland, until 1891, two and a half centuries after they had split.

BUNYAN: A PILGRIM AND A TINKER

John Bunyan's family were tinkers in the English Midlands, members of a craft that used the heat of a brazier to repair or make metallic utensils. In the mid-1640s, as a teenager, Bunyan became a soldier in the English civil war, fighting on Oliver Cromwell's side, though he spent few days in the actual fighting. In an era when Christianity was discussed intensely by all kinds of people, Bunyan experienced long periods of spiritual fear and doubt, but his first wife – her name is not known – was reassuring. We know that his oldest child, Mary, who was blind, experienced infant baptism in 1650. His own views on baptism were to change.

Bunyan's complexion was ruddy, and that colour was deepened by a touch of red in his hair. His wavy locks curled around his ears, and his eyes were sympathetic and even pleading. An easy mixer, he was walking along a street in Bedford when he came across 'three or four poor women sitting at a door'. Caught by the sunlight, they were speaking to one another about the way God had recently 'visited their souls'. Bunyan learned that they were members of a Baptist-like congregation, which he eventually joined, being baptised by immersion. Becoming a preacher and speaking in houses, barns and simple meeting rooms, he persuaded many to change their way of thinking and feeling.

When Charles II became king of England in 1660, the Baptists and other sects fell from favour. Their preachers and informal services were often declared illegal, but Bunyan went on preaching. Refusing to be silenced, he was sent to prison for a long term. Occasionally permitted to leave prison and see his family, he seized those opportunities to preach to others, thus endangering his own freedom. His fortunes changed in 1672, when Dissenters were licensed to preach, and he was elected as the minister of the Bedford separatist church.

His most celebrated book was written partly during his time in prison. He called it *The Pilgrim's Progress*, though he must have realised that a pilgrimage was a relic of Catholicism and that 'pilgrim' was therefore a questionable word. The book's full title was more revealing: *The Pilgrim's Progress from this World to That Which Is to Come*. Bunyan began the book with a dream. He imagined that he saw a man 'clothed with rags', turning his back on his own home and setting out with a book in his hand and 'a great burden upon his back'. The man opened the book, obviously the Bible, and 'wept and trembled', and called aloud, 'What shall I do?' The trembling man really was asking, 'What shall I do to be saved?'

Many of the episodes describing the troubled man's long pilgrimage caught the imagination of readers and were to become part of everyday English speech. Here lay in wait a cruel and burly fellow, the Giant Despair, who lived in Doubting Castle. Here was an outwardly charming witch, Madam Bubble, 'a tall, comely dame, somewhat of a swarthy complexion', who announced to pilgrims she met, 'I am the mistress of the world, and men are made happy by me.' Much admired by readers were Great-heart, Mr Valiant-for-Truth and the pilgrims named Hopeful, Standfast and Christian. On the long pilgrims' way lay such landmarks as the Delectable Mountains, Vanity Fair, the Valley of Humiliation, and muddy ground called the Slough of Despond, into which the pilgrim could sink in body or spirit. Readers were stirred when the pilgrimage seemed to be almost over, but dismayed to find a wide river blocking the pilgrims' final approach to the Celestial City. In the end the leading pilgrim, having deep religious faith, safely crossed the river: 'So he passed over, and all the trumpets sounded for him on the other side.' Several million English people, both adults and children, could recite that sentence by heart.

The Pilgrim's Progress appeared in bookshops in two parts, the first in 1678. It was translated into Dutch and then into French, but its main market was amongst the Dissenters in Britain and the United States, where demand for it was so persistent that local printers supplied a small avalanche of new copies. Adults read Bunyan's work to their children, who, when they grew up, read it to theirs.

John Bunyan's prose had vitality, the common touch and echoes of the King James Bible, which had first been published during the lifetime of Bunyan's father. But serious critics were inclined to dismiss the book. The rumour spread that in the printing works an editor had been forced to correct Bunyan's spelling and grammar. Wealthier readers were put off by the cheap paper on which it was usually printed. Even evangelical readers felt uneasy because *The Pilgrim's Progress*, while based heavily on the Bible, was largely a work of the imagination: all the imaginative arts were looked on with suspicion by Puritans. Curiously, Bunyan's chief pilgrim, a working man named Christian, was a foretaste of Harry Potter, conceived three centuries later.

For a century or so it was a favourite of ordinary readers but not of the literary critics. The wheels of fashion began to turn in its favour when Dr Samuel Johnson, an Anglican and esteemed as a man of letters, gave it high praise. Late in the eighteenth century the arrival of the Romantic movement, which enthroned simple and earthy people, thereby exalted Bunyan. Sir Walter Scott, when he was the most renowned novelist in Europe, vowed that *The Pilgrim's Progress* was his delight when as a Scottish boy he had to fill in puritanical Sunday afternoons. That Bunyan was a genius or close to one was an opinion shared by writers as diverse as Wordsworth, Keats, Coleridge, Dickens and Thackeray of England, and Ralph Waldo Emerson of New England. Once revered for his spiritual message, Bunyan was now admired for his artistic flair.

In his last years Bunyan was invited to give sermons in London. Word of mouth would announce that on a certain day he was coming, and audiences would gather long before the doors of the building were opened. His friend John Doe recalled him setting out to preach at 'seven o'clock on a working day in the dark winter time', and about 1200 people waiting there to hear him. One Sunday about 3000 people crammed into a big London building, and were unable to create even a tiny pathway along which Bunyan could move from the front door to the high pulpit. He had to be lifted up and carried above the heads and shoulders of the crowd. Many of the people who heard him speak felt an inner peace take hold of them.

In 1688, while riding through the driving rain on an act of mercy, Bunyan caught cold and was soon dead. In the following year an era of increased religious toleration dawned in England. He had done much to bring forward that era, though his rivals, the Quakers, had been even more forward.

THE QUAKERS

The 'Quakers', for such was their nickname, were seen as stormbirds not only by Bunyan but by most English churchgoers. They flew over England in a disorderly formation, making loud cries, and the popular wish was that they would not land in one's own village. In a remarkable turnaround they were to become the apostles of silence.

Their founder, George Fox, was an apprentice to a shoemaker at the time when the English civil war began. The Church of England did not satisfy him, nor was he attracted to any of the Christian sects that flourished. After long struggles and much listening and arguing, he saw the light and began preaching outdoors, where he attracted converts. In 1649 he was first sent to prison for interrupting a sermon in a church: he was never afraid to disagree in a loud voice. Again and again he appeared in churches, usually listened to the sermon and then gave his own. If the preacher aroused him he constantly interrupted. When people hit him with sticks or hustled him out of the church he did not retaliate.

He had many religious experiences, which he recorded simply: 'One day when I had been walking solitarily abroad, and was come home, I was taken up in the love of God, so that I could not but admire the greatness of His love.' And another day: 'as I was sitting by the fire, a great cloud came over me, and a temptation beset me; but I sate still.' After a time he felt full of hope and heard a voice within him saying, 'There is a living God who made all things'. In his journal he recorded that the cloud vanished and the temptation too: 'my heart was glad, and I praised the living God.' He did not know that his mystical experiences belonged to a wide and old Catholic tradition, of which Bernard of Clairvaux, Catherine of Genoa, Teresa of Avila and many others were exponents.

After gathering more converts, Fox decided to give them a name, The Friends of Truth. Later they were simply called Friends and, much later, the Society of Friends. To the public they were known as Quakers.

The first of the 'Quaker' preachers in London, Oxford and Cambridge were women. Mrs Margaret Fell of Swarthmore Hall in Lancashire became an early supporter and organiser, and in 1669, long after she became a widow, she agreed to marry Fox, who was ten years younger. By then he was dignified and courteous, spoke in an arresting way, and could write a compelling pamphlet in favour of his version of Christianity. He often wrote in the middle of the night for he needed little sleep. A biggish man, his most conspicuous feature was his long, straight hair, which fell in rats' tails.

If an imaginative doctor of theology had set out to devise doctrines that were outrageous in the eyes of his fellow countrymen, he could not have outshone George Fox. The annual calendar he emphatically disliked, pointing out that January was named after a Roman idol and Wednesday was called after Woden, who was a heathen god. Fox did not think a magistrate deserved respect: he refused to take off his hat in the presence of high officials or aristocrats. He did not believe in celebrating Christmas: every day was Christ's birthday. He did not believe in Holy Communion: the Lord's supper should be celebrated at every meal.

Warfare was opposed by him and his band of followers in a century when war was widely seen as necessary – how else could England drive out Spanish or Dutch invaders and guard its own sea lanes? While many of their views – especially their pacifism – are more fashionable today, they were not fashionable then. In the words of a famous nineteenth-century historian, Thomas Macaulay, the Quakers in in their early years 'were popularly regarded as the most despicable of fanatics'. The word 'fanatic' was a vogue word of the 1650s. Those who knew their Latin realised that the English word was derived from *fanum*, a temple. Fanatics were people turned by their religion into a frenzy of enthusiasm.

Fox read the Bible closely but also had no hesitation in arguing with it. If his own inner light outshone several verses in Matthew's gospel, his inner light won. He sent out his travelling preachers in pairs, and soon thirty pairs were at work in England; but eventually he saw little need for clergymen, because every man and woman, once they had dedicated their lives to Christ, could serve as their own pastor.

Fox had little time for the rules that nearly every other Christian sect saw as indispensable. He thought a church should be simple and unadorned – not an architectural affirmation of the importance of Christ. He preferred to call his own church a 'meeting house', while rival churches were labelled as 'steeple houses'. In the meeting house a set program of hymns and prayers and a sermon was not needed. The spirit of worship was everything, and silence would foster that spirit. In the silence, God would fill each of them with his spirit, or his 'Inner Light'. The spirit of God was everywhere, waiting to be found. Quakers believed, unlike the Calvinists, that everybody with willpower and humility was capable of breathing that spirit.

After the monarchy replaced the short-lived republic in England in 1660, the Quakers and other Puritans were persecuted. A punitive law of 1663 even banned private religious meetings if they did not conform to the practices and liturgy of the Church of England, and if more than four adult visitors, not being members of the household, were present. Quakers had not the least intention of obeying such a law. They met openly and were arrested. Since they sometimes met publicly in complete silence, it was not always clear to a jury whether they had actually been conducting a religious service. Nevertheless, many were imprisoned, at which time their children regularly conducted the Quaker religious services in their meeting houses: being sixteen years of age or younger they were exempt from the law. In London at times the big jail at Newgate was almost full of Quakers. In all, 450 died in English prisons before the Toleration Act of 1689 was passed.

Their triumphant spirit, their visible joy, was secretly admired by many Christians, and their courage became legendary. When they visited or migrated to several North American colonies in the 1650s and utterly offended other Puritans with their teachings, they were not deterred by a public flogging or the threat of execution. On Boston Common in 1659 and 1660, four Quakers were hanged. The neighbouring colony of Rhode Island, however, was kinder, even exempting the Quaker men from compulsory military service.

In 1667 the Quakers found a prize recruit. William Penn, the owner of large rural estates on both sides of the Irish Sea, was in his early twenties when he decided to join the society. A genuine believer, he spent most of his spare time publicly promoting the Quakers' message and went to prison rather than restrain his tongue. Here was the son of an admiral, well known for fighting battles at sea, actually rejecting warfare.

The young Penn was not the typical Quaker. Living in style, he and his wife and daughter were driven in a fine horse-drawn carriage. They were far removed from the traditional Quakers in their old-fashioned clothes, and enjoyed access to high places. In 1681 William Penn, partly because of his father's connections, received from King Charles II the right to set up a colony in North America.

Situated well to the south of New York harbour, the new colony was called Pennsylvania in honour of Penn's father. Its main town – on the shores of a freshwater bay – Penn christened Philadelphia, a name signifying brotherly love and rich in biblical associations. The ancient Philadelphia, situated in what is now Turkey, was the site of an important early Christian Church, named in the Book of Revelations as one of the 'Seven Churches of Asia'.

Penn's Pennsylvania was designed to be a permanent home for Quakers and other persecuted sects. Offering that unusual privilege, freedom of religion, it promised to give almost every male citizen a share in the government. Not militarily inclined, Penn hoped to foster harmony with the native Amerindians. Another advantage for Penn was that he could sell his own entitlements to land and so reduce his personal debts, which were very large.

In August 1682, Penn set out on the long voyage to his Quaker paradise. By the end of the year, twenty-three shiploads of colonists arrived, and were buying land and planning their meeting houses and chapels, for German and Swedish Lutherans were also present. Soon the Quakers were outnumbered. Called by Penn a 'holy experiment', Pennsylvania retained its spirit of experiment. It was a leader, nearly a century later, in the movement to set up the United States of America.

The Quakers in the United States and Britain, though relatively few, were to lead the movement against the slave trade and against slavery itself, even though many American Quakers at one time had owned slaves. The Quakers were to initiate the movement for reforming every prison, the squalor of which, in their rebellious years, they had personally experienced. They were to lead a crusade for the abolition of the death penalty. They tried to abolish war between nations. In proportion to numbers, they were to be the most influential of all Protestant sects and groups.

25

TWO OPEN-AIR VOICES: WESLEY AND WHITEFIELD

In England in 1740 the Dissenters or Puritans – so powerful a century previously – were in slight decline. They still possessed their strongholds but held the loyalty of barely one in twenty of the English. They were stronger in town than in countryside, and more visible amongst shopkeepers and tradesmen than amongst the very poor. Anglicans presided over the life of the nation, holding all the important offices, dominating the nobility, supreme in the universities, in the courts, and in the navy and army. Except in Scotland, they were the established church, their activities financed by the public purse, and their clergy present in nearly every village in England and Wales and many in Ireland.

It was John Wesley who shook the Anglicans. He was born in Lincolnshire, where his bookish father, Samuel, a rural clergyman, wrote a history of the Old and New Testaments in prose, and a life of Christ in verse. His mother, Susanna, was a strong-willed Christian. Giving birth to nineteen children, of whom John was the fifteenth, she firmly shaped their beliefs.

As a very young man, John Wesley was not discernibly ambitious. His diaries, in shorthand or cipher, mention horse-riding, swimming, dancing, cards and shooting: he liked to carry a gun and hunt birds in the marshy country called The Fens. Becoming an Anglican clergyman in 1725, he spent two years helping his father before returning to Oxford University as a fellow of Lincoln College and a teacher of classical Greek. There he joined a cell of like-minded men, of whom his younger brother Charles was a leader. These young men met for prayers and serious discussions on most evenings. On Wednesday and Friday they ate very little food. On Sundays they preached in village churches, if invited. Known as the Holy Club, they were given the nickname of Methodists, their approach to life being so serious and methodical.

AT A QUARTER TO NINE

In 1735 John and his brother Charles felt a call to migrate to Georgia, the last British colony to be founded in North America. It was designed to be a moral colony, and it prohibited slavery and banned the trade in rum. Charles went as secretary to the young governor, Colonel James Oglethorpe, and John went as a pastor and as missionary to the local Amerindians. In the course of their slow voyage they met a party of young German Christians. In German-speaking lands the zeal of Luther's era had largely faded, but the Moravian Brethren were reviving it. Their calmness in the face of a storm in the Atlantic impressed the Wesley brothers.

John Wesley had an eccentric charm and unusual good looks: his portrait reveals auburn-tinged hair worn long, a pointed nose and inquisitive blue eyes. In Savannah he had the chance to exercise his looks and charm, especially among women. He soon fell in love with one of his parishioners, Sophy Hopkey, the seventeen-year-old daughter of a storekeeper. When she decided to marry another man, he was emotionally devastated, as his private diary affirmed: 'No such day since I first saw the sun!' He hoped that, as long as he lived, God would not let him 'see such another' day.

Gossiped about by his parishioners and blaming himself, he began to examine his heart. He came to believe that at the deepest levels of his heart he was not fully a Christian. Troubled and sometimes depressed, he sailed home prematurely, landing at the English port of Deal on 1 February 1738.

His brother Charles, in ill health, was already back in London and had renewed his connection with the Moravian Brethren, whom he found inspiring. At their meetings he witnessed their flashes of insight, followed by their calm assurance that they were at one with God. One night, at their meeting in Aldersgate Street, Charles suddenly felt that same flash of insight and calm assurance.

Three days later, on the evening of Wednesday 24 May 1738, his brother John attended 'unwillingly' a similar meeting. There he heard, read aloud, the preface that Martin Luther, more than 200 years before, had written for a newly translated edition of *St Paul's Epistle to the Romans*. Luther explained that true Christians must trust in Christ's love rather than in their own worthiness. The message sank deep into John's soul. It was at a quarter to nine – he remembered the time exactly – that a flash of illumination came to him. Like Luther before him, he realised for the first time in his life that his own efforts were not enough to save him, and that he must 'trust in Christ, Christ alone, for salvation'. He remembered that his 'heart was strangely warmed'. He looked back on that night as the turning point in his life.

That same summer John Wesley travelled to the villages of

Marienborn and Herrnhut in what is now eastern Germany. There he was inspired by the primitive version of Christianity recreated by the Moravian Brethren in the German countryside. These Moravians, under their various names, never became a major Protestant group, but their influence was strong on those who became Methodists.

Home again, John Wesley felt reborn. He began to visit gaols and speak earnestly to the prisoners. In every Anglican church that would welcome or tolerate him, he spoke of his enthusiastic faith. Invitations for him to preach in churches did not multiply, for he was not yet a skilled preacher. He was compelled, if he wished to reach an audience, to find it elsewhere.

At Bristol in April 1739, he heard a younger evangelist, George Whitefield, preach in the open air for the first time: 'I could scarcely reconcile myself to this strange way of preaching in the fields,' he recalled. With some embarrassment he too began to preach in the open air. Without the atmosphere of a church, the presence of altar and pulpit, and the reverential silence of the congregation, he felt lost; he had to summon all his willpower to ignore the coming and going of members of his audience. His reputation as an open-air preacher soon spread and he won a large personal following.

A few people inquired where exactly was his home church or parish. 'The world is my parish,' he airily proclaimed, but he also found a temporary parish. Near Finsbury Square in London his supporters bought a big vacant building called 'The Foundry', where brass artillery had been made for the navy and army. Renovated to hold a congregation of 1500 people, it also held apartments, in one of which Wesley's widowed mother lived. She too became a convert.

After his mother's death in 1742, he visited Newcastle and the north, which was not yet industrialised by the textile industry. In the following year he stirred Cornwall, which was to become the most

Wesleyan corner of the British Isles. He did not cross the sea to Ireland until 1747 and did not visit Scotland until 1751, but returned to them again and again in the years that followed.

A HORSEBACK PREACHER

For years it had not been certain whether John Wesley would leave a lasting mark on England. A committed Anglican, he hoped to rejuvenate that church, not create another. He trusted that his followers would attend their local Church of England on Sunday morning and then attend their own Wesleyan meeting in a private home or hired building at a later hour.

A tireless organiser, he led and supervised his converts and made the rules that guided them. Rising soon after four, he read, preached, prayed or conversed nearly all day, and in the course of a year he spent maybe 1000 hours on horseback. He slept when he felt the need for it: he had the ability 'to sleep immediately'. In surviving archives his height is rarely mentioned, but it was just five feet three inches or 153 centimetres, which placed him slightly below the average height of that time. When standing at the pulpit, at the zenith of his preaching powers, his magnetism was such that he seemed to stand six feet tall.

Early on he enlisted helpers, eventually engaging them by the hundreds. His willingness to appoint laymen as official preachers was unusual. The sergeants of his part-time army were those who conducted his class meetings. First employed in Bristol in about 1742, and modelled partly on a Moravian idea, the class meeting was a weekly gathering of the devout with sometimes the addition of a few eager beginners. Ideally, each class or team held ten or twelve members and the early tendency was to conduct separate meetings for women and men. Held on a weekday evening, the class meeting began with a hymn and then an off-the-cuff prayer, during which the members knelt. The class leader then spoke, earnestly describing anything that had uplifted or upset his spiritual mood during the week. Members in turn reported on their own wellbeing and sought the prayers or comfort of the others. There was little room for privacy or shyness.

If the leader of the class meeting was diligent, he visited members who were sick or were backsliders. He also collected the small sum of one penny a week from each member, and the shilling that was expected quarterly. In the early years Wesley himself supervised the meetings, for most were held around Bristol and London and were few in number. He appointed or approved of the leaders, and he also banned those people who were likely to be disruptive or whose personal lives did not stand up to scrutiny. In his lifetime the class meetings enlisted scores of thousands of members – on the American frontier, on the sugar island of Antigua, at the busy British ports, and in countless other places.

Many of his disciples thought that the weekly class meeting was the backbone of their religious life and more rewarding than the actual services held on Sundays. But some time after Wesley's death, when personal privacy became one of the desires of a section of society, the popularity of the class meeting was to fade. Moreover, its typical members had altered, being mainly the second or third generation of Wesleyans rather than enthusiastic converts.

An optimist, Wesley believed that nearly all people were capable of loving God and all mankind. Unlike Calvin, he believed that heaven was open to all who loved God and who tried to live a worthwhile life. Hell was not prominent in his later sermons. From his diaries and other writings a variety of exotic opinions emerge. He believed that witches existed; that demons could take possession of people; and that the spirits of the dead would sometimes reappear and 'manifest themselves' to the living.

For years Wesley rarely was invited to preach in an Anglican church but on 19 January 1783 he noted in his journal: 'The tide is now turned.' Usually he preached straight from the Bible, but some critics thought that he took liberties with the New Testament. A later theologian, a Methodist himself, marvelled at the ease with which Wesley lifted the words of Jesus or Paul from their context and so altered their meaning.

In Italy at the very same time, Catholics admired a priest who, in his essentials, was another John Wesley. Alphonsus Liguori was a successful Naples lawyer who in 1726, at the age of thirty, entered the priesthood. Six years later he founded the Redemptorists, a highly successful order encompassing monks and nuns. Father Liguori shone as theologian, preacher and writer, and wrote the words of the Italians' popular Christmas hymn, 'Tu scendi dalle stelle' which means 'From Starry Skies Descending'. The personal faiths and precepts of Liguori and Wesley, reached independently, were alike. The Italian had a strong sense of the duties that must be fulfilled, and he displayed a warm-hearted attitude to people. His ardent love went to the Virgin Mary, whom he addressed as 'O my most sweet Lady and Mother Mary'. He died in 1787, aged ninety.

John Wesley, outliving Liguori by four years, died at the age of eighty-eight. On the eve of his death, Wesley is reported to have said twice: 'The best of all is God is with us.'

He was pleased to stand in the long line of Christian preachers extending even into the Catholic epoch, and so the nameplate on his wooden coffin was not in English but in Latin. On the morning of his burial in London such a throng of his followers was expected that, to prevent an unmanageable crush, the funeral began at five. At his request the service was unassuming; and six old and poor men were each paid the large sum of twenty shillings to carry his coffin to the burial ground.

WHITEFIELD THE CROWD-EXCITER

George Whitefield, himself an entrepreneur of religion, showed Wesley how to preach in the open air. Taller than average, Whitefield was a powerful speaker. His bearing and gestures seemed extravagant in the enclosing walls of a church, but they were well suited to a hillside or natural amphitheatre. A slight squint in one of his small, blue eyes – said to be the legacy of the measles – in no way detracted from the impression he created, for in a vast audience only spectators standing in the front rows could see his face. His voice was his compelling feature; it had unusual resonance, and his slowly spoken sentences were 'audible at immense distances'.

When he was speaking in the centre of the town of Philadelphia late in 1739, that practical genius Benjamin Franklin walked around the outskirts of the crowd and carefully calculated how many people actually heard Whitefield, as distinct from seeing him or merely being present in the hope of hearing him. That day at least 30 000 heard his message. He virtually paved the way for the mass oratory that was vital for the rise of popular political movements in the United States and Britain in the nineteenth century.

The orthodox Anglican Dr Samuel Johnson concluded that there was such a flavour of the circus in Whitefield's antics that even if he were silent he would command attention: 'He would be followed by crowds were he to wear a nightcap in the pulpit or preach from a tree,' mused Johnson. Whitefield's retentive memory – he used no notes – and his sense of drama became talking points. In one sermon delivered in a church he described in gripping detail how a blind man was stumbling towards a precipice. A listener was so transfixed by the fear that the blind man would fall to his death that he leaped from his seat and called aloud, 'Good God! He's gone!' Such anecdotes, told wherever Whitefield went, declared that he was a celebrity.

A clergyman with the common touch – partly the result of an uncommon childhood – Whitefield was born in Gloucester, and seemed likely to follow his mother's occupation of innkeeper. Later he concluded that he had narrowly avoided going to hell. Believing, later, that his daily life was scrutinised by God, he felt guilty when he remembered that he had often attended the theatre and 'the common entertainments of the age'. He did not realise that his love of the theatre yielded a long-term dividend, for his effectiveness as a preacher depended on dramatic skills.

A turning point in his zigzag life occurred in the riverport of Bristol, where, inside a church, God filled him 'with such unspeakable raptures' that he felt almost carried away. In Oxford he worked as a servitor in a university college and, like an ascetic monk, deliberately wore patched clothes and dirty shoes. After becoming a deacon and then a priest of the Church of England, he eventually joined the little Holy Club in which the Wesley brothers were prominent at Oxford. Eleven years younger than John Wesley, Whitefield followed him to Georgia, where he founded an orphanage to which he devoted much thought, no matter where he was travelling.

Soon back in England, he preached in magnetic style and aroused such hysteria that he was considered unseemly. If excluded from a church he would preach nearby, sometimes standing on a tombstone. In February 1739 – he was then aged twenty-four – his speeches to coalminers and their families at Kingswood near Bristol were a sensation. He was soon capable of speaking in the open air to more people than any British cathedral could hold on a normal Sunday morning.

Whitefield returned to North America, where his talent as preacher and actor was appreciated by a people who were more at ease with informality. A Congregationalist theologian of Massachusetts, Jonathan Edwards, had recently lent his voice to the religious revival later known as the Great Awakening, and Whitefield now became the chief awakener in a crusade that not only aroused New England but stretched from Nova Scotia to Georgia and far inland. It is doubtful that the religious fervour experienced there between 1740 and 1743 had ever been seen on such a scale in England. Whitefield played boldly on his audiences' emotions, whipping up guilt and fear until many felt on the brink of hell. Offering the hope of God's mercy to those who truly repented, he and his fellow preachers effected many mass conversions. It did not worry him that theologians in both the Harvard and Yale universities denounced his tactics.

Whitefield's favourite dish, when a trifle of luxury seemed justified, was the cooked heel of a cow. His whole routine was spartan. Each morning before 4.30 he was busy, praying and reading and, if necessary, preparing to begin his day's travel. He shared John Wesley's early-rising energy. Not one minute was to be wasted, but both men found almost enough time for marriage. Neither man lived very contentedly with his wife – not surprisingly, for they were rarely home. A bluff clergyman who welcomed both evangelists to his Bedfordshire pulpit also chanced to meet the two wives, and he labelled them 'a brace' of ferrets. Here, a doctoral thesis awaits a feminist author.

While Whitefield created no sect of his own, he promoted the Welsh Calvinistic Methodists and a sect called the Countess of Huntingdon's Connexion. The countess, who had been widowed in her late thirties, hailed Wesley and later Whitefield as her personal mentors. She and her supporters founded at least sixty churches and chapels, initially at fashionable resorts such as Brighton, Bath and Tunbridge Wells. Wealthy people also attended: they came to taste, some staying to savour.

Whitefield once said that he would 'rather wear out than rust out'. In September 1770, at the age of fifty-five, he delivered his final sermon, two hours in length. He died the following day and was buried beneath the pulpit of the Presbyterian church in Newburyport, Massachusetts. In fame he was not unlike a medieval saint, and hundreds of dissenting congregations on both sides of the Atlantic would have relished the privilege of guarding his tomb.

After the news of his death reached London, a memorial service was held in the large 'tabernacle' that his disciples had built for him in Tottenham Court Road. The sermon was given by John Wesley, though he had moved apart, personally and theologically, from his Calvinistic friend. It was a momentous day in the history of Protestantism, for Whitefield and Wesley between them were transforming the religious mood of the English-speaking peoples.

ITINERANT PREACHERS ABROAD

When the North American colonists declared their independence from Britain in 1776, not many thousands of their citizens were followers of Wesley. By 1850, however, one in every three of the 'religious adherents' in the United States was a Methodist. Their Sunday or weekday services relied heavily on itinerant preachers, who had little training, little book-learning, and who willingly accepted low salaries. Each itinerant preacher had charge of a small district or circuit, and tried in the course of a month to visit every church and every group that met in private houses. Most of the early preachers who went about on foot or horseback were unmarried and willing to spend weeks away from home. They suited newly settled rural districts where large towns were few and families were poor.

As most congregations could not expect the itinerant preacher to appear more than once a month, their members – perhaps a farmer or a shopkeeper – served as part-time preachers for the normal Sunday or even the weekday services. Some were sheer amateurs who, through dedication and organisational ability, out-performed many professional pastors.

Australia was not so easily organised as North America by religious leaders, because it began as a convict colony and was so distant. It was in 1787, when Wesley was still alive, that the British government despatched a fleet carrying armed marines and convicts – and a Christian chaplain – to the east coast of Australia. Those who selected the chaplain for that difficult task included William Wilberforce, leader of the campaign against slavery, and John Newton, a former captain of a slave ship who became a prominent London clergyman. The hymn 'Amazing Grace', popular again in the late twentieth century, was written by Newton.

As chaplain they chose Richard Johnson, a young evangelical clergyman who was influenced by Wesley's teachings. At first Johnson's chubby features were the face of Christianity in the vast continent. In February 1788, on his second Sunday ashore, he stood on the side of a grassy hill near Sydney Harbour and spoke to the hundreds of male and female convicts arranged in front of him. He chose his text from Psalm 116: 'What shall I render unto the Lord for all his benefits towards me?' The convicts were not sure whether they shared in the benefits. At least they heard in their adopted land that specialty of Whitefield and Wesley: earnest preaching in the open air.

When Johnson a few weeks later conducted his first Holy Communion, he borrowed a wooden table from a naval lieutenant who was sufficiently devout to hope that his table would someday become a sacred object in the history of Australia. 'I will keep this table also as long as I live,' he wrote.

THE SWIFT SINGERS

A hymn sung to a colourful or solemn tune and relying heavily on rhymes was a simple way of spreading a Christian doctrine. The rhymes helped people to remember the words in an era when so many churchgoers, being illiterate, depended solely on their memories. But in the early years of Protestantism, the combined impact of words and tune and the voices of the whole congregation – rather than those of a small male choir – were not yet appreciated. The chapels and meeting houses that hailed Calvin as their inspirer agreed with him that singing should not dominate religious ceremonies. Only the psalms were sung, usually without an organ or violin to accompany them.

In England this rule was weakening, thanks to Isaac Watts. He came from a family of devout Dissenters; indeed, Isaac's father, a Southampton clothier, had been imprisoned for his religious views in 1675, the year of his son's birth. By the time Isaac was in his twenties, he and his family were attending a Congregational chapel in which new hymns were welcomed. In the chapel the verses of his latest composition were read aloud, in turn, by the clergyman from a sheet of paper, and then the people would sing them one by one. At the time of World War I most Britons and Australians and New Zealanders above the age of ten knew at least the first verse of Watts' hymn 'Our God, Our Help in Ages Past', and tens of millions knew every verse of his Easter hymn 'When I Survey the Wondrous Cross'. Watts did not admire Methodism, which, when he died in 1748, was still an infant.

The Wesley brothers, even more than Watts, composed hymns, knowing that an impressive hymn was more persuasive than most sermons, and much shorter, too. Within twenty years Wesley believed that his congregations sang like no others. The males and females usually sat on opposite sides of the church – if they possessed a church – and sometimes all the males and then all the females sang a verse, after which they combined their voices for another. Initially without an organ to accompany it, the singing was described as 'swift'. The early Methodist tunes were often borrowed from popular songs – this annoyed other churchgoers – but later the serious German tunes were chosen for many of the several thousand hymns written by Methodists.

John Wesley produced his first hymn book for his Church of England congregation in Georgia in 1737. He translated from the German language five of the hymns in the book. He continued to write occasional hymns – vehicles for his theology – but his brother Charles became the prodigious writer. Some of Charles's catchy hymns celebrated the act of communal singing. 'Oh For a Thousand Tongue to Sing My Great Redeemer's Praise', sung to the tune of 'Lydia', was to appear in crowd scenes in two celebrated novels by Thomas Hardy and George Eliot.

Whitefield also compiled a hymn book for his followers, and it was so much in demand that it was reprinted thirty-five times before the end of the century. He had no hesitation in revising the words and even the theological message of hymns written by others. One of his happier ideas was to alter the opening lines of Charles Wesley's popular Christmas hymn 'Hark! The Herald Angels Sing'. Wesley had originally written 'Hark, How All the Welkin Rings' – a line which would have weakened the prospect of the hymn surviving today.

Most of the evangelical and Calvinist groups were not sure whether to permit a violinist or organist to accompany the singing. Many began to permit a musician to play a pipe or violin, just to acquaint the audience with the tune and to set the singing on its way. Sometimes a soloist – called a precentor – led the singing. By 1800 a pipe organ was common in many churches but not yet normal, and some congregations walked out or started a new sect rather than submit to a musical sound that competed with the biblical words for attention. Presbyterians living in Scotland and in distant British colonies remained wary of the organ or any other instrument, but by 1850 the radicals were winning. They discovered that the barrel organ or harmonium or grand pipe organ, played with sensitivity, could enhance the words and make them easier to remember.

Numbers of ordinary churchgoers developed a tenacious memory for the words; some could recite 500 hymns, every single verse of them, by heart. Popular singing and off-the-cuff praying became the hallmark of the Sunday services conducted by Wesley and other revivalists, and they contrasted with the formality of Catholic, Anglican and Lutheran churches. Whereas in 1500 serious Christians could feel at home and know the procedures and rituals of any church in Europe, in 1800 they were likely to feel at sea if by chance they joined one of the newer congregations.

Wesley's creed and methods, which he had hoped would not be the basis of a separate creed, eventually led to a separate sect that became worldwide. Though initially he organised it minutely and even dictatorially, as if only one man were capable of running it, it actually flourished even more when he was dead. One century after his death, Methodism was the largest church in the United States. It was probably second in England and Wales, if measured by attendances every Sunday. In Australia and New Zealand it was fourth, and in many other lands it was prominent.

The religious revival led by Wesley deeply impressed a later French historian. He argued that the main reason why England did not undergo a version of the French Revolution was that Wesley had brought stability, and even conservatism, to sections of the nation. In the eyes of a distinguished Oxford historian, Wesley could be likened to Napoleon and Gandhi as a shaper of modern history. Other historians might not offer such unstinted praise but few would deny his influence. An unusual and posthumous tribute was extended to him by the poet Robert Southey: 'I consider him as the most influential mind of the last century – the man who will have produced the greatest effects, centuries, or perhaps millenniums hence, if the present race of men should continue so long.'

26

TURMOIL IN PARIS

France was the most populous country in Europe in 1780 and the showcase of civilisation. It was also the most powerful country on land and perhaps even on the sea. One of the two vigorous colonial powers, its overseas possessions stretched from the West Indies and Louisiana, on the American mainland, to the rich island of Mauritius in the Indian Ocean and to the east coast of India. French seafaring explorers were legendary, and in the 1780s were exploring more of the Pacific Ocean than were Britons.

The French language was especially prized. Since the Treaty of Rastatt in 1714, French was the language of diplomacy. Almost equally prized was French food: French chefs were sought by the monarchs of Europe. While English technology was superior, French science saw itself as superior. In staging a grand public spectacle the French had few if any equals. The grand palace at Versailles was imitated in Prussia and Austria, where the terraces and avenues at the new Potsdam and Schönbrunn palaces were the work of French designers. In the new St Petersburg, French architecture flourished.

Even Russia's statue of its own Peter the Great on horseback was modelled on one designed to glorify King Louis XIV of France.

THE CHURCH IN FRANCE: A CARRIAGE WTH FINE HORSES

And yet in the 1780s France was troubled. The monarchy, the nobility, the Catholic Church, agriculture and finances were under strain, and the monarch's and the country's debts, difficult to separate, had been alarmingly enlarged by France's support for the United States in its war of independence. More intellectuals of influence lived in France than in any other western country, and one of their targets was their own country's institutions. Hostility to the church and its priests was widening.

The French king – Louis XVI – and his church were almost one. If the monarchy collapsed, the bishops and priests could collapse too. Christianity in France could fall with them. In contrast, the church in England and in the United States was much more diverse. In both countries there was not one church or sect but many, and disunity gave strength. If the Church of England fell, a host of other Christian sects would survive and might flourish more than before.

On the eve of the Revolution, more Christians lived in France than in any other country. Large numbers of French people spent their working lives as officials, priests, monks, nuns and servants of the Catholic Church. The Church urged the young to devote their lives to Christ, and the first rung of the stepladder leading to the priesthood could be climbed as early as the age of seven, though most joined the priestly ladder at the age of nine or ten. A vital step, normally taken at the age of twenty-one or twenty-two, was the vow or personal promise of lifelong celibacy. Formal entry to the priesthood might follow about three years later.

Tens of thousands of French boys who initially wished to be priests changed their minds after spending their childhood in the Church. Some preferred to accept the prestige of the Church but not its responsibilities. These halfway priests, known as Abbés, even wore their own style of clothing that, by 1750, included a wig, which could be 'impertinently curled', and a hat that was shaped by three or four corners.

Some were men about town and might be seen applauding at the theatre, or posing in literary or artistic salons. If given a small sum or gift, they gladly enhanced the prestige of a funeral by marching in the procession in their religious garments. Some taught in schools, their title giving them a touch of distinction. A few were rakes and sexual prowlers, their half-priestly appearance helping them gain entree to a woman's heart. Even at the age of seventy they were still gravely addressed as Abbé. On the whole, they were not a very attractive advertisement for the French Church, for similar groups were virtually unknown in England, Italy, Russia and Spain.

The parish priests were more creditable. Some 30 000 in all, most probably did their duties faithfully and many were held in high esteem. Thus, in June 1762 in Brittany, a priest celebrating his fiftieth anniversary in charge of that parish could humbly recall, 'I have lived and live still without trouble and in peace with all men. But I have every reason to fear the terrible judgements of God who has confided to me, over so long a period, the care of thousands of souls – a perilous task.' On the whole the French clergy were 'better behaved and better educated than ever before', wrote one historian. Many even offered agricultural and medical advice in villages that no scientist or doctor visited. While most priests were diligent in carrying out duties, others had to be rebuked by the bishop because they drank too much, especially at festivals, wasted time by hunting, indulged in coarse jests or lent money at high interest.

One complaint was that, in their haste to resume more interesting pastimes, priests omitted part of the day's religious service they were obliged to conduct. A few priests earned lasting affection despite their misconduct. In Lorraine in 1757, one was condemned to death for the crime of sodomy, but he partly redeemed himself by delivering a noble speech in his last minutes. In time to come, people made pilgrimages to the place of his execution.

Priests were answerable to their bishop, though some did not have to answer if the bishop was lazy. In 1789, France supported 130 bishops, each with his own diocese or territory. In his realm he was often the most influential inhabitant. Many were able administrators, vital for an organisation so large, and nearly all were of noble birth. In the preceding forty years, just one commoner had been chosen as a bishop. This sole exception was the Abbé de Beauvais, son of a lawyer and much admired by the king's daughters, an admiration that aided his advancement. In 1774 he became the bishop of Senez, a poor mountainous district in which the parishes were perched on hilltops or lay at the end of long valleys. His heart and mind remained in Paris, and eventually he resigned.

Two centuries previously, the Council of Trent had ruled that a bishop must visit his many parishes at least once every two years. If old, sick, lazy or absorbed in a pleasant life, he either delegated this duty or neglected it. In 1778 the new bishop of Le Mans entered a village that had been last visited by a bishop more than thirty years previously. At one town he confirmed more than 1600 people who had come especially from neighbouring parishes to receive this important sacrament not previously offered to them. While on tour he solved disputes.

A wealthy bishop travelled in a style befitting an aristocrat. He might set out with a procession of riding and carriage horses and various helpers, including his own cook. If not wealthy, he might travel in a carriage drawn by two black mules. At the end of his travels he was glad to return to the bishop's palace, where there was everything he needed. Back in 1683 it was explained that a bishop, to be respected, should employ two valets, a surgeon, a private chaplain, a manager of the palace, a man to look after the horses' stables and another the wine cellar – not to speak of table-waiters in fine uniform, skilled cooks who baked the bread and made the meals, and a boy whose task it was to turn the roasting spit. The servants also supplied food to the poor, who regularly called at the gate, for famines were frequent in France. Finally, a carpenter had to be permanently employed to keep the bishop's house, stables and fences in repair. It was slightly incongruous that all this comfort was provided in the name of that other carpenter who had founded the bishop's religion.

High above each cluster of French bishops was an archbishop: there were twenty-eight in all. At the very top were the French cardinals. So close were the ties with the monarchy that a churchman on occasions actually governed France on behalf of the monarch. In effect, Cardinal Fleury was prime minister of France until 1743, a total of seventeen years. The son of a tax collector, he knew about money.

The Catholic Church in France had many virtues. Whether its zeal and effectiveness in preaching the gospel was one of its main virtues is a matter for debate amongst historians. Certainly, its enormous wealth – it owned one-sixth of all the land in France – enabled it to be a generous patron of many of the arts. The finest choirs in France were to be heard each Sunday in the cathedrals and larger churches. In Paris since 1725 the Concert Spirituel was one of the musical events of Holy Week and a succession of Sundays. French composers – and also the talented Italian Pergolesi – wrote music for such occasions. The young Mozart once visited France to take part.

One English tourist, Thomas Bentley, reported eagerly in his 1776 *Journal of a Visit to Paris* that he had just heard a choir 'chanting the service, which I think the finest and most devotional music in the world'. Intensely moved, he said that he was 'fixed fast in a fit of devotion'. Paris was the most glamorous city in the world to many sophisticated people, and also to many church officials who lived in the provinces. Whenever the canon of the Sainte-Chapelle of Dijon visited Paris he felt elated by the rich musical and spiritual experiences. A biblical scholar who read Hebrew and ancient Greek, he vowed that every other book, when compared with the Bible, was nothing but 'whipped cream'. Not all his priestly colleagues agreed, and on their visits many preferred the whipped cream itself.

On one topic, which once was tempestuous, nearly all Catholics agreed: the Protestants, who mostly lived in the south of France, were no longer a threat. The laws kept them in submission. In 1700 they were not allowed to meet in public for religious purposes, not allowed to marry except in Catholic Churches, and not even allowed to make brief visits to Geneva, Holland or England in order to be baptised by Protestant pastors or bishops. Some religious offenders were sent to the galleys. By 1750 these laws were not enforced, unless a local official was overly officious.

EXPELLING THE JESUITS

In France the arguments directed against the core beliefs of Christianity were probably the most serious, politically, since those made by the Roman pagans in the decades before the conversion of the Emperor Constantine in the fourth century. But victory for the new attackers seemed unlikely. Christianity was entrenched in France, though less amongst the people than amongst those who governed. It was also defended by powerful intellectuals, especially the Jesuits.

In Europe and elsewhere their Society of Jesus provided the most learned debaters of religious topics. Recruiting talented young men for lifetime service, the Jesuits trained them in their excellent colleges and seminaries. They also taught the elite, including the sons of the nobility and high officials. Jesuit colleges numbered 133 in Italy, 105 in Spain, and eighty-nine in France, according to the official census of 1749. When monarchs and even popes faced difficult diplomatic issues, they sometimes turned to the Jesuits for advice. If in that century Nobel Prizes had been awarded for scholarship and learning, Jesuits would have won many of them, though not perhaps the Peace Prize, for they stirred the political pot too vigorously. The Jesuits were absolutely vital for a church increasingly under attack, but they were increasingly under attack themselves.

They were opposed partly for their success. They had the permanent support of Rome, and were also envied as magicians who could open locked doors in remote courts. Thus, in China they had infiltrated the palace of the emperor, and had made themselves, through their skills and learning, almost indispensable. They became the Chinese emperor's advisers on astronomy, and could predict with some accuracy the date of an eclipse of the moon or sun. In mechanics and mathematics they were probably the best consultants and teachers in Beijing. They increased their influence on the Chinese people by adapting certain Christian doctrines to such local preferences as the worship of ancestors and the admiration for Confucius. That was exactly what the most effective missionaries had long been doing in Asia and the Americas, but when the Jesuits did it, so far from home, the resentment expressed by their rivals became intense.

In Portugal the Jesuits were denounced as too influential for their own good and for the good of the monarchy. Pombal, the civilian who ruled Portugal with the consent of the king, fell out with them and duly expelled them from Portugal and Brazil in 1759. That they might also be expelled from France seemed unthinkable – or was it? More than a century before, as a sign of official favour, the Jesuits' grand church in Paris had been opened and blessed by the great Cardinal Richelieu, who was then almost the ruler of France. But even then the Jesuits were seen as too close to the throne, and indeed they allowed the monarch to take both bread and wine at the Eucharist as if he were a priest.

By 1760 the Jesuits in France, as in Portugal, were under attack. Criticised for their commercial activities in the French colony of Martinique in the West Indies, and for the debts they incurred, they were the subject of an official Paris inquiry, which was not altogether impartial. In 1762 it reported unfavourably, declaring the Jesuits to be 'destructive of all principles of religion, and even of honesty'. Soon their property was confiscated and they were driven from France. Their two main sins were obvious: they were too talented and powerful, and they were seen as the voice of Rome, not of Paris.

In Spain, their real birthplace, the Jesuits were now regarded as a challenge to the monarchy. As they made a special vow of obedience to the pope, they were seen as outsiders and occasionally as meddlers by many Spaniards. Other religious orders, especially the Dominicans, were also wary or even jealous of them. Spain supported the huge number of 200 000 priests, monks, friars and nuns in a total population of ten million; and in this long-robed procession the Jesuits formed only a small minority. Alas, a riot in Madrid in

1766 was believed to have been stirred by them. A year later 5000 Jesuits were formally expelled from Spain and its empire. Of the fifty-six bishops in Spain, forty-two approved of the expulsion. The government gladly approved, for it became the new proprietor of the Jesuit lands, schools and other properties.

In barely a dozen years the Jesuits had been toppled. All the way from the shores of the Baltic Sea to the high country of South America they had been expelled, though they were left alone by several monarchs who were not Catholics. Finally, in 1773 Pope Clement XIV, under pressure from France and Spain and various Italian states, dissolved the very organisation of these priests known within the Catholic Church as 'the blacks'. Indeed, the head of the Jesuits, always resident in Rome, had long been known as 'the Black Pope'. This was 'the papacy's most shameful hour', wrote one historian calmly.

In punishing the Jesuits, the Catholic Church punished itself. It was like a nation expelling its experienced generals on the eve of a major war. The Jesuits continued to do their work in Prussia, Russia, England, Maryland and other countries where the pope had no influence, but they were now humiliated and almost leaderless. In Catholic lands they were not to be reinstated until 1814 by Pope Pius VII. Meanwhile the French Catholic Church urgently needed the help of those intellectual Jesuit torchbearers whose light had been snuffed out.

PHILOSOPHERS, ATHEISTS AND OTHER DOUBTERS

There had always been criticism of certain of the basic beliefs of the Christians. In the two centuries after Luther's death, numerous priests and pastors must have thought dangerous and heretical ideas. Those scholars who held doubts about the divinity of Christ, referring to him rather as a saintly man than the Son of God, were careful not to speak too loudly. Philosophers, happy with abstract ideas, might express doubts in a prose that was not easily understood even by the educated. Probably in Catholic countries a few priests might reveal their doubts in a secluded rural church where the congregation hardly saw the implications, while in Protestant circles a brave Unitarian pastor might wonder whether the Holy Ghost existed.

The Reformation had really paved the path for atheists and other kinds of doubters to walk on. By attacking the authority of the Catholic Church, it quietly inspired other thinkers to attack the authority of the new Protestant churches. By encouraging debate about the meaning of many sentences in the Bible, the Protestants indirectly encouraged debate about the core principles of Christianity. Was Christ really the Son of God? Did he really rise from the dead? Did God intervene incessantly in daily life or did he stand aside for much of the time? The mainstream Protestant leaders, devout as they were, had unintentionally enabled these deeper attacks directed against Christianity itself. While believing firmly in the presence and power of amazing miracles during the life of Christ, they were wary of believing in miracles said to have happened in their own lifetimes. Thus, they had prepared the way for other thinkers to criticise – if they dared – the concept of a miracle.

Deism, a doctrine often formulated by doubters, gained influence in France and Prussia and England in the eighteenth century. God existed, but he presided over the universe rather than interfered; deists, in their theology, tended to dispense with a personal God. While some deists were atheists in disguise, most were religious and, by today's standards, would be called true believers. The majority decided that God had created the universe in all its beauty and majesty, set in place the oceans and lands, launched the sun and moon on their predestined courses, created the climates of the different continents, created mankind, and then stepped aside, to intervene rarely, if at all. In other words, God was not dead but was often resting. Or perhaps he remained all powerful but was content simply to preside over the marvellous universe and the slightly less impressive human race he had created.

The discovery of important natural laws by Copernicus of Poland, Galileo of Italy, Newton of England, Descartes of France, Huygens of the Netherlands, and other scientists and mathematicians helped to underwrite deism. These discoveries suggested that the natural world obeyed its own laws and rhythms and had no need for God's intervening hand. Thus, God could not be expected to save passengers in distress in a stormy sea, or a city endangered by a flood or fatal plague. Such a doctrine challenged the concept of prayer.

Versions of deism, while not winning converts in huge numbers, shaped important parts of the intellectual world, and even politics in the few democracies that were emerging. In the 1770s four of the notable founders of the United States – George Washington, Thomas Jefferson, Benjamin Franklin and Tom Paine – were deists; deism even affected many people who might be expected to know little about recent theology. Captain James Cook, exploring the east coast of Australia in his ship *Endeavour*, reflected this theological trend. When young he had been influenced by the Quakers in Yorkshire, but now, under the daily influence of the free-thinking young scientist Joseph Banks, he was not certain whether God ruled the wind and sea.

In August 1770, Cook's sailing ship was, for a second time, almost wrecked on the Great Barrier Reef, and was saved only by a short-lasting puff of wind at the moment of highest danger. One of Cook's colleagues wrote privately that without God's help in sending that puff of wind, 'there would have been no hopes of saving one single life in so great a surf'. At first Cook more or less agreed, writing in his official journal that it had pleased God 'at this very juncture to send us a light air of wind'. Later, contemplating the event from a safe distance, Cook reassessed God's role. Perhaps God had not sent a puff of wind to save the endangered ship. It was almost as if deism had grasped Cook's hand and pen.

Shaping the new atmosphere of religious doubt were critics who bravely took their scissors to pages of the Bible. Thus, Pierre Bayle, who taught philosophy and history at a French Protestant university in Sedan and later at Rotterdam, dissected the Old Testament. In what he called his *Critical and Historical Dictionary*, he repeatedly warned that you could not believe everything the Bible said. Most of his pages could be safely read by the French official censor, for Bayle had cleverly incorporated the book's more explosive points in the side notes, in small print. Only after Bayle's death in 1706 was his work publicised and translated widely. We know that towards the end of that century the American father-figure Thomas Jefferson owned a translation of Bayle's work in five large volumes.

The basic idea of Christianity was that man was sinful and needed God's grace in order to be redeemed. Jean-Jacques Rousseau, originally a Calvinist from Geneva, challenged the very idea that mankind had been tainted by sin ever since the Garden of Eden. In his view mankind was originally good but had been corrupted by civilisation. It had been corrupted by the very civilisation of which Christianity was now the vital strand. 'Man was born free', wrote Rousseau in 1762, 'and everywhere he is in chains.' In removing the chains Christianity was not needed.

Another Frenchman, Voltaire, spread a radical message about religion. As far as can be ascertained, he did believe more or less in the existence of God, but his deism stood far from the main Catholic creed. The most celebrated man of letters in Europe, Voltaire spread his opinions, in print or by word of mouth, to a vast audience. In 1807 – long after Voltaire's death – the English critic Robert Southey lamented that even the stalls at country fairs were selling Voltaire's 'atheistic' tracts, printed with worn metallic type on grubby paper. In accusing Voltaire of hating Christ, Southey called him 'of all the authors the most mischievous and the most detestable'. After the French Revolution and its outbursts of atheism, Voltaire was widely condemned as one of the causes. Nonetheless, his writings did concede that fear of God was an essential policeman in a disorderly world. 'If God did not exist, it would be necessary to invent him', wrote Voltaire.

The critics and rationalists known in France as the 'philosophes' dismissed the afterlife. They believed that the life lived here on earth was more important and fulfilling than the next life – if it existed. There is some truth in the bold assessment, made long afterwards, that 'the key invention of the eighteenth century' was the idea that mankind could be, and should be, happy on this earth. More than anywhere else, France was the home of this invention, and the French church was its earliest victim.

WHICH MIRACLES DO YOU BELIEVE IN?

In the second half of the eighteenth century a few talented authors were writing a version of history not approved in the cathedrals. They insisted that human beings, and geographical and other factors, were the main shapers of the past. David Hume, producing in

1754 the first of his six volumes on the history of England, had no place for God. He implied that if God did exist, he was impotent in the face of the current political and religious upheavals in Europe. Hume also saw religious enthusiasm as a dangerous passion. That was not what Francis of Assisi and Bunyan of Bedford had preached.

How far could a secular critic venture when attacking the Christian creeds? That was a slippery question in an age of censorship. David Hume was on safe ground in noting that individuals who incessantly worried about their own salvation were self-absorbed and therefore not necessarily Christian in spirit. That comment was seen by many as constructive, and promoting Christianity. But Hume himself was seen as destructive when he ridiculed the trust that most Christians, especially Catholics, invested in miracles. After 1748, he became a bogeyman in the British Isles, though a hero in the secular corners of Paris, where he lived for some years. He was accused of heresy, deism, scepticism, atheism. He probably would have written stronger criticisms of Christianity but his friends warned him of the consequences. Amiable and gregarious, he had a quiet rather than a burning desire to change people's opinions.

A Scot, David Hume gave Edinburgh a reputation as the haven of atheism. The terror and confusion with which everyday Christians viewed atheism are hard to imagine today. Even before he died in 1776 – probably of cancer – there was anxious speculation about Hume's state of mind during his last weeks alive. Did he, they inquired, face his death calmly? Or did he repent on his deathbed? Many expected that he would have chosen to become a Christian again. There was an expectation that no person, not even David Hume, would dare to face their maker calmly, while the taint of atheism or blasphemy was still on their lips. At his funeral, a small hostile group assembled, alongside his friends. At the burial ground at Calton Hill a guard stood beside his grave for eight nights, for fear that an act of vandalism or an unruly public demonstration might take place.

One generation after David Hume's first volumes of history were published, Edward Gibbon, in his massive book *The Decline and Fall of the Roman Empire*, attributed the Empire's decline partly to Christianity, about which he wrote with some amusement. Since most scholars thought highly of the Roman Empire, Gibbon was accusing Christianity of committing a serious mischief in helping to undermine it. The conversion to Christianity of the Emperor Constantine was, in his judgement, a decisive blow to the Empire's prospects of longevity. He thought that the Christian Empire, influenced by ideas of self-denial and humility, was unlikely to remain strong militarily. On the other hand, he praised Christianity for mollifying 'the ferocious temper' of the barbarians who overran the Empire in its final, feeble phase. The last pages of his book were written in 1787 on the shores of Lake Geneva, but he had long ceased to attend its Calvinist churches.

NEWS FROM AN AMERICAN UTOPIA

In most of the major and minor states of Europe, one religion was dominant and received privileges not available to the others or, in some cases, even occupied a monopoly in religion. Even before the American War of Independence began in 1775, most of the British colonies sitting along the Atlantic seaboard received a degree of freedom unknown in Europe. Of the thirteen colonies that were soon to form the United States of America, the four colonies of Rhode Island, New Jersey, Pennsylvania and Delaware had already granted religious liberty to their inhabitants and a sense of equality to the various sects. Most of the other colonies moved towards this new pattern of religious liberty as the war went on.

When the thirteen colonies united federally under the name of the United States of America, they endorsed the principle of religious freedom. A federal law of 1786 confirmed that any person, irrespective of religion, could become the president of the new republic. A Quaker or a Catholic could be a legislator or a judge. Even an atheist, so long as he was born in the United States and was not a slave, could become the chief of its armed forces. Under its federal constitution, no Christian denomination could receive preferential treatment from the central government. In creating and maintaining, perhaps for the first time in the Christian era, a nation that affirmed the value of religious freedom, the new United States made a bold experiment.

Later, a popular theory explained that the freedom arose because so many of the early American immigrants were fleeing from 'the relentless sword of religious persecution' in Europe and were eager to create a new haven of freedom. This interpretation feels right but should not receive too much credence. People escaping persecution often set up a regime that persecuted their old enemies. New England, the first haven for those refugees, was not at first a fortress of freedom.

In explaining the rise of religious freedom in the new United States, at least two other factors were vital. In the thirteen colonies that formed the United States, a wide variety of sects and churches had established themselves, largely through migration, and by 1750 not one sect held as much as one-quarter of the total population. This was conductive to a policy of live and let live. Equally important was the fact that the Catholics at first were not numerous, and for that reason most Protestants were willing if not eager to grant them toleration. Incidentally, nobody could then imagine that Catholics by the year 2000 would become the largest single church in the United States, as a result of successive inflows of migrants from Ireland, Italy, Poland and Mexico. Another important factor favoured religious toleration. If the American colonies rebelling from Britain were to become one patriotic nation, they had to treat every religious and ethnic group with respect. So emerged this unusual policy of religious toleration. Meanwhile, a few state governments still imposed religious preferences, the last survivor being Massachusetts, which in 1833 was to cease to bless Congregationalism as its official church.

What happened in the new United States of America was a revelation to European radicals in the 1780s. The United States showed how politicians, discussing and arguing and voting, could shape a nation's destiny. Here was a form of equal opportunity and religious freedom not available in any European kingdom. No king reigned in Philadelphia, the temporary capital city, nor in Washington. No American nobility lived in style along the Atlantic seaboard and in the inland valleys. No branch of Christianity received special favours from the federal government or from the typical state government. Reason, rather than tradition, seemed to be the uncrowned king. The lesson was not lost on those French radicals who were seeking to transform their country. France's fascination with the infant United States and its claim to be a political and religious utopia was increased by the knowledge that French forces had helped to create it.

THE REVOLUTION'S HAMMER AT WORK

In France the first stage of the Revolution began in 1789. New laws and edicts followed the speech-making. In the following year the reshaping of the French Catholic Church was underway. It had so many enemies and lukewarm friends that it could not deflect the blows of the hammer by appealing to public opinion.

Under the new regime, the national church of France would no longer bow to the king and the pope. People of each district would virtually elect the bishops. Even a selection of Protestants, Jews and atheists could have their say in electing bishops of the reformed Catholic Church. Hitherto the Protestants had barely been tolerated in France, and it was only in 1787 that they were allowed to be married by their own clergymen.

Several of these radical changes appealed to the Catholic clergy of lower ranking. They were promised higher salaries and security of office. The existing bishops had no such reason for rejoicing. Their prestige, status and income were diminished. They thought they had been appointed bishops for life, with the right to be absent from their diocese or territory for much of the time; instead, they now had to face an unsympathetic secular electorate. Moreover, the number of bishops was to be reduced from 135 to eighty-three, one for each civil department in France. This news was not welcomed by the fifty-two whose prestige and territory were to vanish.

The National Assembly, the new ruler of France, challenged its clerical opponents. In November 1790 the clergy had to swear that they would uphold the new French constitution or lose their positions in the church. The French bishops – with seven exceptions – resigned, and many emigrated. At first maybe half of the parish priests and other working clergyman tried to adapt to the changes they had vowed to accept. Those bishops and priests who hesitated to transfer their oath of allegiance to France and its new constitution had to go into exile.

The church's traditional right to collect tithes – a tax for the benefit of religion – was abolished. The vast properties of the Catholic Church were being confiscated. The remaining priests were in danger of being punished or deported against their will. If six citizens laid a public complaint against the 'uncitizenly behaviour' of a priest, they set in motion an investigation that could result in his arrest. At the end of 1792 three ships, carrying 550 convicted priests, set sail for a desolate place of exile on the Atlantic coast of Africa.

King Louis XVI was willing to make concessions but not on religion. At Easter 1791 he and the queen set out to participate in the Eucharist at the church at St Cloud, but a mob prevented their carriage from proceeding. Resenting the widening assault on Christianity, he decided, with the queen, to flee from France. They did not reach the border. Captured on 21 June, they were brought back to Paris. The king's own life was now in peril, for he showed no loyalty to the new France. In January 1793 he was beheaded by the new French republic. When the news reached Rome, Pope Pius VI decided that the king had devoutly sacrificed his life, a martyr to the Catholic faith.

Who was to blame for this upheaval in what for centuries had been the most populous Catholic country in the world? The pope blamed the rationalists and 'factious, Calvinistical men', but also factions within his own church. That the church as a whole had failed, though not in every way, was too painful a conclusion for the pope to reach.

Atheism seized the pedestal in revolutionary France in the 1790s. The secular symbols replaced the cross. In the cathedral of Notre Dame the altar, the holy place, was converted into a monument to Reason. In the cathedral of Reims, an ornate and historic vessel held the holy oil that had anointed a succession of French kings. Now the holy oil was viewed as poison; during the Terror of 1792–93 it was discarded. Marriage was no longer seen as essentially a religious event: a clergyman did not have to preside at a wedding. Many citizens resented the small changes affecting their daily life. By order of the revolutionaries, the old Christian calendar and even the day called Sunday were abolished. Instead came the week of ten days, of which the last was the day of rest now called *décadi*.

Meanwhile, monasteries, convents and their buildings and estates were taken over, and monks and nuns were ordered to leave. The French Government needed the money, and hoped it would pay off the national debt. In Burgundy, the splendid monasteries – a glory of the middle ages – were dissolved, and the monks walked out. At Cluny, the lofty church that was once the most capacious in all Christendom was mostly pulled down, and the building stones carted away. For 700 years it had been a mecca for worshippers or a staging house for passing pilgrims, but the new republic of France had no place for pilgrims. For Catholics the upheaval was more dislocating than the rise of Martin Luther nearly three centuries earlier. The Reformation had disowned the pope but this revolution virtually disowned Christianity in Europe's most powerful country.

In 1801, France's new ruler, the brilliant soldier Napoleon Bonaparte, resolved to restore the church, or as much of it as could easily be restored; the confiscated lands were not returned. Napoleon even signed a Concordat or formal treaty with Pope Pius VII. At the grand ceremony where Napoleon was to be crowned as emperor, the pope himself was invited to preside. Napoleon then showed who the supreme authority was by accepting the jewelled crown from the hands of the pope and then crowning himself.

The Catholic Church was revived, though it was now under Napoleon's control. Soon, Catholic schoolchildren were regularly reciting a catechism which affirmed that 'to honour and serve the Emperor' was to serve God himself. Most of the self-exiled or deposed bishops – those who were alive – came back to their homeland. Vitality returned to religious life. The disruption of the church and the persecution of many of its priests had been bitterly resented by crowds of humble people who valued their religion, but numerous other French people were now aloof from Christianity, and would remain aloof or even hostile for generations to come.

27

CHRISTMAS CAROL

Those mighty events – the swift-moving French Revolution and the slow-moving Industrial Revolution – were transforming Europe and the Americas, mentally and materially. The steam engine shrank distances on land and sea. New fields of knowledge were being ploughed, especially in science, but of the older fields of knowledge, public ignorance was often profound. The new mental climate and the emphasis on materialism raised fears amongst many Christians, and yet by some measures this was one of the most dynamic periods in their long history.

NORTHERN PROPHETS

Most of the old mainstream churches flourished and new creeds multiplied, some exerting a wide influence only decades after the death of their founder. Emanuel Swedenborg founded such a sect. Born in Stockholm in 1688, the son of a Lutheran clergyman, he was almost too versatile for his own good. He refused a chair of mathematics at Uppsala and turned his mind to physiology, zoology, the sea tides, mining and metallurgy, differential calculus, and coinage. At the age of sixty, spiritual matters absorbed him.

Swedenborg saw three heavens and three hells. In his view those people who were vain and self-loving went straight to one of these hells. The angels concerned him deeply. Who were they? he inquired. Originally the inhabitants of the earth, they had been transported to heavenly cities, he believed, where they lived happily in a married state. Swedenborg himself was a bachelor but he understood that marriages sometimes took place in heaven. He understood that the angels spoke their own language, though it had been diffused into numerous dialects. One of their vital duties was to destroy evil spirits. Swedenborg was one of the few Protestants of his era who wondered about the routine of daily life in heaven. A popular pastime was listening to wonderful sermons delivered by a preacher who faced east towards a crowded congregation, with the wisest listeners sitting in the middle of the church and the less wise on the wings: apparently, intelligence tests or wisdom tests were conducted in heaven. In the list of those admitted to heaven he included unbaptised babies, but thought that Catholics were less likely to be admitted.

In his imagination Swedenborg roamed through outer space. He said he conversed with souls living on the moon, and claimed that he had frequent contact with many people long dead. He believed that Christianity had served its purpose and would give birth to a new religion, of which he was the doorkeeper and herald.

He died in England in 1772, with only a few followers. Sixteen years later in the London suburb of Clerkenwell a church was founded honouring his name. Called the New Church, or Swedenborgian Church, or Church of the New Jerusalem, it spread to other cities and attracted writers and intellectuals. In England and New

England many clergymen were swayed by his novel creed, while remaining in their own parishes. People inclined to spiritualism liked parts of his voluminous works, while others observed an imagination that made most novelists seem unimaginative. Amongst his admirers was the poet Elizabeth Barrett Browning, who, living her last years in Florence, told friends that his intellect had few equals. Two centuries after his death his churches were still alive – but breathing faintly – in cities as far apart as Boston and Adelaide.

In the cities of the Protestant world, tucked away in side streets but sometimes in main streets, were the chapels and churches of unusual sects. The large and handsome chapel of London University in Gordon Square was originally the home of the sect spurred by Edward Irving, a close friend of Thomas Carlyle, who was the secular prophet of England and parts of Germany. Irving, a tall and magnetic Scot, hoped to be a missionary in Persia, but he became a kind of missionary in London. On arriving there he became the minister of a small Caledonian church in Hatton Garden, where he predicted that Christ would soon return to earth. His engaging personality and strong intellect widened his circle of friends – the poet Coleridge, author of 'The Rime of the Ancient Mariner', was close to him – and London celebrities of the day hurried to hear him in the packed church, especially after he began to speak 'in tongues' and thank the Holy Spirit for descending on him. His fame spread. On a return visit to Scotland he agreed to preach next day at 6 a.m.; long before the doors were thrown open, a crowd eager to hear him milled outside.

Eventually, he was expelled from his London church on a charge of heresy and, in 1833, from the Church of Scotland, of which he was still nominally a minister. After he died of tuberculosis at the age of forty-one, a sect was created by his disciples. It took the formal name of the Catholic Apostolic Church, though it was far removed from Catholicism. It blended a rich high-church liturgy punctuated by spontaneous outbursts in unknown tongues. On Sunday the high altar could be seen through a cloud of incense and bright religious lights. Attracting prosperous and talented families, including the Earl of Northumberland, it founded a string of large city temples extending from Manchester and Birmingham to North American cities and even the southern hemisphere. In Melbourne, influential institutions, ranging from Wesley College to the Hawthorn Football Club, held a strong Irvingite strand in their early history. Eventually, the Irvingites became stronger in Germany than in Britain.

They felt such a deep conviction that the Second Coming of Christ was within sight that they made no provision for keeping alive their sect. In the beginning they appointed twelve 'apostles' as governors, with no plan for succession. Each apostle was in charge of one 'tribe' – an echo of the twelve tribes of Israel. When the last of the twelve apostles died at a ripe old age in England on 3 February 1901, the church almost came to an end. The founders had confidently assumed that by then Christ himself would be reigning on earth.

One of this church's main predictions was long remembered. Winston Churchill's first firm intimation that a great war might be approaching actually came to him from his young Irvingite friend Lord Percy, in or about the year 1902 – twelve years before the outbreak of World War I. Political allies in the House of Commons, they were holidaying, together with Germany's young Crown Prince, at Percy's country estate of Dunrobin. Percy began to talk frankly about his religion, mentioning that the last apostle of his church had recently died and recalling the prediction that the world would endure a time of troubles and even calamities before the new millennium reigned. As they walked Percy talked of Armageddon, that biblical concept, and 'predicted with strange assurance an era of fearful wars'. Churchill, who would not be called a very religious man, had strong reason to remembered the Irvingite prediction, for he was the political head of the British navy in 1914 when that momentous war against Germany commenced.

PROFESSOR CHALMERS AND CARDINAL NEWMAN

In influence, Irving paled beside Thomas Chalmers, to whom he had been an assistant in Glasgow. Now forgotten outside Scotland, Chalmers was one of the preaching giants at a time when oratory was the equivalent of the television of our era. Born in 1780 – about twelve years before Irving – Chalmers held a different mixture of views. Under the influence of the tide of ideas crossing the North Sea from revolutionary France, he briefly became a kind of rationalist, but by the age of twenty-three he was the minister of a Presbyterian church in Kilmany in rural Fife. At first he had little impact on the people to whom he ministered. Like many recruits to the ministry, he saw it as a safe and useful career rather than a spiritual adventure.

Books, not in theology, sometimes absorbed him on weekdays, and he was accused of neglecting his duties to his congregation. He spent four months in bed, a sufferer of tuberculosis. It was Carlyle who described Chalmers, even when in sound health, as 'a man capable of much soaking indolence, lazy brooding and do-nothingism'.

A religious book by the English anti-slavery campaigner William Wilberforce helped to stir Chalmers from his do-nothing life. Though the book had the uncatchy title of A Practical View of the Prevailing Religious System of Professed Christians, it persuaded Chalmers, then aged thirty, that he had a duty to change the world. Fire and urgency entered his preaching. The annual Sunday when his parishioners in rural Kilmany took part in the ceremony of Holy Communion showed his growing influence. In 1810, a total of 270 adults took part, but the next year 458 received communion. In 1815 he was invited to be the minister of the large church at Tron in Glasgow.

As he was somewhat ungainly and his clothes were a bit crumpled – even after his new wife took an interest in his appearance – he gave an ambiguous image to many who saw him for the first time. William Hazlitt, an English essayist, hearing him preach, weighed up his virtues: 'He has neither airs nor graces at command; he thinks nothing of himself; he has nothing theoretical about him.' Unlike most evangelists, he actually read his sermons line by line, his finger resting on each line before slowly moving down the page. He was slow to warm up as a speaker, and his sentences were disturbingly long, but after the sermon was underway he could mesmerise listeners, especially when he leaned over the side of the pulpit as if trying to reach them. Then his kindly face became taut and his eyes, it was said, bulged.

People who heard him for the first time wondered why they were so entranced. Henry Cockburn, a Scottish lawyer, listened to every phrase 'with a beating heart and a tearful eye'. When later he had an opportunity to read the same sermon in cold print, he realised that it was less the words than the personality that achieved the effect. For a few weeks Chalmers preached in London, where his sincerity was infectious. A future prime minister, George Canning, was 'quite melted into tears', according to a neighbour seated near him. 'All the world is wild about Chalmers,' wrote William Wilberforce in his private diary for 1817. By 'the world' he meant London, which was now the world's largest city.

Thomas Chalmers blended the evangelical and the rational. His powerful intellect respected the Enlightenment and its emphasis on reason – Scotland was one of its strongholds – but he thought that reason and logic did not change people's hearts. People could not live a fulfilling life unless they totally accepted that Christ was their 'Saviour'. Whereas the goal of Chalmers was to reform the individual, his opponents wished first to reform the social environment, to which the individual would then respond. This is still one of the key controversies in the social sciences, law courts and prisons; those who wish first to reform the social and economic environment are, at present, the more numerous. Criminals, they argue, are merely the children of their poor environment, an argument with which Chalmers disagreed.

In fast-growing Glasgow, where rich merchants lived near streets of deep poverty, Chalmers tried to alleviate social ills. He induced trusted laymen to take over sections of his parish and perform some of his pastoral and social work. As new churches were needed to serve what was now Scotland's largest city, he and the wealthy book-publisher William Collins devised ways of gathering money. If every worshipper provided at least one penny a week, and the wealthier provided a gold sovereign, large sums could be anticipated. Corinth must have used similar funding schemes in the era of the apostle Paul. The same organising enthusiasm was applied in the 1830s to other Scottish districts, and 200 churches were built.

Chalmers tried to bridge the gulf between Protestants and Catholics. Previously he had not met Catholics in those rural parts of Scotland that he knew well, but now in Glasgow he met many who had left troubled Ireland to find work in the cotton mills and ironworks. He set out to meet them, was welcomed occasionally into their cottages, and was pleased to see numbers of Catholics sitting in his weeknight church services at Tron. He was inclined to conclude that many of his fellow Scots were ill-informed, for they criticised medieval Catholic traditions that were no longer practised. In their criticisms of Catholics, they singled out those doctrines that were accepted by peasants rather than by priests who had been trained in the seminaries. When at the age of forty-two Chalmers was appointed to the chair of moral philosophy at St Andrew's University, he outlined his distinctive theology. As people were natural sinners, they must rely on their own awakened consciences. He called it 'the authority of the conscience'.

The government paid the salaries of the thousand and more ministers of the all-powerful Church of Scotland. It also governed the church indirectly, approving its theology and setting out the procedures by which each individual congregation selected its parish minister. In these selections the rich landholders often exercised a firm voice, but Chalmers and his supporters wanted the members of the congregation to have more power in selecting the clergymen who would preside over them, year after year. The Scottish landholders, however, had the support of the English Government, led by Sir Robert Peel. They also had the initial support of most congregations and clergymen in Scotland. Called 'The Disruption', the dispute shook the Scottish church. Families were split, and clergymen who had been lifelong friends indignantly or quietly parted.

If the wound could not be healed, the protesters resolved to form their own sect called the Free Church of Scotland. It would be a sacrifice, for they would have to build their own churches and somehow find funds for the salaries of clergymen. Meanwhile, they promised to preach 'in the highways and hedges, in barns and stables, in sawpits and tents', and so 'regenerate Scotland'.

On 18 May 1843 in Edinburgh, the general assembly of the whole Church of Scotland met at St Andrew's Church, its galleries packed with spectators. There the Chalmers party, consisting of clergymen and elders, was clearly outnumbered. After reciting at length their formal arguments, and protesting at 'the dishonour done to Christ's crown' by their critics, they left the building in an orderly way and walked four abreast along a street lined with spectators, some of whom cheered and a few of whom hissed. At a large hall hired at Canonmills, hundreds of supporters waited to greet the arrival of their fellow seceders. So the Free Church of Scotland was formed with Dr Chalmers as its leader.

In all, 474 of the 1203 clergymen of the Church of Scotland resigned so that they could join the new sect. In the history of Protestantism during the preceding three centuries it would be hard to recall any other major secession that embraced four of every ten clergymen working within a sect. Scotland now experienced a flurry of church-building. The expelled congregations themselves set up new churches all the way from the smoky cities to the western islands. Others decided to emigrate across the world. In New Zealand they helped to found the city of Dunedin; and its deep harbour is still named Port Chalmers.

Such was Chalmers' fame in his final years that he realised how corrupting fame could be. On occasional Sunday mornings he wondered for an instant whether he was preaching partly to please his own vanity, but his humility stepped forward to save him. Though he had divided Scotland into two camps and created a phalanx of enemies or critics, he won from his followers an admiration of an intensity such as few Scots had received. To witness his funeral procession in Edinburgh on a bleak misty day in 1847, just four years after the secession, it is estimated that 100000 people lined the route. Behind them were empty shops and offices, closed for a few hours in tribute to him. In the fields around the cemetery at Grange the mourners were countless. It seemed as if an army of women and men had assembled there in silence.

Meanwhile, in England the Wesleyans or Methodists were suffering from their own disruptions. John Wesley himself had believed in unity and hoped that his church would remain part of the Church of England. After his death it became fully independent, with its own characteristics and theology. Those walkers who happened to pass a Wesleyan chapel on a warm Sunday, when the windows were opened to admit fresh air, were often surprised by the power of the singing and the evangelical preaching, but many of those sitting inside argued that the fervour was weakening. One large group formed the Primitive Methodists, who were politically radical and later provided leaders for the rising Labour Party. Another, centred in Cornwall, called themselves Bible Christians; many of them migrated to the new Australian mining fields, where their chapels could be counted by the scores. Other new sects called themselves the United Free Methodists and the Methodist New Connexion. In 1930 in Britain all were to reunite in imitation of an earlier Australian merger.

The Anglicans, too, were shaken in the 1830s and 1840s. A group of bright young men at Oxford University tried to return their church to what they saw as its medieval splendour. They insisted that its architecture, layout and rituals should mirror the Catholic traditions of centuries ago. They even called on young clergymen to fast rigidly and to abstain from marriage. They were highly spiritual, they tried to lead holy lives, and they had a certain warmth of personality rather than the solemnity of some brands of puritanism. Their influence at first was more amongst the educated. Their printed tracts or booklets – the eager readers came to be known as Tractarians – were widely debated at dinner tables. Professor Edward Pusey, one of the young leaders of the Oxford movement, thought the excitement that was generated by the tracts was almost a contagion: 'The tracts found an echo everywhere. Friends started up like armed men from the ground. I only dreaded our becoming too popular'.

His fears were premature. Those little theological pamphlets did not shake most towns in England, but the reform movement gained strength. Half a century later its influence could be seen in the outer and inner architecture of new English churches, in the increasing preference for the ceremonial and for candles and incense, and in the willingness of young Anglican clergymen to work in the poor suburbs and even the slums – areas where their church had been weak.

The Reverend John Henry Newman was the star of the Oxford movement. Of French Calvinist and Dutch heritage, and absorbed in spiritual and scholarly matters from a tender age, he overcame his shyness and became a public man. His four o'clock sermons and lectures at St Mary's Church were considered the most awakening intellectual performance to be witnessed in Oxford. Like others, he wished to recover, hidden behind the stained glass of the formal church, the essence of early Christianity. He sought it through historical research and a visit to Rome, which he initially decided was 'idolatrous'. Of the Anglican Church, he wrote privately to a female friend, 'I do so despair'. He despaired less about Catholicism and increasingly said so.

Accused of trying to entice the whole nation in the direction of Rome, John Henry Newman and his Anglican colleague Henry Manning confirmed, by their behaviour, that these accusations were correct. They openly resolved to become Catholics. The conversion of Newman was highly newsworthy in 1845, for he was well known as a leader of reform, a sophisticated and subtle writer and preacher, and as the author of the hymn 'Lead kindly Light, amid the encircling gloom'. For a leading Protestant to become a Catholic was a rare event; in present-day terms it was like the foremost intellectual in atheism becoming an eloquent pastor of the Assemblies of God. In his journey of rebellion Newman was eventually followed by several hundred clergymen of the Church of England.

Newman's conversion was a vital step in restoring the prestige of the Catholics in Britain, a land they had once dominated. Moreover, the Irish were emigrating in their tens of thousands, at first to the western ports such as Glasgow and Liverpool, and they needed priests. Members of several minor Catholic religious orders were also arriving, amongst them the Passionists, who had been founded in Italy by an eloquent preacher named St Paul of the Cross just over a century previously. Reaching England in 1841, the Passionists, though few, were especially noticed, being the first Catholic group since the Reformation to wear publicly in English streets their distinctive uniform or habit – a black garment on which was displayed a white heart surmounted by a cross. When Newman decided to become a Catholic, who should receive him into his new church? A newly arrived Passionist, Father Dominic Barberi, stepped forward. Soon Newman was importing to Birmingham another Catholic religious order, the Oratorians, which had been founded by Philip Neri, an all-rounder and earlier Italian model of Newman.

England had possessed no cardinal and no Catholic bishop for some 300 years. In 1850 the pope conferred on London a Catholic archbishop, Cardinal Wiseman, who could hold his own in theological discussions with his Anglican rivals and usually outshine them in his ability to reconcile science with religion. The uproar in London at the very idea of a high Catholic prelate performing his offices in a heartland of Protestantism, and claiming the rank of archbishop, was echoed in hundreds of churches and chapels all the way from Cornwall to Yorkshire. When in the 1870s the two prized converts from Anglicanism, Manning and Newman, were enthroned by the pope as cardinals, the challenge was reinforced. It was not yet predicted, and not even foreseen, that in Britain in the year 2000 the active Catholics would outnumber the active Anglicans.

In Europe, Catholics nourished new organisations that went out to meet the world: as always, the Catholic innovators tried to operate inside the church. Amongst the influential orders now emerging was the Society of Mary, founded in Lyons in 1824 and popularly called the Marists, which was entrusted with the Christianising of the western part of distant Oceania. In the same decade in Italy arose the Pallottine Fathers, who trained missionaries. In the 1830s in France emerged the Society of St Vincent de Paul. Founded by Antoine Ozanam, a distinguished scholar who later held a chair at the Sorbonne, it defended Catholic doctrines against attack from freethinkers, who were multiplying in France more than in any other major nation.

In 1859 in Turin, a congregation of priests and teachers was formed, the Pious Society of Francis de Sales, better known as the Salesians, who specialised in rescuing and educating the young in the hope that many would become priests or Christian laymen. By the 1870s it supported a sister congregation known as Daughters of Our Lady Help of Christians, while in South America it was beginning the work that would make it one of the main missionary organisations in the world. Other Catholic orders that came to prominence as teachers were the Sisters of Charity, the Sisters of Mercy, the Christian Brothers and the Loreto Sisters. A hallmark of several new Catholic orders was the enlisting of people who still pursued their everyday work while giving leisure time to the church.

SECTS AND SAINTS IN THE BACKWOODS

The United States, in religion as in commerce, produced a torrent of entrepreneurs. Those Americans clasping a new religious idea had a chance to disseminate it to new audiences, for potential converts arrived every week in European migrant ships, while to American farming regions in the west flocked new settlers only too willing to attend a church of any Protestant denomination – so long as it was the nearest to their new farm. In the United States far more than in Europe, the new rural church was often the main meeting place and the upholder of law and order in the face of local drunks, petty thieves and brawlers.

In Dresden, in New York State, lived William Miller, who read the Old Testament anxiously and closely. He was strongly affected by the belief, powerful in the first decades of the nineteenth century, that Christ would soon return to earth or that the earth would be shaken or even ended dramatically. The eighth chapter of the Book of Daniel, and its reference to the cleansing of the sanctuary, underwrote Miller's prophecy. He came to the conclusion, which he preached through his journal *The Midnight Cry*, that Christ would return to earth on 22 October 1844. In certain Protestant circles in the United States, the public interest in this prophecy was intense. The failure of Christ to return on the expected day did not deeply perturb a section of his followers. Christ would come, they reassured themselves, in his own good time, and then would reign for 1000 years. Determined to purify themselves in time for the Lord's Second Coming, they lived the good life, gave generously to the Church and its missions, and treated their bodies as if they were holy temples. They vowed not to drink alcohol nor smoke tobacco, and most shunned tea, coffee and meat; their emphasis on a vegetarian diet led them to manufacture breakfast cereals. The modern western breakfast is their monument.

Called the Seventh-Day Adventists, following a conference at Battle Creek in Michigan in 1860, they chose to observe their Sabbath from sunset on Friday. Confined at first to the United States, they gained such a foothold in other countries that their total membership reached several million.

From the same generation of young Americans came the Mormons: most of their early members were rural workers and under the age of thirty. Most were kept poor by the depressed years experienced after the Napoleonic Wars ended in 1815. Joseph Smith Jr, the magnetic founder of the Mormons, lived on a New England farm that had failed. He felt a grievance towards the economy and also the existing churches. They had nothing to offer him and his neighbours in their distress.

Of the major religions to emerge in the United States, Joseph Smith's was unique. It combined mainstream Christian beliefs with the novel idea that the United States had been a part of the long history recorded in the Old and New Testaments. Smith claimed to have discovered in the 1820s the 'Book of Mormon' – ancient writings preserved on gold plates – that revealed missing truths. It told that a lost tribe of Israel had settled in the USA in 600 BC, and that Christ, soon after his resurrection, had walked near the lands that the Mormons now ploughed. In the near future, Christ would return not to Palestine but to the city of God that would be founded in the USA, in a place and at a time still to be announced.

Smith enlisted 190 followers in the Mormons' first year. After they migrated from New York State to Ohio and then to Missouri, their membership reached 2000. Expelled by the Governor of Missouri, they numbered at least 10000 after they found refuge in Illinois in 1839. Fervent and tightly knit, they were willing to drill and arm themselves when necessary in their own defence. Believers in

Christ's power to transform, they hoped to sit alongside him when he returned to judge. The Mormons formally called themselves the 'Church of Jesus Christ of Latter-Day Saints'.

Increasingly, the Mormons were convinced that the United States – 'a land which is chosen above all other lands' – was sliding into chaos. It had lost all sense of justice and failed – the Mormons said – to exercise its power to punish evil. The victory of evil could now be seen everywhere, for crusaders against slavery were being shot dead, Catholic convents and churches destroyed, 'black men burned at the stake or tree', and the Mormons themselves treated – or so they assumed – the worst of all. Perhaps their founder, Joseph Smith, the prophet, could win the presidential election of 1844 and save the nation. Instead, not yet forty years of age, he was killed by a mob.

The Mormons decided to allow polygamy, though finally disowning that practice after intense public pressure and indignation had been applied to them in 1890. As Mormons were willing to baptise people who had died before Joseph Smith discovered the Book of Mormon, they became experts in genealogy and family trees, and remain so. In other facets of behaviour their church demanded high levels of personal responsibility from its members, even insisting that they donate one-tenth of their income to the church and, if possible, spend two years as missionaries.

In 1847 most of the Latter-Day Saints moved with their new leader, Brigham Young, to Salt Lake City in faraway Utah, which was a territory and not a state and so could evade more easily the prying eyes of Washington. In grand isolation they established their way of life and continued to attract enthusiastic migrants from the British Isles, Prussia, Sweden and Switzerland; but they were warned that when at last the transcontinental railway reached Utah in 1869 they would be overrun by newcomers and their creed would weaken. The famous American philosopher Emerson disagreed, calling 'Mormonism' one of the world's three religions 'which, right or wrong, are full of force'. Emerson's intuition was sound. This unusual sect still expands, many Pacific Islanders being amongst its recent conquests.

Spiritualists, seen as almost as exotic as the Latter-Day Saints, emerged in New York about 1848 and soon flourished in England and most western nations. It is more than coincidence that they arose in the first years of the electric telegraph – only four years after Samuel Morse transmitted the first message along a thin and mysterious thread of wire from Washington to Baltimore. In the next two decades the sending of messages by cable across the seabed of the Atlantic and overland by pole-held wires to India and China stimulated the concept that thoughts could be sent through the atmosphere without even the aid of wires. Perhaps a message might be sent by new techniques from the living to the dead and back again. Spiritualists, like Christians, believed that there was life after death.

Several notable British physicists sympathised with spiritualism and hoped that the dead might be able to contact the living, with the help of empathetic persons who acted as go-betweens. It became fashionable to sit around a table and await a message; a mysterious sound of tapping on the table was greeted as evidence of contact. While many of the go-betweens were later condemned as frauds or fools, the idea of the dead effectively sending messages to the living retained a serious following. Sir Oliver Lodge, head of Birmingham University and one of the world's leading physicists when that discipline was hailed as king of the sciences, lost his son Raymond on a battlefield in World War I; the father gained notoriety by trying to contact the spirit of his dead son.

Four centuries previously, an attempt to make direct contact with the dead would have been shunned by priests. It was assumed that most of the dead were in purgatory and beyond all contact. To try to make contact, moreover, might have been condemned as sacrilege. In short, spiritualism was both a revolt against Christianity and an imitation of it. Like many religious movements of the times, it attracted both sides – the Christians looking for a spiritual explanation of the mysterious messages, and others who thought there must be a material explanation, to be found maybe in the realm of physics.

HAVE YOU SEEN THE CHRISTMAS TREE?

The evangelical wings of Christianity rarely celebrated Christmas because they insisted that every day should be a holy day. In England the Puritans briefly banned it, and Massachusetts in 1659 fined people who celebrated Christmas, whether with merriment or fasting. Even in living memory, many of the major Protestant sects did not open their church on Christmas Day – unless it fell on a Sunday. Methodists and Presbyterians in their different ways preferred to honour New Year's Eve. While many Scots made merry on that evening, around the world the Methodists organised a watch-night service and sang in the new year at midnight with a solemn hymn.

In the middle years of the nineteenth century the first signs of the modern free-spending and semi-secular Christmas arrived. As late as 1850, maybe only one in three children received a gift at Christmas. But Santa Claus, a jolly bearded man, increasingly arrived with a sleigh and a sack of toys and climbed down the chimney – with no soot on his clothes – early on Christmas morning. About this time the Christmas bonbon or cracker was invented by a London manufacturer of confectionery, and Christmas cards also appeared, being popularised by the British innovation of cheap postage stamps and a daily delivery of letters in the towns.

The symbolic Christmas tree enjoyed a long history before it reached Britain. In medieval plays the Germans celebrated around a Paradise tree, which was a fir tree decorated with apples, a reminder of the Garden of Eden in which Adam and Eve had played. Wealthy German Catholics had long celebrated the feast day of Adam and Eve on 24 December by erecting a cut-off tree inside their house with a lighted candle as the symbol of Christ. Many Lutherans continued to set up a small fir tree as their Christmas tree, and it must have been a seasonal sight in Bach's Leipzig at a time when it was virtually unknown in England, and little known in those farmlands of North America where Lutheran immigrants congregated.

In 1848 the popular *Illustrated London News* boosted the profile of the Christmas tree. It printed a black and white drawing of the English royal family gathered around a tree loaded with small decorations. Queen Victoria's husband, Prince Albert, a devout Lutheran, had initiated the practice seven years earlier when, in readiness for Christmas, he had imported fir trees, presumably in tubs, from his home castle at Coburg in Germany.

As England's royal family was then more popular than it would be for perhaps a whole century, its private Christmas trees were soon imitated in the hallways or dining rooms of many prosperous households. There was then no prejudice in borrowing ideas from Germany, for England and especially Prussia lived in peace and had much in common. The German words of the Christmas carols 'Silent Night' and 'Away in a Manger' were happily translated into English and learned by heart.

Amongst English-speakers, the idolising of Christmas owed much to Charles Dickens and his story *A Christmas Carol*. He wrote this pint-sized novel in a hurry towards the end of 1843, and it appeared in the bookshops almost too late for Christmas, with only six shopping days remaining. The villain of the story was the mean-spirited owner of a warehouse who employed many clerks. Dickens, calling him Scrooge and thereby adding a vivid word to the language, depicted him as a frugal and heartless employer. But on this Christmas Eve, Scrooge was suddenly transformed when, escorted silently through the streets of London, he saw his own lowly-paid employees unselfishly spreading the message of love. He saw the curtains of a house veiling a flickering coal fire, and from the house children 'running out into the snow to meet their married sisters, brothers, cousins, uncles, aunts, and be the first to greet them'. Escorted to a ship in rough seas, Scrooge was shown the officers of the watch, every one of whom 'hummed a Christmas tune, or had a Christmas thought, or spoke below his breath to his companion of some bygone Christmas Day, with homeward hopes belonging to it'.

Dickens, if he was anything specific in religion, could almost be called an Unitarian. A spectator, he stood on the very edge of Christianity, but his little book made its way to the foot of Christmas trees in thousands of homes on both sides of the Atlantic. With scarcely a direct hint that Bethlehem had even existed, he expressed a universal spirit of love and merriment in his exultant prose.

At the same time Handel's sacred oratorio *Messiah* was becoming a favourite at Christmas. It had not been sung often in his lifetime, and rarely if ever at Christmas. First performed in Dublin in April 1742, it was heard a total of only five times in the British Isles in its initial two years, not once in its third year, and not often in the following ten years, except in those expensive fundraising performances at the large new chapel of the Foundling Hospital 'For Exposed and Deserted Young Children' in London. The composer and his work, however, were seen with some suspicion by the evangelicals – the very group that a century later were to love him. They knew that he was a voracious eater and drinker and a loud swearer too. They did not know that he was a committed Lutheran, and that in his last years – when blind – he was to be seen publicly praying on his knees in St George's Anglican Church in Hanover Square, London.

The *Messiah* mingled baroque music with vivid sentences taken straight from the King James Bible. Its words as much as its music appealed to evangelicals in the 1850s. They called it *The Messiah*: for them there could only be one Messiah. The oratorio was regularly staged in the great town halls of England at Christmas and the male and female choirs singing it were huge, compared to the fifteen or twenty men and boys forming the chorus in Handel's day. To go out on a cold dark night to a town hall or big church to hear the *Messiah* was the closest most Protestants came to making a pilgrimage, and many made it with uplifted spirits. In northern Europe, Bach's *Christmas Oratorio* enjoyed a similar revival, thanks to Felix Mendelssohn, who rediscovered it.

As extreme poverty was diminishing, most English people could afford a Christmas dinner. The consumer society, with its busy advertising in newspapers and on billboards, and its brilliant displays of gifts in the gaslit windows of shops, was invading nearly all households. Gifts were still called 'Christmas and New Year presents' but they were now bought in the weeks before Christmas. In New York in December 1867, Macy's new department store remained open until midnight for the very first time and, more astonishingly, December for the first time supplanted May as the busiest shopping month.

Initially, the early Christians had borrowed an ancient pagan festival that marked the year's shortest day and converted it into their annual celebration of Christ's birth. By the twentieth century, the pagans were recapturing Christmas.

Easter was changing less as a celebration of the church. Like Christmas, it was celebrated more by Catholics, Orthodox Christians, Anglicans and Lutherans than by evangelical Protestants. In England the Puritans were quiet at Easter: the event and the way it had long been celebrated smacked of papacy. Most of the young Puritan British colonies of what became the United States did not extol Easter, though Anglican Virginia and Catholic Louisiana were exceptions. In the 1860s the American Civil War served to elevate Easter Sunday as a significant day for Protestants, for that day was chosen by many churches to commemorate young men who had died in the war. As white was the liturgical colour for Easter, white flowers were picked to decorate the pulpits, the seats and the windows of Baptist, Disciples of Christ and other Protestant buildings. The Bermuda lily, appearing in many vases, became known as the Easter Lily.

THE HEYDAY OF SUNDAY

Sunday, too, was about to be liberated in the English-speaking world. That day had long emitted a solemn flavour and feeling, and ever since the reformation English and Scottish laws stipulated what could *not* be done on Sunday. An Act of 1677 even prohibited travelling by horse or boat. A German woman visiting London during the Napoleonic Wars was astonished to find that on Sundays the theatres and shops were closed, dancing was forbidden, and in most households the playing of cards was frowned upon. She did not realise that in stricter families even the children's toys and books were put away. On the other hand, the working people of the Continent, she wrote, knew Sunday as 'a wonderful day' with perhaps a visit to church and to a theatre or inn, and 'dancing under the lime trees' in summer.

In 1848, Queen Victoria was returning to London in the new steam train and feared that she might be publicly criticised if she was seen to be travelling on Sunday. From Scotland she accordingly travelled through the night, intentionally reaching Euston Station in London at 10.30 a.m. on Sunday. She was then driven unnoticed through the quiet streets to Buckingham Palace in a horse-drawn coach, but without her normal official escort in order 'to keep everything quite quiet'. Respect for 'observing the Sabbath' was especially strong in those British colonies where the English and Scots were dominant. In the United States the north-east states knew the silent Sunday, as did Ontario in Canada and Christchurch in New Zealand. Melbourne was probably the first large city in the world to become obsessed with spectator sports, but even there public sport in the parks was banned on Sundays, as indeed it was in every English and Scottish city worthy of respect.

A farmer who ploughed on Sunday, in the period when it was widely known as the Lord's Day, was likely to be punished by a poor harvest. In the world's richest gold mines, opened near Johannesburg in South Africa in the 1880s, work on Sunday was banned by the Calvinists who ruled the republic of Transvaal, and the ban persisted even into the 1990s. In many cities public transport did not operate on a Sunday morning and no newspapers were published, and museums and public libraries were closed. Buying and selling on that day was frowned upon. Even the visiting of the sick was discouraged, especially during hours of divine service. Methodists, amongst others, were advised not to travel on a Sunday, except by foot, so that more railway and tramway employees could be free to attend church or take rest on that day. There was the strong belief that people should use the day primarily for spiritual purposes, 'by God's authority' and in keeping with the Jewish tradition.

Respect for Sunday as a holy day was called Sabbatarianism. In Protestant nations it gave the churches a virtual monopoly on Sunday entertainment, which eventually they were to lose. In the second half of the twentieth century, the family car, the Sunday 'drive' and the arrival of television in the home were to reshape Sunday in the western world. Catholics moved in the same direction, and the mass on Saturday evening was often preferred to that on Sunday morning.

The reverence for Sunday is now so out of keeping with the present desire for personal liberty that it calls for further explanation. For hosts of people their religion was the centre of their lives, and on at least one day of the week it had to be given full priority and so allow their attendance at church, private prayers, the 'perusal of the Scriptures', and the teaching of religious lessons to the young in Sunday schools. A simple physical reason also helped to enthrone Sunday as the day of rest. Before 1900, and even some time after, most people worked long hours on six days of the week and did their work while standing up. As far more did physical than mental work, by Saturday evening they were exhausted and ready for a day of quiet, free from any manual work.

THE UNSEEN GUEST

The history of Christianity does not simply encompass the lives of those who became known for preaching new doctrines. It is primarily about the everyday life of the people who practised – or neglected – their religion. Tens of millions found comfort, inspiration or rejuvenation in Christianity. Others looked at their lives in the mirror and temporarily made New Year resolutions. Hosts of others called themselves Christians and rarely visited a church, but from time to time their lives were uplifted or their fears calmed by Christian doctrine or snippets of it.

Here is an English village on Christmas morning, about the year 1850. Frost has blackened the grass, and George Eliot describes how 'the bells rang merrily', summoning to the church its largest crowd of the year. She explains that the Christmas hymn and anthem 'brought a vague, exulting sense, for which the grown men could as little have found words as the children, that something great and mysterious had been done for them in heaven above and in earth below'.

In the same decade, people in a village in Ceylon met regularly in their large new church, whose roof was supported by lofty columns. They had largely paid for it from their savings. On this day a visiting Englishman was to preach, and such was the crowd arriving on foot or in bullock wagons – it was not even a Sunday – that children were quickly sent elsewhere to make room for the adults who were eager to attend: 'The sight was novel and affecting. The many colours of women's dresses made them like garden beds of lilies and dahlias; and the trinkets on their necks, arms, and ears, gave a glitter to the scene.' While the women and the better-dressed men occupied the body of the hall, crowds of men who stood against the walls or in the doorways and windows wore no clothing on the upper parts of their bronze-coloured bodies. When the liturgy was read aloud from the pulpit, the people knew when and how to respond. Their responses were 'loud as the sound of many waters'. Many had been converted from Hinduism but still owned, from their past, metallic charms and ornaments, which they presented to the visiting English preacher and his wife.

A few decades later an author, on a walking tour in the Tyrol, saw the crucifixes erected by people on the side of the mountain roads, every fifty or 100 paces apart. The wind carried to his ears a droning sound, and he realised that it came from the Austrian peasants 'mumbling their rosaries as they march to work'. In Portugal a funeral procession was assembling, and the air of excitement amongst the surrounding children was as visible as the sombre ways of the mourners and the cluster of priests.

In Budapest in the early 1840s, a band of Scottish workmen building a bridge across the Danube was delighted when a Scottish clergyman, whose main work was to convert Hungarian Jews to Christianity, arrived to preach to the bridge-builders on Sunday. In the same decade, a letter-writer in the Sydney *Herald* called for the repairing of an early Anglican church so that a congregation could again assemble for what he described as 'the best and dearest purpose on earth' – divine service. In Europe and the Americas, millions of people thought that the buildings in which they worshipped were as precious as their own homes. Every day, all the way from Poland to the Philippines, fathers or mothers turned to the family at mealtime and asked whose turn it was to give thanks to Christ for the food. In many kitchens, just above the dining table, was a sign stitched in coloured threads and reminding all that 'Christ is the unseen guest at every meal'. Hundreds of such episodes could be recounted.

In Russia, the novelist Leo Tolstoy, several of whose earlier lives were wild and dissipated, was trying a seventh life, living as he imagined Christ's disciples had once lived in Galilee. His new life was inspired by a visit in 1878 to a dynamic Orthodox monastery, Optina Pustyn, near Moscow. On his large rural estate at Yasnaya Polyana, he gave up meat and ate simple peasant meals, and tried to manufacture his own leather boots, which proved to be almost unwearable. He discovered that the Sermon on the Mount was a hard taskmaster.

On the other hand, many millions living in Christian countries, whether in remote farmlands or smoky industrial towns, knew almost nothing about religion. In the early 1840s, in the new cities of northern England, a public investigation revealed the width of their ignorance. James Taylor, aged eleven, in reply to questioning, vowed that he had never heard the name of God, except when coalminers used it as a swear word. An eighteen-year-old woman said that she 'never heard of Christ at all'. Children who had been instructed to say the Lord's Prayer before they went to sleep were able to remember only the two words 'Our Father'. Many children did not know that Christ was part of Christmas.

It was widely believed in the nineteenth century that Christianity was still at the heart of civilisation. What was new was the growing idea that a specific brand of Christianity was no longer crucial.

28

A TASTE FOR TOLERATION

Governments had traditionally supported Christianity but endorsed or financed only one particular branch of the Church. Thus, Spain and many others supported only the Catholic Church. England supported the Church of England, Denmark the Lutheran Church, Russia the Orthodox Church, and Scotland the main Presbyterian Church, which was usually called the Church of Scotland. In most countries of Europe, the official church retained its favoured position, including the formal right to crown and bless an incoming monarch at the coronation ceremony. Here and there, experiments were made in treating all Christian and Jewish churches as equal, and the USA and revolutionary France led in such experiments. Where the experiments were leading was still uncertain.

DISMANTLING THE FENCES

In 1790, Ireland was not ruled by the Irish and the Catholics. Anglicans formed only 10 per cent of the population but controlled the parliament in Dublin and owned the lion's share of the land. Another 20 per cent of the people were Presbyterians, and mainly occupied the region standing closest to Scotland. The remaining 70 per cent were the Catholics, and most were poor, landless and not eligible to vote, though at least they were served by their own Catholic priests.

A few of the disadvantages imposed on the Catholics were whittled away. From the early 1790s they were allowed to practise law, serve as officers in the army, attend a university, and vote – if they owned property – in elections for the Irish House of Commons. The outbreak of war between England and France in 1793 increased the danger of Irish Catholics welcoming a French invasion of their island, and three years later a force of 15 000 French soldiers actually reached Bantry Bay. Henceforth, it was clear that Catholics must be given more concessions or they might rebel.

In the British Isles, most of the Protestant sects also nursed their grievances. As late as 1800, their members, like Catholics, were not eligible to be prime minister or to lead the navy or army. As late as 1850 they, along with Catholics and Jews, could not be admitted to Oxford or Cambridge universities. In England for long the Quakers, Baptists and other dissenters could not be formally married in their own church by their own pastor. In Scotland the schoolmasters and professors – until 1853 – had to profess publicly that they believed in the official Confession of Faith. Curiously, in such British colonies as Canada and Australia, the freedom to worship and the equal standing of all Christian Churches were established earlier than in the British Isles. By 1900 most of the official forms of religious discrimination in the British Isles had been repealed.

Several other nations had travelled further than Britain towards religious neutrality. France led and continued to lead. In 1905, amidst burning controversy, Catholic bishops and priests ceased to receive financial support from the French Government. The Portuguese-speaking world abandoned its long tradition. After its revolution of 1889, Brazil separated church from state but permitted Catholics to retain their valuable properties in city and countryside. In Portugal in 1910 a more aggressive revolution disowned the Catholic Church and deported priests who refused to conform.

In a few newly settled British lands the government had actually subsidised churches and sects on a neutral basis. In 1850, most of the six Australian colonies were giving annual grants to aid the main churches and their schools, especially those in remote places, the money being apportioned according to each church's share of the total population. Thus, the Anglican, Catholic and Presbyterian churches, because they possessed the most adherents, received a large share of the total subsidy and Quakers and Jews a smaller share. The Congregationalist churches, in which Oliver Cromwell the republican leader and John Milton the poet had worshipped, refused subsidies. Rightly, they called themselves the Independent Church. These subsidies eventually ceased, and each religion paid its own way.

JEWS AND OTHER OUTSIDERS

Across Europe, toleration was extended in fits and starts. In the Balkans the Muslim rulers strongly favoured their own religion, though they did make concessions. The Bulgarians, for example, were allowed to create their own breakaway branch of the Orthodox Church in 1870. Russia made guarded concessions to other Christians and virtually none to the Jews, but they did allow them to conduct their own synagogues in their own crowded enclaves. By 1830, France and most principalities of Germany gave citizenship to Jews. Italy, being a land of many governments, lacked a uniform policy, but in the first half of the century it tended to penalise Protestants and Jews, both of whom were few. In the 1840s Florence had the only university that admitted Protestants.

The same free winds, blowing across western Europe, reached the alpine slopes of north-west Italy and gave heart to the Waldensians. Perhaps no other Christian group in the heartland of Europe had been persecuted for so long. Founded in the late twelfth century by Valdes or Valdesius, a merchant of Lyons, the Waldensians were known as 'the poor men of Lyons'. Like the Franciscans, their contemporaries, they initially rejoiced in their own poverty and gave money to the poor. Eagerly they preached along the roads and byways, but Rome was wary of giving them formal approval.

The Waldensians eschewed the Cathars, who were busy in the same regions at the same time. While the Cathars were heretics, the Waldensians generally were not. Their real act of defiance was quietly to deny the existence of purgatory. Amateurs but often more effective than the professional priests and friars, they simply preached the essential Catholic message in their own way. A target of the Inquisition – that incessant Catholic search for heretics – they survived in small groups in scattered places, and in Bohemia they briefly were allied with the Hussites.

More than three centuries after the death of their founder, they were rejuvenated by the Reformation. Their Bohemian followers made contact with Luther, and their alpine-Italian followers in Piedmont turned to Calvin. In periods of hardship in the mountains, their children emigrated, and new colonies of Waldensians could be found in Calabria and Apulia in Italy and Provence in France. In Catholic countries they were careful to attend the parish church while privately retaining their own doctrines. In the spirit of the

Protestant reformers, the Waldensians resolved that their pastors could marry. They retained, however, most of their other beliefs, including their hostility to warfare.

After a brief taste of liberty, the alpine Waldensians were again a military target for their Catholic ruler. In 1655 the English poet and diplomat John Milton wrote a sonnet deploring their recent sufferings, and in Britain thereafter the Waldensians rarely lacked sympathisers. In thundering verses entitled 'On the Late Massacre in Piedmont', Milton proclaimed:

Avenge, O Lord, thy slaughtered saints, whose bones
Lie scattered on the Alpine mountains cold

More than a century and a half passed, with occasional periods of hope. Then a British officer, whose leg had been amputated after the Battle of Waterloo, went to live amongst the Waldensians and became their protector, setting up 120 schools in Piedmont. At last in 1848 they were officially given their freedom, which they celebrated by erecting a handsome neogothic 'evangelical temple' in one of the noble boulevards of Turin. The city whose rulers had long persecuted them became their home, but many of their families preferred to emigrate. It was a sign of the rising toleration shown by Catholic nations in Spanish America that Waldensian temples and Sunday schools began to flourish in Argentina and Uruguay. In 1900, for every three Waldensians who remained in the old 'mountains cold', one lived in South America.

In the new air of liberty, the Jews were viewed with friendlier eyes. In many districts of Eastern Europe they continued to live in their designated areas and to crave in vain for a few civic privileges, but in central and western Europe they were increasingly liberated.

By 1830 they held rights of citizenship, including religious freedom in France and several German kingdoms and principalities. They had long possessed religious freedom in Holland and England, though they did not vote or sit in parliament. In Florence in the mid-nineteenth century they were treated almost civilly, and in their ghetto by the river in Rome their freedom was slowly increasing. During the previous century they had formed perhaps 4 per cent of Rome's population, and the pressure on them to convert to Christianity was intense, though frequently resisted.

In Piedmont the Jews were liberated at the same time as the Waldensians; and in the local city of Turin their huge Moorish-style synagogue eventually arose, just one street away from the Waldensian temple. By 1870, in Austria, Hungary and Spain and the new united Italy, the rights of Jews were positively affirmed. Only four years later Benjamin Disraeli, a politician of Jewish ancestry, became not only the prime minister of England but also the favourite politician of Queen Victoria.

The rising tide of toleration – hailed as a hallmark of the western world in the last 150 years – is not easily diagnosed. For much of its history the Christian Church had been intolerant, and each branch of the religion had been intolerant towards other branches. This reflected the fact that Christians thought religion was the most important matter in the whole world. It was their belief that rival creeds, because they did not hold the correct keys to heaven, were depriving people of the opportunity to share in the most important gift of all: the opportunity to commune with Christ and share in what they called 'eternal life'. Such creeds did not deserve, in their opinion, to be tolerated. The rise of toleration is partly a sign of the decline in religious convictions. But a section of the world's people – so long as the human race survives – will hold strong convictions on certain topics or ideologies, and if their convictions are very strong, they will be accompanied by intolerance.

Certainly our generation will be seen as highly intolerant in some ways; and if we each lived long enough, we would probably be surprised to find ideas that now please us being widely denounced as reprehensible or dismissed as a sign of our deeply rooted intolerance by a later generation.

'ROLL, JORDAN': HOPE AND SLAVERY

For several thousand years, slavery had been accepted by moralists. The early Christians accepted slavery as part of the human condition. So far as they knew it had always existed. The Roman Empire held millions of slaves, and St Augustine of Hippo thought those slaves, of whom he had knowledge, lived a more comfortable life than did many of the poor. In most parts of the world at any one time people were enslaved, but by 1800 the white slave was no longer so common.

Quakers were probably the first religious group in Europe to condemn slavery outright. In 1774 John Wesley also condemned slavery, insisting that 'the African is in no respect inferior to the European'. Six years later, on the other side of the Atlantic, the annual Methodist conference that met in Baltimore took half a step towards disowning slavery by decreeing that its itinerant preachers should not own slaves. Hitherto, some used a slave to care for their horse, which was their only means of transport.

Meanwhile, the slave ships crossing the Atlantic from West Africa to the American coast formed the busiest long-distance passenger fleet in the world. By the year 1820, more African slaves than European free migrants had been carried to the United States. Likewise,

Brazil had received eight times as many African slaves as it received free migrants from Europe. While probably more than half of these slaves had been captured and enslaved by Muslims in Africa, they were purchased there by Europeans and carried away in ships whose captains and owners were nominally Christian, and sometimes intensely Christian.

Most slaves were pagans when they left the African coast, but in the United States most became Christians. In their knowledge of the Bible, they were at least as well-informed as the typical white American. They did not necessarily have to adopt the church of their owners. In the lowlands of South Carolina, most of the slave-owners were Episcopalians – in short, they were American Anglicans – but the slaves themselves preferred to join the Baptists, Methodists or other evangelical sects.

On Sunday nearly all slaves dressed in their best, their favourite colour being red. They might wear no boots on weekdays but on Sundays they liked to wear shoes, which, being expensive, they treated with care. Some put on their precious shoes only when they approached the church door. To be stylish inside the church was a privilege for those who had few privileges.

In the American slave-owning states, and on the westwards frontier, a new style of worship was emerging. It was not confined to the black congregations but they expressed it most distinctively with the stamping of feet, the clapping of hands, the swaying of bodies and loud spontaneous cries, to which the preacher often responded. This style was visible in slave congregations and in new independent churches with their free black pastors. Probably the first such congregation was the African Methodist Episcopal Church, founded in Philadelphia in 1816. That the sect bedecked Methodism with bishops' robes was an idea that would have pleased Wesley. Soon the south of the United States had more and more black clergymen and independent black churches.

Fanny Kemble was one of the best actresses in the English-speaking world in the late 1830s when first she visited her husband's cotton plantations in Georgia. Hearing that a young black man bearing the Old Testament name of Shadrack had just died, she provided a cotton cloth to serve as a winding sheet for his body; when she arrived for the funeral, she found the coffin resting on trestles outside a cottage and a slave named London, 'a Methodist preacher of no small intelligence and influence amongst the people', waiting to conduct the ceremony. The mourners, gathering around, had come in daylight from all around: they would go home in the darkness.

The mourners began to sing, London himself giving out the words, presumably line by line. No musical instrument was to be heard, just the voices. In modern films evoking the era of slavery, the hymns are often sung as part songs but here the congregation sang as one. They commenced their singing with a sad, high wailing note that, Fanny Kemble recalled, 'sent a thrill through all my nerves'. Following a prayer, during which all kneeled on the bare ground, the procession was ready to move in the thickening darkness towards the burial ground; and as the people walked with the aid of 'the light of pine-torches and the uprising of a glorious moon', they chanted a hymn.

It was forbidden to teach slaves how to read and write, but this preacher was literate, and he recited parts of the burial service and told the biblical story of Lazarus rising from the dead. There was something deeply impressive about the ceremony and the mood of the people. Fanny wrote to a friend: 'how I prayed and cried, for those I was praying with'. Before long she herself became a crusader against slavery.

The hymn sung in that funeral procession was probably a

'spiritual', though that word was not likely in circulation for another thirty years. The message of a spiritual, its imagery and geography culled from the Bible, was typified by 'Roll, Jordan, Roll'.

> *He comes, he comes, The Judge severe,*
> *The seventh trumpet speaks him near,*
> *Roll, Jordan, roll,*
> *Want to go to heav'n, I do.*

The Jordan was a slow trickle compared to the Mississippi, but John the Baptist had made his prophecies on its banks and Jesus had been baptised there; and many American slaves believed that they would cross the Jordan and finally reach freedom in the next life. That freedom finally arrived in this life was the result of a long campaign led primarily by Protestants.

A CRUSADE AGAINST SLAVERY

In the 1780s a few evangelical Anglicans – along with a group of Quakers – inspired the movement that finally abolished slavery in the British Empire. They formed an Abolition Society in 1787, and often their campaign in the English parliament was led by the young William Wilberforce. Twenty years later they had a major success, for a new law banned the importing of new slaves into the West Indies and other British colonies, where tens of thousands of slaves already worked on the large sugar, cotton and other plantations. Existing slaves could continue to work but replacements could no longer be imported from Africa. Slavery, however, remained a disgrace in the eyes of abolitionists, and they maintained their crusade. To own slaves and to trade in slaves 'are the greatest crime that any nation ever committed', said T. Fowell Buxton, the husband of a Quaker and strongly influenced by her family's views. In 1823 the 37-year-old crusader informed the House of Commons that 'no nation under heaven has ever been so deeply tainted' with these crimes as Britain, and accordingly many Britons would shudder when 'that day comes which shall disclose all secrets and unveil all guilt' – the Day of Judgement.

Finally, in 1833, slavery in the British colonies – the West Indies held the most slaves – was abolished. A triumph for Protestant churches more than for any other group, it exerted pressure on other slave-owning countries. In 1848 France permanently abolished slavery in its colonies, but French-owned ships were still permitted to be active in the slave trade. Portugal had banned slavery in most of its colonies but still allowed its ships to supply independent Brazil with African slaves. In effect the trade in slaves was diminished.

The nation where slavery now aroused the most publicity and indignation was the United States, one of the most vigorously Christian countries in the world. It had ceased to import slaves – only a tiny fraction of its workforce consisted of slaves – but its southern sub-tropical states were determined to retain slavery. At last, in December 1865, after the long Civil War between north and south, slavery was abolished in the United States, but it persisted in Cuba and Brazil until the 1880s, and was still practised in many parts of Africa and Asia, and especially in Muslim countries, in the twentieth century.

WAS GOD DISAPPEARING OR DYING?

The deepest fear inside most of the churches focused on the rise of doubt. Claus Harms, a Lutheran preacher in north Germany, made his name by responding to the clamour of rationalism. In 1817 at Kiel, on the 300th anniversary of Luther's protest at Wittenberg, Pastor Harms published his own ninety-five theses for these stirring times. He singled out Reason for attack. Argumentative and all-knowing, Reason had climbed into the pulpit and, taking in hand the Bible, had tried to trash it.

The Germans, now becoming the leaders in theology and philosophy, led these forces of Reason. They studied critically the Bible and also the mental processes that readers brought to the Bible. Why, they asked, do we know that we know? Immanuel Kant and a long line of notable thinkers, many from Lutheran backgrounds, led these debates. They were heightened in 1835 and 1836 when the theologian David Friedrich Strauss wrote his *Life of Jesus*. He dissected the stories and parables of the New Testament one by one, especially those that dwelt on the miracles of Christ. Some saw it as the most devastating religious book of the century. He was like a tornado, tearing down trees on both sides of the once-safe road. His prose style magnified the power of his book, and one of his German successors called it 'one of the most perfect things in the whole range of learned literature'. At first his book, widely translated, had more effect on intellectual circles than on Sunday congregations, and very little effect on Catholics.

The restless research by geologists and biologists increasingly disputed the authenticity of important verses of the Bible. The traditional Christian belief was that God had made the world and everything in it, that the planet called Earth was its centre, and that all creatures had been made by God in precisely the same form that they displayed today. In the next generation more and more thinkers questioned the idea that God, single-handed, had made the universe and that it remained unaltered. Some critical thinkers were careful in their choice of words and their selection of those to whom they confided. Other scholars replied that the universe was so astonishing, so systematic, and so varied that it must have had a divine maker. Criticisms of the accuracy of the Book of Genesis were therefore illuminating but minor.

The Old Testament was explicit in describing the creation of the world and the human race, in the space of six hectic days. Archbishop Ussher of Ireland, reading the Old Testament with care, set out an exact chronology. The world itself was created by God on Sunday 23 October 4004 BC. On the following Friday, Adam and Eve – the first male and female – appeared in the Garden of Eden, which was understood to lie somewhere in the Middle East. The world, according to this chronology, was only 6000 years old. But now research by Sir Charles Lyell, himself a Christian, and other British geologists showed that the present shape of the mountains and seas and silted plains had evolved over a vast span of time. The earth, moreover, was much older than mankind.

Archbishop Ussher's timelines, hitherto accepted by most theologians, were now in trouble. His idea that the history of human beings was brief was also given intense scrutiny. John Lubbock, who was the neighbour and friend of the scientist Charles Darwin in rural Kent, issued in 1865 his remarkable book *Pre-historic Times* and made the confident declaration that man had first appeared in Europe so long ago that history was unable 'to throw any light on his origin'. In short, the Old Testament recorded only a fraction of the long history of mankind. Adam and Noah and Moses were latecomers. To this discovery was added another, mistakenly attributed to Charles Darwin. Mankind was not created by God in one day. Indeed, human beings had not appeared straight from the hand of God. They were more likely to have evolved, with an incredible slowness. They were not unique amongst all living creatures, but closely related to the apes.

As late as 1850, these sceptical ideas reached only a tiny minority of people. Most of the devout or sometimes-devout Christians said their prayers each morning and night, and believed those prayers would be answered or at least heard. The dispute about the exact history of mankind was a sidelight for most Christians. Moreover, the scientific sceptics were merely challenging the first pages of the Old Testament and not the essence of the New Testament. If the Book of Genesis had not gone into such vivid detail, and instead affirmed simply that God had made the earth and all that was in it, this particular debate might not have cast such wide doubt on the literal accuracy of the Bible.

Even in 1850 Charles Darwin had not expressed his religious doubts in public. As a young man on the naval ship *Beagle* he had completed in 1836 his stimulating voyage to South America, New Zealand, Australia and South Africa, but safely home in England he remained a hesitant believer in orthodox Christianity. In the following twenty years, in a slow and barely noticeable series of steps and shuffles, he changed his views. In his *Autobiography* he claimed that he ceased to believe in the Old Testament story of how the world and mankind were created so speedily; he ceased to believe in 'the miracles by which Christianity is supported'; he decided that the Gospels were not necessarily eyewitness accounts; and he concluded that the concept of hell and eternal punishment formed 'a damnable doctrine'.

This recollection of his own change of mind suggests that he himself, on his own initiative, was mentally exploring his religious dilemma. The intellectual world, however, was alive with these ideas, potentially disturbing to Christians. His grandfather, Dr

Erasmus Darwin, poet and country doctor, was called a 'freethinker' because he had voiced several of these major doubts a few decades before Charles Darwin was born. Even in 1859, in his path-finding scientific book *The Origin of Species*, Charles largely held his tongue on religious matters.

Darwin would not even have published that book and stirred the pot of science but for the arrival from the Indonesian archipelago of a rival essay written by the brilliant naturalist A. R. Wallace. So Darwin, great man that he was, is grossly overrated as the sower of seeds of religious doubt. He was more the harvester of seeds that others had sowed. Even his remarkable theory of biological evolution did not necessarily lead to the conclusion that religion was dead. His fellow discoverer, Wallace, retained his questing spirit and later blossomed as a spiritualist.

It is often argued that hosts of mainstream Christians were disturbed by the new scientific research because they had long believed that every single sentence in the Bible was divinely inspired. And yet the Bible, verse by verse, was not seen as sacrosanct by orthodox theologians. For hundreds of years it had been disputed in subtle or forthright ways: the Reformation itself was such a dispute. St Augustine, dictating ceaselessly to his secretaries in North Africa nearly 1500 years ago, had challenged the Book of Genesis and its sequence of events. Scholars, long dead, had frequently weighed one chapter of the New Testament against another when events in the life of Christ were reported differently. In Europe, century after century, more mental effort had been devoted to detailed debates about facets of Christianity than to any other topic. This age-old and continuing debate had exposed acute disagreements about the spiritual importance and accuracy of one gospel compared to another. For most Christians, moreover, the path to salvation, road-mapped in the New Testament, was infinitely more worthy of debate than the history of the earth and its inhabitants, as set out in one pithy page of the Old Testament.

Christianity had dominated all fields of knowledge for so long – most of the early universities were its creation – that its leaders were slow to realise that in new fields of research they had no innate advantage. In retrospect, mainstream Christians should have been willing to concede some ground to the well-equipped forces of science. After all, it did not necessarily matter that Christians had been seriously mistaken in their chronology of the history of the earth. That topic was not central to their beliefs. Central for them was whether God had created all living things or had merely laid down the design that was followed by the process of evolution. On such questions the most learned scientists threw serious doubts, but they were not able to prove the new notion that all living things had slowly and painfully evolved on their own. Nor could the most learned Christians prove definitely the truth of their contrary beliefs.

Eminent scientists themselves proved to be woefully mistaken in the new chronology they confidently drew up: they underestimated the age of life on earth a hundredfold. Moreover, they underestimated the earth's likely future, for they believed it was growing colder and would, in the far future, be unable to support human life. Such is the present prestige of science that its failures in this vital debate have been forgotten while those of Christian leaders are vividly recounted in most history books that touch on the topic.

New science was over-confident. Christianity had also been too confident, and its leaders were slow to realise that the spiritual and unseen realm, not the measurable and physical realm, was their home ground.

One influential group of Christians came to accept evolution.

Whether God did or did not intervene in nature, creating a flood here or an earthquake there, did not perturb them. Cardinal Newman quickly absorbed the new idea of biological evolution without altering his Christian faith. Frederick Temple, the archbishop of Canterbury, told his faithful adherents in 1896 not to worry about these criticisms but to accept them and rejoice in them. 'I speak of evolution as a fact,' he informed a congress of churchmen. Christians should rather say, 'You have set before me what was not so well known a hundred years ago; you have set before me a proof that God works in a particular manner which people formerly did not generally understand.' Likewise, some gifted scientists, devout Christians, simply maintained that the earth and all within it were so marvellous and intricate that surely 'the Lord God made them all'. Please, rejoice in the design and the designer! So said Lord Kelvin, one of the most versatile scientists of the nineteenth century.

'CAPTAIN OF MY SOUL'

Intellectuals who felt nagging doubts about the traditional Christian doctrines did not necessarily derive their doubts from scientific research. John Stuart Mill, philosopher and economist, an eloquent exponent of individual liberty, including the liberty of women, was guided by his father up the stairs of atheism. A child prodigy, taught mostly in the course of long walks with his father through rural areas of outer London, he had no need to go to a school. By the time he was ten, he was far advanced in Latin, ancient Greek and arithmetic. On religion he inherited his views. His Scottish father had been licensed to preach in the pulpit when young, but abandoned the calling because he did not believe in God or any other 'supreme governor of the world'. When, almost half a century later, John Stuart

Mill was completing his autobiography he confided chirpily that he was one of the few living Britons who had 'not thrown off religious belief'. He did not have to throw it off. He 'never had it', he confessed.

He was proud to be an unbeliever. He informed his readers that they would be astonished if they knew how many of Britain's 'brightest ornaments – of those most distinguished even in popular estimation for wisdom and virtue – are complete sceptics in religion'. Mill was probably writing about the top fifty or so intellectuals, most of whom he knew. At a guess maybe half of the fifty were sceptics. Many of these sceptics were hesitant to express their religious doubts in public because they firmly believed that the common people must still be encouraged to believe in heaven and hell. Otherwise, human society would fall to pieces. The French Revolution had shown that anarchy rumbled just below the surface.

A few dozen of the powerful intellects in the British Isles, Germany and France said openly what they thought about Christianity. Foremost amongst the English doubters were the poets Matthew Arnold and William E. Henley, whose verses eventually were reprinted even in poetry books for the schoolroom. It was Henley who announced:

I am the master of my fate:
I am the captain of my soul.

Thomas Carlyle, a Scot, was the major doubter in the eyes of British and German readers. His father was a clever stonemason and builder, and his mother, when not caring for the children, infused her favourite son with her biblical viewpoint. The sect to which they belonged was the New Light Burghers, which was a breakaway from yet another sect that had left the powerful Church of Scotland.

In Ecclefechan, not far from the English border, the sect's simple church building – at one time roofed with thatch – could hold 600 people at a time when the town barely held twice that number. To this most popular church in the town, 'pious weavers' and rural folk arrived each Sunday, some having walked for 10 or 15 miles. Thomas Carlyle, long after he had left Scotland, did not forget Preacher John-stone and the devout atmosphere in the bare but crowded church. He said that all the listeners, presumably he amongst them, were 'lit up by tongues of authentic flame from Heaven'.

Carlyle once thought of becoming a clergyman, but after suffering a religious crisis he became a teacher and then, in the seclusion of the Scottish countryside, a serious author. With his wife, Jane, he moved to a house only a few minutes from the banks of the Thames, in inner London, where he expressed his thoughts about the state of the world in simmering, staccato sentences. Carlyle's first bestseller, *The French Revolution: A History*, was published in three volumes in 1837, the first year of Queen Victoria's reign. Soon the young fell at Carlyle's feet, seeing him as a lighthouse in the troubled times.

While he no longer believed that Christ was divine, he remem-bered Christian principles from the Scottish kirk of his youth. The poor were as worthy as the rich, perhaps more so. The humble poor were worthier than the ordinary poor. For businessmen to pursue what Carlyle called 'Mammon', and to relentlessly make money, was to suffer from a curse. At the end of their lives, all individuals had to answer for their actions. For Carlyle no heaven existed, but he envisaged a judgement seat where all had to sit and face their own conscience. During his long life his writings tended to increase reli-gious disbelief, and yet he retained respect for the spirit of religion: 'The Church: what a word was there; richer than Golconda and the treasures of the world! In the heart of the remotest mountains rises the little Kirk; the Dead all slumbering around it, under their white memorial stones, in hope of a happy resurrection.'

This was the kirk or church of his parents and his childhood. He also felt a sympathy for Muslims, who, like the simple Scots of old Ecclefechan, were unwavering in their faith: 'these Arabs believe their religion, and try to live by it!' The official and formal stream of Christianity no longer had an appeal for Carlyle when he was wearing his logical hat but his emotions were still more vulnerable than he realised. In old age he walked one afternoon in Battersea Park near his home, and hearing a child play the hymn tune 'Pilgrim of the Night', he was overwhelmed by the emotion stirred in him. Christianity tugged at his sleeves but he had to walk away from it, which he did with difficulty. Upon his death in 1881, the Dean of Westminster Abbey offered a burial place for the body of this troubled prince of agnostics, but Carlyle had already expressed his wish to be buried, without funeral speeches, alongside his parents in Scotland.

Other critics of Christianity were also the children of families who were deeply devout. In the 1840s the English novelist Marian Evans, who later wrote under the name of George Eliot, had to explain to her father that she no longer believed in God and now regarded the Bible as 'mingled truth and fiction'. Moreover, she told him that she no longer wished to attend church. It was one of the most embarrassing meetings in the life of both daughter and father, for they loved each other. Partly because of her bravery and radicalism, George Eliot had a degree of fame – she was seen as almost the successor to Goethe in the grand court of European literature – that is now difficult to imagine.

The new unbelievers often displayed a deep sense of the mystery of life. John Morley was a Wesleyan who turned Anglican and then gave up his ambition of becoming a clergyman, instead becoming a man of letters, a leading politician, and a dissident member of the British cabinet that made the decision to go to war against Germany in 1914. Of him, George Meredith the novelist said: 'Cut him open, and you will find a clergyman inside.' Emotionally but not intellectually he was still close to his old religion.

THE WALLS OF DOUBT

Today it is widely assumed that most of the leading scientists nursed these religious doubts. And yet in 1850 most probably believed in God. Gregor Mendel was almost as important as Charles Darwin in probing the tantalising question of the origins and evolution of new species. He did most of his experiments with pea plants in a monastery garden near Brno in central Europe. An Augustinian priest, he retained his faith.

Michael Faraday did as much as anybody to unravel the principles of electricity. He built, in 1821, a simple electric motor, and later lent his surname to the Faraday Laws and the celebrated Faraday Effect. In London on Sundays he took his place as an elder of an unusual sect, the Glasites or Sandemanians, who had arisen in Scotland just before the start of Wesley's crusade. It was not the kind of sect likely to attract one of the world's great scientists, for it demanded unanimity of thought on religious matters, and even prohibited its members from praying in company with those of other sects. Faraday died in 1867, by which time the Darwinian ideas were being heatedly debated, but he was still a leader of his sect.

In the year of Faraday's death only a tiny minority of people in the western world said aloud that no God existed. It took courage to say so, and many did not declare what they really thought to their own families. It was easier for intellectuals to make their stand in the relative safety of a German or French university or in a book published in a big city where a prosecution – atheism was against the law in some lands – was less likely to be initiated.

In some European countries those bold enough to say that they were atheists might not be appointed to the positions, public and private, that their talents merited. When they died, they might not always receive permission to be buried in consecrated ground, alongside their relatives. If they had to swear an oath, in court or in other official places, they had to refuse to hold a Bible in their hand as a sign of their sincerity. A controversy was sparked in England in 1880 when Charles Bradlaugh, who had risen from the ranks of errand boy to that of popular lecturer, won a seat in the House of Commons. He was denied entry because, being an atheist, he would not swear the official time-honoured oath. Twice the people of Northampton had to re-elect him before he was permitted to take the oath and occupy his seat in the House. As late as 1900, nearly all the political leaders in the western world formally shunned atheism.

Several learned observers concluded that midway between Christianity and atheism lay a wide strip of vacant ground. Neither side could capture it. Neither side could demolish its rival, intellectually. Christians, relying more on faith, intuition, imagination and a sense of wonder and mystery, could usually prevail in debates on their home ground – religion. Scientists, with their insistence on evidence and measurement, and their search for general theories and for certainties and predictability, usually prevailed on their home ground, though more in the physical sciences than the natural sciences. As for the deep question – is there a God? – Christian intellectuals could not prove the existence of God, and scientists could not disprove it.

The deadlock seemed permanent. It was the French Jesuit Teilhard de Chardin who expressed it distinctively. His posthumous book, *The Phenomenon of Man*, was to argue in 1959 that science and religion were two sides of the same phenomenon, a quest for perfect knowledge, and that each side was vital. And yet each side often insisted that there was only one truth, and that it could be seen perfectly clearly in the mirror that it had selected.

The truths on which Christianity rested – that Jesus was the Son of God, that he had risen from the dead, and that one day he would return to this earth to judge the living and the dead – were challenged more often. In fringe Christian chapels, especially those of the Unitarians who flourished in and around Boston and once controlled Harvard University, many of the attenders doubted the divinity of Christ. These doubters had tended to be informal members of churches in 1800 but they rarely entered them in 1900 – unless a wedding or funeral demanded that they attend. These critics were more and more influential, because now they dared to speak publicly.

Many young men who thought of entering the church as a lifelong career felt moments or even months of religious doubt. Even in the times of St Francis or Luther, many must have held these doubts, but now the doubters multiplied. William Temple, a brilliant Oxford philosopher, decided in 1906 to follow his father into the Anglican ministry – his ambition since childhood. But the particular bishop who initially blocked his entry felt obliged to explain that Temple did not fully believe in the Virgin Birth and in the bodily resurrection 'of Our Lord'. Temple persisted and was finally admitted to the Anglican ministry. Eventually, he became the archbishop of Canterbury, at a time when Christianity and intellectual freedom and the whole western world were in more peril than any prophet in the nineteenth century could have imagined.

29

THE AGE OF STEAM AND HASTE

In the few lands of freedom, almost anything and everybody could be analysed and criticised, and so the pope was a simple target. Pius IX, elected in 1846, seemed likely to survive such criticism. In some ways he knew the world. As a young Italian priest he had visited Chile, thus designating him as probably the first pope who, at some stage of his life, had set eyes on the Pacific Ocean, the world's largest. Soon after becoming pope he showed signs of being a moderate liberal, and in Italy he was praised by graffiti in the streets. Revolutionary ideas were in the air. Perhaps he would listen to them.

THE POPE STANDS TALL

When the revolutions ran from the Mediterranean to the Baltic in that tumultuous year of 1848, the pope became firmer. He feared that the revolutionary tide might tumble ashore and sweep away the cathedrals and bishops' palaces and erode the foundations of Catholicism.

Pope Pius IX saw liberalism and the growth of democracy as dangerous enemies. While the mass of people tended to see democracy as a blazing rocket of hope, the pope saw it as a noisy display of fireworks, signifying confusion. Attacking democracy in December 1864, in what he called 'The Syllabus of Errors', he also criticised another modern movement: the rising nationalism, of which the newly united Italy was an exponent. He stood rather for internationalism, being the head of what was almost certainly the most universal body in the whole world. The voice of traditional authority, he was apprehensive about the new political mood in parts of Europe, and the rising hostility to priests and the Catholic Church. The mood was described by a word freshly coined in the 1860s – anticlericalism.

The pope's nervousness was increased by the rise of Garibaldi and his crusade to unite Italy. Most Italians hoped for one government, ruling a united nation. That, however, would end the papacy's right to control its own Papal States, spanning the centre of Italy. For centuries the papacy had been a secular power with its own tax collectors, its own courts, and its own troops guarding its own substantial Italian territories and cities. By 1860 the evidence was strong that the people living in the Papal States wished to join the fast-uniting Italy. The pope had little chance of defending his own territory. His army was small, the artillery weak. Even the arrival of Irish volunteers disguised as 'navvies' did not really strengthen his armed forces. After a brief campaign, nearly all the area he governed – stretching from the port of Rome to the Adriatic – was captured by Italian armed forces. All that remained in his hands was part of the city of Rome.

Worse was to come. In August 1870 the French soldiers who guarded the Vatican were called home: their own nation was being invaded by Prussia. In the following month the forces of King Victor Emmanuel of Italy seized the Vatican: they were occupiers, not caretakers as the French had been. The pope remained the main spiritual ruler in the world but was no longer a civilian ruler in his own right. The Vatican ceased to be a nation. For the next half-century, even the dome of St Peter's was not on papal territory. In Catholic circles it was feared that the pope might cease to be so powerful, spiritually, because he was no longer an independent monarch protected by his own territory.

In this unique crisis Pius IX saw an opportunity to enhance his prestige and the authority of all the popes who came after him by declaring their major edicts and pronouncements to be 'infallible'. Admittedly, a pope's pronouncements on 'faith or morals' had always been close to infallible, for on earth he was the servant of Christ and the purported spokesman 'for all Christians'. Several medieval popes, including Gregory VII, had pursued the same goal of infallibility, their aim being to make every king answerable to the pope on religious matters. Now, in a more democratic era, Pius IX called in a different way for a higher level of obedience and respect. As one of the foremost leaders in the history of the papacy, and the only pope to reign for more than twenty-five years, he was almost certain to enlist the Catholic support he needed.

A council of the church was summoned, and archbishops and bishops poured into Rome. Their task was to resolve the question: is the pope not only supreme but also infallible? They were expected to answer 'yes'. In short, they must affirm that the pope 'possesses that infallibility with which the Divine Redeemer was pleased to invest his church'. A minority of bishops thought the time was not politically ripe for a decree that defied the European trend towards liberalism. On 17 July 1870, one day before the vote was taken, about sixty bishops left Rome rather than publicly proclaim their dissent. Only two opponents remained: the final tally was 533 votes to two.

The vote had been taken during a thunderstorm. The thunder did not go away. While the massive supporting vote bolstered the authority of Pius IX, it did not win him Protestant friends, for it proclaimed the supremacy of Catholic doctrine over that of all other churches. The claim that the pope was infallible vexed the patriarchs of the Orthodox Church in Constantinople and Moscow. It stung the learned William E. Gladstone, the prime minister of England, who was himself an amateur theologian, and it stung the strong Prussian leader Otto von Bismarck: both were firm Protestants. In Germany a minority of Catholics, led by Dr J. J. Dollinger of Munich, also opposed the doctrine of infallibility on theological grounds. Dollinger was excommunicated.

The papacy represented a very long tradition of conservatism. A source of strength, conservatism could also be a hazard in a quick-changing world. For many Catholics, the Church's error was to attack too many modern trends. In 1878 the papacy condemned communism and facets of socialism, and then condemned facets of capitalism after the twentieth century dawned. It also criticised birth control.

Some ardent Catholic worshippers argued that their church was making a mistake in isolating itself in this era of change and haste. In fact, by standing firm it seemed to maintain, in the following 100 years, a higher proportion of its adherents than did those Protestant sects who changed sail in the wind.

PILGRIMS IN AN AGE OF STEAM

For centuries an everflowing stream of people possessing intellectual ambitions or talents had embraced the Church as their lifelong profession or calling. That stream of inflowing talent was no longer so wide. New professions were open to talent. Christianity, however, was still a topic of high intellectual interest, and the bookshops of Prague and Amsterdam reflected it. In Europe more books of theology were sold than the combined books of travel, biography and history. In England until 1900, half of the new books published each year were on religious topics. The Christian Church in most of its shapes and shades was in sound health.

There was a quickening desire by Catholics to make pilgrimages. Railways enabled them during a long weekend to visit shrines that, five centuries earlier, could be reached only on foot or horseback. French crowds went in long steam trains to the shrine at Lourdes, where many of the pilgrims – blind, deaf, lame or suffering from incessant pain – prayed for a miracle. Italian trains carried crowds to Rome, Assisi, Loreto and other holy places. Russian women went on railway excursions to the notable monasteries within reach of Moscow and felt an inward peace or even ecstasy when they stood on soil where a saintly monk was said to have trodden. It is fair to say that pilgrimages of, say, 200 miles were far more frequent than even during the peak years of the medieval crusades, but then again, the Catholic and the Orthodox populations were higher than ever.

Jerusalem became a frequent goal, thanks to the steamers that carried passengers across the Mediterranean Sea and the new French-built railway that conveyed them from the coast to the heights of Jerusalem in 1892. For the last six centuries Jerusalem had been permanently in the hands of Muslims, but now the Ottoman Turks readily accepted the Christian pilgrims who arrived in large parties. Week after week in the tourist season the Russian pilgrims arrived – a journey of a lifetime that was recreated in several of the great Tolstoy's tantalising short stories. Small parties of Protestants – an ideology that did not believe in pilgrimages – frequently visited the sacred or exotic sights in the Holy Land, and sent home to the USA the postcards they had bought from street hawkers. They did not call themselves pilgrims but they were.

From Jerusalem the overseas pilgrims made short excursions to see Bethlehem and its vineyards and cornfields, and to the banks of the River Jordan, in whose sacred waters they soaked the shrouds in which they hoped, after safely returning home, to be wrapped on their day of burial. Those who knew their Bible gained inspiration by walking along the road to Nazareth or ascending the Mount of Olives. Items carved from olive wood were amongst the souvenirs they tenderly carried home.

England and Prussia had combined to finance their own resident bishop of Jerusalem, who would minister to Protestants trading or sightseeing in Ottoman lands. The first bishop, chosen in 1841, was Solomon Alexander, a Jew from the Grand Duchy of Posen on the Baltic coast. As a young rabbi he was converted to Christianity in England and then ordained as an Anglican clergyman with the mission of converting Jews to his new religion. Having served faithfully as missionary to the Jews around Danzig and preached often in the Episcopal Jews' Chapel in Palestine Place in London, and having held the chair of Hebrew at King's College in the same city, he was considered to be the ideal choice as bishop of a diocese that it was hoped might extend even to Abyssinia. The British Government farewelled him, his wife and many children – and two accompanying clergymen and a physician – as they boarded the steamship *Declaration*, specially hired for their voyage to Jaffa.

The bishop arrived in cold Jerusalem in January 1842. He must have been dismayed to find that Protestants held no foothold and not even a prayer-mat in the major shrines, whereas unfamiliar Christians such as Coptics, Armenians and Russian Orthodox owned three of the four chapels inside the large church on the site where Jesus was said to have been buried.

In the following decades the Ottoman Turks permitted Christian groups to build more churches, chapels, hospitals, convents and memorials at the places where Jesus had preached. Kaiser Wilhelm II of Germany, in his successful visit of 1898, acquired a large site for a German Catholic Church on Mount Zion, and a site on which the Church of the Redeemer could be built for German Protestants. The Kaiser, dressed in the white mantle of the Teutonic Knights, took the opportunity to remind the world that the heavenly light originating in Jerusalem had made Germany a 'great and glorious nation'. Such was the glamour and accessibility of Jerusalem in the age of steam that some pilgrims predicted that one day the pope himself might decide to spend part of his summers or autumns there.

THE RED CROSS AND BASKETBALL

Social movements founded by the young for the young are essentially modern. It was in London in 1844 that George Williams, in his mid-twenties, formed perhaps the most successful young peoples' movement that Christians had seen so far.

The son of a west England farmer, Williams had been amongst the tens of thousands of young people who flocked from towns and villages to the big European cities to work in the expanding white-collar occupations such as shop assistant and office clerk. At first he lived with 140 other young men in the large dormitories provided by the London draper employing them. Though they worked long hours, the young men had free time on certain evenings and throughout Sunday, especially during those hours when no church services were held. As many must have come from deeply religious backgrounds, for most white-collar firms liked to employ such people, George Williams had no trouble in forming a small religious club where they could discuss serious topics, read the Bible, pray and sing. A drapery firm lent them the room, where their Young Men's Christian Association was born. The dozen founders were equally divided between Congregationalists, Wesleyans, Anglicans and Presbyterians: normally, that was not a formula for success.

Outgrowing their original room, they rented a large building in which they set aside a library and newspaper room, and a lecture hall for evangelical addresses. Foreign languages were taught. Sofas and armchairs gave a relaxed air. On Sundays from 5 to 8 p.m., hot cups of tea or chocolate and plates of refreshments were handed around by the club's servants, and the friendly atmosphere and novel amenities attracted other young unmarried men.

London members travelling on business to other English cities inquired, 'Why don't you have a YMCA?', and gave advice on how to create one. Young German businessmen eagerly set up their YMCA clubs. Scots already had them under another name, and eventually united with the English association. By 1850 South Australia had two such clubs, in the following year Amsterdam and Montreal and Boston founded theirs, and even the clerks of tropical Calcutta opened their own in 1854.

A year later Paris was to stage an exciting trade fair that displayed the latest machines, patents and commercial novelties. As it was likely to fascinate spectators just as the earlier Crystal Palace, the world's first great exhibition, had excited them in London, the various branches of the YMCA agreed to hold a combined meeting in Paris, which many of their members were already planning to visit. In Paris the ninety-nine delegates, coming from both sides of the Atlantic, agreed to form a world organisation to govern or guide the

YMCA. They not only wished to set up practical meeting places around the world but to spread a Christian message. 'We seek,' they said, 'to unite those young men who, regarding Jesus Christ as their God and Saviour, according to the Holy Scriptures, desire to be His disciples in their faith and in their life.'

To the founder, George Williams, alcoholic spirits and gambling and even tobacco were demons waiting to trap his friends, the shop assistants. Another demon was hidden in the cheaper racks of the bookstalls. John Fairfax, an Australian newspaper-owner, warned the members of the YMCA who met regularly in Sydney in 1856 that one of the 'greatest curses of the present day is the reading of sensational novels'. In his opinion, the 'heroes and heroines of these tales are often nothing less than adulterers and adulteresses'.

Women were not yet employed in these big offices and shops and so were outside the ambit of the new YMCA. But here and there, young women felt a need to set up their own societies on similar Christian lines. In the south of England in 1855, Miss Robarts formed a prayer union, and Lady Kinnaird set up houses where young business women could meet and talk in their leisure hours, or even reside. Eventually, the two female groups united to form the Young Women's Christian Association. It too became global.

The older all-male YMCA, while Puritan in spirit, displayed an outer cheerfulness and heartiness. In the United States, eventually its stronghold, many of its members favoured athletic activities. In 1891 the branch at Springfield in Massachusetts actually invented the game of basketball, and a neighbouring branch four years later invented the game of volleyball. In east Asia, in many cities stretching from Tokyo to Singapore, the YMCA became a training ground for potential national leaders. The first president of South Korea, Syngman Rhee, had worked when young with the local YMCA, while the political master of modern Singapore, Lee Kuan Yew, had his own reasons for praising it. As a struggling university student, he reached London in a troopship after the end of World War II and temporarily needed a bed. From the phone book he found a local address for 'The Y', as it was now called, and hurried there: 'The receptionist was a good Christian, friendly and sympathetic. He gave me a room for a fortnight.'

The Red Cross was conceived by this same religious movement, which was attracting young businessmen on both sides of the Atlantic. Henry Dunant, born into a Calvinist family, was a leader of a small Evangélique group in Geneva. His group became part of the YMCA; and it was Dunant who actually suggested that its first international conference be held at the time of the Paris Exhibition in 1855. His letter of invitation to all the branches of the YMCA expressed his own hopes, and those of his Geneva friends, to 'spread abroad that ecumenical spirit' that embraces all Christian Churches, sects and groups. 'I believe in the Communion of Saints and in the Holy Catholic Church,' he wrote, to which he added the rarely stated affirmation that all Christians should be friends.

Dunant's own business interests were in French Algeria; four years after the Paris conference he tried to arrange a meeting with the French emperor, who was then in north Italy, directing his troops in their short war against an Austrian army. By chance, Dunant, always an optimist, strayed almost to the edge of the battlefield at Solferino, just south of Lake Garda. There, to his dismay, he saw the carnage of the heaviest fighting experienced in Europe since the Battle of Waterloo, forty-four years before. The short battle was almost over, thousands of Austrian, French and Italian troops were lying wounded, and the modern rifles and artillery had spilled blood on such an unprecedented scale that the medical services were unable to help all the wounded and the dying. Dunant tried briefly to organise help for the wounded. Later, in his hometown of Geneva, he and a few friends from the YMCA and other groups created a small organisation called the Red Cross. At first it was primarily a Protestant group, but in time it welcomed Catholic, Jewish, Buddhist and other volunteers, eventually becoming the largest humanitarian organisation in the world.

George Williams' original London group, beginning humbly amidst the smell of fresh linen and cotton, was like a tiny shop that became a global emporium. It turned its attention not only to clerks but eventually to university students, whose numbers were soaring. Once again it acted globally. In 1895 John Raleigh Mott, a young Methodist American who held the grand title of travelling secretary of the YMCA, joined with Swedish and other student leaders to form the World Student Christian Federation, under a banner proclaiming 'the evangelisation of the world in our generation' – surely one of the most ambitious mottos in the history of Christendom. Its leaders had the feeling – widespread in the generation before the First World War – that they could achieve the impossible.

John R. Mott, as the first secretary of this new group, eventually saw other opportunities to Christianise the world. He was to lead the group that set up the first International Missionary Conference, which met in 1910. More than one-third of a century later, he did more than anybody to set up the World Council of Churches, the most effective attempt so far to unite the long-divided Christians. That was one of the remarkable results springing from the meeting of a few homesick shop assistants in London one century previously.

'A WOMAN'S PREACHING'

If young men could become leaders of Christianity, so perhaps could young women and even old women. The female demand for the right to preach had been spurred by the radical wings of the Reformation. In the English language, the first book to justify that right, with a trelliswork of arguments in support, was *Women's Speaking Justified*, published in 1667 by Margaret Fell, a Quaker who was later to become the wife of George Fox. Her book presumably had few readers, for nearly all women then thought that a female preacher was 'out of place' and 'uncalled for'.

Even one century later, the sight of a woman preaching spurred unease or amusement in most circles. In 1763 in London, Dr Samuel Johnson, when informed that women had recently been seen preaching in public, made a prompt response: 'Sir, A woman's preaching is like a dog's walking on his hinder legs. It's not done well; but you are surprised to find it done at all.'

In the United States half a century later, it was done well, especially by a sect called the Shakers, but not often. In 1835 in the southern USA, another popular open-air preacher was Mrs Jarena Lee, whose black face and neck were clothed by a white bonnet and shawl. To those who said that she should not preach, her reply was snappy: 'If a man may preach, because the Saviour died for him, why not the woman?' In that year alone she preached about 600 sermons. One obstacle facing the few women who wished to speak in public was that usually they had to preach in the open air, because most church buildings were not open to them.

The much-publicised crusade against slavery in the United States was initially a white male crusade. Angelina and Sarah Grimké, members of a respected Charleston family who employed slaves as servants in their house, decided that slavery was an outrage and resolved to oppose it. Moving to Philadelphia, they found the Quakers were a more sympathetic forum, but even they did not permit female members to speak in public against slavery, nor were they fully sympathetic to the idea of black Quakers. In the public arena the mainstream American Anti-Slavery Society did not enrol women as members, and so Angelina joined the new Philadelphia Female Anti-Slavery Society. Moving to New York, she hoped as a dedicated crusader against slavery, Angelina planned to speak in churches, but only a few radical ministers were willing to invite her, and then only on condition that her audience consisted solely of women. She responded in 1837 by announcing that she would lead a new campaign for the rights of women. In the United States the two Grimké sisters were probably the first to publish a systematic argument for women's rights.

The abolition of slavery in the United States in 1865 owed much to the American Civil War and much to the campaign led by Christian women as well as men. Whereas those women initially had to campaign outside the mainstream churches, their next campaign harnessed many of those churches. They now worked from within, though not yet on equal terms. The rising movement to reduce the consumption of alcohol relied heavily on these female orators, writers and petitioners who came mainly from the Baptist, Methodist, Presbyterian, Congregational, Disciples of Christ, Salvation Army and other denominations.

In the 1880s, their Women's Christian Temperance Union, a major forerunner of modern political feminism because it demanded the right to vote, became a vigorous movement amongst Protestants in the English-speaking world. Its members argued that if only women could receive the vote, they would elect politicians willing to enact laws restricting the sale of alcohol. They proved to be powerful campaigners. More women spoke in public than ever before. Their united voice strongly helped New Zealand in 1893 to become the first country to give women the vote, and helped Australia, nine years later, become the first country to give them the right both to vote and to stand for parliament. In the following quarter-century women in many European nations and the United States, too, were enfranchised.

American women of an evangelical spirit hoped that the USA, as the birthplace of their Women's Christian Temperance Union, would be the scene of another victory. Almost at the same time as American women won the right to vote, they were to the fore in seizing the opportunity to sway public opinion decisively against alcohol. They helped to impose an absolute prohibition on the sale of alcohol in the United States in the 1920s. It did not usher in the paradise they had planned.

'OUR EYES SHALL SEE THE GLORY'

At a time when the hymn book was a manual of Protestant theology, more and more women wrote hymns. Thus, in 1862, during the American Civil War, a leading opponent of slavery had written 'The Battle Hymn of the Republic', publishing it not in a hymn book but in the big-selling *Atlantic Monthly*; millions of Americans still sing Julia Ward Howe's vow that our 'eyes shall see the glory of the coming of the Lord'. In Ireland, Mrs Cecil Frances Alexander, the wife of the archbishop of Armagh, was acclaimed long before her death in 1895 as an inspiring writer of hymns: 'There is a green hill far away, without a city wall' was an early favourite, as was 'Jesus calls us o'er the tumult of our life's wild restless sea'. Possibly half of the ten-year-olds in the English-speaking world knew Mrs Alexander's refrain:

All things bright and beautiful,
All creatures great and small.
All things wise and wonderful,
The Lord God made them all.

Charles Darwin, the English scientist – almost her exact contemporary – would have disputed her simple account of how the living world was created, but it was her view of Creation, not his, that prevailed amongst adults as well as children.

Meanwhile, a few women had been allowed, before 1850, to be the pastor or leader in Unitarian churches and Quaker meeting houses. In the Primitive Methodist congregations – another English breakaway from the Wesleyans – chosen women were encouraged to deliver sermons. But the main branch of Methodism, the Wesleyans, remained almost as reluctant as the Catholics to allow women to preach inside a church. In Australia in 1890, they tactfully explained why a woman's role as preacher was in the open air rather than in a church: 'We are of opinion that, in general, women ought not to preach – 1. Because a vast majority of our people are opposed to it. 2. Because their preaching does not seem necessary. But, if any woman among us thinks she has an extraordinary call of God in public (and we are sure that it must be an extraordinary call that can authorise it), we are of opinion that she should, in general, address her own sex alone.'

In England, Mrs Catherine Booth of the new Salvation Army had already worked hard to make the female preacher acceptable, if not yet fashionable. Salvation Army women, in their bonnets, spoke from the pulpit or at the noisy street corners of cities. Those listeners who heard the most fluent speakers were often entranced.

A VOICE FROM DARKEST ENGLAND

The Salvation Army was ingenious in welding the new to the familiar. It was founded by William Booth and by his wife, Catherine, whose contribution was vital. The daughter of an English coach-builder, she was – in the crucial phrase of her time – 'respectable and refined'. She met William Booth in 1848 at a Wesleyan congregation in the London suburb of Brixton. He was three months younger, a pawnbroker who was reared by an impoverished family in Nottingham. His education was hit-and-miss, except for the Bible, which he read closely. Even when young he showed determination, sympathy with people in trouble, and a voice that expressed his emotions with penetrating volume and empathy. His mother was said to be of Jewish ancestry and he himself was often described as having 'strong Jewish features': a handsome man with densely black and shining hair. When he preached, a certain fierceness was sometimes evident. His height added to the powerful effect.

Breaking away from the Wesleyans, William Booth joined a young sect called the Methodist New Connexion, for which he became a full-time itinerant preacher, especially in the north of England. Both he and Catherine were aged twenty-six when they married; eight children followed. While they were living in Gateshead, an industrial port across the Tyne from Newcastle, Catherine sometimes stepped forward at the end of William's thundering sermons and said the closing prayers in a refined voice and reverent manner. Before long, in front of her reluctant husband, she delivered her own sermons. When in 1860 a Congregationalist pastor said that women should not preach, she responded with a courteous pamphlet. She really had no need to reply. She had already shown in public the talents she possessed.

William Booth's practice, after one of his emotional sermons, was to invite members of his audience to confess their sins and to place their trust publicly in God. In the front of his church was a penitents' form where they could sit, then kneel in repentance, and finally be calmed by the Holy Spirit. His manner hinted that he was clothed in a layer of gloom, but those he converted seemed almost unusually happy.

At his wife's suggestion, he left the Methodist sect in 1865 and formed a new church in the poor London suburb of Whitechapel. Eventually he called it the Salvation Army. Its members wore distinctive military-like uniforms and were immaculate in dress and cleanliness, for he hated grubbiness. He called his churches 'citadels'. Military titles were also adopted by their officers, male and female, for both were equal. To the dismay of professional soldiers in the British Army, William called himself General Booth.

One innovation was to seek public donations in pubs and bars – places that were increasingly seen as sinful by dissenters. A startling idea was to employ a band instead of an organ at religious services in their citadels. The brass band, then at the height of its popularity, was ideal for street marches, at which the Salvation Army excelled. In open-air services the bands required no amplifier – it was not yet invented. In the Salvationists' early years, their dashing methods of publicity seemed quite foreign to Christianity.

By 1890, on weeknights or Sundays, the sound of the cornet, drums, tambourines and cymbals could be heard in streets or citadels in a thousand cities and villages extending from Adelaide to Cape Town and Cardiff. By 1910 the red banner and the marching bands could be seen and heard in places as far apart as Argentina and Japan. The Salvation Army combined sincerity and show business. While a few Anglican bishops quietly applauded, the Methodists were not so sure about their prodigal son. After all, he was John

Wesley brought to life again, travelling in trains and eventually in motorcars rather than on horseback, and preaching in the open air to those outcasts and outsiders whom the Methodists, now respectable, could rarely reach.

William Booth had no time for cricket, football or other simple activities that gave pleasure. He also resented poverty: he said it was unnecessary. His book of 1890, *In Darkest England and the Way Out*, was a sobering exposure of the extent of poverty for those who wanted to know. He and his wife were already experts in helping people who had no work and scant clothing and inadequate food. The soup kitchen and the cheap sixpenny meal became city trademarks of 'The Army'.

At Catherine Booth's funeral service in 1890, in the huge arena called the Olympia in London, 36 000 people and numerous brass brands were present. Many people, standing or sitting within that crowd, could testify that they had been lifted from poverty by her work and encouragement. Some of the mourners were London women engaged in the dangerous work of making matches tipped with yellow phosphorus, a chemical hazard that Mrs Booth had tried to eliminate. If she had lived longer, she would have succeeded her husband as leader of this global sect. She was probably the woman most prominent, so far, in the history of Protestant churches.

MRS EDDY'S CHURCH OF CHRIST THE SCIENTIST

One of the few major churches founded by women emerged in the United States, at the same time as the Salvation Army was emerging in England. Known as Christian Science, its founder was a New Englander, Mary Baker Eddy, who, unusual in that era, had been married three times. Dissatisfied with orthodox medicine after her spine continued to give her pain, she came to the conclusion that the Christian faith, if applied correctly, was a safer healing force than the latest medicine. In 1875, when in her mid-fifties, she completed a book, *Science and Health*, which in the eyes of her few followers was a vital supplement to the Bible. Four years later her new sect was born in Boston. There, her first simple building – followed by a grand one – was called the First Church of Christ, Scientist. Women were especially attracted to this religion and were often the leaders in the hundreds of new congregations that quickly arose in North American cities.

Christian Science survived the death in 1910 of its founder, Mary Baker Eddy, who lay in her grave in a parkland cemetery in Boston, a telephone reportedly beside her so that she could communicate if awakened. The phone proved to be one of the myths that stalked her in death as in life. Meanwhile, her wealthy estate provided free copies of her books to a host of public libraries, and her church's daily newspaper, the *Christian Science Monitor*, founded in 1908, became perhaps the first semi-global newspaper; within a decade or more it circulated in San Francisco and London as well as its home city of Boston. By then the Christian Scientists possessed 1900 congregations in the United States, and 300 more in England, Canada, Germany and other lands. Its members became active in social welfare – in prison and army camps and of course in the hospital, an institution of which they did not fully approve. It was their belief that faith and prayer, not doctors, were the wholesome healers. For the first time women were leading several vibrant – some critics preferred to say 'eccentric' – branches of Christianity. There were few signs yet that they would have an opportunity to be ministers, let alone bishops, in the major churches.

HELL AND HEAVEN REVISITED

A message spreading slowly amongst a few circles of Protestants was that hell did not exist. For 1500 years or more, people who did not believe in the divinity of Christ and those who gravely and frequently offended his precepts were warned that, after death, they would suffer eternal torment in hell. This terrible fate was depicted in novels, poems, stone carvings, paintings, and coloured glass in cathedrals and churches. Hell was the subject of a thousand warnings and a shelf of quotations. By 1900, however, millions of Protestants ceased to believe in perpetual punishment and in the existence of hell.

Heaven was not to be jettisoned so easily. It was a consoling, heart-warming belief. In an era when so many children died before they reached the age of five, and when the typical father and mother did not reach the age of sixty, the idea of a final reunion in heaven was intensely appealing. Moreover, death was usually quick or sudden: no miracle drugs were available to halt illness. The persisting belief in heaven was aided by the increasing belief that God was full of love, that sin was easily forgiven, and that nearly all Christians would find a way to heaven. Whereas Calvinism had insisted that human beings were selfish, self-loving and not necessarily deserving of mercy and therefore few would go to heaven, its doctrine was in fast decline in the late nineteenth century. Now the prevailing belief – especially in Protestantism – was that most human beings were decent at heart. Why, then, should they be deprived of a place in heaven?

God, in the eyes of those who believed in him, was no longer quite justified in judging behaviour sternly or in expressing anger. If he did, was his judgement well-informed and compassionate? It became common for churchgoing people, when facing an unexpected tragedy in the family, to ask why God was so unjust to them.

Old-time Calvinists would have been astonished to hear such a protest. For them God was awesome and almighty, and his wisdom dwarfed whatever a human genius, let alone an ordinary soul, might possess. Why, then, in the opinion of such Calvinists, should God's judgement and wisdom be challenged so glibly? Their argument was heard less often.

The self-esteem and the 'rights' of human beings were rising at the very time when the status of God was falling. This increasing optimism about human nature was not entirely a surprise. The nineteenth century, materially, seemed like a miracle for the peoples of the western world. Famines became fewer; and if hunger did seem likely to set in, grain-ships were summoned by the electric telegraph from distant ports. The standard of living was higher, and the new steam engines shortened the weekly hours of labour. Housing and hygiene improved, and by the end of the century most children on both sides of the North Atlantic were formally educated to the age of twelve or fourteen. For the first time, pain was eased by that remarkable invention, the anaesthetic. Fewer women died in childbirth, fewer children died in infancy, and a growing proportion of adults reached the age of fifty. Even wars were shorter, especially those fought in Europe.

This optimistic mood reached Protestants and secularists before it reached Catholics. It was visible in north Germany, reaching the United States soon after. Lutheran theologians – aided by the new sciences and the linguistic X-raying of key words of the Bible – propelled the new attitude. Their liberal theology rested on an optimistic assessment of human nature, an assessment that had occupied only the slimmest place in medieval theology. Now it almost seemed as if mankind could manage on its own, with little help from God. Now viewed as rarely, if ever, interfering in the world, God was the absentee owner of the universe.

WHO GOES TO CHURCH?

In some nations there was intense discussion on the recent decline of churchgoing without a realisation that the Christian Church, almost since its beginning, had been rising or falling in public esteem and enthusiasm. In several other periods, the Christian Church as a whole had been declining far more markedly than it was in Europe around the year 1900.

Even a century previously, in many cities, the poorer people rarely went to church. London, the biggest city in the world, had extended so far that many new suburbs possessed very few churches. Paris and Berlin, though not Milan, were similar. When Glasgow became a fast-growing industrial city it held churches capable of seating only a fraction of its population. In 1820 Glasgow had 120000 inhabitants, mostly Presbyterians, but that denomination owned churches with seats for only 21000 worshippers; the best seats were permanently rented by the wealthier attenders. Generally, people of middling wealth were more likely than tradesmen or the poor to attend church, and women more likely than men. Of the various nationalities, the Irish and Portuguese were more regular than the French in attending, the Welsh and Cornish more than the English, the Poles more than the Swedes. Churchgoing was usually less frequent in the city than in the countryside, where it was a social as well as a religious occasion. On the other hand, North America was a land of churchgoers, probably even more than were certain republics of Latin America, where a hostility towards priests and nuns was growing.

One danger sign was noticed, by observers of white Protestantism on both sides of the Atlantic Church, for the well-dressed. Late in the nineteenth century, attendance at fashionable churches in large Protestant cities conveyed some of the prestige attached, one century later, to the possession of seats at a prime table in a five-star restaurant. The fashionable church usually engaged a magnetic preacher who delivered bright sermons, in which theological reasoning was rationed to a degree that would have dismayed an old churchgoer. A well-trained choir, topped up by one or two professional singers, enhanced the music. People felt they were privileged to have a seat in such a church, but it was really a form of consumerism, in the opinion of one American historian, because 'attendance came to count for more than genuine adherence'.

Early in the twentieth century, certain Christians had a robust attitude to religious decline. They almost welcomed it, explaining that too many congregations now consisted of people who went to church because it was fashionable. Others went out of habit, their parents and grandparents having taught them the practice. Some serious critics thought it preferable if Christians became fewer but more genuine in their faith.

In keeping with the call to modernise, startling architecture appeared in a few newly built churches. Thus, the celebrated Frank Lloyd Wright designed the Unity Church at Oak Park near Chicago in 1906. Of concrete made with a pebble aggregate, square in shape, it resembled a mausoleum from some angles and the latest public library from others. Dominikus Böhm, an expressionist, designed a Catholic Church at Bischofsheim, near Mainz, in 1926 that seemed to resemble France's new aircraft hangar at Orly. Of the 1920s architects it was noted that their extreme rationalism 'made it difficult if not impossible for them to provide ecclesiastical edifices which differed in any expressive way from meeting halls'.

There was much discussion of the famous Barcelona architect Gaudí, whose version of primitivism and Art Nouveau astonishes many viewers even today. His big church, the Temple of the Holy

Family or Sagrada Familia, initially intended to be a conventional building of the Gothic Revival, became more and more exotic as it grew. In many big cities the grand church no longer was such a vital part of the skyline. One of the little-known signs of the new challenge to Christianity is the chronology of tall buildings. In 1880 the two tallest buildings in the western world were the cathedrals of Cologne and Rouen. Thirty years later, in New York and Chicago, the tallest church spire, when seen from the baby skyscraper next door, resembled a doll's house.

30

COMING OF THE LIGHT AND THE DARKNESS

Many observers who detected signs of decline in Christianity in 1900 tended to be looking at their own nation, district or suburb. If they had toured the world, they would have reshaped their argument. In recorded history, few invasions of ideas have matched the global spread of Christianity during the period from, say, 1780 to 1914. Sometime during this period it probably became, for the first time, the largest religion in the world.

In trying to persuade peoples of faraway lands, Protestants had lagged behind Catholics, but now they were winning the contest in many regions. Whereas in 1600 the two far-reaching colonial powers, Spain and Portugal, were both Catholic, 300 years later Britain, Germany and Holland were amongst the most vigorous colonial powers, and the United States was joining them. These four were primarily Protestant. Ever since the time of the emperor Constantine, political support was vital if Christianity was to expand into new territories; in the nineteenth century especially, Protestant churches gained globally from the political and economic power exercised by Britain, Germany and the United States.

CAN ASIA BE CONVERTED?

The Protestant attempt to convert people in India was sluggish. It was almost two centuries after the Lutheran rebellion that the first of its missionaries crossed the equator. In 1706 King Frederick IV of Denmark sent one such missionary to south India. There, Pastor Ziegenbalg translated the New Testament and parts of the Old into Tamil and printed them on an imported press. Influenced by the Pietist movement and its stronghold in the north German university of Halle, the Lutherans and Moravians sent more missionaries to India and the Americas. On the other hand, the largest Protestant kingdom in the world, England, was a laggard. There, at last, three important missionary groups were founded between 1792 and 1799: the Baptist, the London, and the Church missionary societies.

On this wave of enthusiasm came William Carey, a Baptist missionary who was a cobbler by trade. His initial zeal owed much to Joseph Banks, the young botanist who sailed with Cook in the exploring ship *Endeavour*. Banks then was marginally a Christian – he was probably a deist – but he wrote so grippingly about the heathen people he met in the Pacific and New Zealand that young Carey was amongst those Christian readers who felt a craving to respond. After studying at night and learning five foreign languages, he knew that he could master others. In 1793, at the age of thirty-two, he sailed to the east coast of India, where, in Danish territory, he translated the Bible into Bengali. His was the voice that did more than any other to terminate the Indian custom whereby a widow did not live beyond the time of her husband's funeral.

More missionaries, male and female, sailed to remote lands. For the first time, a popular Christian hymn embodied in verse a map of the whole world. Bishop Reginald Heber's hymn marvelled at Greenland's icy mountains, India's coral strand, Ceylon's spicy breezes and Africa's sunny fountains; his verses exulted that heathen inhabitants were soon to receive the Messiah's word. Arriving in Calcutta in 1823, Heber served in theory as the Anglican bishop of Bombay and Colombo, and Australia and South Africa: a bishopric so vast that he could visit only a fraction of it. In the area under his supervision more languages were spoken than in Europe, and so a regiment of linguists would be needed to provide a copy of the Bible for everyone. Nearly ninety years passed before the first Indian, Samuel Vedanayakam Azariah, became an Anglican bishop. In his diocese of Dornakal he built a cathedral that resembled a south Indian temple. When he died in 1945, the 250 000 people in his charge were served entirely by Indian clergymen.

Several dozen different churches, sects and religious orders joined in the quest to convert Asians and Africans. It was like a gold rush, and the first to arrive was often the winner. Remarkably, the German-speaking Moravians won so many converts in the Dutch colony of tropical Guiana that in 1900 they formed the largest religious group. French Catholic missionaries went to many parts of Asia and tropical Africa, where later they were joined by Catholic and Lutheran Germans. The Pacific islands of Fiji and Tonga were virtually taken over by the Wesleyans, while early visits to New Zealand were made by Samuel Marsden, an irascible Anglican clergyman who had settled in Sydney. The Dutch Reformed Church increased its taskforce in the Indonesian islands, and today an exotic sight in the Javanese city of Semarang is an ornate Calvinist church of the 1750s with its airy ceiling and lofty pulpit.

Many regions of East Asia had long been out of bounds to Christian missionaries. In 1858 the Treaty of Tientsin allowed them to enter the interior of China, and a stream of North Americans arrived. In the 1870s Japan was again open to European and American missionaries, and soon they were permitted to live permanently in Korea, where ultimately they won more success than in any other part of the East Asian mainland. Missionaries did not understand the hidden resentment they sometimes aroused in parts of Africa and Asia, for they were seen as accomplices of the ruling European powers. In Korea missionaries were welcomed as allies against the invading Japanese.

Those Christians willing to adapt to the new lands and people were more likely to succeed. Hudson Taylor reached China in 1866 to set up the celebrated China Inland Mission at a time when most pastors and priests lived in the safety of Shanghai and other coastal cities. Travelling up the canals, with his wife, four children, an English nurse and at least six unmarried 'lady-missionaries', he was fortified by the passage in Psalm 68: 'The Lord giveth the word: the women that publish the tidings are a great host.' Thinking that female missionaries were most likely to convert Chinese women, he instructed them to wear Chinese costumes and adopt Chinese ways. He hoped an era would come when Chinese pastors and teachers, using their own language and building 'edifices of a thoroughly native style of architecture', would convert all the Chinese.

That policy had been pursued in west Africa, where a black man, Samuel Adjai Crowther, was the first Anglican bishop. Briefly a slave, he attended school in Sierra Leone and studied at an Anglican theological college in London, where he was presented to Queen Victoria. After serving as a missionary along the Niger River, he was enthroned in 1865 as bishop of those regions of West Africa lying outside the British possessions. The Church of England then showed less hesitation about appointing a black bishop than in contemplating a gay bishop, nearly a century and a half later. After his death, at the port of Lagos in 1891, Crowther was succeeded by a European-born bishop, a decision that displeased numerous African Christians.

FROM TAHITI TO PAPUA

The South Pacific island of Tonga experienced one of the speediest conversions, and in the thirty years after 1826 virtually everyone became a Christian, whether enthusiastic or lukewarm; even today its royal family is Methodist. But the first wave of conversion carried a cultural shock. The missionaries tried to impose not only Christian principles but their own English social values. Idleness was now frowned upon, whereas the Tongans enjoyed being idle because they grew food with such ease on their tropical island that they normally had time for dancing, boat races, face-painting, love-making, and the improvised music called *tukipotu* that was played with the instruments used for beating the handmade cloth. The traditional Tongan priests and priestesses, whose offices were hereditary, also resented the authority soon gained by the newly arrived clergymen. In this rearranging of prestige, the Tongan 'commoners' were the gainers overall, and most recognised that truth.

In the post-colonial era, many tropical and subtropical peoples held divided and strong opinions about the merits of the incoming European religion and its allied culture. In the Torres Strait Islands, sitting between Australia and New Guinea, the arrival of the Congregational missionaries is still called 'The Coming of the Light' and is seen as the highlight of their long history. Some modern anthropologists, however, view the same highlight as virtually the Coming of the Darkness, for it dropped a shadow over the local culture. This argument will rise and fall for decades.

By 1900 Christian preachers and teachers had reached almost every part of the inhabited world except remote parts of Africa and parts of the highlands of New Guinea. The new missionaries were to gain most influence in the Pacific Islands and the accessible parts of New Guinea. In Ceylon and some other lands, however, they converted many of the upper class but not the masses. In few corners of Asia and Africa did they convert more than 5 per cent of the population during their sustained efforts in the nineteenth century. The Philippines remained the most Christianised country in south and east Asia, a tribute to Spanish priests and monks and nuns of earlier centuries.

Success in spreading Christianity often came to those churches that were willing to employ local converts as pastors. The London Missionary Society, Congregationalist in origin, ran crusades in the Pacific Islands with the help of Polynesian pastors, some of whom had first to learn the local languages. The society had astonishing success all the way from Tahiti in the east to Papua in the west.

Doctors and nurses, linguists and teachers came with the missionaries, and sometimes a printing press so that the freshly translated New Testament could be issued in the local language. These efforts were financed largely by silver and copper coins subscribed by European and North American citizens, many of whom were relatively poor. Higher sacrifices, however, were made by the missionaries, their wives and children, who left their homelands, not sure whether they would ever return. The fleets of mail steamers now plying regular routes on the Pacific and Indian Oceans increased the chance that missionaries would return home, perhaps in old age.

In a few mission fields the rate of failure was noticeable. Some pastors and teachers failed to learn the new language, some succumbed to the hot climate, some became domineering in their manner towards the people they taught, some were quarrelsome, some were hopelessly homesick, and some did not find the glamorous way of life they had expected. Some lost their faith and some pretended they hadn't. For countless others it was the unforgettable time of their lives. Hudson Taylor, writing to his sister in England in 1869, explained that in China the 'last month or more has been, perhaps, the happiest of my life'; he wished he could adequately express 'what the Lord has done for my soul'. Like most others he selected a sentence from the Bible to serve as his explanation: 'Whereas once I was blind, now I see.'

Europe suffered from a drought of Christian martyrs but the far-away mission fields supplied them: pastors eaten by cannibals in Fiji; young women killed in China by anti-foreigners; pastors wounded by surprise attacks in New Guinea just when they were taking comfort from early successes; and medical missionaries dying from disease or sheer exhaustion in tropical Africa. David Livingstone, a medical missionary from Scotland who became an explorer and a campaigner against African slavery, disappeared for so long in the jungles and grasslands of east Africa that a costly search for him was led by H. M. Stanley, a reporter of the *New York Herald*. A few missionaries were becoming red-hot news.

Livingstone, when he was lost and when finally he was found, was one of the most discussed people in the western world. In the public mind he came as close as a Protestant could to sainthood. After his death in Africa, his body was conveyed home in a steamship to England, where in 1873 he was buried in London's cemetery supreme, Westminster Abbey. The 1860s and 1870s are now painted as decades when the veracity of Christianity was under siege from philosophers and scientists; but most of those who read the high-circulation penny newspapers, now printed by steam-driven presses, viewed events differently. Dr Livingstone outshone any intellectual celebrity and thrust Charles Darwin into the shadows. Of course, Africa was more mysterious and romantic than Canada, and even the medical care provided in Labrador one generation later by the missionary Wilfred Grenfell – and all the hospitals and nursing stations and hospital ships he created – did not fully fire the imagination of Europeans.

Amidst all this Protestant activity, the Catholics continued to build. France, with its widening empire in Africa, Indo-China and the Pacific Islands, sent out more missionaries in the nineteenth century than the other Catholic countries combined. Catholic heroes continued to emerge. Joseph de Veuster, a late teenager, voyaged from Belgium to Honolulu to become a missionary. Ordained as a priest in 1864 he felt deep sympathy for the lepers living on Molokai Island, nearby. Becoming their priest and leader – he was known as Father Damien – he improved their simple houses, tapped a source of fresh water, and even became a handyman, digging the soil for their vegetable gardens, and even digging their graves. His death from leprosy at the age of forty-nine made him almost a saint, and in Europe three books about him were published within a year of his death. It was a sign of the lowering of sectarian barriers that many Protestants silently thought of admitting him into their private pantheon of heroes.

Latin America remained a tantalising Catholic prize – there the contest was between the rival Catholic religious orders. In Peru, Paraguay and Guatemala missionaries showed skill in adapting and adopting. After the Jesuits observed Brazilian dances and songs, and the way the dancers clapped their hands and tapped their shoes, they devised a role for Christ in the dancing room. An altar was erected, and the native dance called the *cururú* was accompanied by the sounds of viola and tambourine, and songs in praise of the saints. Some of the popular songs were not in praise of the saints. Anti-clerical feeling was growing, especially in Mexico.

EIGHT MINUTES IN A SCOTTISH HALL

In the zeal to win converts, dog ate dog, Catholic nipped Protestant, and the nips were repaid. As rival churchmen did not necessarily agree with one another when living in Belfast, why should they agree in Korea? Facing the hardships of a strange land, they could cooperate. In the slow zigzag movement towards finding a formula for promoting Christian unity, missionaries working far from home were influential. Perhaps they should cooperate because their rivals erecting a new church or hospital just over the next hill faced identical problems of isolation, shortage of supplies, and the difficulty of learning new languages and understanding tribal customs. Most Christian missionaries also faced rivalry from Muslims in the northern half of Africa. The Protestant gains from helping one another were clear.

Whenever Christians formed a small and troubled minority, they thought of cooperating with their fellow Christians in a rival church or sect. Cairo was now said to be the most ecumenical city in the world, because a committee of liaison was formed by the Roman Catholic, Coptic, Maronite, Greek Orthodox, Greek Catholic and various Protestant churches. They shared a problem: its name was Islam. In India a few churches not only cooperated but decided to merge. In 1908 the local Presbyterian, Congregationalist and Dutch

Reformed pastors and congregations formed the South India Uniting Church, into which came Anglicans and Methodists a generation later. No such wide-spanning merger had been seen in Europe. The merger gave heart to one of the YMCA's wandering organisers, John R. Mott, and he organised a remarkable gathering in Edinburgh in June 1910.

The conference probably brought together as wide a variety of churches as any previous conference in the history of Christendom. They represented sixty different denominations and missionary societies. It was a sign of the fast-changing Christian world that more delegates came from the United States – 498 in all – than from any other nation, and that an American chaired most sessions. Politely and efficiently John R. Mott tapped the wooden table when a delegate spoke for more than the allocated eight minutes.

Called the World's Missionary Conference, it embraced a Chinese Christian in his bright robes, an Indian, a Japanese, several Australians, and many more who had made long sea voyages to be present. Nearly all acclaimed it a moving occasion and vowed that they felt the divine presence. They also felt, over their shoulders, the presence of Islam as a rival. The delegates publicly regretted that, in deference to Islam, the British Government was impeding the work of Christian missionaries in Egypt, the Sudan and northern Nigeria.

Here in Edinburgh was a glimpse of a more harmonious world. The Great War, however, was only four years away; and one of the delegates who glimpsed its coming was Admiral Mahan, a famous analyst of naval warfare. A glance at the seating list reveals the presence, too, in that packed hall, of Bishop Montgomery, whose son would be the most famous British soldier in World War II.

The United States, now possibly the nation with the largest but most divided Christian population, talked often of Christian unity.

A conspicuous supporter of the idea in 1910 was the Disciples of Christ, which had been founded by Thomas Campbell in west Pennsylvania a century earlier in the hope of rising above the incessant religious disputes. It set up a wide-spanning Protestant alliance that tried to entice all Christian Churches to the same conference hall. Letters and telegrams carried invitations to innumerable churches in many nations and colonies, and even to Pope Benedict XV, who was sympathetic. A major conference was planned for the years 1914 or 1915. By then it was too late, for war had begun.

CALM AND STORM ON THE UGANDA RAILWAY

In Egypt the Christians already worked together. Many missionaries were now willing to shake hands with rivals on foreign soil. In the highlands of Kenya, the Bantu-speaking people were being courted by Muslims as well as rival groups of Christian missionaries. Sensing the gains from a Protestant alliance, representatives of church missions in central Africa met in 1913 at a town on the newly advancing railway to Uganda. It was in a region of Kenya dominated by the Church of Scotland, but invitations went out to the Seventh-Day Adventists, the Quakers, the Africa Inland Mission and many others. Once assembled, the sixty representatives thought of forming a regional Christian federation. Even more unusually, at the end of the conference all attended a service conducted by the Anglican Bishop of Mombasa and took their part in Holy Communion or Eucharist.

Heresy, 'sheer heresy'! That was the lament of many Europeans who heard about this shared ceremony. Indeed, it was the most astounding event since the Reformation, announced the Anglican Bishop of Zanzibar.

At home, the Church of England was forced to intervene in order to meet or allay criticism. Selected archbishops – from York to the West Indies, and Gibraltar to Armagh – applied all their tact as a committee of inquiry. Gently, they concluded that the Lord's Supper free-for-all, which had been movingly shared by diverse Christians within sight of the Kikuyu railway station, should not be viewed as a precedent. In their minds an East African religious federation that bonded different Christian Churches was unthinkable. The Anglicans concluded that their own members should not take part in Holy Communion in other churches, though on occasions they would welcome, say, a Presbyterian to give a sermon in one of their African pulpits. These conclusions were still in the making when the great European war began in August 1914.

ARMAGEDDON

It was widely predicted that the war would be frightening but brief. Perhaps it would be the war of 1914, certainly not the war of 1914–18. The important wars fought in recent decades had been very short, especially when the latest weapons were used, and it was assumed that the next major war would be short. Reassuringly to many observers, the globe was shrinking. Indeed, the first decade of the twentieth century had witnessed the first long-distance wireless messages and the flight of aircraft. The belief was strong that as nations came closer to each other, talked to and traded with each other more often, the chance of war would recede. A more cheerful concept of human nature – a deviation from the mainstream Christian tradition – was almost a hallmark of the nineteenth century and the first decade of the twentieth. It was a rare time of globalisation and exchange in Christianity and commerce. That was one reason why the war, when it came, was so shattering to peoples' hopes and expectations.

The major nations that initially engaged in the war were Christian. The notable exceptions were Japan and Turkey. Significantly, Protestants and Catholics in vast numbers fought side by side, as well as on opposing sides. They were accompanied to battles on land and sea by clergymen known as chaplains, many of whom, being in the line of fire, would be killed in the war.

The First World War was also a sign of the utter disunity in Christendom as a whole. On some of the many battlefronts, Christian nations fought other Christian nations. In the Tyrol mountains, Italian Catholics fought Austrian Catholics. On the Western Front in northern France, Protestant Germans and Protestant Britons killed one another. In the Balkans and Eastern Europe, one army of Orthodox soldiers fought another army composed mainly of Orthodox soldiers.

A few Christian leaders had tried to prevent the outbreak of the war. The Archbishop of Canterbury, Randall Davidson, England's leading churchman, had been perturbed, five years previously, by the possibility that Germans and Britons might fight one another in a major war. He supported the sending of a delegation of four Anglican bishops to Germany, where they met the emperor, Kaiser Wilhelm II, in 1909. Two years later London welcomed the renowned Berlin theologian Adolf von Harnack. He was formally presented by Davidson to the new king, Edward VII, at Buckingham Palace. Davidson remarked that a war between Britain and Germany, countries that had so much in common and shared such long religious traditions, was quite 'unthinkable'. In 1914 the unthinkable happened.

Later in the war, Davidson did not win many friends when he called for Britain to show more mercy to the German soldiers. He criticised the use of poison gas by both sides fighting on the Western Front. In Britain the most courageous criticism of the war was made by that small sect, the Quakers. Many refused to fight on conscientious grounds; some served in the Red Cross; and others worked at sea on the mine-sweepers, arguing that such a task consisted of merely removing dangerous explosives from the sealanes rather than adding to them. After the war was over but not the dislocation, and hunger was widespread in Russia and Eastern Europe, Americans led by Herbert Hoover, a Quaker by religion and a rich mining engineer by profession, organised one of the largest aid programs seen in the world to that time. The Russian famine in the early 1920s was eased by generous external donations from Quakers and other Christian groups, most of which had little sympathy with communism as an economic doctrine and none with its policy of atheism.

During the war, the Vatican was able to display neutrality. No longer a state in its own right, no longer the possessor of an army, no longer in urgent need of an ally to defend its independence, now it could stand to one side. As millions of Catholics were fighting on opposite sides, there was an incentive for the pope to be impartial. Moreover, as Italy was neutral at the commencement of World War 1, Pope Benedict XV did not necessarily offend Italians, on whose soil he lived, by himself proclaiming the merits of neutrality. One month after the war began, he urged Catholics throughout the world 'to leave nothing undone to put an end to the calamity'. Towards the end of the year he urged the main fighting powers to declare a truce during Christmas; he failed to persuade them.

When Italy entered the war on the side of France and Britain and Russia in 1915, it imposed a condition, kept secret at the time, but accepted firmly by her allies. All of Italy's wartime allies agreed that the pope should not be allowed to take part in negotiating the peace treaty at the end of the war. Italy wished to control its own foreign policy. The presence of the pope was not wanted.

He continued to plead for an end to the war, and in 1917 he tried to usher in peace at a time when the door was ajar. He pleaded for fairer treatment for prisoners of war: he even sent Easter gifts to British soldiers who were prisoners. He deplored the new military tactic of using aircraft to drop bombs on enemy cities where women and children were likely to be killed. He denounced the hounding of the Armenian Christians in 1915 by Muslim troops operating inside Turkey. His calm messages, however, passed over the heads of civilian and military leaders, even in Catholic Austria and half-Catholic France.

After World War II, critics were to denounce the papacy, arguing that it should have demanded that Hitler cease to exterminate Jews during that war. The humanity of these critics demands respect, but they were ignorant of the futility of such papal interventions. They did not realise that the papacy again and again during World War I had tried to diminish human misery, with almost no success.

When World War I ended in November 1918, more than six million men had been killed in action or had died of sickness or wounds. The overwhelming majority – probably more than 90 per cent – would have called themselves Christians. Understandably, countless graves in the official war cemeteries in Europe were marked by a Christian cross. Of the soldiers of the British Empire who died in battle but whose bodies could not be identified, most were given a Christian burial, and the words 'Known unto God' were inscribed on their tombstone or collective monument. In contrast, during World War II, the majority of those combatants who were killed in action were not Christians.

After Britain decided to select an unknown soldier from a war cemetery on the Western Front and rebury him in a place of honour, it chose Westminster Abbey. Christened 'The Unknown Soldier', he might have been a loyal Catholic or Salvationist with no wish to be buried in an Anglican abbey, but such a criticism, if made publicly, was dismissed. The soldier was chosen as a symbol of national rather than religious unity.

In England the post-war event that displayed religious unity on the large scale was a football match. Football and cricket had long been seen, in some circles, as games in which a Christian spirit was expected and insisted upon: fair play was at one time the eleventh commandment. Moreover, hymns had long been an emotional link between rival Christian groups, and the words of the most popular hymns were known by heart. In London's new Wembley Stadium, the long-anticipated football match was the FA Cup Final, which – until the World Cup was initiated – was the best-known fixture in the world of soccer. There in 1923, before the start of the match between Arsenal and Cardiff City, the crowd of 91 000 united in the singing of the hymn: 'Abide with me; fast falls the eventide; The darkness deepens; Lord, with me abide.' It was chosen because it was a favourite of King George V, who sat in the grandstand that afternoon. Thereafter, at the same annual event, decade after decade, the hymn was sung, even after most members of the crowd ceased to feel the magic and melancholy of the words and tune, and privately preferred the thump-thump of rock and roll.

When in 1923 they first sang this hymn at the stadium, one passage must have seemed apt to those who had an intuition that the world was more fragile than before:

Swift to its close ebbs out life's little day;
Earth's joys grow dim, its glories pass away;
Change and decay in all around I see.

The previous century and a half had been a golden age for Europe. Its population had trebled and the overflow had gone to North America, Australia and many other regions. Europe had become the richest part of the world, and it was able to rule most of the world. The expansion of Christianity and its global spread owed much to this golden age of the European peoples. But the First World War, really a suicidal contest for European and global supremacy, ended with two distinct losers: Europe was one, and its fragile Christian civilisation was the other.

31

WAR AND PEACE

By the start of the twentieth century, secular creeds were challenging the Christian Churches. Nationalism was a rising god, and the nation and flag attracted the loyalty of citizens to a degree not imaginable previously. In 1914 the opening months of the First World War showed the vigour and the potential fanaticism of nationalist feelings.

Another way of viewing the world came through communism and its half-brothers – socialism and anarchism. They had many of the characteristics of a religion, with command of the loyalty of their members, their vision of a utopia in which neither poverty nor unemployment existed, and their denunciation of the forces of evil that they detected in capitalism. The socialists, communists and even sections of the social democrats were crusaders, like Christians. On the eve of World War I, they seemed likely to abstain from what they saw as a capitalists' war. They even thought of organising a long-lasting general strike, disrupting transport across Europe, and thus forcing the warring nations to the peace table. When war arrived, however, many of their members were engulfed by patriotism. They did not lay down their rifles in protest, but loyally carried them to the frontline.

In Germany and France, the zeal of many socialists had originally come from their Christian principles. Some accused their own churches of tolerating poverty and thus betraying the spirit of Christianity. But most revolutionaries, as distinct from social democrats, were not Christians. Karl Marx, a Jew when a child and then a Christian, became an ardent atheist. One of his memorable sentences of the 1860s insisted that religion was the opium or opiate of the people. It made people feel content, materially, with what they had. Christianity, Marx complained, fixed their hopes on an afterlife, whereas communism would create a paradise on earth in which poverty was unknown. In Paris in 1871, the revolutionaries, who were briefly in power, showed their colours by defacing the interior of the Panthéon. They hung a red flag from the upright of the great cross, having already sawn off its arms. What happened in France was a foretaste of what would happen when communists, further to the east, seized power.

The English historian Professor R. H. Tawney, an Anglican and a socialist, wondered about the reasons for the decline in church attendances in Europe during the decades between the two world wars. 'The alternative to religion is rarely irreligion,' he decided. He realised that in several nations new religions such as communism and fascism were stepping forward in the hope of occupying the 'vacant throne'. These secular religions demanded the same loyalty as Christianity had demanded in the Middle Ages. They set up their own twentieth-century version of the Inquisition, and it was more efficient and deadly.

LENIN, HITLER AND THEIR ANTI-CHRISTIAN FLAGS

The revolutions of 1917 were a blow to Russia's Christians. Lenin, the first leader of revolutionary Russia, denounced their religion as 'one of the most odious things on earth'. The Russian Orthodox Church, known formally as the Orthodox Catholic Church, had been the loyal ally of the tsars and their regime. Once Lenin was in power, he trampled on the Church. In 1918 all theological seminaries were shut, and no priests could be trained. It was a criminal act for an Orthodox priest to indoctrinate a person under the age of eighteen years. Many rebellious priests were killed and the obstinate were imprisoned. In Russian cities and villages, thousands of churches were closed. Some were turned into museums, temples of atheism, or storehouses. In springtime, migratory birds could be heard and seen making their nests and rearing their young inside the grand onion-like domes of empty or rarely-used churches. A bird was more welcome in a church than a young person. The young risked their careers, their chance of gaining further education or a superior job if they attended a Russian Orthodox Church. Islam, which was strong in the Soviet-ruled regions of central Asia, was not penalised as strenuously as the Russian Orthodox Church.

A wave of Soviet propaganda denounced Christianity. In 1923 the Soviet machine denounced the celebrating of Easter and Christmas. Two years later the Soviet Government founded the League of Militant Atheists in order to intensify its crusade. Groups of priests were sent to the deadly labour camps on the shores of the White Sea. This was one of the most vigorous persecutions of Christians in Europe since the heyday of the Roman Empire, and yet here and there in the late 1930s foreign visitors noticed churches that flourished. 'I remember,' wrote an English journalist, 'going to an Easter service in Kiev – the crowded cathedral, the overwhelmingly beautiful music,

the intense sense which, as they worshipped, the congregation conveyed of eternity sweeping in like great breakers.'

In 1942, after Russia was invaded by Germany, the Soviet Government relaxed its campaign against Christianity in the hope of
promoting national unity. The Russian Orthodox Church was given
a reprieve. Thereafter it was not encouraged, nor was it systematically persecuted. After the Second World War had ended, the
atheist messages were again amplified at home, and relayed to the
new communist countries of Eastern Europe. In Poland, Hungary,
Lithuania and other Eastern European countries, Catholic leaders
who were unwilling to submit or to be silent were denounced, publicly humiliated or imprisoned by the communists. Leaders of the
national Orthodox Churches in Romania and Bulgaria had to be
cautious and submissive.

In the whole history of Christianity, few setbacks were as serious
as the swift decline of the Orthodox Church in Russia in the first
half of the twentieth century. Of all the Orthodox Churches, the
Russian was by far the most important. While Constantinople was
seen as the traditional home of that creed, Moscow was now more
influential and was guiding the lives of far more people. Moscow,
in effect, was the heir of the longest strand in Christian history, for
the eastern Church had often been custodian of the birthplaces of
Christianity. Its sacred language – classical Greek – was that of all
the authors of the New Testament; even in Rome the first Christians
had probably said their prayers in Greek.

In earlier centuries, four of the five most powerful Christian bishops had been based in eastern cities, Rome being the exception.
Many of the church's hallmarks originated in the east. In the shaping
of a variety of Christian creeds and institutions, including the Trinity
and the role of Mary and the birth of monasteries and nunneries, the

494

eastern or Orthodox Churches were the more influential. Likewise, the early governing councils of the church were held in cities on or near the eastern Mediterranean, and most of those who attended were easterners. And now the Russian Church, the strongest of all the Orthodox Churches, was suppressed by Russia's atheists.

HITLER ERECTS A NEW ALTAR

The aggressive spread of atheism in the Soviet Union alarmed many German Christians. What might happen to them and their churches if their fatherland were taken over by communists or extreme socialists? In the mid-1920s, Hitler's infant political party became the main opponent of communism and also an extreme exponent of German nationalism. Late in 1932, amidst grave unemployment, his National Socialist Party became so popular that it won 37 per cent of the votes at the national elections, thus emerging as the largest single party. Many Christians had voted for Hitler, relishing his nationalism but not understanding his ruthless ambition. He himself saw Christianity as a temporary ally, for in his opinion 'one is either a Christian or a German'. To be both was impossible. Nazism itself was a religion, a pagan religion, and Hitler was its high priest.

After Hitler completely controlled Germany, and the parliament ceased to meet, he showed his contempt for the Catholic Church in which, as a child, he had been raised. He broke his pact or concordat with the Catholic Church. He divided the main Protestant creed by encouraging Nazi sympathisers to set up their branch of Lutheranism, the so-called 'German Christians'. But a host of Lutheran pastors, many of whom would be viewed as 'fundamentalist' in today's vocabulary, rebelled against Hitler. They paid a high penalty. Hundreds went to prison, The most celebrated – *notorious* was an adjective used by the Nazis – was Reverend Martin Niemöller, who had commanded a German submarine in the First World War. An outspoken Berlin pastor, he was to spend a total of seven years in Dachau and other German concentration camps.

Other Christians suffered. The 30 000 or so German members of a small American-born sect, the Jehovah's Witnesses, stood mostly on the lower rungs of the income ladder. Refusing to declare their loyalty to the German Reich, refusing to be conscripted to fight in the German Army, or any army, they were declared to be enemies. Some risked their lives by sheltering Jews. During World War II, about 6000 Jehovah's Witnesses were to be held in concentration camps. At least 625 were to die of illnesses and malnutrition, and at least another 250 were to be executed.

In Germany in a mere five years, Nazism had replaced Christianity as the dominant creed. Its high altar was not inside a building. Instead, it was Germany itself and the German people, their soil and forests and language and traditions. Hitler was the new Messiah. The cry 'Heil Hitler' was the national halleluiah and prayer.

In Italy, Benito Mussolini, who had gained office in 1922 with a show of strength, was also an atheist. But he could not create for himself the same halo that shone around Hitler's head. More pragmatic, he allowed religion to be taught in Italian schools and finally came to terms with the pope. The Vatican again was set up as a city state, and the pope, in effect, was allowed to pursue his own foreign policy – within strict limits.

STUMBLING TOWARDS UNITY

There was a hope that in a crisis, one united Christian voice could speak for all the churches. In the 1920s the ancient Greek word 'ecumenical', virtually unknown to most churchgoers, was revived. Denoting the whole world or the whole church, it had been used in fifteen different sentences in the New Testament and therefore carried history with it. One strong sponsor of the ecumenical movement was Randall Davidson, archbishop of Canterbury, who, before the war, had denounced the Turks for their killing of Orthodox Christians in Macedonia and Russia and for allowing 'blind and cruel' mobs to rampage against Jews. In Britain after the war he encouraged discussions with Catholics and with the dissenting Protestant churches now commonly known as the Free Churches.

It was fit that Davidson should be the all-church spokesman because he was to be a remarkable survivor, becoming the longest-serving archbishop of Canterbury since William Warham, who had died four centuries previously. In 1922 the church in Russia urgently needed Davidson's help. After the Soviet Union arrested the head of the Russian Orthodox Church, the patriarch Tikhon, Archbishop Davidson responded by organising protests that drew in nearly every British denomination, including Catholic and Hebrew leaders. Possibly they saved Russia's patriarch from a long sentence in prison. It was one of the widest displays of Christian solidarity seen in Europe since the Reformation began.

How could the different churches of Europe be enticed to meet even once, let alone regularly? The first world missionary conference in Edinburgh in 1910 had temporarily united in an exciting way missionaries from nearly every corner of the earth, but especially from the United States and Britain. In 1921 a French cardinal organised a private annual conference with other Christians – and then the pope intervened. In 1925 a world conference of numerous Protestant churches was held in Stockholm: it was just a beginning and other meetings followed. The steps forward were difficult. Europe was fractured politically, and that sometimes harmed negotiations.

A remarkable gesture of Christian fraternalism embraced Jews worldwide. The originator of the gesture was Arthur James Balfour, who was born into a wealthy family in Scotland and for long was prominent in British public life. A philosopher who combined deep learning and gracious and lucid prose, and prime minister of England for three years, he was one of the foremost intellectuals ever to become the leader of a nation. A devoted Presbyterian, and the author of an influential defence of Christianity called *Foundations of Belief*, he also became a quiet enthusiast for the rights of the Jewish people. In November 1917, he used his learning and his position as foreign minister to persuade his colleagues to allow Palestine, once it was safely captured from the Ottoman Empire, to become a national home for the Jews as well as for the resident Palestinians. Balfour also hoped by his plan to persuade the Jews, whom he believed had influence on the new revolutionary government in Russia, to continue to support Britain and her allies in the final stage of the war against Germany and Austria-Hungary.

The Balfour Plan was the slow start of the present nation of Israel, but it was not entirely practical. How would Muslims, truly in the majority in Palestine, accept an increasing influx of Jews determined to remake the rules of daily life? Meanwhile, throughout the world a host of Jews, though far from all, felt grateful to Balfour and his vision. When he died in March 1930, his name received a level of praise such as few if any Christian leaders had ever received from Jews. Already Jewish immigrants were settling in Jerusalem and on the coast, and even taking up land overlooking the Sea of Galilee. Here was a haven they would urgently need as turmoil spread across Europe.

Jerusalem was now wide open to Christian pilgrims, but they did not arrive in the crowds that had been anticipated. For their part, Protestants did not believe in pilgrimages; they thought that the Holy Land should be read about in the Bible rather than visited in person. Orthodox Christians loved to be pilgrims, but after the communist revolution of 1917 those living in Russia ceased to have permission to visit the Holy Land. Catholicism was also the church of the pilgrims, and in the year 1000 or 1500 most Catholics living in Europe would have loved to visit Jerusalem just once in their lifetime; a deep-felt wish was that they should chance to be there on the day Christ returned to earth. By the twentieth century, however, Jerusalem had lost some of its glamour as a place of Christian pilgrimage. Now it was as rewarding and far cheaper for a Portuguese or Italian family to buy a day-excursion ticket and travel by train to a nearby shrine in Europe.

WORLD WAR II AND THE HOLOCAUST

The war commenced in September 1939 with the invasion of Poland. Hitler's forces led the invasion, and Stalin's Soviet Union soon joined in. In 1940 Hitler overran most of western Europe, and by the end of the year most of the Christian inhabitants of Europe were now living under German rule. Generally, the life of the churches was allowed to continue, so long as it remained subdued and took no part in national politics. In June 1941 Hitler invaded the Soviet Union. In December, Japanese forces, already occupying a large area of China, began their lightning conquest of British, French and Dutch colonies in South-East Asia. At the same time, the United States entered the war after the Japanese aerial attacks on Pearl Harbor and American bases in the Philippines. It was now a global war and continued as such until 1945, Germany being defeated in May and Japan in August.

As the war deepened, it became a mirror of human nature. The worst and the best in human beings was displayed but the worst was incredibly conspicuous. One cause of the extreme violence and the brutality is rarely pinpointed but was highly relevant. In Europe during the war, more countries were occupied by an enemy, and occupied more quickly and firmly subjugated, than at any previous time. The military occupation of such a vast area made it easy to punish civilians on a massive scale, if it were so resolved.

Two ruthless dictators, Hitler and Stalin, intensified the evil. They did not hesitate to be violent to civilians living in territories they occupied. In comparison, World War I seems less brutal, except for the massacre of the Christian Armenians in Ottoman territory, a disaster that even today is not widely known.

By 1941 Hitler and other Nazi leaders decided to seize the opportunity to wipe out the Jewish people still living in Europe. Hitler had long hated the Jews. He believed erroneously that they had white-anted Germany in World War I and thus hastened its defeat. The extermination was one of the most heartless decisions ever recorded. It embraced children as well as adults, the very old and the very young. Their crime was to belong to the Jewish race. True, other decisions to wipe out helpless and defenceless people had been made in many places in the course of thousands of years, but they usually involved inhabitants of a relatively small area. Hitler, in contrast, massacred the Jewish inhabitants not only in Germany, where they were relatively few, but also in Poland, Austria, France, Holland and other nations.

While earlier massacres of the people of one tribe or race or religion, whether in Roman times or in the Reformation wars or the Mongol invasions, had usually been impulsive and inefficient, Hitler's was a long-range and efficient plan. It was still vigorously being implemented when the war ended. Under this plan, later called the Holocaust, five million Jews were killed. They were executed with scientific efficiency. Efficient and harsh censorship prevented the knowledge of the tragedy from spreading easily. The intended victims were sent in long trains to the concentration camps where they were killed systematically, using the latest technology. This could not have occurred on a large scale during World War I, partly because few countries were totally held in captivity by an enemy.

For western civilisation it was a self-inflicted wound. The Jews, in proportion to their population, had almost certainly proved to be the most creative and talented people in the world in the century 1840 to 1940. They were achievers in music, art and literature, theology and philosophy and the social sciences, in medicine and science, law and some of the other professions, in mathematics and in physics, which was then viewed as the queen of the sciences. In other fields many Jewish people showed remarkable gifts. Their total achievement was prodigious. Here was western civilisation, in the midst of a terrible war, actually poisoning itself.

Christianity could not escape some indirect blame for the terrible Holocaust. The Jews and Christians had been rivals and sometimes enemies for a long period of history. Furthermore, it was traditional for Christians to blame Jewish leaders for the crucifixion of Christ, even though the evidence suggested that the Roman rulers in Jerusalem were more to blame. At the same time, Christians showed devotion and respect. They were conscious of their debts to the Jews. Jesus and all the disciples and all the authors of his gospels were of the Jewish race. Christians viewed the Old Testament, the holy book of the synagogues, as equally a holy book for them. In long periods of Christian history, more sermons centred on a sentence of the Old than of the New Testament. Even in the early Protestant years, the hymns of Calvinism and many of the sects consisted entirely of Jewish psalms. The two religions had so much in common. It was a Christian, Arthur Balfour, who did more than anybody to provide the Jews belatedly with a national home. Nonetheless, the accusation will linger that Catholics and Protestants in many nations, and even Jews living in the United States, might have indirectly and directly given more help or publicity to the Jews during their plight in Hitler's Europe.

A lesson was learned. In the following forty years, Christians and Jews were to come together more closely than at perhaps any other time since the half-century after Christ had died.

The two world wars were a deep shock to those who tried to view western civilisation impartially. A century of seeming progress had culminated in destruction, death and atrocities on a scale not previously imagined. The nation that was singled out, at the time, as the worst culprit was Germany. In the eyes of many neutral observers, it had been the most civilised nation in 1900. In music the German people had led the western world for several centuries, and they were also amongst the leaders in literature, architecture, painting, the social sciences, and conspicuously in science and technology.

In religion, the Germans had created an impressive tradition. The Reformation had begun in Germany, the first leaders of the Reformation outside Germany were German-speaking people, and in the nineteenth century German theologians were again the pathfinders. Dr Albert Schweitzer, one of the all-encompassing minds of the twentieth century, a kind of Einstein of the humanities, recorded in 1910 his opinion that, when the dust and commotion had settled

down, 'German theology will stand out as a great, a unique phenomenon in the material and spiritual life of our time'. He argued
that only the German temperament possessed the combination of
intellectual and emotional powers – including critical acumen and
religious feeling – that could produce such results. This was the
same Germany that, only a quarter of a century later, revealed by its
own conduct how fragile was European civilisation and how flimsy
the Christian foundations on which it stood.

Arnold Toynbee, the London historian who had been the boldest
in studying past civilisations – he located more than most educated
people had heard of – expanded at length his dismal diagnosis of his
own civilisation after the Second World War ended. He concluded
that the world was now in a new spiritual crisis. In the last 300
years, he wrote, the western world had abandoned a vital part of its
Christian heritage. Since the seventeenth century, a majority of its
citizens had discarded or minimised the 'doctrine of Original Sin',
and they had discarded or allowed to slip from sight human beings'
capacity for evil. The main message of the New Testament had been
watered down by many of the Protestant churches and undermined
by the new secular religions of communism, nationalism and science. Admittedly, Toynbee's book, A Study of History, was sometimes
sweeping in its conclusions, and many historians dismissed him or
decided not to read him, but various theologians felt that he was
revealing an unpalatable truth. The world, by turning to reason and
science, had learned so much in the past three centuries but had
also forgotten so much.

The Christian religion had arisen from the Jewish insight into
human nature and its potential for creating disaster as well as triumph. Ironically, descendants of the people who had provided this
insight had recently been slaughtered by leaders of the modern nation

that had once proclaimed the truth, the insight, but had largely discarded it. Perhaps the Second World War was less an indictment of Christianity than a painful reminder of its basic message.

A SHRINKING WORLD

Christianity was born in an era of simple travel and communication. Christ and his disciples walked everywhere: to ride a donkey or sit in a cart was an unusual experience for them. Jesus did not once travel in an ocean-going vessel, though he did sit in a fishing boat in an inland sea. For about 1900 years, all Christian teachers, lacking the electronic media, used their unaided voices, though the master-preachers knew how to project them a long distance. And now in a rush came the moving picture, long-distance radio, gramophone, microphone, television, fibre cable and satellite.

By 1939 several of the new forms of communicating were changing weekdays and Sundays. Most homes in the more prosperous nations owned a radio, and the leading preachers reached audiences of a size previously unimaginable. In the United States, Archbishop Fulton J. Sheen, who first broadcast his 'Catholic Hour' in 1930, reached the ears of more worshippers in a week than Martin Luther and his unamplified voice managed to reach in his whole life. Sheen was said to reach seven million listeners through his weekly broadcast, while Father Charles E. Coughlin, his rival, was said to employ 150 clerks merely to open and sort his mail. Many families who previously went to church on Sunday evening now listened to a direct broadcast from a leading church.

The radio was probably used more intensively against Christianity than for it. Hitler and Stalin were masters of propaganda, the radio being their favourite instrument, and Christianity one of their targets. Even in free societies the radio and then the television spread indirectly a consumerist and secular message. Hollywood's films gave pleasure and entertainments to hundreds of millions of people, while the lives of the film stars also made divorce fashionable and almost honourable for the first time in western civilisation. More people were persuaded by radio and television to drink Coca-Cola than to take the cup at Holy Communion. On the other hand, Reverend Billy Graham, the young minister of an evangelical sect in the southern United States, was on his way to becoming a television star after the crusade he conducted in Los Angeles in 1949 showed that his face, hairstyle, voice and manner were attractive to a camera. Without radio, television and the jet aircraft, he would not have reached 1 per cent of the worldwide audience he commanded in the space of a generation.

The first effective aeroplane had been invented by a religious American family. The Wright brothers, the sons of a Brethren bishop, had no idea that their innovation would affect Christianity as well as virtually every other human institution. Perhaps the first Christian pastor to use aircraft systematically to extend his work was John Flynn, a Presbyterian, who founded his Australian Inland Mission to carry a Christian message to people living in faraway and lonely cattle stations and mining camps. Once travelling with the aid of camels and then simple motor vehicles, in 1928 he hired a small aircraft from the Qantas airline to launch the world's first Flying Doctor, a medical service that now covers more than half of the Australian continent. It was said of him in 1951, the year of his death: 'Across the lonely places of the land he planted kindness.'

The pope, too, would become an air traveller and visit the western and southern hemispheres for the first time. The ancient idea of the pilgrimage was to be turned upside down. For centuries a host of

Christians had made pilgrimages to Rome to set eyes on the pope, and now he became the pilgrim, visiting his flock in far-off lands.

Leaders of churches knew that the world was shrinking and that they should build bridges. The fast train and the ocean liner enabled people to come from remote places to a central conference. Wars interrupted their plans. Protestants had long tried to form a World Council of Churches, which they achieved at last in 1948, a total of 147 church organisations agreeing to meet in Amsterdam. That city had hosted the last large pre-war conference of Christians from many nations, the World Conference of Christian Youth, in 1939. The ensuing war shaped the new conference and selected its theme, 'Man's disorder and God's design'. Their first gathering was a religious service on Sunday 22 August 1948 in Amsterdam's Nieuwe Kerk, into which crowded the delegates, observers and the media. The delegates came from forty-four countries, Asia being well represented and Africa less so. They described themselves as 'a fellowship of churches which accept Jesus Christ as God and Saviour'.

They did not promise to come closer together with any haste: they were cautious. Considered in the context of their time, their eagerness was only a few steps ahead of those that had tentatively been shown by Luther, Zwingli and other Protestant rebels who agreed to confer – but refused to confer again – at Marburg barely one decade after the Reformation began.

Catholics did not join the World Council of Churches, nor, at first, send official observers, though later they were seated on the sidelines and often sympathetic in spirit. As the largest church in the world, they saw no urgent need to mend a rift that others had created. They were willing to review and revise their own doctrines and attitudes but only inside their meeting rooms in the Vatican. Some of the fundamentalist Christian sects, especially those in the

Americas, also refused to join, but Germans attended gladly while carrying a sense of wartime guilt on their people's behalf. The Orthodox Churches were divided in their attitudes, and the Orthodox Church of Russia and its linked churches in Eastern Europe did not attend. As the Cold War was now intense, the debates sometimes demonstrated the tensions between delegates from Eastern Europe and those from America, one of whose speakers was the Presbyterian John Foster Dulles, who five years later was to become the US secretary of state and a fierce warrior in the Cold War.

Though a symbol of half-unity, the Amsterdam conference for those who attended was a heartfelt experience. Its final reports were humble in spirit: 'We embark upon our work in the World Council of Churches in penitence for what we are, in hope for what we shall be.' They hoped not only for unity, far in the future, but also for a revival of true Christianity: 'there is no gain in unity unless it is unity in truth and holiness.'

THE EAST IS RED

The post-war years were unfavourable for extending the Christian creed. Just as the initial years after the First World War recorded the vast and speedy spread of atheism in the new Soviet Union, so atheism advanced even further as a result of the Second World War. By 1945 the Russian forces had occupied Eastern Europe and were to remain in occupation for almost half a century.

In that huge stretch of territory, the Christian Churches were not always penalised as severely as those of the Soviet Union, but most became minor institutions. Nearly all their schools and many of their church buildings were closed. They lost their traditional role in grand public ceremonies. The young, especially those who were ambitious, realised that their path to advancement in the professions or the government would be blocked if they were active worshippers, and at school they were taught the merits of atheism. In the new regimes, Christian leaders who were outspoken received warnings or penalties. As Rome had long led the verbal attack on communism, retaliation against its leaders was to be expected.

In Lithuania most priests were imprisoned or even deported. In Hungary in 1949, Cardinal Mindszenty was given a sentence of life imprisonment, and in Czechoslovakia the archbishop was sent to an undisclosed place of confinement. At one time 8000 Czech monks and nuns were in prisons. In Poland, one of the most Catholic of European countries, the communist government and the church clashed frequently: the church did not often lose, for it retained massive public support. In Romania, the new constitution of 1948 granted religious freedom, but that was overruled by the resolve of the communist government to interfere in the running of the Romanian Orthodox Church.

In 1949 the final victory of the communists in the civil war in China vastly expanded the anti-Christian zone. It now extended from Berlin to Shanghai, from Prague to Canton, from the mouth of the Danube to the mouth of the Pearl River.

China, for long the home of intensive but not triumphant Christian activity, became the world's most populous home of atheism. At the end of 1949, Catholic schools alone had taught some five million Chinese students, Catholic hospitals and doctors served maybe thirty million people, and the Catholic orphanages alone numbered 1500. Now the schools and hospitals passed into the hands of the government, most of the churches were closed, and the foreign priests, pastors, nuns and medical missionaries prepared to return to their homelands. Most were Americans and Canadians, and they left with sadness.

The leader of the previous Nationalist Government, General Chiang Kai-shek, and his wife were Methodists, and they retreated with their followers to Taiwan. The Buddhists, who had been influential in China for centuries, could still sound their temple gongs in the provincial towns but only the older people answered their summons. Throughout the world, there was valid reason for Christians to wonder whether their golden age had ended. They were no longer a global religion, having been excluded from large areas of East Asia. Further Communist victories were soon to exclude them from North Korea and much of Indo-China.

As Europe lost control of many of its overseas colonies, those liberated peoples and their rulers specified the conditions under which Christian missions could remain. In North Africa and the Middle East, the increasing list of countries now ruled directly by Muslims did not welcome Christian evangelists. The hope of Christianity expanding in Africa and Asia was not considered to be high in the 1950s, on the eve of the first wave of decolonisation. In the western and eastern halves of Europe the habit of regularly attending church was in decline, and the pace of decline would become rapid.

In the United States the churches remained buoyant. That nation was the guardian, militarily, of the 'free world' and the defender of its religion in the face of militant communism. It was also the staunch defender of a new nation, Israel. Perhaps for the first time in their long history, the Jews had a deeply committed guardian and protector.

VATICAN II

Until the two world wars and their aftermath, the Catholic Church had loosely united more races and lands than any governing institution in history. In one sense, however, it was not international. It was controlled by Europeans, all of whom for many centuries had been Italian-born.

After the First World War was ended, Pope Benedict XV called for more Asian-born priests and more respect for the culture they brought with them. But during his lifetime, his church in China, Japan and India possessed no local-born bishop. At last, in 1926 six Chinese bishops were consecrated. Soon the Catholic Church in Africa was to receive its first black bishop – in Uganda. In the following quarter of a century, most of the major Catholic countries in the third world could take pride that at least one of their bishops, and sometimes all, were locally born. By the early 1960s, half of the 2800 Catholic bishops lived outside Europe, and most were Latin Americans, Africans or Asians.

How could this vast global institution be guided in a swift-changing world? It had to change, but not all change would be constructive, and too much change would undermine the continuity that was a quiet strength. Pope John XXIII, elected in 1958, resolved to be a bold navigator. He was aged seventy-six when he moved from Venice to Rome and surveyed the health of his global church. Instead of being the quiet man on duty, he decided to summon the Vatican Council, the church's supreme international parliament, which had not met for more than ninety years. He died of cancer in 1963, soon after the council had assembled, and left his successor Pope Paul VI to preside over a hurricane of change.

The Vatican Council, which met between 1962 and 1965, made more changes than any such conference held since the Council of Trent four centuries previously. It removed Latin from the liturgy, enabling the local or national language to prevail, thus repeating inside the mother church the reform implemented by Hus and

Luther and other Protestants centuries earlier. It delighted many of those worshippers who knew few words and phrases of Latin; but for the traditionalists, especially in Europe, it was an emotional shock whenever the new translation did not possess the rhythms and cadences of the Latin. Lest this reform be seen as too sweeping, Pope Paul VI urged the Benedictines when they met in Rome in 1966 to cling to their Latin.

At the mass the priest now faced the people; hitherto his back was turned so that he could face the altar. A new free-and-easy music was welcomed; many lamented that guitars were superseding the pipe organ, and that songs run up by enthusiastic teenagers were replacing melodies that had come from the noblest composers of Italy and Austria. On the other hand, hundreds of millions of Catholics in New Guinea, Angola, Costa Rica and 100 other lands were tentatively freed from the strong stamp of European culture, and their music or dances were sometimes admitted to the church. It was as if a second Reformation had arrived, this time reshaping the Catholic Church from within.

The Catholic Church now offered a role – a limited role – for men and women who were not priests or monks or nuns. On some of the major committees set up to recommend new policies, women and laymen held seats and expressed their views. The Index of Prohibited Books – a long litany of sins in print – was itself forbidden and placed in the archives. A rule that many Catholics now saw as quaint and outmoded – the eating of fish instead of meat on Fridays – was abandoned. These changes were not entirely approved of by two church leaders who were present at the council and later served as pope.

The Vatican Council's decision to allow Catholics to marry Protestants was applauded: in essence, a Catholic who married in a

Protestant church was no longer excommunicated. If a mixed marriage took place in a Catholic Church, a Protestant clergyman was permitted, after the ceremony, to make a short address to the married couple and to share in the prayers. In extending a handshake to other creeds, the pope apologised to the Jews for the way they had been maltreated or rejected by many Christians over so many centuries. In 1966, in the same spirit, the Archbishop of Canterbury, Michael Ramsey, met the pope, who generously presented the Englishman with the ring he had received when he became a bishop.

That thorny topic of the sixteenth century – whether priests should be allowed to marry – was debated again. In Africa many local priests now lived in marriage, despite the Church's rules. In Europe and North America a minority of Catholics declared that it was unnatural for priests to live a celibate life. The pope refused to yield ground. Perhaps never before was there such an exodus of priests, monks and nuns from the Catholic Church. After Vatican II had formally ended, a large commission or assembly consisting of female and male, and clerical and ordinary members discussed whether a true Catholic couple should be allowed to practise methods of birth control. They knew that Protestants, except perhaps minor sects, had long ceased to oppose birth control. The Catholic commission decided to recommend the modern view, but the pope himself disapproved; he had the last word. All over the world were Catholic couples who ignored the pope. Italy practised birth control with such firmness that it was one of the first European nations to face a fast-declining birth rate and, by 2010, a static population.

This was said to be one of the rare occasions – perhaps the only occasion – in which a papal decree about a facet of daily life had been so widely defied. It is uncertain, however, whether this is true. We know far too little about the daily life and beliefs of ordinary

Christians during the last 2000 years, but evidence suggests that for decades and even centuries, whether in Norway or Peru, many Christians clung quietly to certain ancient beliefs and pagan customs that had long been denounced by their own Christian leaders.

A remarkable event that emerged from this series of meetings was a reunion of long-lost friends. In Jerusalem in 1964, a long-awaited meeting took place. The pope of Rome and the patriarch of Constantinople, now called Istanbul, met for the first time since 1439. During the previous five centuries they had not once exchanged greetings in person. In 1966 they agreed to synchronise their clocks so that two congregations of worshippers could meet simultaneously. At exactly the same hour, in Rome and in Istanbul, religious services designed to reconcile and forgive were solemnly conducted, the Orthodox and Catholics praying together.

In every century, a few voices had implored other Christians to value unity. One voice was that of Cyprian, who was bishop of Carthage in North Africa in the years AD 248 to 258, when the Church was racked with disunity. Christianity, he warned, must remember that it has only one head and one mother: 'Of her womb are we born, by her milk are we nourished, and we are quickened from her breath.' It was also true that much of the vigour and longevity of Christianity had stemmed from a willingness to innovate and argue, and from the determination of new sects to break away and walk alone.

32

THE MOVING EYE OF THE NEEDLE

The fast decline of Europe as the heartland of Christianity was not foreseen in 1900. Even today that decline is not widely recognised, though the evidence is overwhelming. One statistic highlights the rise of the new Christian world. In the year 1000, most Christian baptisms took place in Europe and Asia Minor. In 1999, only a fraction of Catholic baptisms took place in that traditional homeland of Christendom. In that same year in the world as a whole, more than half of all those individuals newly baptised as Catholics lived in Latin America and in Africa. In world Protestantism, the declining role of Europe was just as emphatic.

A WATCHTOWER IN AFRICA

In the 1920s the Christian parts of Africa became, spiritually, more dynamic. In the German colonies, taken over by France and Britain after the end of the First World War, new groups of Christian pastors and teachers, doctors, nurses and schoolteachers arrived. From the

United States and Canada came more Protestant and Catholic missionaries. Even more influential were African-born Christians, who pruned the theology that had been taught to them and grafted onto it their own traditional beliefs and customs.

An American sect, at first called the Watchtower Bible and Tract Society and later called the Jehovah's Witnesses, was to make firm headway in Africa. Founded in 1872 by Charles Taze Russell, a young Pittsburgh draper and Bible student, it rested on the simple prophecy that Christ would return to earth secretly, and the world as they knew it would come to an end in 1914. The people likely to be saved were members of his sect. They had many of the characteristics of minor Puritan religions: a belief that every word in the Bible was true, though the exact truth about the Bible's many predictions could be extracted only by the prophets; a belief that only adults should be baptised; a reliance on laymen as teachers and preachers; a refusal to celebrate Christmas and Easter; and the replacing of Holy Communion by an annual event, which they called the Lord's Meal.

Russell's periodical magazine, *The Watchtower*, found readers in many languages. The outbreak of war in 1914 naturally boosted its circulation. That the months passed and Europe did not blow itself to pieces was somewhat of a disappointment to Russell, who was now in his sixties. He assigned a new date to the time when his prophecy was to come true and pressed on with his work. Self-disciplined like the members of so many sects, his followers took no part in civil society, refusing to vote at elections, abstaining from the swearing of civilian oaths, and accepting no military duties when the United States in 1917 joined in the war. Governments, in their eyes, belonged to the realm of Satan.

Their belief in Christ's Second Coming and their prediction that he would soon arrive were potentially attractive to many people in south and central Africa. Joseph Booth, an Englishman, did more than anybody to introduce the Watchtower message to Africa. In his life, as in his religious opinions, he was itinerant. Beginning as the child of Unitarian and Anglican parents in industrial England, he emigrated to New Zealand and then to Melbourne, where, now a suburban Baptist, he held weekly debates with a prominent Australian atheist, the pair attracting indignant but eager audiences. Back in the northern hemisphere, he was attracted in 1906 by Russell's exciting message – Christ will come again – and carried it to Cape Town.

Soon the Watchtower Society won disciples in South Africa and far inland in Nyasaland – the present Malawi – where 12 000 converts were baptised by one of Booth's converts, Elliot Kamwana, in about the year 1909. Kamwana acted quickly: no time was to be lost, for Christ was said to be setting up his kingdom on earth in five years' time.

As the Watchtower leaders were against governments, wherever they found one, they attracted Africans who were disillusioned with British, French and other colonial rulers and their taxes and forceful hiring of African labour. Booth himself shouted, 'Africa for the Africans,' and Africans raised the level of the shouting and added their own slogans. They linked the promise of the Second Coming in 1914 to the hope that they would become rulers again. In World War I the new African Watchtower leaders took part in unsuccessful rebellions against the British Government in Nyasaland and Zambia. More than perhaps any other branch of Christianity in Africa so far, this sect was a distinctive voice for Africans.

Kamwana, seen as more of a troublemaker than was the fact, was exiled by the British Government to the remote Seychelles Islands and did not return to his homeland until 1937. Other leaders took his place. There was never a dearth of Christian leaders in the southern half of Africa. A congregation had no sooner become a success than at least one member was thinking of starting a breakaway. Links with the parent organisation in New York, Paris or London were easily broken. Eventually, in some African colonies, the Jehovah's Witnesses, increasingly independent, had a level of prestige and influence they gained in no American state.

Some Jehovah's Witnesses in Africa adopted – unlike their American brethren – parts of the new Pentecostal movement from the United States and began to speak in tongues. Many Africans who had long feared witches and other evil spirits welcomed the Holy Spirit as a benign force that could safeguard them.

DOWIE'S ZION CITY

John Alexander Dowie was indirectly a rival of Booth. An itinerant preacher like Booth, of about the same age, he had emigrated from Scotland to Australia, becoming a Congregational minister in two small towns on the Adelaide Plains and then moving in quick succession to Sydney and Melbourne churches and tabernacles. Forceful and provocative, his sermons were backed by a wide knowledge of the Bible and spoken in a resonant voice. After moving to the United States, he founded his own Zion City by the lake near Chicago in the 1890s. Inside he allowed no breweries, tobacco shops, gambling places or hospitals: prayer and faith were seen as the real medicines. He permitted no dance halls and theatres: no theatre was needed, for under the name of Elijah the Restorer he enlightened and entertained his own huge congregation and kept the media spellbound. Increasingly, he was carried away by his own charisma.

In 1904 he caused excitement when he announced that he welcomed the idea of blacks marrying whites. Many of his followers
disagreed, and some were shocked. As headlines in overseas papers
proclaimed, there was now 'Discord in Zion'. Such views made his
sect and theology much more acceptable in Africa, however, and
in 1904 the first Dowie-style church was opened in South Africa,
which was just recovering from the Boer War. Black Africans eagerly
joined, especially in the cities, and independent Zion churches
appeared in their hundreds, many being different to the mother
church and some being eccentric.

Of these, the most influential, called the Zion Christian Church,
was founded by Ignatius or Engenas Lekganyane in 1910 as the
result – he said – of a dream. The temple and sacred town set up
in the northern Transvaal was to become the goal of one of the largest Easter pilgrimages in the world, and was attended eventually by
close to a million people, whose cars and buses caused acute traffic
jams on the incoming roads each Easter. Amongst the cars to be
seen was the founder's own Rolls-Royce.

The town was named Mount Zion Moriah after chapter two of
Chronicles in the Old Testament: 'Then Solomon began to build
the house of the Lord in Jerusalem on Mount Moriah.' Today the
Zion Christian Church is known throughout the nation simply by its
initials, ZCC or 'zed-say-say'. It has empathy with the Jewish people,
and the star of David is its symbol.

The African founder, Pastor Lekganyane, borrowed much of his
theology and some of his marketing from Dowie's sect and its Zion
City near Chicago, and also learned from the rising Pentecostal
movement. His theology found its own distinctive voice. It was puritanical in its disdain of alcohol, tobacco and sexual licence, and like
Dowie and the Jews it disdained pork. Wary of political violence, it

was sympathetic to Nelson Mandela when he sought political power in the 1990s. Its Sunday ritual of shutting the doors and windows of its church buildings and then opening them wide, just before the sermon, was seen as a distinctive feature of Zion churches.

William Blake, the poet and artist, fired the imagination of English people after he imagined that Christ had once visited England:

> *And did those feet in ancient time*
> *Walk upon England's mountains green?*
> *And was the Holy Lamb of God*
> *On England's pleasant pastures seen?*

Like the Mormons in North America, the leaders of the Zion Christian Church in South Africa believed that Christ's own 'feet in ancient time' had walked on the mountains of their homeland. They also believed that their supreme leader in Africa was a spiritual conduit through which worshippers could gain the attention of God. These were clear and subtle forms of nationalism, and attractive to African believers in an age of growing nationalism. By the start of the twenty-first century, one-quarter of the black population of South Africa belonged to the various Zion Christian sects, of which there were said to be 5000. A host of Zion members could be found in other African nations that had once belonged to the British Empire.

MORE AFRICAN MESSIAHS

Born in the Belgian Congo – now the Democratic Republic of Congo – Simon Kimbangu was the son of a leader of a tribal religion. Converted to Christianity by British Baptist missionaries in 1915, Simon's literary skills were so tentative that he was not chosen as an official pastor or teacher, but he was more magnetic than most of his friends who could read and write. His faith in Christ and his determination to disseminate the good news pushed him to the fore. After becoming a faith-healer, in 1921 he healed a sick woman. The news spread, and he helped to spread it too.

Distancing himself from local religions and cultures, Simon denounced polygamy, witchcraft, erotic dancing and the magical drumbeat. His African face was round and slightly chubby, his dress was western, and a blurred photo shows him wearing a pale open-necked shirt and long white trousers. Surrounding himself with twelve apostles, he was increasingly revered as a new Messiah. Amongst the thousands who came to his home village to hear him preach were many followers of the European-led churches in the Lower Congo. The Baptists, while envying his success, realised that he was passing beyond their control.

For five months he was a sensation, but in influence he was feared by those Belgian officials who thought a dangerous nationalism might be emerging from his crusade. He was arrested, charged with sedition and condemned to death. After his case was referred to the King of the Belgians, his sentence was reduced to life imprisonment. He was to spend more years in jail than Nelson Mandela was to spend as a political prisoner in South Africa one generation later. Generous to his fellow prisoners, and a Christian to the end, Simon Kimbangu died in prison in 1951. Today, his 'Church of Jesus Christ on Earth' has some four million members, mainly in Zaire and Angola, and fills a seat in the World Council of Churches.

In the northern third of Africa the Muslims remained dominant. Further south the Christians made headway. They had more freedom than the Muslims to experiment and to adapt and adopt. Near the copper mines of the Belgian Congo, a Belgian missionary named

Placide Tempels closely studied the local religions and philosophy and began to translate, and even adapt, his Franciscan beliefs into central African culture. Soon after World War II, thousands of Africans joined his charismatic movement, which was known as Jamaa, being the Swahili word for family. Though he was summoned back to Belgium, his new creed flourished and spread and became independent.

Kenya was another country where newly converted Christians who wished to retain old customs, including polygamy, formed their own sects. To traditional missionaries who argued that Africans could not retain three wives and keep a special relationship with Christ, the firm Kenyan reply came: 'We'll hold on to them all.'

In many of the new mission fields, two versions of Christianity competed for space. One tried to maintain those costumes, symbols, rituals, rules, hymns, Biblical interpretations and social attitudes brought out by nuns and priests from Europe or pastors from the United States. The other version tried to adapt Christianity to the culture of particular African regions. Hundreds of independent sects and churches springing up in Africa combined tribal religions and local political movements with precepts of the New Testament: after all, the early Christians in Europe had adapted the festival of Christmas in the same spirit.

TONGUES OF FLAME

In Latin America from the 1960s a new version of Protestantism began to challenge Catholicism, which had long been dominant. The challenge was unexpected. In 1900 the Protestants had been relatively few and tended to be new immigrants or the children of immigrants from Europe or North America. It so happened that a few dynamic migrants from the United States had contact with the Pentecostal movement, which was just emerging in Los Angeles. They believed that Christ was about to return to earth and that the Pentecostals were his messengers chosen to foretell this mesmerising event. Named after the Pentecost, the Pentecostals felt that they too were touched by the Holy Spirit, and thus were enabled to speak in foreign or mysterious languages that they had never been taught. Encouraged to read the New Testament and carry it with them, they knew by heart the story, recorded in Acts, of how the Holy Spirit had descended on the apostles in Jerusalem on the Jewish Day of Pentecost and enabled them to communicate publicly in languages hitherto unknown to them.

In the port of Valparaiso in 1908, the largest Methodist church in Chile, with seats for a thousand, was opened on the site of a smaller building recently destroyed by an earthquake. Its pastor, Willis Hoover, visiting the USA four years previously, experienced the new Pentecostal movement and brought it home to Chile. In his new church the congregation came together, as was the Methodist practice, an hour or so before midnight on New Year's Eve, and on this occasion Hoover encouraged a variety of worshippers to kneel and offer their prayers aloud, one after the other. 'But that is not what happened this time,' he recalled. Together they 'began praying in a loud voice, as if it had been planned beforehand'. On the contrary, he said, there was no plan. It was as if unspoken prayers had been pent up, and out they poured, lasting for maybe fifteen minutes. The Holy Spirit was at work: almost everyone agreed on that.

The innovation in prayer spread to smaller Methodist congregations nearby. People began to speak in what seemed to be strange or garbled languages not only at prayer time but also during the congregational singing, which, in Methodism, was one of the more disciplined activities. Boys and girls and shy women too sometimes 'would speak with a power that would overcome their hearers'. In response a few of the hearers would cry aloud or tremble. This excitable, unpredictable expression of the spirit of Pentecost seemed like a return to extreme primitivism; and that was its charm and magnetism in the eyes of the Pentecostals of Chile. For the more traditional worshippers, however, it was emotional chaos. They were not consoled when they were informed that it was perhaps a noisier version of the revivalist meetings of Wesley and Whitefield.

Dozens of distinct Pentecostal churches were founded in Chile, inside and outside Methodism. The spontaneity and vitality of the praying, preaching and singing were attractive. The new movement sometimes appealed to patriotism, and the word 'National' was often in the name of the individual churches. In the cities they enticed a few lapsed or lukewarm Catholics, the first of a multitude. As people flocked from rural regions to the overflowing and anonymous cities, the Pentecostal churches provided fellowship and guidance.

As the most populous country in Latin America, Brazil was certain to attract its share of Pentecostals preachers. Two such preachers, Italians from Chicago, settled in São Paulo – until they were expelled from their congregation. Swedish-American members of the rising sect called the Assemblies of God arrived in north Brazil and tried to spread their message, though they spoke virtually no Portuguese.

Brazilian citizens soon took over the movement. The speed with which they won converts was astonishing. By the year 2000, it was estimated – very optimistically – that 47 per cent of all the people of Brazil had some link with these evangelical Protestant churches. It was easy to erect a little Pentecostal church. No ornamental cross and no altar were needed – indeed, they had no place in this spartan version of Christianity. No carpet and no comfortable seats were required, and no cabinet organ. For seats, fifty wooden boxes and twenty simple plastic chairs might be carried in. Even the pulpit or reading stand from which the preacher delivered the sermon was optional because most preachers spoke without the help of notes. Hundreds of such churches were set up in the front rooms of houses, in abandoned shops and small warehouses, in roofed sheds where cars were repaired, and in picture theatres, which were losing their customers after the advent of television. The poor felt at home in a makeshift church and did not have to wear their best clothes, if they owned any.

Millions of these new worshippers were convinced that Christ was all around them, each day of the week, every morning and every night. Those who read the Acts of the Apostles saw a time ahead – perhaps in their lifetime or centuries away – when the sun would be 'turned into darkness' and, as predicted, Christ would return to reign on earth.

From Latin American cities these sects in all their varieties spread to rural towns. Favoured first by the poor, they began to attract well-off worshippers who preferred to call themselves Charismatics rather than Pentecostals. At first not political, the new churches eventually fostered a generation who influenced national politics; in 1982 a Pentecostal became the ruler of Guatemala, by a coup. Many of their pastors began to hint that God rewarded his followers materially in this world as well as the next. If they attended church faithfully and gave money to worthy causes, they would be rewarded with prosperity. It was noticed that many borrowed too much money to buy a house or start a small business, confident that they would easily pay it back.

While it originated in the USA, the movement had its strongest influence on Latin America, which was the home of almost one-third of the world's Catholics. There, by the year 2000, maybe 350 million Catholics were said to be under challenge from some 170 million Protestants. This ratio was exaggerated, being based on hope of what might happen rather than an actual count of the religious allegiances of people. In the former Spanish and Portuguese colonies in Latin America, the Catholics still prevailed. Only in Brazil and Panama did Protestants form as much as 15 per cent of the population, and only in Chile and Paraguay did they reach 10 per cent. Nonetheless the Pentecostal revival in Latin America was contributing to Protestantism more people, in total, than the original European Reformation had recruited in that half-century dominated by Luther, Zwingli, Calvin and Henry VIII of England. In the era of the jet aircraft, most European scholars, their eyes fixed on their own cities, were inclined to see Protestants globally as the dwindling inhabitants of the half-empty churches, but Latin America and Africa proved otherwise.

MARTIN LUTHER KING ON THE MARCH

In the United States, the 1950s was one of the Protestants' dynamic decades. Most of the twenty million Afro-Americans were Protestants, and now a few of their leaders saw their churches as rallying points. Oratory, as so often in religious history, was their powerful weapon.

In 1955, Dr Martin Luther King Jr was the pastor of a black Baptist church in Montgomery, Alabama. Aged twenty-five, he resolved to be a practical pastor and tackle the plight of the black people of the south and the prejudices directed against them. A visit to India in 1959 convinced him of the virtues of Gandhi's tactic of protesting persistently but shunning acts of violence. After he joined his father as co-pastor of the Ebenezer Baptist Church at Atlanta in Georgia,

Dr King continued with the patient protests, sit-ins and boycotts that helped to modify or end the practice, in the southern states, of segregating black people from whites in buses and eating-houses. Several times he was arrested or imprisoned.

In 1963 in Washington he addressed, from the steps of the Lincoln Memorial, crowds stretched far in front of him, and a hidden television audience too. He spoke of his dream for black people living in 'The South'. Some of his long sentences were a mosaic of metaphors, straight from the Old Testament and instantly recognisable by millions of Americans: 'I have a dream that one day every valley shall be exalted, every hill and mountain shall be made low, the rough places will be made plains, and the crooked places will be made straight, and the glory of the Lord shall be revealed, and all flesh shall see it together. This is our hope. This is the faith with which I return to the South.' He concluded with the emotional words of the old Negro spiritual: 'Free at last! Free at last! Thank God Almighty, we are free at last!'

Not all who campaigned for civil and voting rights on behalf of Afro-Americans relished the tactics and theology of Martin Luther King Jr; the Bible is a violin on which scores of tunes can be played. But his voice was heard the clearest in a land where pulpit-like oratory and the Bible were a vital part of daily life and public debate. It was President Lyndon B. Johnson – known more as a thrusting politician than as an adherent of the large sect called Disciples of Christ – who signed in 1964 and 1965 the federal laws that formally remedied some of the grievances against which Martin Luther King Jr had spoken. King was aged thirty-nine and still a Baptist minister when he was assassinated in Memphis on 4 April 1968. In the United States a national holiday honours him.

THE JESUITS AND LIBERATION THEOLOGY

In South America in the 1960s, many Catholics set out to fight injustices. They insisted that the poor had been the original concern of Christ's teaching but were long neglected by the official Church, which had fallen under the sway of the powerful and power-hungry. Whereas Christ had preached that it could be difficult for rich people to squeeze into the kingdom of heaven, the same rich people in subsequent centuries had walked defiantly through the entrance gate, carrying all their possessions. Now was the opportunity to recapture the Church on behalf the homeless, hungry and forgotten. In the name of 'Liberationist Theology', these new crusaders reread distinguished theologians of the past and discovered overlooked or hidden sentences. They even saw the comfort-happy Erasmus of Rotterdam as primarily the friend of the poor in the sixteenth century.

Led mostly by Jesuits, many parish priests and Catholic teachers expressed sympathy for the black people whose ancestors had come to Brazil and the Caribbean as slaves. In South America the gap between rich and poor, and the bruising poverty of the very poor, was a recruiting ground for communists, but it could also be fertile ground for radical priests. Whereas in Europe the Catholics and communists, because of their experiences in the period 1917–45, were enemies, they were not always bitter opponents in Latin America. There, no communist party had won a major victory until Fidel Castro seized power in Cuba in 1959; and towards the Catholic Church Castro was less aggressive than were communist rulers in Europe. So in Latin America an experimental alliance between groups of armed Marxists and leftist Catholics was not unthinkable. In Colombia the priest Camilo Torres joined the guerrilla forces 'as a sign of true Christian love', in the words of one Jesuit theologian. In February 1966 Torres was killed in battle. Che Guevara, a revolutionary who was shot dead in Bolivia the following year, was praised by the same theologian as shaking 'the conscience of many Christians'.

The new theology entered bishops' palaces, sometimes by the back door. At a conference held at Medellin in Colombia in 1968, various Catholic bishops blamed the rich nations of the west for robbing the hungry, illiterate and often-ill people inhabiting nations of the third world. Pope Paul VI, who opened the conference in the course of the first papal visit ever made to Latin America, was not quite prepared for the conference's final report. It called attention to Latin America's misery, violence, social tensions, 'illness of a massive nature', general misery, 'profound inequality of income', and lack of voting rights for the masses. 'Latin America appears to live beneath the tragic sin of underdevelopment,' the report concluded. With a mixture of Marxist and Jesuit phrases, it called on the people and churches to liberate their nations.

Jesuits, the most intellectual of the Catholic religious orders, sometimes saw Karl Marx as a serious theorist who deserved more than simple condemnation. Concluding that Marx's concern for the poor exceeded that felt by many Christian theorists and theologians, various European and South American Jesuits were prepared, for the time being at least, to overlook his atheism. Meanwhile, they showed their new colours by withdrawing from some of the South American schools in which they had long taught children of the elite. But their new message antagonised Rome, which, for more than half a century, had fought communism in Europe.

Leaders of the Liberationist theology included Leonardo Boff of Brazil, the parish priest and theologian Gustavo Gutiérrez of Peru, and Archbishop Romero of El Salvador. In many countries they worked together with political organisers. The revolution in

Nicaragua in 1979 was fed by Liberationist as well as Marxist messages. When the new Sandinista Government took over, Catholic priests accepted five of the offices in the cabinet.

In nearby El Salvador, a severe critic of the military rulers was Archbishop Romero. He preached that every effort to create a fairer society 'is an effort that God blesses, that God wants, that God demands'. He warned of the moral perils facing rulers who enjoyed social comfort and political prestige but neglected their souls.

On 24 March 1980 he was delivering a sermon pleading for 'justice and peace for our people' in the chapel of a hospital in San Salvador. He seemed to be in the most secure of havens, but a gunman was watching him. As Romero was about to celebrate mass, a shot rang out. His funeral, like his manner of dying, was long remembered. In the huge, swaying crowd of mourners, forty people were crushed to death.

Catholic Liberationists in troubled Nicaragua set out a very radical creed: 'it is imperative to revolutionise society, no matter what the system or regime, and it is also imperative constantly to revolutionise the church itself, that it may be ever more evangelical.' Brazil was the key to the success of that creed, for it was the most populous nation in Latin America and soon to be the second-largest Christian nation in the world. In Brazil at least, of its radical theologians, Bishop Pedro Casaldáliga was willing to defy Rome. Eventually, in 1988 he was summoned to the Vatican, in a manner slightly reminiscent of the summons to Martin Luther to face the Holy Roman Emperor in Worms. Whereas Luther went by wagon with male friends, the bishop flew in the same plane as forty nuns making their pilgrimage to Italy.

In Rome, the bishop was questioned with courtesy by two cardinals, Gantzin and Ratzinger, who inquired of his religious beliefs and whether he had made the statements reported of him. Next, after passing eight guards, he was ushered into the presence of Pope John Paul II, and the two conversed in Portuguese. 'He speaks fluently, a true polyglot,' remarked the bishop. The meeting of fifteen minutes was almost cordial, if the bishop's published account is impartial. Though the theology of the two churchmen was far apart, the pope believed that his response during the meeting was tolerant. To the Brazilian bishop he responded, half in jest, 'So you see that I am no wild beast.'

Leaving Rome, the bishop went on a brief pilgrimage to Assisi, where he was accompanied by admirers. 'In Assisi all was bathed in light,' he explained by post to his colleagues in Brazil. A poet, he rejoiced in the doves and geraniums, and was moved when he stood in the little garden of Clare, where St Francis had recited his 'Canticle of Creatures'. This saint, so often invoked by the Liberationists, was foremost in the Brazilian bishop's thoughts on that summer day, and he found himself addressing his thoughts directly to him: 'What good you do us, and how all of us, followers of the Lord Jesus, miss you!'

The Catholic tradition of dedicated individuals working amongst the poor, in a self-forgetting spirit, continued to flourish at the end of the twentieth century. Mother Teresa of Calcutta was of that tradition. Born in the Balkans in 1910, when it was part of the fading Ottoman Empire, she joined the Sisters of Loreto at the age of eighteen and did not meet her Albanian mother again. Learning to speak English while being trained in Ireland, she then sailed to India, where at first she taught children. She was awakened, spiritually, when travelling on a train from Calcutta to the hill town of Darjeeling. She resolved to re-route her life's journey. Becoming immersed in the plight of the poor and especially the lepers in Indian cities, she launched her Missionaries of Charity in 1950 with the goal of help-ing 'the hungry, the naked, the homeless, the crippled, the blind, the lepers, all those people who feel unwanted, unloved, uncared for'. In her last years, some 4000 nuns and a smaller tally of brothers and laymen were doing her work in many lands.

While she did not seek publicity, television cameras pursued her. A documentary by the English critic Malcolm Muggeridge in 1969 widely publicised her work and her compassion. The long-lasting smile and exuberant kiss of the new television stars did not attract her: she allowed only lepers to kiss her. In the opinion of a discern-ing English critic she remained that rarity: 'one of those people who has taken the commandment of Jesus quite literally, and given up everything'.

A MOSAIC OF RELIGIOUS GROWTH AND DECLINE

In China the communist victory of 1949 was seen by Christians, especially in the United States, as a religious disaster. The most populous country in the world was now out of bounds to new and old missionaries. The strong influence of the Young Men's Christian Association on China, as on other parts of east Asia, suggested that it could co-exist perilously with the all-powerful communist govern-ment led by Mao Zedong. A senior YMCA official, Y. T. Wu, was appointed to preside over the official body set up to compel the sur-viving Christian Churches to work with the communists. It was like a bear and a kitten inhabiting the same room. Wu was finally sent to prison: he died there twenty years later, in 1979. Meanwhile, the Red Guards closed all Christian Churches, and many priests and pastors were imprisoned. Nearly all foreign cultural influences were seen as toxic.

Once the cultural revolution was over, it was slightly easier to be a Christian. Chinese Christians began to assemble in houses privately. There were even Catholic bishops, but the government appointed them and punished those whose loyalty seemed to be pledged to Rome as well as Beijing. By the early 1980s some Protestant congregations were meeting again in those big old church buildings that seemed to have been hauled straight from the main streets of Hamburg, Manchester or Chicago. Foreign visitors could see for themselves the intense feelings of the worshippers, most of whom were old but numerous enough to fill the capacious churches and even their galleries.

The Chinese Catholics – they outnumbered the Protestants – were looked on officially with more suspicion: the Vatican had long been against communism. In 2002 the Vatican estimated that eight million Chinese Catholics worshipped 'underground' rather than risk being seen to pray in public. Some observers of China believe that a religious awakening is quietly occurring, alongside the economic revival, and speak of 100 million Christians or even more, a statistic that should be swallowed with a grain of salt.

India, the second-most populous country in the world, had long ceased to be a land where Christianity was thought as certain to expand. Today Christians form just over 2 per cent of the population but their relative failure has perhaps been exaggerated. There are more Christians than Sikhs in India. Christians outnumber Buddhists in the birthplace of Buddha by three to one. In three of the very small Indian states, Christians form a majority. In Nagaland, near the north-east frontier, nine of every ten people are Christians, primarily Baptists. It is the most Baptist state in the world, even more so than any southern state in the United States, but even this accomplishment would have been viewed by William Carey, the pioneering Baptist in India, as weak compensation for the high hopes he held when he landed in Bengal as a young shoemaker and pastor in 1793.

For long the Portuguese colony of Goa, closer to Bombay, was the heart of Catholicism in India. Its archbishop is still crowned as the patriarch of the East Indies, and its cathedral – holding the remains of Francis Xavier, the Jesuit – is said to be the grandest cathedral in mainland Asia. Even in the port of Goa the number of Catholics has been surpassed by the Hindus in the twentieth century.

In the half-century after the end of the Second World War, Europe and the peoples of European descent, especially in Australia, New Zealand and South Africa, became less Christian. Fewer people went to church. Protestant nations were forced by public opinion to liberate their Sunday, traditionally a monopoly of the churches. Shopping centres and supermarkets were open; major sporting matches were played in the afternoon; and airports, which were relatively quiet on a Sunday in the 1950s, became busy, for people were no longer reluctant to travel long distances on the Lord's day.

Of the tens of thousands of Christian Sunday schools, which had flourished either on the morning or afternoon of that day, nearly all declined, and in many countries simply vanished. The stigma attached by Christians to suicide was peeled away. A tragedy of the late twentieth century was the change of public morality that almost encouraged teenagers to seek attention and dramatically proclaim their temporary mood of misery by taking their own lives.

By the year 2010, half of the babies in Britain and France were not baptised, and the first name conferred on such a child might be culled from a soap opera rather than the Bible. A funeral in a British city was often presided over by a celebrant or a civic official, and even the coffin at a Christian funeral might be draped with a football team's scarf, or other insignia that could be safely described as pagan.

In Eastern Europe a majority of people in most nations had no contact with a church. In Poland, a stark exception, more than nine of every ten inhabitants were Christian and half attended church. In France and Belgium, about six in every ten said they did have a religion, and in Netherlands, Italy and Spain the proportion who felt some religious instinct was slightly higher, but fell well below Poland's. Italy in 2000 yielded the surprising statistic that 92 per cent of children were baptised as Catholics, but less than 25 per cent, judging by the present trend, would regularly attend church when they grew older. Those Europeans who said firmly and confidently that they were atheists were multiplying rapidly.

THE USA, OR GOD AND TWO OCEANS

The 1950s – a boom time for Christian Churches in the United States and Canada – was followed by a slow decline and a difficulty in attracting teenagers during the remainder of the century. A few new Protestant sects defied the downward trend. The Assemblies of God, a twentieth-century creation preaching a Pentecostal message, more than trebled its members, while the powerful Southern Baptists continued to grow. Generally, the fundamentalist sects retained their appeal, while the sects with the more educated preachers tended to struggle.

At least Catholics could rejoice that in 1960, for the first time, one of their members, John F. Kennedy, was elected president of their nation. With the help of Mexican and other immigrants, Catholics were soon to be the most powerful single denomination in the USA. But they suffered from a loss of morale in priests and nuns.

At one cathedral a dozen nuns interrupted a mass to protest against their nation's part in the Vietnam War. Thousands of priests and nuns resigned and the number of new recruits declined. Opinion polls in 1970 showed that Americans as a whole were convinced that religion was becoming less pervasive in the nation's life.

While the United States shared with Europe in the decline of churchgoing, its decline was less startling. At the end of the twentieth century, nine of every ten Americans believed in God, and more than half claimed to be members of one of the 200 Christian groups in the United States. A president of the United States usually went to church on Sunday, and most voters knew the name of his church, whether Baptist or Methodist or Presbyterian. A long-lasting legacy of America's early religious history was that most presidents, even in the last sixty years, belonged to those sects that in Britain were called dissenting or nonconformist.

Why does Christianity, in all its variety, remain a hallmark of the United States? Even in 1750, religion was more vital for Americans than for Europeans. In the pioneering of that vast land, the Christian Churches, especially in new rural districts, had a social as well as a religious role: they were the meeting places, the social hub. Religion acquired some of the characteristics of American business and commerce. Rival Christian Churches were very competitive, and eager to attract new members. Nowhere else in the story of Christianity, until perhaps the rise of Africa, was there such energy in founding new sects or creeds. If worshippers disliked their clergyman they walked out and, gathering hammer and saw, nails and timber, erected their own church. If they could not find a suitable preacher, they themselves became the first preachers. The amateurs and the volunteers gave strength to newborn American congregations.

A pervasive idea within the United States was that their country was unique, and that Christianity was a vital ingredient of that uniqueness. Here was a new Promised Land, washed by the waves of the Pacific and the Atlantic. Americans are conscious of their long history as a strong and independent nation, with rarely an urgent need for allies even after the Cold War commenced in the late 1940s. It is almost as if God was viewed as the only ally. They saw their land as set aside for them by providence, huge in area and resources, and protected by two wide oceans from any dangerous enemy. Most Americans believed, or sensed, that they belonged to 'a covenanted nation', called into being and guided by God. So far their history has not overthrown their belief.

CHRISTENDOM'S NEW HEARTLAND?

Two episodes show how the hub of Christianity has moved from Europe. One is a little-known building, the other is a Christian parable.

The republic of the Ivory Coast, the largest producer of cocoa in the world, has been independent of France since 1960. A nation of some fifteen million people, it is not wealthy, and yet somehow it raised the money to build a massive basilica. For African visitors, this basilica arouses some of the wonder that early Gothic cathedrals in France must have done. Opened in 1989, and blessed by the pope one year later, its light-coloured dome can be seen far across the tropical green fields. Visitors are almost overwhelmed by its walls of Italian marble, glass windows of purple, blue and red, and a sweeping space capable of holding 18000 people, of whom 7000 are seated. It is rarely full, for it stands on the edge of the capital city, Yamoussoukro, where Catholic Churches more human in scale already serve Catholic worshippers. In this corner of west Africa no other buildings outshine it. How can they possibly dominate what is now the largest Christian Church in the world, being slightly larger than St Peter's in Rome?

Another sign of the strength of Christianity in many African countries is the entry of New Testament parables and metaphors into everyday speech. In 1966 Chinua Achebe, the west African novelist, described his fictional hero arriving in a smart government car at a well-guarded hospital in Nigeria. The gatekeeper promptly allowed the car to enter. 'In our country,' added Achebe, 'a long American car driven by a white uniformed chauffeur and flying a ministerial flag could pass through the eye of a needle.' Today the biblical allusion to a camel passing through the eye of the needle is as likely to be familiar in the Christian regions of Nigeria as in the unchristian regions of France.

Even in 1980 Europe still dominated Christendom, though the margin of dominance was very narrow and fast declining. Fifteen years later, Europe held some 557 million Christians, most of whom were half-hearted in their beliefs and practices. Another fifteen years passed, and Latin America and Africa each had overtaken Europe to become the strongholds of Christendom. In the world the two largest Christian nations were the United States and Brazil, and in Africa several nations held more Christians than did Italy.

The year will come when the new pope, for the first time in history, is a cardinal born far from Europe. In Brazil, Nigeria and the Philippines most Catholics will probably rejoice in the ending of the long European reign. The Church of England, another global church, reflects the same trend. Of those who assembled in London in 1998 for that church's high parliament, known as the Lambeth Conference, far more bishops came from Africa than from the British Isles. And who was the typical Anglican worshipper, globally? If all Anglicans were arranged according to age, sex and nationality, the typical worshipper would be a 24-year-old African woman living south of the Sahara.

33

'MORE POPULAR THAN JESUS'

The pope is more influential than in 1500, on the very eve of the Reformation. Then his influence was confined to western Europe and Asia Minor, but today his influence is global and he presides over a population of Catholics that, since 1500, has multiplied a dozen times or more. Indeed, many democrats might argue that such power resting in one man – a leader who cannot be deposed – is a potential weakness in the largest of all Christian Churches. On the other hand, the Orthodox and Protestant churches, except perhaps the Church of England, rarely produce a leader whose words, even in one year, capture a mass audience in a hundred nations.

AN EXTRAORDINARY POPE

The twentieth century produced one of the most notable of all pontiffs. A century hence, Pope John Paul II might well be seen as one of the five most influential popes in the history of the church, but it is too early to know what will flow from his long reign. Born in

Poland, of humble background, he was variously a university student and a worker – in a chemical plant – before he studied for the priesthood. Not many popes in the last 1000 years have come from such a humble background. He was a bishop by the time he was thirty-eight, and recognised widely as a thinker and scholar. Twenty years later he was elected as pope, the first time in four centuries that the pope had come from outside Italy, and perhaps the first time that a pope was a native of Eastern Europe. That he was reared and educated in a communist nation, at a time when the Cold War between capitalism and communism was being waged, made his election the more remarkable.

He was prominent in the eventual defeat of Soviet and European communism, for long the Catholics' main enemy. He spoke against materialism at a time when unprecedented prosperity diverted attention from religious matters. A much-quoted biblical message was that the spirit and the unseen were vital and that 'man cannot live by bread alone', but now for the first time in history several billion people had the opportunity to live by bread alone, and most seemed to applaud material abundance and find it enticing. The Church, maybe temporarily, was the loser. Ironically, the west, at the very time when it was overthrowing communism, was imitating its materialism.

Pope John Paul II expressed forthright views on theology and social customs. His own working life under Nazi and communist regimes made him see the virtues of personal freedom, though not completely. He resented the prevailing tolerance of death, especially in a world that outwardly seemed so disapproving of needless deaths. He opposed contraception and abortion as another form of death, the victims being those who otherwise might have been born. He opposed the ending of life by unnatural means; he criticised euthanasia and also the death penalty when inflicted by law courts. All these came under the label of what he called 'the culture of death'.

His eyes did not gleam when he observed the victories by the liberation theologians in South America. He saw them as too close to the Marxists. In Brazil he silently rebuked the radical Archbishop Arns of São Paulo by slicing off much of his diocese or territory, without consultation, and appointing new bishops. At the same time the pope walked in the footsteps of Francis of Assisi by announcing that the Catholic Church had 'a preferential love for the poor'. While he denounced communism and cast doubt on collectivism, he also denounced facets of capitalism and liberalism. He critically weighed and assayed various streams of thought. In so much of what he did he was a one-man committee.

At a time when women's rights were high on most political agendas he announced that no woman could be ordained as a Catholic priest. The contrast with Protestantism was stark. More than thirty years before he became pope, Protestant women were serving as pastors in the United Church in Canada, in the Lutheran churches in Denmark, and in Presbyterian and Methodist churches in various lands. In the Anglican or Episcopalian churches in the United States, Canada and Hong Kong, the first women were ordained as priests in the 1970s. When the fifth World Council of Churches met in Kenya in 1975, one in four delegates were Protestant women – a startling increase on the previous meeting. By 1990 women even served as bishops in Lutheran churches in countries as diverse as Norway and Nicaragua.

The pope was not impressed. He partly justified his position by explaining that Jesus had appointed not one woman as his disciple. On this line of argument John Paul II might well have resolved, had he been a very early pope, to refuse to sanctify the Blessed Virgin Mary on the grounds that she was a woman. In contrast he did give wonderful publicity to the shrine of Fatima, which honoured a woman. After the attempt in 1981 by a Turkish communist to kill him, the pope presented the bullet, removed by surgeons, to that Portuguese shrine.

In the end he disappointed many admirers by not giving sufficient of his attention to the rising scandal of the priests who had sexually abused boys. After his death the extent of the scandal became more apparent. While at least ninety-nine per cent of the priests living at the time were presumably innocent, the damage to the reputation of the church was already inflicted. The scandal also invited the tough and persisting question: should the Catholic Church continue to be primarily a male domain?

Amidst all the controversies surrounding him, Pope John Paul II was consistent as a thinker: he dovetailed his thoughts. He quietly modified the Church's theology, gave little attention to purgatory or hell, and renewed emphasis on the importance of love. He sought everywhere for those modern lives, both female and male, that might merit a sainthood, and found far more than had any previous pope, for he believed that a saintly life lived in the twentieth rather than, say, the tenth century could be more inspiring to young Catholics. One of his subtle messages was that saints, as human beings, had their faults.

The embarrassing papacy of the Renaissance period and several earlier periods had been redeemed by the popes of the last 200 years: it was widely agreed that most were good and some were great human beings. That was high praise. Pope John Paul II strengthened that impression with his deep faith, kindliness, and simple, rather cumbersome dignity. Mentally and physically courageous, he travelled to foreign lands and spoke to huge crowds when he should have remained at home, in hospital. No other pope had visited so many parts of the world, and it is likely that his foreign travels exceeded the combined mileage of all the other popes during the last 1000 years. When he died in 2005, after the second-longest reign in the history of the papacy, he was mourned globally. Perhaps no previous pope had won the respect of such a high proportion of Protestant and Orthodox pastors and priests. In his own indirect way he promoted the cause of Christian unity.

ATHEISTS AND SCIENTISTS FLY THEIR FLAGS

In the western world, atheists became more active and even militant in the new century. Many expressed their arguments with clarity and skill, though they relied essentially on arguments used by numerous radical Christians since at least the eighteenth century. Most atheists rejected, as did many modern Christians, the idea of a God who constantly intervened in daily affairs. Another effect of Christianity, they argued, was the promotion of war and violence. It tends to be forgotten, however, that the most ruthless leaders in the Second World War were atheists and secularists who were intensely hostile to both Judaism and Christianity. Later massive atrocities were committed in east Asia by those ardent atheists, Pol Pot and Mao Zedong. All religions, all ideologies, all civilisations display embarrassing blots on their pages.

Amongst the most articulate critics of Christianity are those scientists who predict that as the world becomes more educated, the principles of science will supersede Christianity. They usually breathe an infectious optimism about human nature. They predict that the world will become better and better. Thus, in 2010

543

Professor Stephen Hawking, one of the world's most celebrated scientists, explained that 'the human race has been improving so rapidly in knowledge and technology that if people had been around for millions of years, the human race would be much further along in its mastery'. He argued that the fullness of time would enable the human race to fulfil its enormous potential. Meanwhile, he asked, why was 'the world in such a mess'? The main reason, in his view, is that we are not adequately employing our reasoning powers. Fortunately, we will greatly improve, he argues, because we are close 'to an understanding of the laws governing us and our universe'.

A similar optimism was common in educated circles in 1900. A devastating world war, let alone two, was seen as impossible, for progress was on the march. The two world wars wrecked this prediction. They were devastating wars because science and technology had been enlisted to help warfare, as never before. Moreover, two of the new anti-Christian ideologies – Soviet communism and German fascism – placed a low premium on human lives, especially those of their civilian enemies. The deadliest sector of World War Two, the scene of far more atrocities than any sector in the preceding war, was the Russian front, where the two secular creeds confronted one another.

The belief in inevitable progress or the high possibility of progress, so strong in educated circles in 1900, has returned less than a century later. It is as if a terrible phase of human history, contradicting the basis of that optimistic mood, has faded from collective memory.

Many scientists and secularists tend to stand on one side of a high dividing wall. They are optimists about human nature and therefore about human progress: after all, scientists have done so much to create material progress. On the other side of the wall is the mainstream Christian tradition combining pessimism and optimism. It assumes that evil, like goodness, is part of human nature. Accordingly, most of the mainstream Christians were less surprised than secularists when the calamities of the twentieth century occurred. But the secularists' view of human nature is again foremost, especially in learned circles. These two views of human nature sit on opposite ends of a seesaw, and global events and trends favour one view for a time and then swing around to favour another.

NEW VICTORIES FOR ISLAM

As a rival to Christianity, Islam waxed and waned. A younger religion, it became more influential than Christianity by the year 1000 and seemed likely to become the first and only worldwide religion. But the discovery of sea routes across the Atlantic and Indian Oceans by Portuguese and Spanish navigators opened a new field for Christian missionaries. Western Europe also became dominant in science, arms and vitality, and increasingly governed most of the Muslim lands. By 1900 Christianity was far ahead of Islam in the number of its adherents.

After the Second World War, Islam revived. The main Muslim lands became independent: Indonesia and Pakistan with their massive Muslim populations, and India with its huge Muslim minority, became independent nations. Oil became the world's main source of energy, and it so happened that a surprising proportion of the world's oil lay in the Middle East and other Muslim regions. Small but rich Muslim nations became financiers of Islamic activities. Millions of migrants from Muslim lands moved to France, England, Germany, Spain and Holland, where they became confident minorities. Whereas the lands governed by Muslims did not welcome Christians and even curtailed their activities, the Muslims living in

Christian lands gained the right to practise their religion and even sought to introduce their own civil laws. In this new environment Islam flourished more easily.

These rival religions, in their attitudes and values, have drifted apart at a time when a shrinking world has tended to promote sameness. In the space of a century Christian countries have become much more democratic, more materialist, more educated, more zealous for women's rights and more eager for civil liberties than a typical Muslim land. They have also become less puritanical. In 1900 an evangelical Protestant possibly had much in common with a Muslim in social attitudes, but today the gaps have widened. When, on 11 September 2001, a tiny wing of Islam delivered a terrorist attack on two cities of the United States, it seemed that the religious gaps could widen even further.

Islam maintained an intensity of belief and a pace of growth not matched by its main rival in recent centuries. The lands that it dominated tended to be slow-changing. It discouraged debate. Moreover, in the twentieth century, the populations of Islamic lands multiplied rapidly, for the typical family was large. While Christianity continued to be the largest religion with more than 30 per cent of the world's population, Islam was catching up. Possessing 12 per cent in 1900, it possessed closer to 19 per cent in the year 2000. Today, according to certain estimates, Christians probably outnumber Muslims by a ratio of only five to four. If that estimate is correct, then Islam might well capture the lead before the twenty-first century is ended.

WILL CHRISTIANITY FADE AWAY?

The 1960s was the decade of the young and their rebellion against traditions and taboos in religion, politics, sex, music, clothes and much else. No such explosion of values had been experienced in the long Christian era, except perhaps in the opening years of the French Revolution.

The four English 'rock' musicians called 'The Beatles' helped to lead the latest revolution. Their family background in the port of Liverpool was more Christian than pagan, and indeed their leaders, Paul McCartney and John Lennon, first met at a Church of England fete and musical event in 1957. In less than a decade, the Beatles became the most celebrated young men in the world. On both sides of the Atlantic their public appearances induced hysteria and fainting, and the sales of their gramophone records were enviable. They looked so young as to appear innocent.

Miraculously, they danced their way along a thin white line that separated traditional Christian values from those displayed in discotheques and at rock concerts. On 4 March 1966 John Lennon crossed that white line. 'Christianity will go,' he announced in the London *Evening Standard*. 'It will vanish and shrink,' he predicted confidently. 'Jesus was all right, but his disciples were thick and ordinary.' In praise of the Beatles, he cheerfully claimed that 'We're more popular than Jesus now.' In the circles in which he moved, his observation was correct, but in Alabama – in retaliation – bundles of Beatles' records were thrown on bonfires. Preachers said that Lennon had committed blasphemy. Trying to retreat, he intimated that what he had in mind was the waning prestige of Christ in England. In Chicago he finally repented about the comparison with Christ: 'I am sorry I said it.'

In 1900 no celebrity in the western world, least of all a popular entertainer, could have delivered such a slur on Christ and still retained a massive following. And yet the Beatle was partly correct. In Europe the church was in decline, and many intellectuals quietly agreed with his prediction that Christianity would vanish.

Christianity is in decline in the most prosperous, most literate and most materialist nations, though not elsewhere. Its decline in Europe may well be a portent of its long-term future. But even in Europe, a traditional Christian heartland, the decline cannot yet be viewed as permanent. In its heartland, in the course of twenty centuries, it has declined and revived again and again. In AD 300 it was weaker in Europe, Asia Minor and its heartland than it is today. Even in 1000, as a result of the rise of Islam and the tenacity of paganism, it was probably less influential than it is today in that same old heartland. In 1600 it was weaker in the world as a whole than it is today. A conclusion of this book is that Christianity has repeatedly been reinvented. Every religious revival is a reflection of a previous state of decline; but no revival and perhaps no decline is permanent.

In Europe, another profound change has not yet made a universal impression: the decline of its own place in the world. Today, more people and more Christians live in Africa than in Europe, and more people and more Christians live in the Americas than in Europe.

Even when Christianity was on one of its peaks, crowds of people were indifferent or lukewarm, and its influence on many parts of society was faint or patchy. As John Calvin confessed, when his Geneva was seen as the showcase of Christianity, most of its people did not necessarily believe the main religious truths. They did not necessarily believe that God was all-powerful. Calvin insisted that most men and women thought that luck, chance and fortune were the main shapers of their lives. 'If one falls among robbers, or ravenous beasts; if a sudden gust of wind at sea causes shipwreck; if one is struck down by the fall of a house or a tree,' argued Calvin, then most people attributed such mishaps to luck and not to the will of God. Calvin insisted that 'this erroneous opinion' prevailed in all ages and is 'almost universally prevailing in our own day'.

That swearing and blasphemy also persisted during the centuries when Christianity was dominant is another sign that religion could be a veneer. By the late nineteenth century swearing was accepted widely, even by Christians who took their religion seriously. In Russia the devout novelist Tolstoy was addicted to swearing, while occasionally denouncing the habit. Joseph Lightfoot, Bishop of Durham, conceded in the 1880s that those Christian coalminers whom he personally knew did swear, though he assured himself that it was more with their lips than their hearts.

In essence, the western world today should not be compared too harshly with the supposedly more Christian civilisation that preceded it. Christianity, even in its various heydays, was partly a veneer for a multitude of people.

'WISDOM IS THE THING'

In the western world in the first decades of the twenty-first century, Christian doctrine often seems slightly irrelevant. For the first time in history, several of the maladies that made religion helpful or indispensable have been removed or weakened. No longer is there such a variety of illnesses with no known cures, and no longer such frequent deaths of the young, nor such extremes of hunger and poverty. At one time most people who died at the age of fifty were physically worn out, but machines of many kinds have largely dispensed with the incessant hard physical labour that sustained economic life. For all these reasons the incentives to turn to the Bible, when in despair or pain, have weakened, though material success seems to create fresh causes of despair.

In the more formally educated countries, Christianity has also had to face a mental mood that is less favourable. Three hundred years ago people relished supernatural explanations; now they are more often convinced by explanations that appeal – or seem to appeal – to science, logic and reason. Science and technology have a simple and persuasive message: the world's problems are soluble by ingenuity and material innovations; the world's riddles, such as the origins of the universe, can be unravelled by the scientific mind. But while science's achievements have been remarkable, they have not been revolutionary in probing human nature. In some ways the measurable problems analysed by science and technology are more easily dissected than human problems. The moon is more easily explored than is the typical mind and heart.

In the hierarchy of mental virtues, knowledge rides high. The word 'wisdom' is little employed in a century that values knowledge more than ever before. 'Wisdom is the principal thing: therefore get wisdom,' said the Book of Proverbs. Many illiterate Jews of the Old Testament, whether shepherds or water-fetchers, were probably more interested in seeking wisdom than are most of the winners of a Nobel prize some 2500 years later. Wisdom is primarily concerned with human beings and their predicaments. Indeed, wisdom should constitute the arena in which atheists and Christians both compete.

It is legitimate to say that one does not believe in God. But to say no more, and to sideline that debate about human nature that surrounds the whole concept of a god, is to misunderstand why Christianity has absorbed so many minds for so long.

WEIGHING CHRISTIANITY ON THE SCALES

Christianity has reinvented itself so often. Probably no other institution in the history of the world has displayed such diversity. What arguments would break out if eight influential Christians from different centuries met at the same dinner table: Paul the Apostle along with Bishop Nestorius of Constantinople from the early centuries, Francis of Assisi and the nun Teresa of Avila and Martin Luther of Wittenberg from the middle centuries, and Mrs George Fox of the Quakers along with Pastor Lekganyane of the Zionist Church in South Africa and Pope John Paul II? Oddly, one reason why Christianity has been so dynamic for so long is its eagerness to argue, almost as a matter of life and death.

It is not easy to evaluate such a huge and longstanding religion, many of whose regiments marched out of step. Certainly it has shaped and sometimes misshaped much in the modern world. Not only morality and ethics have been influenced but also the calendar, holidays, social welfare, spectator sports, architecture, language and literature, and the names fixed to the globe's maps. Perhaps no other institution – except for modern governments – has cared so diligently for the sick, the poor, the orphans and the old. In some centuries the Church was the predecessor of the welfare state. For centuries it was the main teacher in most of Europe and the founder of most of the early universities. Christianity affected the public role of women, the status of the family, and – some historians would say – the rise of capitalism and socialism. Christianity has both spurred and retarded the sciences and the social sciences. Indeed, most of the modern debates of profound significance were originally dialogues with or within Christianity.

The rise of modern democracy, very different to that elite version practised in the open air in ancient Athens, owed much to the early Christian plea of Paul that all souls were of equal worth in the eyes of God. Democracy also owed much to that wing of early Protestantism that, obeying no pope and no bishop, gave real power to the congregation assembled each Sunday. The rise of freedom of expression owes much to the battles fought inside Christianity in the last five centuries. Even modern atheism is largely the by-product of Christianity, and far more successful than was predicted.

Christianity helped to carry out much that was regrettable during the history of the last 2000 years. While it was one of the forces propelling European navigators to discover or rediscover the Americas, Australia, New Zealand and a constellation of Pacific Islands, the resulting spread of European culture to those distant lands was both beneficial and destructive to their peoples. While Christianity could be a force for peace, it could also be a force for war.

Christianity inflicted far, far more wrongs than its first Apostles could have imagined. Many of those wrongs were committed by those who spoke in the name of Christ but were lip-servants. It has been a difficult and tantalising creed. Of the billions, now dead, who had some understanding of Christ and tried to follow his precepts, most probably would have admitted that they had largely failed in some phases of their lives or perhaps in all. If Christ himself was to judge the world's erratic response to his message in its first 2000 years, he might have responded, 'Remember: I told you so.' It was he who had once spoken the prophetic words: 'Many are called: few are chosen.'

And yet Christianity probably has been the most important institution in the world in the last 2000 years. It has achieved more for western civilisation than has any other factor; it has helped far more people than it has harmed. So much of what seems admirable in the world today comes largely or partly from Christianity and from people who practised it. On the other hand, scholars and commentators living in 2200 and holding another set of values might conclude differently. There is rarely a final and unanimous verdict on whether the really major changes of the past were or were not beneficial to the world as a whole.

It is remarkable that a man who lived 2000 years ago, who held no public office and owned no wealth, and who travelled no more than a few days' walk from his birthplace should have exerted such influence. 'I am the way, the truth, and the life,' he declared. His precepts, prophecies, warnings and parables have deeply influenced hosts of people. They believed that Christ was and is everywhere. They took heart from his words: 'For where two or three are gathered in my name, there am I in the midst of them.'

The debate about Christ's message and influence will continue. Long after we are all dead and the twenty-first century is lost behind passing clouds, the fascination with him will persist; and many will still see him as triumphant.

ACKNOWLEDGEMENTS

I express my gratitude to two friends who read the whole manuscript. I give thanks to John Day (of Wangaratta), who has an eye for sentences and arguments that don't stand up to inspection, and to Michael Costigan (once of Rome and now of Sydney), who often gave me the benefit of his wide experience and insights in church matters: amongst many activities, he sat through long weeks of Vatican II in the 1960s. I am deeply indebted to four specialist theologians and church historians who generously, and at short notice, read certain chapters and offered forthright comments on them: to Francis Moloney, who held chairs in church history at American and Australian universities, and Ian Breward, who held chairs in New Zealand and Australian universities; and to Austin Cooper, who has long lectured at Melbourne's Catholic Theological College, and Dorothy Lee, who is the new dean of Trinity College's Theological School at the University of Melbourne.

Each of these generous readers will probably disagree with some of the assumptions and arguments in this book. My calculation is that there must be at least 27 000 separate 'facts' or inferences in the preceding pages. On some, alas, I will be mistaken. I accept full responsibility for my errors and dubious interpretations.

My thanks must go to Bob Sessions, of Penguin Books, who encouraged me to write this book, and to Anne Rogan, a patient and alert editor. For guiding me to particular books and other sources, I am also grateful to Rex Harcourt, David Runia, Raymond Flower, Winston Lim, Max Suich, Sir Rod Carnegie, Rob Nave, Richard Hagen, Mario Panopoulos and Anna Blainey. I am grateful to my wife, Ann, who has carried in her head, ever since she was a teenager, a detailed history of theology, which she has expanded in the last three years, to my great benefit.

I pay tribute to the State Library of Victoria, the Baillieu Library at the University of Melbourne, and the Mannix Library of the Catholic Theological College in the same city. I also gained from visits to a variety of cathedrals, chapels, history museums, art galleries, and sacred sites extending from Assisi to Zanzibar.

SELECTED SOURCES

The literature on the history of Christianity is massive and almost overwhelming. The endnotes in the following pages cover a tiny fraction of it. They refer only to the more important and sometimes the out-of-way sources that I found useful. They rarely refer to sequences of events that are well-known and can easily be consulted in standards works and encyclopaedias. If an actual gospel is mentioned in an episode in the narrative, it is rarely specified in the following endnotes. For gospel quotations I usually prefer the *Holy Bible: Revised Standard Version* (London, 1952 edition.) If a quotation is widely known and appears in the *Oxford Dictionary of Quotations* or similar works, I rarely include it in these endnotes. Sometimes, if the title or subtitle of an article in a learned journal is very long, I condense it.

ABBREVIATIONS OF GENERAL REFERENCE WORKS
(especially those cited more than once in these endnotes)

AR: The Annual Register, London, 758–2000.
Bettenson: Henry Bettenson (ed.), *Documents of the Christian Church*, London, 1943.
CEHE: Cambridge Economic History of Europe, Cambridge, esp. vol. 3 'Economic Organisation and Policies in the Middle Ages' (1965); vol. 4 'The Economy of Expanding Europe in the Sixteenth and Seventeenth Centuries' (1967).
CHC: Cambridge History of Christianity, Cambridge: esp. vol. 3, 'Early Medieval Christianities' (2008); vol. 5, 'Eastern Christianity' (2006); vol. 9, 'World Christianity c. 1914 – c. 2000' (2006).
CHJ: Cambridge History of Judaism, Cambridge, esp. vol. 3 (1999).
DNB: Dictionary of National Biography, the first series except where designated.
EB: The Encyclopaedia Britannica, Cambridge, 1910–11, 11th edition, esp the three vols (30, 31, 32) at the end of the unusual and little known 12th edition, 'dealing with events and developments of the period 1910 to 1921 inclusive'.
EHD: English Historical Documents, London; in 12 vols, spanning c. 500 to 1914, esp. vols 11 (parts 1, 2), 12.
NCMH: New Cambridge Modern History, Cambridge, 1957–, 14 vols.
New Grove: The New Grove Dictionary of Music and Musicians, Stanley Sadie (ed.), Macmillan, London, 1998 edition, in 20 vols.
ODCC: Oxford Dictionary of the Christian Church, F. L. Cross (ed.), Oxford: 2nd edition, 1974; revised 3rd edition, 2005.

CHAPTER 1. THE BOY FROM GALILEE

6 A very present help in trouble: Psalm 46:1.

8 And have come to worship him: Matthew 2:2.

8 Columbus, Tasman and three kings: for Cuba, see Richard C. Trexler, *The Journey of the Magi*, Princeton, 1997, p. 137; for New Zealand, see Tasman's journal in Andrew Sharp (ed.), *The Voyages of Abel Janszoon Tasman*, Oxford, 1968, pp. 138 ff. Tasman discovered the islands on Epiphany or Three Kings' Day.

8 Planets and Jesus's birth: Raymond E. Brown, *The Birth of the Messiah: A Commentary on the Infancy Narrations*, New York, 1993, pp. 170–1.

9 Evidence against Bethlehem as birthplace: C. J. Cadoux, *The Life of Jesus*, West Drayton, 1948, pp. 30–1.

9 Jesus the Nazarene: Matthew 2: 23; Allen Brent, *A Political History of Early Christianity*, London, 2009, p. 25.

9 No known birthplace: W. D. Davies & E. P. Sanders, 'Jesus: from the Jewish point of view' in *CHJ*, vol. 3, p. 623.

9 Possible brothers, sisters and cousins : Mark 6: 3.

9–10 Jesus's literacy and trade: David Fiensy, 'Leaders of Mass Movements and the Leader of the Jesus Movement', *Journal for the Study of the New Testament*, issue 74, 1999, pp.15–17.

10 Jesus and 'must': Gerald O'Collins, *Jesus: A Portrait*, London, 2008, pp. 16–18; Luke 2: 49.

11 Jesus and John the Baptist: John 1: 24–34; Luke 3: 1–22; Kurt Rudolph, 'The Baptist Sects' in *CHJ*, vol. 3, p. 477–9.

13 Preaching at Capernaum: Mark 1: 22.

13 Theologian on Jesus as rival : Francis J. Moloney, *The Gospel of John: Text and Context*, Boston, 2005, pp. 52–3, 62.

14 The harvest truly is plenteous: Matthew 9: 37.

14–15 Let the dead bury their dead: Matthew 8: 22.

14–15 Sabbath made for man: Mark 2: 27–8; 3: 1–6.

15–16 Sermon on Mount and Lord's Prayer: Matthew 5: 1–14; 6: 9–13.

16 The kingdom in Lord's Prayer: O'Collins, op. cit., p. 20.

18 But woe unto you that are rich: Luke 6: 24–26.

CHAPTER 2. THE DEATH AND REBIRTH OF JESUS

20 Women and Jesus: Paul Johnson, *Jesus: A Biography from a Believer*, London. 2010, pp. 134–42.

20–21 Herod's temple and its amenities: Dan Bahat, 'The Herodian Temple' in *CHJ*, vol. 3, pp. 54–8.

21 God too mighty to be confined to a temple: Shaye J. D. Cohen, 'The Temple and the Synagogue' in *CHJ*, vol. 3, p. 310.

22 The widow's coins: Mark 12: 42–44.

22 Jesus disrupting temple's activities: Davies and Sanders, op. cit., *CHJ*, vol. 3, pp. 650–1.

23 From the ends of the earth to the ends of heaven: Mark 13: 24–27.

24–25 Interpretation of anointing : Mark 14: 3–9; O'Collins, op. cit., pp 155–6. There were possibly numerous such anointing gestures by women in Jesus's brief preaching life. Others are in Luke 7: 37–38 and John 12: 3.

25–26 Last Supper: *ODCC*, p. 801.

26 'I tell you', said Jesus: Matthew 26: 29.

26 Jesus eventually reveals himself as Messiah: *ODCC*, 1st edition. p. 906.

26 Accusation of blasphemy: Mark 15: 64.

27 Unnamed disciple at crucifixion: John 19: 26.
28 Jesus's last words in Aramaic: O'Collins, op. cit., p. 170.
30 Luke and Emmaus: Luke 24: 28–31; Francis J. Moloney, *The Living Voice of the Gospel: The Gospels Today*, Mulgrave (Aust.), 2006, pp. 220–222.
32 Main cities of Roman Empire in AD 14: Angus Maddison, *Contours of the World Economy, 1–2030 AD: Essays in Macro-Economic History*, Oxford, 2007, p. 42.
33 Jewish percentages of total population: William Horbury in Ian Hazlett, *Early Christianity: Origins and Evolution to AD 600*, London, 1991, p. 40.
33 Asia Minor and Jews: William Horbury in Hazlett, op. cit., p. 42.
33 Jews in Egypt: J. Gwyn Griffiths, 'The Legacy of Egypt in Judaism' in *CHJ*, vol 3, pp. 1028–30.
33 Synagogue as social centre: Griffiths,.S. H. D. Cohen in *CHJ*, vol 3.
33 Septuagint: William Horbury in Hazlett, op. cit., p 47.

CHAPTER 3. 'WHO CAN BE AGAINST US?'

37 Damascus road: A. N. Wilson, *Paul: The Mind of the Apostle*, London, 1997, p. 68.
38 Paul hated by some Jews: Davies and Sanders, op. cit., *CHJ*, vol. 3, pp. 678 ff.
38 Hebrew of the Hebrews: Davies and Sanders, op. cit., *CHJ*, vol. 3, p. 730.
40 Anti-christ: 1 Thessalonians: 9, 10.
41 Paul on Christians of 'counterfeit faith': 2 Timothy: 4.
41 Your hearts and minds in Christ Jesus: Philippians: 4.
42 Epistles to Timothy: Timothy 1 and 2 probably not written by Paul: Brendan Byrne, *Paul and the Christian Women*, Homebush (Aust.), 1988, p. 86.
42 Female tutor: 'Apollos' in ODCC, p.73.
42 Women in Caesarea: Patricia Ranft, *Women and Spiritual Equality in Christian Tradition*, New York, 1998, p. 5, Acts 21: 8–9.
42–43 Role of women: *CHJ*, vol. 3, pp. 370–5.
43 Female helpers: *Women and Spiritual Equality in Christian Tradition*, op. cit., pp. 17–19. Paul later modified the church's radical attitude to women. Byrne, op. cit., p. 98.
43 I have fought: 2 *Tim.* 4:7.
43–44 Paul viewed as first romantic poet: A. N. Wilson, *Paul: The Mind of the Apostle*, op. cit., p. 221.
44 'Who can be against us': Romans 8: 31.
44 Rome and Lyon worshipped in Greek: Hazlett, op. cit., p. 148.
45 Greek words remain important: Owen Chadwick, *A History of Christianity*, London, 1995, pp. 33–4. See also *ODCC* for apostle, bishop, dogma, apostle etc.
45 Pope Victor writes in Latin: David Wright in Hazlett, op. cit., p 151.
48 Tatian: ODCC, p. 1590.
48 Selecting the books of the New Testament: Chadwick, op. cit., pp. 49–51; Diarmaid MacCulloch, *A History of Christianity*, London, 2009, pp. 128–9; John M. Court, 'The Growth of the New Testament' in *Oxford Handbook of Biblical Studies*, Oxford, 2006, pp. 532–40.
50 Liking for older religions: Rita N. Brock & Rebecca A. Parker, *Saving Paradise: How Christianity Traded Love of This World for Crucifixion and Empire*, Boston, 2008, p. 445 n.
51 Mani: Kurt Rudolph in Hazlett, op. cit., pp. 193–4.
51–52 Bardesanes in Edessa and Armenia: Martin Marty, *The Christian World: A Global History*, New York, 2007, pp. 31–2.

CHAPTER 4. BREAD, WINE AND WATER

54 The ideal bishop: Timothy 3: 1–7 and Titus 1:7.

54 Rome's forty-six presbyters: Stuart G. Hall in Hazlett, op. cit., p. 108.

54 Seven deacons: Acts 6.

55 Saturday worship: David E. Duncan, *Calendar*, New York, 1998, p. 54.

56 Bread and water: Edward Foley, *From Age to Age: How Christians have Celebrated the Eucharist*, Collegeville (USA), 2008, pp. 63–5.

56 Jesus's joyful meal: Gilles Quispel, *The Secret Book of the Revelation*, New York, 1979, p. 37.

56–57 Easter day: *ODCC*, pp. 1037–8 (see Paschal Controversies).

59–60 Holy water: F. C. Conybeare, 'Holy Water' in *EB*, vol. 13, p. 623.

60 Baptism of blood: *ODCC*, p. 881.

61 Three times: F. C. Conybeare, 'Baptism' in *EB*, vol. 2, esp. pp. 364–6.

62 Baptism: *EB*, vol. 2, esp. pp. 365–7.

63 Aim of fasting: Brock & Parker, op. cit., p. 123.

63 'Your fairest robe': cited in Brock & Parker, op. cit., p. 1240.

65 'Old men shall dream dreams': Acts 2: 17.

CHAPTER 5. IN THE EMPEROR'S HANDS

66 Persecution of Christians: M. I. Finley, *Aspects of Antiquity*, London, 1968, pp. 141–2.

66–67 Perpetua as martyr: Patricia Ranft, *Women in Western Intellectual Culture, 600–1500*, New York, pp. 29–34.

67 Churches like a welfare state: Chadwick, op. cit., pp. 36, 38.

68 Number seven: *ODCC*, pp. 1264–5 lists these and other special sevens, but has no explanation why number seven was important. Chadwick, op. cit., p 126 explains how eight sins became seven.

69 Onset of new diseases: William H. McNeill, *Plagues and Peoples*, New York, 1976, pp. 116, 122. On Christian rituals and spread of epidemics: Keith Thomas in *The New York Review*, 30 Sept. 1976, p. 4.

69 Healing the sick with prayer and with oil: Mark 6: 12–13.

70 Popes under Decian: Eamon Duffy, *Saints and Sinners: A History of the Popes*, Yale, 1997, pp. 14–15.

71 Eucharist and 49 arrests: W. H. C. Frend in *English Historical Review*, Sept. 2002, vol. 117, p. 896.

72 Christianity's assets for empire: Massey H. Shepherd, Jr, 'Before and After Constantine' in Jerald C. Brauer, *Essays in Divinity*, Chicago, 1968, vol. 2, p. 30.

73 Christians in army: Chadwick, op. cit., p. 61.

73 Constantine no longer divine: Peter Brown cited in Brock & Parker, op. cit., p. 450, n. 61; Massey H. Shepherd, Jr, 'Before and After Constantine' in Brauer, op. cit., vol. 2, pp. 17–38.

73 Riches of pagan temples to Christians: Peter Salway, *Roman Britain*, Oxford, 1986, p. 341.

74 Emperor's right to interfere: Massey H. Shepherd, Jr, 'Before and After Constantine', Brauer, op. cit., vol. 2, p. 33.

74 Constantine's burial: Massey H. Shepherd, Jr, 'Before and After Constantine' in Brauer, op. cit., vol. 2, p. 32.

75 Julian's persecution: Brock & Parker, op. cit., pp. 85, 96.

76 Pilgrims' choices in Palestine: Carolyn L. Connor, *Women of Byzantium*, New Haven (US), 2004, p. 30.

76–77 Egeria: 'Travel Journal', in Bart D. Ehrman & Andrew S. Jacobs (eds), *Christianity in Late Antiquity 300–450 C.E.: A Reader*, New York, 2004, pp. 333–347.

77 Shrine of St Menas: David H. Farmer (ed.), *The Oxford Dictionary of Saints*, 1978, p 276; visit to British Museum in June 2007.

77 Gregory's warning scenery: Ehrman & Jacobs (eds), op. cit., p. 349.

CHAPTER 6. THE GANG OF HERETICS

81 Council of Nicea: Joseph F. Kelly, *The Ecumenical Councils of the Catholic Church: A History*, Collegeville (USA), 2009, pp. 23–7.

81–82 Lutherans and Hitler: Rowan Williams, *Arius: Heresy and Tradition*, 2nd edition, London, 2001, pp. 237–8.

83 Goths: *ODCC*; Catholic Dictionary.

85 Augustine and sea: Garry Wills, *Saint Augustine*, New York, 1999, p. 36.

85 Augustine's conversion: ibid., cited p. 47.

86 Augustine and predestination: ibid, p. 109.

87 Pelagius: Bettenson, p. 75.

87 The Devil: Robert Nisbet, *History of the Idea of Progress*, New York, 1980, p. 72.

89 Ravenna and Arian regime: Lawrence Gowing (ed.), *A History of Art*, London, 1983, p. 366.

90 Making the glass cubes: J. H. Middleton of Cambridge in *EB*, vol. 18, pp. 884–6.

91 Depictions of Christ in Arian Baptistery: Giuseppe Bovini, *Ravenna Mosaics*, Oxford, 1978; Giuseppe Bovini, *Ravenna: its Mosaics and Monuments*, Ravenna, 1987, esp. pp. 71, 114; E. H. Gombrich, *The Story of Art* (12th edition), London, 1973, pp. 95–7. After three visits to Ravenna I find that my view is no longer the same as Gombrich's.

CHAPTER 7. MONKS AND HERMITS

94 William Shakespeare on 'cloister': *Measure for Measure*, Act I, Scene 3.

95–96 Saint on pillar: Edward Gibbon, *The Decline and Fall of the Roman Empire* (Everyman edition), London, 1994, vol. 4, ch. 37, pp. 23–4; Bishop Theodoret's narrative is in Ehrman & Jacobs (eds), op. cit., pp. 381–6.

97 Women form groups: Chadwick, op. cit., p 71.

98 Jerome on women: Ehrman & Jacobs (eds), op. cit., p. 273. Far from deriding women, Jerome loved their companionship.

98 Jerome's letter to women: ibid., p. 286.

99 Elvira: ibid., pp. 244–51; G. C. Coulton on celibacy, *EB*, vol. 5, p. 601.

99–100 Council of Tours: Hermann Josef Vogt in Hubert Jedin (ed.), *History of the Church*, vol. 2, esp. pp. 652–4.

102 Benedictines and medicine: Albert S. Lyons and R. J. Petrucelli, *Medicine: An Illustrated History*, New York, 1978, pp. 283–6.

102 Monte Cassino: C. H. Lawrence, *Medieval Monasticism: Forms of Religious Life in Western Europe in the Middle Ages* (3rd edition), Harlow (UK), 2001, p. 36.

103 Irish monks and Easter: Frank Stenton, *Anglo-Saxon England* (3rd edition), Oxford, 1971, pp. 119–20.

104 Gall: Anselmo M. Tommasini, *Irish Saints in Italy*, Covent Garden (UK), 1937, pp. 252–64.

105 Bede not a traveller: Leo Shierley-Price in intro. to Bede Le Vénérable, *A History of the English Church and People*, p. 18.

105 Imperfections: ibid., p 33.

105 Bede praised as 'greatest historian': MacCulloch, *A History of Christianity*, op. cit., p. 337.

106 Bede and comets: Bede Le Vénérable, op. cit., p 330.

CHAPTER 8. THE RISE OF ISLAM

108 Nestorius: *ODCC* (2005 edition), pp.1145–6.

110 Nestorians: Marty, op. cit., pp. 34–5.

110 Influence of Nestorius in Europe: George Yule (ed.), *Luther: Theologian for Catholics and Protestants*, Edinburgh, 1985, p. 98.

110–111 The monophysite zone of influence: MacCulloch, *A History of Christianity*, op. cit., p. 243.

112 Economic and religious motives of invading Arabs: Bernard Lewis, *The Arabs in History* (revised 6th edition), Oxford, 1993, pp. 45–51.

114–115 Recent historian on Spanish battle (Guadalete): David L. Lewis, *God's Crucible: Islam and the Making of Europe, 570–1215*, New York, 2008, p. 123 ff.

115 Rome pillaged: Duffy, op. cit., pp 78–9.

116 Koran on Christ: cited in Sidney H. Griffith, *The Church in the Shadow of the Mosque: Christians and Muslims in the World of Islam*, Princeton, 2009, pp. 17–18.

117 Islam and sex: Jean Guitton, *Great Heresies and Church Councils*, London, 1965, p. 111.

118 Muslim converts to Christianity: Griffith, op. cit., pp. 148–9.

118 No horse riding: Steven Runciman, *A History of the Crusades*, London, 1991, vol. 1, p. 22.

118 Marriages in Spain: Hugh Thomas, *An Unfinished History of the World*, London, 1979, p. 146.

118 Arabic as language of worship: Griffith, op. cit., pp 49–50.

118 Percentage of Christians in AD 700: ibid., p. 11.

119 Church pillaged by Vikings: Robert Ferguson, *The Hammer and the Cross: A New History of the Vikings*, Penguin, 2009, pp. 41–2.

119 Hamburg: ibid., p. 379.

CHAPTER 9. BATTLE OF THE ICONS

123 Gulf between eastern and western churches: Mary B. Cunningham & Elizabeth Theokritoff (eds), *The Cambridge Companion to Orthodox Christian Theology*, Cambridge, 2008, pp. 4–5; Judith Herrin, *Byzantium*, London, 2008, pp. 45–48.

125 Long controversy about arts and icons: Paul C. Finney, *The Invisible God: The Earliest Christians on Art*, Oxford, 1994, esp. pp. 15–60; Jaroslav Pelikan, *The Christian Tradition: A History of the Development of Doctrine*, Chicago, 1974, vol. 2, pp. 132, 142, 145; Mariamna Fortounatto and Mary B. Cunningham in Cunningham & Theokritoff (eds), op. cit., pp. 4–5; Herrin, op. cit., ch. 9.

125 Icon protecting Constantinople's walls: Herrin, op. cit., pp. 101–4.

126 Triumph of Orthodoxy and defeat of iconoclasm: Hugh Honour and John Fleming, *A World History of Art*, London, 1982, p. 242.

127 Zoe's icon: 'The Culture of Lay Piety in Byzantium 1054–1453', in Michael Angold (ed.), *CHC*, vol. 5, 'Eastern Christianity', p. 92.

128 A dove slaughtered on tomb: ibid., p. 99.

129 Prayer of Leo the Wise: Ephrem Lash in Cunningham & Theokritoff (eds), op. cit., pp. 4–5; Herrin, op. cit., pp. 38–9.

130 Early monasteries of Constantinople: Herrin, op. cit., p. 43.

131 Ethnic mix of monasteries at Mt Athos: *Westermann Grosser Atlas Zur Weltgeschichte*, Braunschweig, 1972, p. 45.

132 'I beg you': Connor, op. cit., pp. 275–6.

133 Theodora's daughter, 'bride of Christ': ibid., p. 287.

134 Apportioning of convent food: ibid., p. 298.

135 Vladimir flirts with Judaism: Fernand Braudel, *A History of Civilization*, New York, 1994, pp. 532–3.

135 Mt Athos's influence: Cunningham & Theokritoff (eds), op. cit., pp. 16, 146, 167, 190, 293.

CHAPTER 10. BEHIND FRENCH MONASTERY WALLS
136 Violence at the Papacy: Duffy, op. cit., pp. 83–87.
138 Children and monastic vows: Lawrence, op. cit., pp. 34–5, 38 n.
138–139 Helpings of food: Paul Delatte, *The Rule of Saint Benedict: A Commentary*, London, 1950, pp. 270–6.
139 The rise of Cluny: Joachim Wollasch, *New Cambridge Medieval History*, vol. 3, pp. 174–83.
139 Cluny as hostel for wealthy: Lawrence, op. cit., pp. 118–9.
141 Vanity: ibid., pp. 149–52.
144 Bernard and Lake Geneva: Henry Mayr-Harting, 'Two Abbots in Politics', *Transactions of the Royal Historical Society*, series 5, 1990, vol. 40, p. 233.
144 Bernard and Judgement Day: Lawrence, op. cit., p. 182.
146 Wordsworth on Tintern Abbey: William Wordsworth, *The Poems of Wordsworth*, Oxford, 1926, pp. 205–7.
146 Lay brothers: David Knowles, *Christian Monasticism*, London, 1969, pp. 106–7.
146 Appearance of lay brothers: Delatte, op. cit., pp. 365–6.
147 Water wheels: Jean Gimpel, *The Medieval Machine: The Industrial Revolution of the Middle Ages*, London, 1977, pp. 16–20, 56–61.
148 Rule 39 of St Benedict: Bettenson, pp. 169–70.
148 Monks and navigation: Robert Miller, 'The Early Medieval Seaman and the Church: Contacts Ashore', *The Mariner's Mirror*, vol. 89, no. 2, May 2003, pp. 132 ff.
149–150 Grand conferences: Lawrence, op. cit., pp. 33 n., 97, 187–9.
150 Iron works: William Rosen, *The Most Powerful Idea in the World*, London, 2010, p. 137.

CHAPTER 11. GRENADIERS OF GOD
152 Carving at Cologne: Honour & Fleming, op. cit., p. 271.
153 Mostly monks will be saved: Christopher Brooke, *The Twelfth Century Renaissance*, London, 1976, pp. 45, 161.
153 The new word 'purgatory': Jacques Le Goff, *The Birth of Purgatory*, Chicago, 1984, p. 364.
153 1274 Council of Lyons: *ODCC* (1974 edition), p. 1145.
156 Popularity of the Blessed Virgin Mary, especially in art: Rachel Fulton, *From Judgement to Passion: Devotion to Christ and the Virgin Mary, 800–1200*, New York, 2002, ch. 2; Chadwick, op. cit., pp. 84–90.
157 Mary on the Thames: A succession of Mary churches is described in Peter Ackroyd, *Thames: Sacred River*, London, 2007, esp. pp. 91–94.
158–159 Golden Legend on Mary Magdalen: Jacobus de Voragine, *The Golden Legend: Readings on the Saints*, Princeton, 1993, vol. 1, p. 376.
160 Transubstantiation and the call for an annual confession: Duffy, op. cit., p. 112.
161 Kippel: ceremony witnessed there in 1999.
162 Juliana of Liege: *ODCC* (2005 edition), 917.
162 Mass at Bolsena: Ranft, *Women in Western Intellectual Culture, 600–1500*, op. cit., pp. 174–6. The influence of this Bolsena miracle is much debated.
162 Medieval love of miraculous: Thomas Goldstein, *Dawn of Modern Science: From the Ancient Greeks to the Renaissance*, New York, 1995, p. 132.
162–163 Pope Joan: Google the words 'Pope Joan', and you find fascinating details,

including the *Catholic Encylopedia*'s response. An English pop group adopted her name.

163–164 Early Cathars, esp. in Balkans: Bernard Hamilton, *Monastic Reform, Catharism and the Crusades*, London. 1979, p. 17.

164 'Massif Central' and Cathars regime: Jonathan Sumption, *The Albigensian Crusade*, London, 1999, pp. 54, 250.

164 Heresy like poison: Sumption, ibid., p. 41.

165 Cathars' outer garment: Sumption, ibid., p. 235.

165–166 Cheese-making: Emmanuel Le Roy Ladurie, *Montaillou : Cathars and Catholics in a French village 1294–1324*, London, 1978, pp. 112–13.

166 Lechery of priests: Le Roy Ladurie, ibid., p. 177.

166 Excommunication for those who failed to pay tithe: Le Roy Ladurie, ibid., p. 262.

166–167 Quarryman's heresy: Le Roy Ladurie, ibid., p. 319.

167 Ladurie's evidence on the Cathars came from an inquisition conducted (1318–1325) in south-west France, especially in villages where the Cathars were numerous. In all, nearly 600 people were interrogated. Of the accused, twenty-five lived in Montaillou (Le Roy Ladurie, ibid., p. xiv). Confessions were demanded, one being obtained by torture.

167 Cathar goodmen: Le Roy Ladurie, ibid., pp. 81–3, 254.

167–168 Idea of the size of heaven: Le Roy Ladurie, ibid., p. 260.

168 Who caused the pleasing harvest: Le Roy Ladurie, ibid., p. 260.

CHAPTER 12. THE MAGIC OF GLASS AND PAINT

170–171 Building castles with stone instead of timber: Jurgen Brauer & Hubert van Tuyll, *Castles, Battles and Bombs: How Economics Explains Military History*, Chicago, 2008, pp. 47, 50.

171 Demand for big churches: Christopher Brooke, op. cit., pp. 97–8.

171–172 Early vaulting in Speyer Cathedral : Honour & Fleming, op. cit., p. 289.

172 Rise of Gothic cathedrals: Goldstein, op. cit., pp. 156–64; Gombrich, op. cit., pp. 137–42.

173 Glass in Augsburg Cathedral: Chadwick, op. cit., pp. 147–8.

173–174 Rise of stained and painted glass: Lawrence B. Saint & Hugh Arnold, *Stained Glass of the Middle Ages in England and France*, London, 1913, pp. 5–7.

174 Glass mellowed with age: Lewis F. Day, 'Glass, stained', *EB*, vol. 12, p. 107.

175 Vellum from eighty lambs' skins: Fernand Braudel, *Capitalism and Material Life 1400–1800*, New York, 1974, p. 296.

176 Finding the date of the new moon: Prayer book of c. 1451 at Ballarat Fine Art Gallery, Victoria, Australia.

177 Waterwheel at Florence: Margaret M. Manion and Vera F. Vines, *Medieval and Renaissance Illuminated Manuscripts in Australian Collections*, Melbourne, 1984, pp. 82, 92–3.

177 Innovations of paper and movable type: Braudel, *Capitalism and Material Life*, op. cit., pp. 295–8.

179 Religious symbols in art: George Ferguson, *Signs & Symbols in Christian Art*, London, 1961, esp. pp. 119, 125, 134, 137, 139.

180 Medical school at Salerno: Charles H. Haskins, *The Renaissance of the 12th Century*, Cleveland, 1968, p. 323.

181 Lecture resembled a sermon: ibid., p. 393.

181 Christian influence on early universities: Colin Brown, *Christianity and Western Thought*, Illinois, 1990, vol. 1, pp. 103–4.

CHAPTER 13. A STAR ABOVE ASSISI

183 Joachim and Columbus: Nisbet, op. cit., pp. 98–100.

184 The mineral alum: John Clapham in J. B. Bury, H. M. Gwatkin & J. P. Whitney (eds), *Cambridge Medieval History*, New York, 1911, vol. 6, pp. 488–9.

187 Francis's appearance, voice, and love of music: introduction by T. Tokey in *The Little Flowers of St. Francis* (Everyman edition), New York, 1947, p. xvii.

188 Francis's food: Jay M. Hammond (ed.), *Francis of Assisi: History, Hagiography*, New York, 2004, esp. essays by Marilyn Hammond and Michael Cusata, pp.198, 220.

188 Francis's 'white robe of chastity': *The Little Flowers of St. Francis*, ibid., p. 330.

188–189 Choice of biblical quotations: Jacques Le Goff, *Saint Francis of Assisi*, London & New York, 2004, p. 69.

189 Bernardino of Siena: Peter Burke, *Popular Culture in Early Modern Europe*, London, 1979, p. 101.

189 A few poor coverlets: Rosalind B. Brooke, *Early Franciscan Government: From Elias to Bonaventure*, Cambridge, 1959, p. 147.

189–190 Francis's few personal possessions: Bettenson, p. 182.

190 New medieval coins: P. Spufforth, 'Coin and Currency', *CEHE*, vol. 3, pp. 600–1; Jacques Bernard in Carlo M. Cipolla (ed.), *The Fontana Economic History of Europe: The Middle Ages*, London, 1972, p. 289.

190 Coins like pebbles: Le Goff, op. cit., p. 61.

191 Poor Clares expand: John Moorman, *A History of the Franciscan Order: From its Origins to the Year 1517*, Oxford, 1968, pp. 34–9; Lawrence, op. cit., pp. 268–9.

193 St Anthony's fishes and token of reverence: *The Little Flowers of St. Francis*, op. cit., pp. 71–2.

194–195 Stigmata: Richard C. Trexler, *Religion in Social Context in Europe and America, 1200–1700*, Arizona, 2002, pp. 195 ff.

195 Brother Sun, Sister Moon: Le Goff, ibid., pp. 61–2.

195 Farewell and death: *The Little Flowers of St. Francis*, op. cit., pp. 392–3; Rosalind B. Brooke (ed.), *Scripta Leonis, Rufini et Angeli Sociorum S. Francisci*, Oxford, 1970, p. 282; Moorman, op. cit., pp. 32 ff.

195 The morning star: Ecclesiasticus 50: 6.

196 Elias on saddle: Rosalind B. Brooke, op. cit., pp. 151–2.

196–197 Bequests to the Franciscans: Moorman, op. cit., pp. 200–4.

197 Where Franciscans preached: ibid., p 121.

199 Emphasis on studying: R. W. Southern, *The Making of the Middle Ages*, Yale, 1965, p. 191.

199 Dominicans: Norman F. Cantor, *Civilization of the Middle Ages* (revised edition), New York, 1994, pp. 428–9.

200–201 Friar bird: W. Sansom (ed.), *The Australian National Dictionary*, Melbourne, 1988, p. 262.

CHAPTER 14. THE CRUSADERS

203–204 Pope Urban II calls for crusade: Cantor, op. cit., p. 292.

205 The French 'Peter the Hermit': Runciman, op. cit., vol. 1, pp. 113–15, 121.

206 Capture of Jerusalem: ibid., pp. 286–8.

206–207 Rivalries of Venice, Genoa etc.: Jacques Bernard in Cipolla (ed.), op. cit., p. 293–4.

208 Orthodox people hate Italian Christians more than Turks: *CHC*, vol. 5, p. 155.

208–209 Franciscan friars lament western crimes: *CHC*, vol. 5, p. 55.

209 Pope Innocent III on 'the proud to the humble': Duffy, op. cit., p. 113.

209 Crusades commercial as well as spiritual: R. De Roover, 'The Organization of Trade', *CEHE*, vol. 3, pp. 60–4.
210 Distinguished British scholar: Sir Ernest Barker, 'The Crusades' in *EB*, vol. 7, p. 550, whose view was sought out with respect by Steven Runciman in *A History of the Crusades*, op. cit., vol. 1, p. xi.
211 Religious incentives for non-crusaders: Duffy, op. cit., p. 113.

CHAPTER 15. ROME, AVIGNON AND THE GOLDEN HORN
214 The church as 'the welfare state': Richard Roehl in Cipolla (ed.), op. cit., pp. 128–9.
215 Christ's attitude to commercial activities: Luke 6: 24–35.
215 Long-distance traders: Gabriel Le Bras in *CEHE* , vol. 3, pp. 564, 566.
216 Penalties for ecomomic immorality: R. H. Tawney, *Religion and the Rise of Capitalism*, London, 1948, pp. 42, 49–50, 58–9.
217–218 Wool-wash fountains: visit to Aquila in September 2004.
219–220 Pope at Avignon: Duffy, op. cit., pp 122–3.
221 Gregory XI moves to Rome: John Jolliffe (ed.), *Froissart's Chronicles*, London, 1967, pp. 224–5.
222 Two rival popes: Duffy, op. cit., pp. 126–7.
224–225 Wycliffe's career and protests: Bernard M. G. Reardon, *Religious Thought in the Reformation* (2nd edition), London, 1995, pp. 4–7.
225 Wycliffe's teachings: Bettenson, pp. 245–51.
225 Anne of Bohemia: *DNB*, vol. 16, p. 1033.
226 The Hussites: Norman Davies, *Europe: A History*, New York, 1998, pp. 428–9.
229 Shrubs hide Hus's monument in Autumn 2010: photo from Tim Warner.
230 The defensive geography of Constantinople: Steven Runciman, *The Fall of Constantinople, 1453*, Cambridge, 1965, pp. 87–92.
230 East and West conferred at Ferrara: Michael Angold (ed.), p. 131.
231 Christian army defeated near Black Sea: Michael Angold (ed.), op. cit., p 77.
231–232 Light of Christendom extinguished: Duffy, op. cit., p. 150.
232 Role of emperor: Borys A. Gudziak, *Crisis and Reform: The Kyivan Metropolitanate, the Patriarchate of Constantinople, and the Genesis of the Union of Brest*, Cambridge (US), 2001, p. 11.
232 Fifty-four different patriarchs in a century: ibid., p. 21.
233 Former patriarch wept bitterly: Michael Angold (ed.), op. cit., p 192.
233 Exempt from Ottoman call-up: Gudziak, op. cit., pp. 19–20.
234 Money from Dniester River: Michael Angold (ed.), op. cit., pp. 166–8.

CHAPTER 16. THE PILGRIMS' PATHS
235 Pardon for their sins: Runciman, op. cit., vol. 1, p. 33; Hugh Kennedy in Thomas F. X. Noble & Julia M. H. Smith (eds), CHC, vol. 3, p. 189.
236 Cologne and the arrival of three kings: ODCC, p. 858; Brown, *The Birth of the Messiah: A Commentary on the Infancy Narrations*, op. cit., pp. 170–1.
236–237 Feelings of millions of German pilgrims: ibid., p. 197.
237 Pilgrims at Compostela: Diana Webb, *Pilgrims and Pilgrimage in the Medieval West*, London, 1999, p. 17.
238 Growing a pilgrimage beard: ibid., p. 171.
239 Goals of Lubeck pilgrims: ibid., pp. 135–6.
239 Pilgrimage as a punishment or reform school: ibid., pp. 52–3.
240–241 Pilgrims carried palm branches or shells: ibid., pp. 8, 124, 125.
241 Palm Sunday procession: *ODCC*, p 1025.

242 Wooden donkey or Palmesel: Historical Museum in old Barfüsserkirche, Basle, visited in June 2007.
244 The head of St. Andrew: Florence A. Gragg & Leona C. Gabel, *Memoirs of a Renaissance Pope: The Commentaries of Pius II*, New York, 1962, pp. 246–254.

CHAPTER 17. THE HERALDS OF CHRISTENDOM
247 Criticisms by Pope Pius II: ibid., p. 357
249 'Patron of Seafarers' : *ODCC* (2005 edition), p. 637. Francis of Paolo was declared patron in the war year of 1943, by which time much of Italy's own navy was out of action.
250 'Soft, warm, and delicious': cited in James Froude, *Short Studies on Great Subjects*, London,1891, vol. 2, p. 81.
251–252 Erasmus on his own translations: István Bejczy, *Erasmus and the Middle Ages: The Historical Consciousness of a Christian Humanist*, Boston, 2001, p. 135.
252 'Christ lives': cited in Reardon, op. cit., p. 31.
252 'Christ's living temple': Euan Cameron, *The European Reformation*, Oxford, 1991, p. 66.
252 Who is a Christian?: Nisbet, op. cit., p 109.
253 Memorial in Basle: Visit to cathedral in June 2007.
255 Luther's growing disenchantment: R. H. Fife, *The Revolt of Martin Luther*, New York, 1957, esp. pp. 164–5, 174; attack on Tetzel: p. 249; finance for Torgau bridge: p. 249–50.
258 Selling forgiveness: Bettenson, p. 264.
258 Luther demands debate in 1517: Timothy F. Lull (ed.), *Martin Luther's Basic Theological Writings*, Minneapolis, 1989, p. 8.
259 Students carry home the message: 'Die Studenten der Universitat Wittenberg', *Westermann Grosser Atlas zur Weltgeschichte*, Braunschweig (Germany), 1972, p. 91.
259–260 The 600 copies: Fife , op. cit., p. 463.
260 Rumour of Hus: ibid., p. 464.
260 The 'puppet of the Roman pontiff': Bettenson, pp. 274–6.
260 Burning the printed word: Fife, op. cit., pp. 568 ff., 580.
260–261 Luther and Pope and purgatory: Hans J. Hillerbrand, *The World of the Reformation*, London, 1975, p. 111.
261 'God's generosity: see 'Justify' in *Shorter Oxford English Dictionary*, Oxford, 1956, vol. 1, p. 1076.
262 Luther's journey to Worms: James Atkinson, *The Trial of Luther*, London, 1971, pp. 142 ff; Fife, op. cit., pp. 359–60. See also Geoffrey Blainey, *A Short History of the World*, Melbourne, 2000, p. 335.
265 The dilemma of whether to fight Islam: Hillerbrand, op. cit., pp. 201–3.
265 Franco-Spanish wars: William C. Atkinson, *A History of Spain and Portugal*, London, 1960, p. 139.
267 German printers: A. G. Dickens, *The German Nation and Martin Luther*, New York, 1976, pp. 102–5, 110–13.
268 Luther's 'I believe': Bettenson, pp. 287–9, with his translation slightly modernised in several places.

CHAPTER 18. A SWISS SWORD-CARRIER
269 Zwingli's village: Visit to Wildhaus, 17 June 2006.
270 Preaching transformed: J. Rilliet, *Zwingli, Third Man of the Reformation*, Philadelphia, 1964, pp. 43ff.
271 Zwingli wept: ibid., p. 54.

272 Reformation in Zurich: Cameron, *The European Reformation*, op. cit., pp. 108ff.; Reardon, op. cit., pp. 88–97; G. R. Potter, *Zwingli*, Cambridge, 1977, passim.
273 Unpaid Swiss soldiers: Rilliet, op. cit., pp. 149–54.
275 Luther's half apology at Marburg: ibid., p. 264.
276 Obstinacy at Marburg : Reardon, op. cit., p. 100; Joseph Lortz, *The Reformation in Germany*, London, 1968, p. 466.
277 Death of Zwingli: Diarmaid MacCulloch, *Reformation*, London, 2004, pp. 175–6.
278 New faith reaches Scandinavia: N. K. Andersen in *NCMH*, vol. 2, pp. 135–6, 147, 155, 156.

CHAPTER 19. A TEMPEST ACROSS ENGLAND

280 The English monasteries: G. M. Trevelyan, *English Social History*, London, 1942, pp. 106–09; Paul Johnson, *The Offshore Islanders*, London. 1998, pp. 146–9.
281 Little rage expressed: David Hume, *The History of England*, (Uni. of Chicago Press edition), Chicago, 1975, p. 120.
282 Most new English books printed in Latin: David Daniell, *William Tyndale: A Biography*, New Haven, 1994, pp. 45–60.
282 Printing the Tyndale Bible: ibid., pp. 108–10.
283 Tyndale's masterly translations: ibid., pp. 3, 135.
284 'In my Father's house': John 14:2. In his original translation Tyndale actually wrote: 'In my father's house are many mansions.' See N. Hardy Wallis (ed.), *The New Testament Translated by William Tyndale 1534*, Cambridge, 1938, p. 218. Tyndale's use of architectural terms and spaces is unusual. Thus, in his 1525 translation of Acts 5, he wrote 'Solomon's hall' which became 'Solomon's porche' nine years later (Wallis, p. 615).
284 King James Bible's debt to Tyndale: Isaac Foot, intro. to Wallis (ed.), ibid.,p. xi.
285 Ten people prosecuted: Daniell, op. cit., p. 183.
285 Maid of Kent: ibid., p. 184.
286 Changed meaning of treacle: *Shorter Oxford English Dictionary* (3rd ed. rev.), vol, 2, p. 2237.
289 David Whitehead: DNB, vol. 21, p. 97.
290 Robert Horne the inconoclast: DNB, vol. 9, p. 1255.

CHAPTER 20. JOHN CALVIN'S REALM.

291–292 Calvin's book: Cameron, *The European Reformation*, op. cit., pp. 184–5.
292 Sunday services in Geneva: E. G. Rupp in *NCMH*, vol. 2, p. 110.
294 Calvin on predestination and eternal damnation: John Calvin, *Institutes of the Christian Religion*, London, 1953, vol. 2, p. 206.
294 Bucer influenced Calvin: R eardon, op. cit., p. 176.
294–295 God's ways are past finding out: Bettenson, p. 80.
295 Attraction of Predestination: Cameron, *The European Reformation*, op. cit., pp. 129, 131.
295 Calvin on guardian angels and Satan: Calvin, op. cit., vol. 1, pp. 146–47, p. 151.
296 Collected works in the German edition: *ODCC* (2005 edition), p. 269.
296 Calvin's views: on honouring Sunday: Calvin, op. cit., vol. 1, p. 341; on attending church: p. 180; on praying: p. 201.
296–297 'Farewell, kind reader': Calvin, op. cit., vol. 1, p. 26.
297 Geneva or 'Breeches' Bible: Genesis 3:70; *EB* 1910–11, vol. 3, p. 901.
299 Life in Calvinist Jersey: Marguerite Syvret & Joan Stevens (eds), *Balleine's History of Jersey*, Chichester (UK), 1981, pp. 83–9; sand-eeling: p. 88.

300 Boston's psalm-singing: New Grove, vol. 15, pp. 348–53.
301 Isleworth and psalm-singing: John Adamson, *The Noble Revolt: The Overthrow of Charles I*, London, 2007, pp. 117–18, 581 n.
303–304 Lithuanian senators and magnates became Calvinists and Lutherans: Borys A. Gudziak, op. cit., pp. 80–1.
304 Poland a Catholic kingdom: Hillerbrand, op. cit., pp. 170–2.
304 French bishoprics sold 'like cinnamon and pepper': H. G. Koenigsberger in *NCMH*, vol. 3, p. 281.
305 Persecution of Huguenots: A. Cobban in *NCMH*, vol 7, p. 232.
305 Truce at Nantes: Hillerbrand, op. cit., pp. 161–2.
306 London's 'clampering' bells: Daniell, op. cit., p. 183.

CHAPTER 21. TRENT: THE ENDLESS MEETINGS
309 Bishop spoke German as mother tongue: Hubert Jedin, *A History of the Council of Trent*, London, 1957, p. 567.
309 Bishops mostly Spanish and Italian: ibid., p. 529.
309 Rival Franciscans attend: ibid., pp. 574–5.
309 German Protestants first attend Trent in 1552 : Kelly, op. cit., pp. 138.
310 Fear of Turkish forces: Jedin, op. cit., p. 516.
310 Bishop of Bergamo's eyes: ibid., pp. 548–9.
312 Achievements of Trent: T. M. Parker in *NCMH*, vol. 3, pp. 44–5, 52–4, 64–5; Chadwick, op. cit., pp. 219–20. A reading of a variety of historians leaves one with the impression that the importance of the Catholic Reformation is perhaps downplayed because it is judged against the Protestant Reformation. To reform an existing institution is perhaps the more difficult mission.
313 Catherine dei' Ricci: *ODCC*, p. 253.
313 Teresa of Avila: Bernard McGinn (ed.), *The Essential Writings of Christian Mysticism*, New York, 2006, pp. 110–16.
314 Ochino the wandering exile: *DNB*, vol. 14, pp. 795–7.
314 Capuchins working amongst Muslims: Fernand Braudel, *The Mediterranean*, London, 1973, vol. 2, pp. 800, 888.
315 Neri the man and 'clubman': Frederick William Faber, *The Spirit and Genius of St Philip Neri*, London, 1850, passim.
315 Rome's 'Untouchables': Hanns Gross, *Rome in the Age of Enlightenment*, Cambridge, 1990, esp. ch. 8.
317 Baroque: Nikolaus Pevsner, *An Outline of European Architecture*, London, 1945, ch. 6; Jacques Barzun, *From Dawn to Decadence*, New York, 2000, esp. pp. 143, 210, 336–7, 388; Gombrich, op. cit., ch. 19.

CHAPTER 22. TO THE ENDS OF THE EARTH
319–320 Montserrat and other Christian-church names: Hugh Thomas, *Rivers of Gold: The Rise of the Spanish Empire*, London, 2003, p. 118.
320 Priests with Columbus in second voyage: ibid., p. 115; no priest had sailed in the first voyage: p. 77.
320 Magi's homeland anticipated in Cuba: Trexler, *The Journey of the Magi*, op. cit., p. 137.
320 Columbus in Franciscan dress on return to Spain: Thomas, op. cit., pp. 144–50.
321 Gold panners and friars: ibid., p. 150.
321 Columbus finds Garden of Eden, North-east Brazil: ibid., pp. 153–5, 171.
321 Naming of Los Angeles: It commemorates the Feast of the 'Perdono' at the little Assisi chapel that the young St Francis had repaired.

323 Survival of pagan idols and customs in Catholic Mexico City and Peru: Chadwick, op. cit., pp.187–9.

324 Slave trade and its Catholic opponents: *ODCC* (2005 edition), 'Las Casas', p. 957.

324 High culture in Puebla cathedral: *New Grove*, vol. 15, p. 441.

325 By 1800 another 15 000 'Indies' churches built: Claudio Veliz, *New World of the Gothic Fox: Culture and Economy in English and Spanish America*, Berkeley, 1994, p. 73.

325 Ignatius de Loyola appearance: Philip Caraman, *Ignatius Loyola*, London, 1990, p. 10; early religious life: p. 49.

326 Congo emperor was Christian: ibid., p. 181.

327 Xavier in Japan: Carl G. Gustavson, *A Preface to History*, New York, 1955, p. 48.

327 Ignoble self-interest: cited in David Chidester, *Christianity: A Global History*, New York, 2001, p. 438.

328 Franciscans in Beijing: Moorman, op. cit., pp. 236–8, 429–32.

329–330 Missions and conflict in East Massachusetts: D. W. Meinig, *The Shaping of America: A Geographical Perspective*, Yale, 1986, vol. 1, p. 94.

330 Ursulines conduct services in France: Mary T. Malone, *Women and Christianity: From the Reformation to the 21st Century*, Dublin, 2003, vol. 3, p. 99.

331 Marie Guyard in Canada: ibid., vol. 3, p. 137.

331 'Poor Heathens': *Oxford English Dictionary*, vol. 5, p. 171, columns 2, 3.

CHAPTER 23. A REFORMATION UNTANGLED

336 'Unspecialised folk': Quirinus Breen in Brauer, op. cit., vol. 2, p. 170.

337 Reading the Bible: John T. McNeill in Brauer, op. cit., vol. 2, p 185.

337 Notable Biblical scholar: Albert Schweitzer, *The Quest of the Historical Jesus*, London, 1926, pp. 270–1.

338 Praise of women's daily work: Hillerbrand, op. cit., p. 210; Ranft, *Women and Spiritual Equality in Christian Tradition*, op. cit., p. 214.

339 Witches: Robin Briggs, *Witches and Neighbours*, London, 1997, passim.

339 Problem of defining a 'war of religion': Richard A. Preston, Sydney F. Wise, & Herman O. Werner, *Men in Arms: A History of Warfare*, London, 1962, p. 103; Geoffrey Blainey, *The Causes of War*, London, 1973, pp. 146–56, 306 n. My book challenges the wide emphasis on religious, commercial or other motives as the main causes of wars.

340–341 Galileo: Karen Armstrong, *The Case for God*, London, 2009, pp. 178–84.

341 Toleration in Poland: William A. Clebsch, *Christianity in European History*, New York, 1979, p. 185; P. Skwarczynski in *NCMH*, vol. 3, pp. 390–2.

342 Portuguese Jews and atheism: Armstrong, op. cit., pp. 183.

343 Spinoza's defiance: Yirmanyahu Yovel, *Spinoza and other Heretics: The Adventures of Immanence*, Princeton, 1980, passim.

345 Cromwell and Dutch Jews: George A. Brake in Brauer, op. cit., pp. 270, 282.

345 Toleration in Prussia: W. H. Bruford in *NCMH*, vol. 7, pp. 302, 306.

CHAPTER 24. PILGRIM BUNYAN AND QUAKER FOX

352 The killing of Felix Manz: T. M. Parker in *NCMH*, vol.3, p 121.

353 Rembrandt and the Mennonites: Marleen Blokhuis in Albert Blankert (ed.), *Rembrandt: A Genius and his Impact*, Melbourne, 1997, p. 24.

353 Dutch shape English Baptists: T. M. Parker in *NCMH*, vol.3, p. 124.

354 Bedford separatist church: Michael Mullett, *John Bunyan in Context*, Keele

(UK), 1996, pp. 101–2. The young Bunyan: B. R. White in N. H. Keeble (ed.), *John Bunyan: Conventicle and Parnassus,* Oxford, 1988, pp. 4–5; Ian Breward (ed.), *John Bunyan (1628–1688): A Commemorative Symposium,* Melbourne, 1988, passim.

355 'So he passed over': John Bunyan, *The Pilgrim's Progress* (Relgious Tract Society edition), London, c. 1890, pp. 572.

356 Bunyan becomes fashionable in literary circles: N. H. Keeble in Keeble (ed.), op. cit., pp. 249–56.

357 Bunyan carried above shoulders of crowd: G. B. Harrison, foreword to John Bunyan, *Grace Abounding* (Everyman edition), London, 1925, p. xii.

357–358 George Fox interjecting in church: George Fox, *The Journal of George Fox* (Everyman edition), London, 1924, p. 9.

358 'I praised the living God': ibid., p. 15.

358 Fox in Catholic mystical tradition: McGinn (ed.), op. cit., pp. 110–16.

358 Hair 'fell in rats' tails': *DNB*, vol. 7, p. 560.

359 Macaulay on the 'most despicable of fanatics': Thomas Macaulay, *Macaulay's History of England* (Everyman edition), London, 1966, vol. 1, p. 123. Macaulay is kinder to Fox in vol. 3, pp. 283 ff.

362 The 'holy experiment' of Pennsylvania: Mary Dunn, *William Penn: Politics and Conscience,* Princeton, 1967, p. 77 ff.

CHAPTER 25. TWO OPEN-AIR VOICES: WESLEY AND WHITEFIELD

363 Dissenters were a small minority: H. D. Rack, *Reasonable Enthusiast: John Wesley and the rise of Methodism,* London, 1989, pp. 35–6 .

364 Wesley's facial appearance: ibid., p. 183, 527.

365 'No such day': Wesley cited by ibid., pp. 125 ff.

365 Wesley's conversion in 1738; Elisabeth Jay, *The Journal of John Wesley: A Selection,* Oxford, 1987, pp. 34–5.

366 Wesley in eastern Germany: ibid., pp. 35–8.

366 Wesley's open-air preaching: Rack, op. cit., p. 194.

368 Wesley's class meeting: John H. Wigger, *Taking Heaven by Storm: Methodism and the Rise of Popular Christianity in America,* New York, 1998, pp. 80–8.

369 Wesley's misreading of Bible: Glen O'Brien in Renate Howe (ed.), *The Master: The Life and Work of Edward H Sugden,* Melbourne, 2009, pp. 112–113.

369 Alphonsus Liguori and Wesley: Clebsch, op. cit., pp. 224–8.

369 'The best of all': Wesley cited in Rack, op. cit., pp. 522–3.

370 How many could hear Whitefield: Benjamin Franklin, *Autobiography and Other Writings,* Oxford, 1993, p. 111; H. W. Brands, *The First American: The Life and Times of Bemjamin Franklin,* New York, 2000, p. 147.

370 Samuel Johnson on Whitefield: James Boswell, *Life of Johnson* (World's Classics), 1980, p. 409.

371 Whitefield shabby in Oxford: 'Memoirs', *AR, 1770,* part 2, pp. 58–9.

372 Two wives like a 'brace' of ferrets: *DNB*, vol. 21, p. 89.

373 Countess of Huntingdon's influence: Rack, op. cit., pp. 284–6; Alan Harding, *The Countess of Huntingdon's Connexion,* Oxford, 2003, passim.

374 Wesleyan lay preachers in USA: Wigger, op. cit., p. 60 ff.

375 Anglicans enter Australia: Geoffrey Blainey, 'Sydney 1788'. in D. J. Mulvaney and J. P. White (eds), *Australians to 1788,* Sydney, 1987, pp. 428–9; Bruce Kaye, *Anglicanism in Australia: A History,* Melbourne, 2002, esp. pp. 7–14.

376 Isaac Watts on Methodism: Rack, op. cit., p. 325.

376 Thomas Hardy and George Eliot: Wesley's hymn, to the tune 'Lydia' appears in Hardy's *Return of the Native* and in Eliot's *Scenes from Clerical Life.*

377 Charles Wesley's altered 'Herald' hymn: *Oxford Dictionary of Quotations* (2nd edition), 1977, p. 565.
378 Historians assess John Wesley: J. H. Plumb, *England in the Eighteenth Century* (1714–1815), London, 1953, p. 90.
378 Southey's letter on Wesley: cited in *EHD*, vol. 11, p. 664.

CHAPTER 26. TURMOIL IN PARIS
381 Brittany priest's 'perilous task': John McManners, *Church & Society in Eighteenth-Century France*, Oxford, 1998, vol. 1, pp. 382–3, 744 n.
381 The French clergy: ibid., vol 1, p. 282.
381–382 Complaints about priests: ibid., vol. 1, pp. 365–367.
382 Council of Trent ignored: ibid., vol. 1, p. 265.
385 Jesuit colleges in 1749: A. V. Judges in *NCMH*, vol. 8, p. 166.
385 Jesuits in China: Mary W. Helms, *Ulysses' Sail: An Ethnographic Odyssey*, Princeton, 1988, pp. 105–9.
386 French king and Eucharist: Olivier Chaline in John Adamson (ed.), *The Princely Courts of Europe 1500–1750*, London, 2000, p. 88.
386 Jesuits denouned in France: A. Cobban in *NCMH*, vol. 7, p. 233.
386 Spanish clergy: J. Lynch in *NCMH*, vol. 8, p. 362.
387 The papacy's 'most shameful hour': Duffy, op .cit., p. 194.
388 Changed attitude to miracles: *ODCC* (3rd edition), p. 1098.
389 Deism and natural laws: Clebsch, op. cit., pp. 188–9.
389 The four famous U.S. Deists: Winthrop S. Hudson & John Corrigan, *Religion in America*, New York, 1992, p. 92.
390 Cook's puff of wind: Geoffrey Blainey, *Sea of Dangers: Captain Cook and His Rivals*, Melbourne, 2008, pp. 296–7.
390 Bayle in five large volumes: Barzun, op. cit., pp. 360–1.
391 Southey on Voltaire: Robert Southey, *Letters from England*, London, 1951, pp. 399–400.
391 Invention of happiness: J. M. Roberts, *The Penguin History of the World*, London, 1995, p. 667.
392 Death of Hume: *DNB*, vol. 10, pp. 216–226.
393–394 Religious liberty in North American colonies: Hudson & Corrigan, op. cit., p 99.
394 'The relentless sword': ibid., p. 101.
396 Huguenots and marriage: ODCC, p. 675.
396 Conflict of church and state: A. Goodwin in NCMH, vol. 8, pp. 687–90.
397 Priests deported to Africa: William B. Cohen, *The French Encounter with Africans*, Bloomington (US), 1980, p. 170.
397–398 Revolution's treatment of church: Roberts, op. cit., pp. 708–9.

CHAPTER 27. CHRISTMAS CAROL
401 Angels and others in heaven: John Casey, *After Lives: A Guide to Heaven and Purgatory*, Oxford, 2009, pp. 346–7.
403 Expansion of Irvingites: O. Eggenberger in Erwin Fahlbusch et al, *The Encyclopedia of Christianity*, Grand Rapids (US), 1999, vol. 1, pp. 110–11.
404 Lord Percy and premonition of World War I: Winston Churchill, *My Early Life, 1874–1904*, New York, 1996, pp. 370–1.
404 Carlyle on Chalmers: Stewart J. Brown, *Thomas Chalmers and the Godly Commonwealth in Scotland*, Oxford, 1982, p. 109.
405 Chalmers, the man and preacher: ibid., pp. 55–9, 393; *AR*, 'Chronicle', 1947, pp. 235–6.

405 Canning and Wilberforce on Chalmers' preaching: *DNB*, vol. 3, p. 1359.

406–407 Chalmers and Catholics: Brown, *Thomas Chalmers and the Godly Commonwealth in Scotland*, op. cit., p. 112.

408 Chalmers leads the Disruption: *AR*, 1843, pp. 250–1.

409–410 Pusey's fear that Tractarians becoming too popular: Alec Vidler, *The Church in an Age of Revolution: 1789 to the Present Day*, Harmondsworth (UK), 1961, p. 52.

413 US frontier churches and 'petty thieves and brawlers': W. W. Sweet cited in G. S. Métraux & F. Crouzet (eds), *The Nineteenth-Century World*, New York, 1963, p. 334.

414 Early Mormons: Kenneth H. Winn, *Exiles in a Land of Liberty: Mormons in America, 1830–1846*, Chapel Hill (US), 1989, esp. pp. 47, 200.

416 Emerson on the Mormons: cited in Charles Dilke, *Greater Britain* (1885 edition), London, p. 123. Dilke had visited Utah.

417–418 Christmas cards: Steve Roud, *The English Year*, London, 2006, p. 377; crackers: p. 388.

418 Christmas tree: ibid., pp. 400–1; Elizabeth Longford, *Victoria R. I.*, (Pan edition), London, 1966, p. 211.

419 Charles Dickens on Scrooge's glimpses of a cheerful Christmas: Charles Dickens, *A Christmas Carol and the Chimes*, Oxford, 1944, pp. 78, 81.

419–420 Handel's 'Messiah': Newman Flower, *George Frideric Handel: His Personality and His Times* (revised edition), London, 1959, pp. 290–3.

420 The chorus in Handel's day: Winton Dean on Handel in *New Grove*, vol. 8, p. 101.

420 Rise of Christmas shopping: Daniel J. Boorstin, *The Americans: The Democratic Experience*, New York, 1974, p. 158.

421–422 Germans 'dancing under the lime trees': Ruth Michaelis-Jena & Willy Merson (ed. and tr.), *A Lady Travels: Journeys in England and Scotland from the Diaries of Johanna Schopenhauer*, London, 1988, p. 161.

422 Queen Victoria and Sunday travel: Longford, op. cit., p. 267.

422–423 Methodists and Sunday travel: *The Laws and Regulations of the Australasian Wesleyan Methodist Church* (revised edition), Melbourne, 1890, see rules 23, 23, 246.

424 Eliot's frosty Christmas: George Eliot, *Silas Marner* (Collins Library of Classics edition), London, first pub. 1860 or 1861, p. 127.

424 A church in Ceylon: Frederick J. Dobson, *Australia: with Notes on the Way* (3rd edition), London, 1862, pp. 85–6.

425 Austrians march to work : John Evans (ed.), *Abroad: A Book of Travel*, London, 1968, pp. 344–5.

425 Divine service near Sydney: James Jervis, *The Cradle City of Australia: A History of Parramatta 1788–1961*, Parramatta, 1969, p. 68.

425 A newly devout Christian peasant: A. Wilson, *Tolstoy*, London, 1988, pp. 297–301.

426 English children's ignorance of God: AR, 1843, p. 56; Ann Blainey, *The Farthing Poet: A Biograhy of Richard Hengist Horne 1802–84*, London, 1968, p. 112.

CHAPTER 28: A TASTE FOR TOLERATION

428 Ireland's civic anomalies: R. R. Palmer, *The Age of the Democratic Revolution*, Princeton, 1964, pp. 491–2.

428 French reached Bantry Bay: ibid., pp. 497–9.

430 Struggles of Waldensians: Euan Cameron, *Waldenses: Rejections of Holy Church in Medieval Europe*, Oxford, 2000, pp. 202–8.

430 Waldensians emigrate to Italy and France: Cameron, *Waldenses: Rejections of Holy Church in Medieval Europe*, op. cit., pp. 202–3.

432 Jews in Rome: Gross, op. cit., pp. 85–6.

432 Rights of Jews postively affirmed: J. Katz, 'Jewry and Judaism' in G. S. Métraux and F. Crouzet (eds), op. cit., p. 351: also *NCMH*, vol. 10, p. 243.

433 Wesley on the African: Wigger, op. cit., p. 134.

434 Slaves and free migrants to Brazil: Blainey, *A Short History of the World*, op. cit., pp. 464–6.

434 Slaves' choice of religion: Eugene D. Genovese, *Roll, Jordan, Roll: The World the Slaves Made*, London, 1975, pp. 189, 232.

435 Slave's burial: Frances Anne Kemble, *Records of Later Life*, London, 1882, vol. 1, p. 230; Frances Anne Kemble, *Journal of a Residence on a Georgian Plantation in 1838–1839*, New York, 1863, pp. 112–13.

436 'He comes': James C. Downey & Paul Oliver in Stanley Sadie (ed.), *New Grove*, vol. 18, p. 4.

437 Buxton's speech against slavery: *EHD*, vol. 11, p. 806.

438 German's praise of Strauss's 'perfect' book: Schweitzer, op. cit., p. 78.

439 Ussher versus Lyell on the earth's antiquity: Geoffrey Blainey, *The Great Seesaw: A New View of the Western World, 1750–2000*, Melbourne, 1988, pp. 60–3.

440 Darwin's views: Steve Wilkens & Alan G. Padgett, *Christianity and Western Thought*, Illinois (US), 2000, vol. 2, p. 91.

441 Darwin holds tongue on religious matters: Christopher Ralling (ed.), *The Voyage of Charles Darwin*, London, 1978, pp. 161–5.

443 Frederick Temple on evolution: *EHD* , vol. 12(2), p. 245.

443 Mill's Scottish father: Bruce Mazlish, *James and John Stuart Mill*, London, 1975, p. 53; John Stuart Mill, *Autobiography*, London, no date, p. 2.

444 England's hidden sceptics: John Stuart Mill, op. cit., pp. 24, 26.

445 A 'flame from Heaven': Ian Campbell, *Thomas Carlyle*, London, 1974, esp. pp. 8–9.

445 Carlyle on Judgement Seat: John Clubbe (ed.), *Froude's Life of Carlyle*, pp. 329–30.

446 A 'happy resurrection': Thomas Carlyle, *The French Revolution*, Boston, 1885, Book 1, chapter 2.

446 Carlyle on Arabs: A. N. Wilson, *God's Funeral*, London, 1999, p. 76.

447 George Meredith on Morley: ibid., p. 28 n.

449 William Temple Jr as candidate: F. A. Iremonger in *DNB*, 1941–1950, p. 870.

CHAPTER 29. THE AGE OF STEAM AND HASTE

451 Growth of anticlericalism: Owen Chadwick, *The Secularization of the European Mind in the Nineteenth Century*, Cambridge, 1975, pp. 115, 118.

452 Gregory VII on religious matters: Cantor, op. cit., pp. 257–9.

452 Bishops on the Pope's infallibility: Alex R. Vidler, op. cit., p. 156.

454 Railways and pilgrims: Chadwick, *The Secularization of the European Mind in the Nineteenth Century*, op. cit., p. 123.

454–455 Pilgrims to Jerusalem: James Hingston, *The Australian Abroad*, Melbourne, 1886, pp. 405–7, 425.

455 Protesant Bishop of Jerusalem: Michael S. Alexander in *DNB*, vol.1, pp. 275–6.

456 Kaiser visits Jerusalem: *AR*, 1899, pp. 256–8.

458 Williams and the rise of Y.M.C.A.: Raymond Flower, *The Y: First Hundred Years in Singapore, 1902–2002*, Singapore, 2002, chs 2–3.

458 Fairfax on sin: Gavin Souter, *Company of Heralds*, Melbourne, 1981, pp. 46–7.

459 Dunant the man: Caroline Moorehead, *Dunant's Dream*, London, 1998, passim. After Dunant went bankrupt, losing much of his reputation, other Swiss churchmen built up the Red Cross.

459 Belief in the Holy Catholic Church: Ruth Rouse and Stephen C. Neill, *A History of the Ecumenical Movement, 1517–1948* (2nd edition), Philadelphia, 1967, p. 327.

461 Margaret Fell: Wilkens & Padgett, op. cit., vol. 2, pp. 209–10.

461 Jarena Lee's preaching : Wigger, op. cit., pp. 122.

462 Grimké sisters: Edward T. James; Janet Wilson James & Paul S. Boyer, *Notable American Women: A Biographical Dictionary 1607-1950*, Cambridge (US), 1971, vol. 2, pp. 97–99.

462 Women, temperance and the vote: Anna Blainey, *The 'Fallen are Every Mother's Children': The WCTU*, PhD. Thesis, La Trobe University, Melbourne, 2000.

464 Wesleyan women should not preach: Rule 352 in *The Laws and Regulations of the Australasian Wesleyan Methodist Church*, op. cit., p. 91.

467 Booths and their Salvation Army and its impact: William Booth in *DNB*, 1912–21, pp. 50–2; Roy Hattersley, *Blood and Fire: The Story of William and Catherine Booth*, London, 1999, passim; Catherine Booth in *DNB*, vol. 22, pp. 233–5; K. S. Inglis, *Churches and the Working Classes in Victorian England*, London, 1963, pp. 212–13.

469 Decline of hell: Maurice Wiles in John McManners (ed.), *The Oxford History of Christianity*, Oxford, 2002, p. 583.

472 American historian on church-attendance: Ann Douglas, *The Feminization of American Culture*, New York, 1988, p. 7.

472 Genuine in their faith: Ross Terrill, *R. H. Tawney and His Times*, Cambridge (US), 1973, p. 248.

473 The new architects: Henry-Russell Hitchcock, *Architecture: Nineteenth and Twentieth Centuries*, London, 1968, pp. 202, 248, 321, 345. 422.

CHAPTER 30. COMING OF THE LIGHT AND THE DARKNESS

475 Carey and Banks: Keith Farrer, *William Carey, Missionary and Botanist*, Melbourne, 2005, passim.

476 First Anglican bishop in India: *DNB*, 1941–50, pp. 30–31.

476 Semarang's Dutch Reformed Church: visited in February 2010.

477 Adopting Chinese ways: Howard Taylor, *Hudson Taylor and the China Inland Mission*, London, 1918, pp. 89–90.

477–478 Bishop Crowther in Africa: *DNB*, vol. 22, p. 518.

478 Tonga: Sione Latukefu, 'The Opposition to the Influence of the Wesleyan Methodist Missionaries in Tonga' in *Historical Studies*, Melbourne, no. 46, April 1966, pp. 252–8.

478 Torres Strait and 'Coming of the Light': a monument outside Anglican church, Thursday Island, visited in January 2008.

480 Hudson Taylor's letter: Taylor, op. cit., p. 173.

482 Brazilian dance: Gerard Behague, 'Brazil' in *New Grove*, vol. 3, pp. 231, 236.

483 Edinburgh missionary rally: *Christian Century* (USA), 7 July 1910; *Sydney Morning Herald*, 15 & 23 June, 19 August 1910.

484 Ecumenical conference planned for 1914, 1915: Georges Florovsky in Rouse & Neill, op. cit., pp. 214–215.

486 Communion on Uganda railway: F. R. Cana in *EB* (special 1922 edition), vol. 30, pp. 676–7; vol. 31, pp. 678–9.

488 Pope Benedict XV in wartime: J. Moyes in *EB* (12th edition), vol. 30, pp. 684–5.

488 Christian soldiers dying in each world war: My own rough estimates, for I can find no reported calculations.

489 Hymns at Wembley: Information from historian of football Roy Hay of La Trobe University, Australia.

CHAPTER 31. WAR AND PEACE

492 Mutilating arms of the cross: Chadwick, *The Secularization of the European Mind in the Nineteenth Century*, op. cit., pp. 159.

492 Need for alternative religion: Tawney quoted in Terrill, op. cit., pp. 138–40.

493 Lenin sees religion as odious: quoted in A. N. Wilson, *God's Funeral*, op. cit., p. 94.

493 Soviet atttack on Christianity: A. G. Mazour, *Russia:Tsarist and Communist*, Princeton, 1962, pp. 600 ff.

493–494 Journalist in Kiev: Malcolm Muggeridge, *Tread Softly for You Tread on My Jokes*, London, 1972, p. 38.

494 The Orthodox Church as Christendom's traditional 'custodian': Johannes Feiner in *Commentary on the Documents of Vatican II*, London, 1967, vol. 2, pp. 130–5.

495 Pastors rebel against Hitler: H. Stuart Hughes, *Contemporary Europe; A History*, New Jersey, 1976, p. 290.

496 Jehovah's Witnesses executed: Tim Kirk, *Cassell's Dictionary of Modern German History*, London, 2002, p. 186.

497 Davidson's protests; G. K. A. Bell in *DNB*, 1922–1930, pp. 240–8.

498 Balfour plan: Geoffrey Blainey, *A Short History of the Twentieth Century*, Melbourne, 2005, pp. 92, 317–8.

503 High praise for German theology: Schweitzer, op. cit., p. 1.

503 Toynbee's diagnosis: E. W. F. Tomlin, *Arnold Toynbee: A Selection from His Works*, Oxford, 1978, pp. 282–3.

505 Electronic media and churches: Colleen McDannell in CHC, vol. 9, pp. 249–51.

505 John Flynn in Australia: Graeme Bucknall in *Australian Dictionary of Biography*, Melbourne, 1981, vol. 8, p. 533.

507 Ecumenical concept: Willem Adolf Visser 't Hooft, appendix 1 in Rouse & Neill, op. cit., pp. 735–9.

508 Czech Christians in prison: Tony Judt, *Postwar: A History of Europe since 1945*, London, 2010, p. 178.

508 Christians in China in 1949: *UNESCO's History of Mankind*, New York, 1966, vol. 6, p. 86.

511 Removal of Latin: *Britannica Book of Year*, 1967, p. 162.

512 Catholics and birth control: MacCulloch, *A History of Christianity*, op. cit., pp. 969–76.

513 Cyprian on unity: "De catholicae ecclesiae unitate', Bettenson, p.103.

CHAPTER 32. THE MOVING EYE OF THE NEEDLE

517 Africans and evil spirits: Chidester, op. cit., pp. 431–5.

517 Dowie in Australia: H. J. Gibbney in *Australian Dictionary of Biography*, Melbourne, 1972, vol. 4, pp. 95–6. In Australia, Dowie's main pulpits between 1872 and 1888 were three Congregational – Hamley Bridge in S.A., and Manly and Newtown in Sydney – and two Melbourne 'Tabernacles' in Sackville St, Collingwood and Johnston St, Fitzroy.

518 'Discord in Zion': Launceston *Examiner*, Tasmania, 8 Sept. 1904.

518 Mt Zion Moriah and Easter: Web http://countrystudies.us/south-africa/54.htm. Source is U.S. Library of Congress.

519 Symbolic shutting and opening doors: Chidester, op. cit., p. 431.

520 Simon Kimbangu: McManners (ed.), op. cit., p.666.

524 South American Pentecostals: Ondina E. González & Justo L. González,

Christianity in Latin America: A History, New York, 2008, esp. pp. 272–4, 281–3.
524–525 Catholic and Protestant numbers in Latin America: ibid., pp. 269, 294.
526 'I have a dream': Martin Luther King Jr in William Safire (ed.), *Lend me Your Ears*, New York, 1992, pp. 535–6.
527 Linking Erasmus with the poor: Bruce Mansfield, *Erasmus in the Twentieth Century*, Toronto, c. 2003, pp. 17, 42.
527–528 Che Guevara: Alfred T. Hennelly (ed.), *Liberation Theology: A Documentary History*, New York, 1990, p. 44.
528 Bishops in Colombia: ibid., p 90.
529 Posts in cabinet: Duffy, op. cit., p. 284.
529 Romero on fairer society: Hennelly (ed.), op. cit., p. 305–6.
530 Visit to Assisi: Bishop Pedro Casaldáliga, 'Letter to Brazilian Bishops' in Hennelly (ed.), op. cit., p. 540.
531 Mother Teresa and lepers: Hugh McLeod in *CHC*, vol. 9, p. 620.
531 The trials of Y. T. Wu: Richard F. Young in *CHC*, vol. 9, pp. 461–2.
532 Christian population in India: Census of 2001, Ministry of Home Affairs, Government of India, esp. Nagalad and Goa.
534 Statistics of Christianity in Europe: Hugh McLeod in *CHC*, vol. 9, pp. 324–5. For Poland's Christians see www.nationmaster.com/europe/pl-poland.
534 Baptists grow in USA: Hudson & Corrigan, op. cit., p. 409.
535 Catholics' troubles in USA: ibid., pp. 391–4.
536 USA, a 'covenanted nation': Marty, op. cit., p. 403.
537 'In our country': Chinua Achebe, *A Man of the People*, London, 1966, p. 63.
538 Typical Anglican is an African woman: David Maxwell in *CHC*, vol. 9, p. 403.

CHAPTER 33. 'MORE POPULAR THAN JESUS'
540 A revolt against Christianity: Basil Mitchell in McManners (ed.), op. cit., p. 624.
541 Arns of São Paulo: Duffy, op. cit., p. 284.
541 Pope negates women's rights: Duffy, op. cit., p. 285.
541 Women as Protestant pastors and bishops: Pirja Markkala in *CHC*, vol. 9, pp. 560–1, 567.
543 Atheists' avenues of attack: Christopher Hitchens (ed.), *The Portable Atheist; Essential Readings for the Nonbeliever*, Philadelphia, 2007, pp. xv, xxiii.
544 Hawking on human beings and the world: Stephen Hawking & Leonard Mlodinow, *The Grand Design*, New York, 2010, pp. 124, 133, 181.
546 Resurgence of Islam in twentieth century: Blainey, *A Short History of the Twentieth Century*, op. cit., pp. 487–92.
547 Lennon's interview in 1966: Bob Spitz, *The Beatles: The Biography*, New York, 2005, p. 615; American protests: pp. 626–32.
548 Calvin and luck: Calvin, op. cit., vol. 1, p. 173.
550 'Wisdom is the principal thing': Book of Proverbs 4:7.

MAPS
Map 8 The estimate of the Christian population and the ten largest nations comes from 'Wikipedia – Christianity by Country'. It is an estimate, and it is not clear whether it refers to 2010 or a combination of years in the period say 2005–10. It is probably to be preferred to the *Atlas of Global Christianity* (Edinburgh, 2009, p. 8), which tends to favour China and India, inflating them to fourth and ninth place.

INDEX